Nund Rishi

Nund Rishi (1378–1440) is considered one of the most important Sufi poets from Kashmir. He is revered as the 'flag-bearer of Kashmir' (*'Alamdār-e Kashmir*), and his poems draw upon the hyperlocal imagery of the Kashmiri literary universe. Despite his popular status as a spiritual successor of Lal Ded, Nund Rishi's poetry has received next to no attention in modern scholarship.

This book embodies Abir Bazaz's enduring engagement with the poetic corpus of Nund Rishi. By unpacking the cryptic philosophical and philological riddles in the poems, Bazaz unearths a negative theology in Nund Rishi's mystical poetry. He argues convincingly that the themes of Islam, Death, the Nothing and the Apocalyptic in these poems reveal an existential politics. Bazaz further suggests that the apophatic style of Nund Rishi's poems is in turn mirrored in mystical poetry across South Asia and the larger Indo-Persian world.

Abir Bazaz teaches English at Ashoka University, Sonepat, India. He holds degrees from Jamia Millia Islamia and the Universities of Chicago and Minnesota. He studies the intersections of mysticism and politics in Kashmiri literature. Other areas of Abir's research include Indian cinema, religion and literature, and violence studies. A volume he edited along with Alexandra Verini, *Gender and Medieval Mysticism from India to Europe*, is coming out in 2023. Abir has also made documentary films.

Nund Rishi

Poetry and Politics in Medieval Kashmir

Abir Bazaz

CAMBRIDGE
UNIVERSITY PRESS

CAMBRIDGE
UNIVERSITY PRESS

Shaftesbury Road, Cambridge CB2 8EA, United Kingdom

One Liberty Plaza, 20th Floor, New York, NY 10006, USA

477 Williamstown Road, Port Melbourne, VIC 3207, Australia

314–321, 3rd Floor, Plot 3, Splendor Forum, Jasola District Centre, New Delhi – 110025, India

103 Penang Road, #05–06/07, Visioncrest Commercial, Singapore 238467

Cambridge University Press is part of Cambridge University Press & Assessment, a department of the University of Cambridge.

We share the University's mission to contribute to society through the pursuit of education, learning and research at the highest international levels of excellence.

www.cambridge.org
Information on this title: www.cambridge.org/9781009100458

First published 2023
Reprint 2025

Printed in India by Repro India Ltd.

A catalogue record for this publication is available from the British Library

ISBN 978-1-009-10045-8 Hardback

For
Haneefa, Shamshad, and Trilok

Hachivih hāṛinji petsiyuv kān gōm
Abakh chān pyōm yath rāzdānay
Manz bāg bāzaras qulphu' ros vān gōm
Tīrthu' ros pān gōm kus māli zānay

A grass arrow to a lightwood bow I have become
An unskilled carpenter fell upon this capital
A shop without a lock, in the middle of the bazar, I have become
A self without a future, who knows my state?

—Lal Ded

You could not be born at a better period than the present, when we have lost everything.

—Simone Weil

Contents

Acknowledgments

I must begin by thanking my teachers. From Ashok Koul in Green Vale School to Miriam Hansen at the University of Chicago and Ajay Skaria at the University of Minnesota, I would not have found the courage to think and reflect on the life and work of a great Kashmiri teacher if it had not been for my own teachers. I owe a huge debt of gratitude to my teachers: Anisur Rahman Sahib, Pratap Pandey, Shohini Ghosh, and Sabeena Gadihoke at Jamia Millia Islamia University; Miriam Hansen, Tom Gunning, and Muzaffar Alam at the University of Chicago; and Ajay Skaria, Simona Sawhney, Thomas Adam Pepper, and the late Qadri Ismail at the University of Minnesota. I must also take this opportunity to thank my other teachers and mentors: Agha Shahid Ali and Rahman Rahi. I am also indebted to the scholarship and insight of Muneebur Rahman Sahib. A special thanks to Shafi Shauq Sahib for his generous help when I first started to study Kashmiri literature. I am also grateful to G. N. Khaki of the University of Kashmir for his warmth and hospitality when I visited Markaz-e Nūr (Shaikh-ul-Alam Centre for Multidisciplinary Studies) at the University of Kashmir.

My journey started from a small school in Srinagar (Green Vale), a childhood idyll for those who remember it, and I thank Vivek, Aurobindo, Sandeep, Prabhjyot, Vishal, and Tushar for sharing the memories and the dreams. I must also thank the founder of the school, Girdhari Lal Ogra, and our principal, Raj Laxmi Ogra, who inspired us with their vision of education. The loss of this school is one more entry in the register of all that Kashmir lost and has been losing. Speaking of Kashmir and loss (Shahid always used to quote his favorite line from *Gilgamesh*: What have you known of loss/That makes you different from other men?), it would have been impossible for the heart to survive without the love and friendship of my Kashmiri friends. Irfan Rahim Guru has been a friend and comrade since our school days when we shared an intense love for Bollywood music. I first met Hilal Mir on the recommendation of a common acquaintance because I learned of his love of Dostoevsky. I showed up at his office one day to speak about Dostoevsky, and he met me as if this was the most natural thing to have happened in the world. He left his office to join me for a walk, and since then we have been walking together. I also shared long walks in early 1990s with Mehmood-ur-Rashid, from whom I learned the meaning and value of a sustained dialogue. I first met Zahid Rafiq when he was just starting out on the path of writing. My conversations with Zahid about life and literature have helped me grow as a person and a writer. I have learned so much from his stories about everyday Kashmiri life and found my own lostness reflected in the lostness of his Kashmiri characters.

A special thanks to Masroor Malik. His honesty, sincerity, and commitment are what I strive to live up to in my own small ways. I owe a huge debt of gratitude to Masroor for introducing me to Rahi Sahib in the early 1990s. Many thanks also to Massarat Malik. I will not be able to find the right words to thank Anmol Tikoo. Anmol Tikoo, Irfan Guru, Masroor Malik, and Vivek Koul are simply brothers who have helped me through difficult times.

Among other friends in Kashmir, I must thank Asghar Qadri, Idris Bhat, Naseer Ganai, Javeed Ahmed Mir, Muzamil Jaleel, Shahnawaz Majid, Suvaid Yaseen, Arif Ayaz Parrey, Syed Tariq, Ruhail Nazir, Zubair Nabi, Vanessa Chishti, Ajaz-ul-Haque, Showkat Motta, Khurram Parvez, Najeeb Mubarki, Bilal Bhat, Wasim Yousuf Bhat, Waseem Khalid, Mufti Mudasir, Shoaib Bhat, Feroz Rather, Azhar Qadri, Baba Umar, Inshah Malik, Uzma Falak, Arshi Javed, Muzaffar Karim, Muzammil Karim, Wajahat Peer, Gowhar Fazili, Shahnaz Bashir, Arshad Malik, Shahid Ikbal, Ifthikar Bashir, Showkat Katju, Hakeem Irfan, Faizaan Bhat, Jasir Haqani, Nazish Mir, Ifrah Javaid, Samreen Mushtaq, Faisal Fehmi, and Salik Basharat. Maroof Shah, my Sufi friend, has always been exemplary with his sage advice and generous with his love.

I have no words to thank Rita Kothari, "friend, philosopher and guide," to use an expression from my college days. Rita taught me what the insistence in Nund Rishi about *bōzun*, listening, is all about. Thanks also to Rita for soul-lifting conversations on Bollywood music, Indian literatures, the Sindhi–Kashmiri dispossessions, and the saints of everyday life. I hope this book lives up to her high standards. I also thank Abhijit Kothari and Shamini Kothari for their love, warmth, and friendship.

Madhavi Menon and Jonathan Gil Harris welcomed me with an open heart to Ashoka University. I am deeply grateful to them for helping me settle in at Ashoka and for their support and friendship over the years. I thank Suvir Kaul for his help and sincere encouragement from the time I first applied to graduate school to his detailed and thoughtful comments on my manuscript. I would also like to thank Aparna Vaidik and Anil Sanweria for their friendship.

I thank Asha Gaur, M. S. Gaur, Deepali Gaur, Iqtidar Khan, and the Nizami family for providing me a home away from home in Delhi. I first met Manash Firaq Bhattacharjee in the late 1990s Jawaharlal Nehru University. His first collection of poems was titled *Ghalib's Tomb and Other Poems* and my experience of friendship with him has been best described by Ghalib: "Dekhnā taqrīr kī lazzat ki jo us ne kahā/Maiñ ne ye jānā ki gōyā ye bhī mere dil meñ hai." Many thanks also to Richa Burman.

My sincere thanks for conversations past and present to Madan Gopal Singh, Sanjay Kak, Mrinal Kaul, Prashant Keshavmurthy, Soumyabrata Choudhury, Venugopal Maddipati, Gaurav Banerjee, Prasanta Chakravarty, Maaz Bin Bilal, Aditi Saraf, Saiba Varma, Rajarshi Ghose, Saitya Brata Das, Luther Obrock, Tyler Williams, Anjum Hasan, Aruni Kashyap, and Anubhuti Maurya. I thank Neeti Nair for her friendship and solidarity over the years. My heartfelt thanks to Pothik Ghosh for long conversations on all things philosophical and the future of a Communism without Communism (though he might not put it exactly in these words). I first met Asghar Qadri and Idris Bhat in Delhi, and they have made the city come alive with their friendship.

In Karachi, I must thank my aunt, Dilshad Mir, and her lovely family. In London, I must thank Meenu Gaur, Mazhar Zaidi, and my love Sarang. I am also grateful to Muhammad Hanif, Nimra Bucha, Mirza Waheed, and Ananya Jahanara Kabir. In Turkey, I must thank Matteen Rafiqi and Shazia Naqshbandi. In Japan, I would like to thank my colleagues Satoshi Ogura and Toru Tak. In Germany, I would like to thank Max Kramer (a true *dost*), Sarah Lina Ewald, and Jeurgen Schaflechner. In Bangalore, I would like to thank my brother Amir Bashir Bazaz, Poulomi Pal, and my niece Zuni. I would also like to express my gratitude to Ajay Raina for his films and our conversations.

My years in the United States were made easy by the friendship and generosity of Manan Ahmed, Prithvi Datta Chandra Shobhi, Bret Beheim, Junko Yamazaki, Dianna Oles, Rehanna Kheshgi, Raquel Valadares, Casandra Silva Sibilin, Nancy Hammond, and Lyubomir Uzunov. I would also like to thank Emily Durham, Sravanthi Kollu, Joya John, Sucheta Kanjilal, and Aniruddha Dutta. Many thanks also to my Kashmiri friends and comrades in the United States: Nishita Trisal, Mohamad Junaid, Rakshanda Aslam, Hafsa Kanjwal, and Sonam Kachru. Sonam's work on Kashmiri pasts and presents is a source of constant inspiration for me. I simply cannot wait to read his translations of Lal Ded. I am also grateful to Suad Joseph and Sudipta Sen for a memorable year spent at the University of California, Davis.

In Minneapolis, I am extremely thankful to Shiney Varghese, Richa Nagar, David Faust, Vinay Gidwani, Joseph Allen, Jason McGrath, Christine Marran, Suvadip Sinha, and Nida Sajid. I thank Suvadip, in particular, for long conversations about films, Kashmir, Shah Rukh Khan, Iqbal, Bergson, and everything else under the sun. I owe a special debt of gratitude to Harshit Rathi, Quỳnh N. Phạm, and María José Méndez. I also want to thank Miranda Brist, Lalit Batra, Hale Konitshek, Sristi Bhattarai, Courtney Gildersleeve, Maheen Zaman, and Akshya Saxena. Omar Tesdell and Elizabeth Tesdell have been like family to me in Minneapolis.

Ashoka University has been an intellectual home for me for the last six years. I owe more than I can express in words to my conversations with Pratap Bhanu Mehta. I will miss his inspiring presence on the Ashoka campus. A special thanks to my colleagues in the Department of English: Johannes Burgers, Subhasree Chakravarty, Geetanjali Chanda, Amit Chaudhuri, Aparna Chaudhuri, Mandakini Dubey, Saikat Majumdar, Vivek Narayan, Alexander Phillips, Janice Pariat, Sumana Roy, Arunava Sinha, Mali Skotheim, and Alexandra Verini. Many thanks also to Harjot Malik. I am also extremely thankful to B. P. Prakash, Bibhuti Nath Jha, and the Ashoka library staff.

At Ashoka, I would also like to thank Aniket Aga, Rajendra Bhatia, Abhinash Borah, Swargajyoti Gohain, Ali Khan Mahmudabad, Mahmood Kooria, Ratul Lahkar, Clancy Martin, Gautam Menon, Pratyay Nath, Amin Nizami, Bikram Phookun, Bittu, Srinath Raghavan, Bharat Ramaswami, Mahesh Rangarajan, Anuradha Saha, Vinay Sitapati, Ravindran Sriramachandran, Gilles Verniers, Matthew Baxter, Upinder Singh, and Malabika Sarkar.

I am extremely thankful to my editors at Cambridge University Press, Qudsiya Ahmed, Anwesha Rana, and Aniruddha De, who believed in this book from the start. A version of Chapter 4 was first published in *South Asia: Journal of South Asian Studies*. I thank the journal, and its editor Kama Maclean, for permission to reproduce a revised version of the article.

Last but not least, I thank all my students at Ashoka University. I have no doubt that I have learned more from my students than they have from me.

Introduction

On May 25, 1995, at the end of a two-month-long siege, the shrine and tomb complex (*astān*) of Nund Rishi (1378–1440), Kashmir's most revered Sufi and the founder of a fifteenth-century Kashmiri Sufi order called the Rishi Order, was destroyed in a gun battle between the militants of the Ḥizb al-Mujahidīn, a pro-Pakistan Kashmiri guerilla group, and the Indian Army.[1] The Ḥizb al-Mujahidīn and the Indian Army kept accusing each other of destroying one of the most popular Sufi shrines of Kashmir even as most Kashmiris retreated into shocked silence and mourning. The gratuitous destruction of a revered Sufi shrine, a center of Kashmiri Rishism, epitomized the everyday fate of Kashmiris in the early 1990s at the receiving end of a low-intensity war between India and the different Kashmiri nationalist, pro-Pakistan, and Islamist groups over the future of the disputed territory of Jammu and Kashmir. The central Kashmir town of Chrar was also destroyed in the gun battle.[2] The shrine at Chrar symbolized the distinctive history of Islam in Kashmir for some (in a less academic and more political variant, it was seen as a symbol of the multireligious, even syncretic, Kashmīriyat, or Kashmiriness) and the beginnings of Islam and Islamic culture in Kashmir for the others. But for most Kashmiris, the shrine evoked the everyday life of faith in Kashmir across different religious traditions. The Chrar shrine was, and remains, clearly one of the most sacred religious spaces for Kashmiris and one of the few that commands respect across the sectarian divide. It is no surprise then that the pro-independence Kashmiri nationalists (as well as Kashmiri nationalists who are pro-India), pro-Pakistan Islamists (as well as the supposedly "apolitical" Islamists), and the Indian state (with its official ideology of secularism at the cornerstone of its claim on Kashmir) all lay claim to Chrar as a center of Rishi thinking and philosophy.[3] For the Kashmiri nationalists (secessionist or subnationalist), the Rishi thinking and philosophy is the Kashmiri way of life. For the Islamists, the Rishi thinking and philosophy is merely the precursor of a pure Islamic culture that is yet to be fully instituted. But neither the Kashmiri nationalists nor the Kashmiri Islamists have articulated any serious understanding of the religio-political movement of the saint who lies buried at Chrar. His movement, known in Urdu scholarship as the *Rishī tahrīk* and in English scholarship as the Rishi movement, has been a unique phenomenon in the history of religion in Kashmir after the advent of Islam there in the fourteenth century. What makes Nund Rishi, and his movement, so fundamental to Kashmiri ideas of self and sovereignty? We will attempt to answer this question in this book through a close reading of the mystical poetry of Nund Rishi.

Kashmir, as is well known, is a disputed territory, and the region remains divided between India and Pakistan.[4] The claims of both India and Pakistan on Kashmir depend on the way these two nation-states approach its status as a Muslim-majority region (for India, the inclusion of Kashmir as a Muslim-majority region in the union ratifies its official ideology of secularism; for Pakistan, a country created as a homeland for South Asia's Muslims, the state's Muslim-majority status is essential to the political claim it advances on the region). It is not at all surprising then that the history of Islam in Kashmir is a controversial subject. The Rishis, central to Kashmir's transition from a Hindu–Buddhist society to an Islamic society from the fourteenth to the sixteenth century, are fundamental to that history. Nonetheless, most accounts of the Rishis in Kashmir have focused on religious and political history, and few have examined the thinking of Nund Rishi. There have been only a few book-length studies of the history of the Rishi Order of Kashmiri Sufism; of these, Mohammad Ishaq Khan's *Kashmir's Transition to Islam: The Role of Muslim Rishis* remains the most influential, even if controversial.[5] The collections of Nund Rishi's mystical poetry have also been published since the arrival of the printing press in Kashmir in the early twentieth century. But there has been no detailed critical study of the mystical poetry of Nund Rishi beyond a few confessional commentaries that situate Nund Rishi's mystical poetry within the Qur'ānic hermeneutic.[6] Nund Rishi left behind no written records or mystical theology other than his mystical poetry. The task I set myself in this book is to explore certain dominant themes in the mystical poetry of Nund Rishi. I focus, in particular, on the themes of death, the Nothing, the apocalyptic, and the meanings of Islam in the mystical poetry of Nund Rishi in order to trace a complex history of the relations between mysticism and politics in the region that complicates our understanding of the beginnings of Islam in Kashmir (the possibility of reading I retrieve here, it is hoped, is one that resists either an easy nationalist or an Islamist appropriation of the complex legacy of Kashmiri mysticism). My reading of the themes of death (Chapter 2), the Nothing (Chapter 3), and the apocalyptic (Chapter 4) in Nund Rishi's mystical poetry is preceded by a long reflection on the meanings of Nund Rishi's Islam (Chapter 1) that disclose his thinking as an irruption of a negative political theology in the religious and political firmament of medieval Kashmir. We shall return to this critical dimension of Nund Rishi's thinking toward the end of this Introduction.

The history of Islam in Kashmir, including the role played in it by the Rishi Order of Kashmiri Sufism, has attracted some attention in recent years because of the persistence of violent conflict in Kashmir. Kashmir is the site of the oldest and most dangerous political conflict in South Asia. The nuclear-armed states of India and Pakistan have already fought two wars over the future of Kashmir (in 1948 and 1965) and came perilously close to a third war (in 1999 and 2002). The genesis of the conflict and its trajectory is in itself a complex subject.[7] The dispute over Kashmir can be traced back to the moment of the birth of the two nation-states of India and Pakistan in 1947. The modern State of Jammu and Kashmir, a princely state of British India, had emerged at the end of the Anglo-Sikh war with military help from the British.[8] This was hardly the coherent political entity it appears in retrospect. Many of the Muslim subjects of this new princely state challenged the legitimacy of this rule and agitated against the Jammu-based ruling Dogra monarchy from the early twentieth century. But it was only in the 1930s, after a massacre of protesting Kashmiri Muslims by the Dogra state, that Kashmiri Muslims launched a popular movement for sovereignty that also received support from many Kashmiri Hindus and prominent Indian nationalists agitating against British colonial rule. This movement was interrupted by the Partition of British India and the rapidly unfolding events in its aftermath (communal strife that spread from Punjab into the Jammu region, the revolt against the Dogras in Poonch, the arrival of the Indian Army on October 26, 1947, in Kashmir to ward off infiltrating Muslim tribal irregulars from West Pakistan backed by the Pakistan Army, the first India–Pakistan war of 1947–48, and another war in 1965).[9] The princely state of Jammu and Kashmir ended up divided between India and Pakistan (India retained control over the scenic Kashmir Valley). Generations of Kashmiris faced routine political suppression since the 1930s as the anti-Dogra movement metamorphosed into a nationalist movement demanding self-determination. Even though there were tensions in the region in the 1950s and 1960s, things settled into an uneasy calm by the late 1970s and early 1980s with the defeat of Pakistan in the India–Pakistan war of 1971. But the barely suppressed unrest in India-administered Kashmir, catalyzed by the widespread allegations about rigging in the 1987 Jammu and Kashmir Legislative Assembly elections and riding on a wave of new Islamist sentiment after the Soviet withdrawal from Afghanistan in 1989 as well as the euphoria around national self-determination after the end of the Cold War, exploded into a violent anti-India insurgency in 1990, which continues unabated and has already claimed more than 60,000 lives.[10] The killings, extrajudicial executions, rape, torture, and disappearances are the more visible signs of death and destruction that have haunted contemporary Kashmir in endless cycles of insurgency and counterinsurgency.[11] Most of Kashmir's Hindu minority has been displaced from the Kashmir Valley by the violent conflict and lives in difficult exile in different regions of India and scattered across the world in the Kashmiri Hindu diaspora.[12]

What is of significance to us here in recounting the modern tragic history of Kashmir is the persistence of the symbolic centrality of Kashmir to the postcolonial states of India and Pakistan (not only in politics but also in culture), which is one of the fundamental causes of the intransigence of the conflict. If Kashmir is the crowning example for India of its distinctive secularism, for Pakistan it is the unfinished business of India's Partition that paved the path for the creation of an independent homeland for India's Muslims. The political claims of India and Pakistan on Kashmir not only go back to the tumultuous events of the Partition of British India but also pass through the history and memory of the sectarian conflict between the Hindus and Muslims of South Asia. For Kashmiris, negotiating the bitter legacy of this Hindu–Muslim sectarian conflict has involved making sense of a complex history of the religious and the political in Kashmir. Kashmir is one of the few South Asian regions like Punjab, Sindh, and Bengal that had seen large-scale conversions from Hinduism to Islam in the medieval period. The history of Islam in Kashmir as such has been fundamental to the negotiations of the cultural pasts in Kashmir and remains deeply contested. The significance of the Rishi Order to most historical accounts of medieval Kashmir places Nund Rishi, and his Rishi Order of Sufism, at the center of these controversies and contestations about the history of Islam in Kashmir. The Indian state, for instance, has often cast the Rishi Order as the forerunner of its ideology of secularism in discourses that surround such symbolic gestures as the naming of the Srinagar airport as the Shaikh al-'Ālam airport (*shaikh al-'ālam* – the teacher, or wisdom, of the world – is one among the many epithets with which Kashmiris remember Nund Rishi). For the Pakistani state, Kashmiri Sufism appears in continuity with the practices of imagining a South Asian Muslim paradise.[13] The role played by the migrant Kubrāwiyyā Sufis in the conversion of Kashmir to Islam in the fourteenth and the fifteenth centuries prompted General Zia-ul-Haq, the former president of Pakistan, to eulogize the work of the Kubrāwīyyā Sufi missionary Mīr Sayyid 'Alī Hamadānī (popularly also remembered as Shāh-e Hamadān, the King of Hamadan) in a conference organized in Pakistan-administered Kashmir in 1987 (interestingly the year the first few groups of young Kashmiris began crossing over to Pakistan-administered Kashmir to prepare for an anti-India insurgency).[14] As General Zia-ul-Haq reiterated, without men like Mīr Sayyīd 'Alī Hamadānī, "we would have had not Pakistan today nor Azad Jammu and Kashmir."[15] Most historical accounts of Kashmir are in agreement that the Kubrāwiyyā Sufi missionaries catalyzed conversions to Islam in Kashmir.[16] As we shall see, the Rishi Order of Kashmiri Sufism takes a different approach to Islam in Kashmir than the Kubrāwiyyā Sufis, who remain preoccupied with conversion.

The state of affairs, so far as the representations of the history of Islam in Kashmir is concerned, has been hardly any different in India. In 2009, for instance, Pratibha Patil, India's then president, invoked Kashmiri Sufism on an official visit to Kashmir as she called Kashmir the abode of the Rishis and a symbol of "liberal values, religious harmony, mutual co-existence and brotherhood."[17] For India, Kashmir is the trophy of a triumphant secularism and the Rishi movement is one of the many forerunners of Indian secularism. The Kashmiri nationalists, in turn, see Nund Rishi as one of the first Kashmiri spiritual leaders to express the national sentiment of the oppressed in Kashmir.[18] Divided between a loyalty to the Pakistani state and a future, post-*jihād* caliphate, the Kashmiri Islamists, on the other hand, have a complex, but not always uneasy, relationship with Kashmiri Sufism. Yet central to most of these narratives about the beginnings, and the subsequent trajectory, of Islam in Kashmir is the Rishi Order of Kashmiri Sufism.

Much of our information about the Rishi Order, and Nund Rishi, is based on accounts written by the Sufis of the Suhrawardī and Qādirī Orders.[19] None of these are contemporaneous to Nund Rishi. But if the Sufis of other orders (in some sense, the rival orders for the Rishis) held the Rishis in such great esteem, one can only imagine the extent of their popularity in Kashmir.[20]

The Kashmiri historian Abdul Qaiyum Rafiqi draws our attention to the accounts of awe and veneration inspired by the Rishis among Kashmiris in Mughal courtier Abul Fazl's *Āʾīn-e Akbarī* in the reign of Akbar and in *Tuzūk-e Jahāngīrī* by the Mughal Emperor Jahangir (1569–1627). Writing about a century and a half after Nund Rishi's death, Abul Fazl gives us this account of the enduring popularity of the Rishi Order at the time of the Mughal annexation of Kashmir under Akbar (the Mughals conquered Kashmir in 1586):

> The most respected class of people in this country (Kashmir) are the Rishis. Although they have not abandoned the traditional and customary forms of worship (*taqlīd*), but they are true in their worship. They do not denounce men belonging to different faiths. They do not have the tongue of desire, and do not seek to attain worldly objects. They plant fruit-bearing trees in order that people may obtain benefit from these. They abstain from meat and do not marry.[21]

This brief portrait of the Kashmiri Rishis is nonetheless striking in its detail. In the memoirs of the Mughal Emperor Jahangir (1569–1627), *Jahāngīrnāmā*, we come across a similar reference to the Rishis:

> There is a group of fakirs called *rishi*s. Although they have no knowledge or learning, they profess simplicity and unpretentiousness and speak ill of no one. They do not beg or practice mendicancy. They do not eat meat, and they do not take wives. They plant fruit-bearing trees in the wilderness with the intention that people might enjoy the fruits, although they themselves do not derive any enjoyment from the practice. There must be atleast two thousand of these individuals.[22]

As we shall see, the "lack of knowledge" alludes here to controversies over the relations between Sufism and theology in Kashmir, which I shall discuss in Chapter 1. Abdul Qaiyum Rafiqi also writes that the fifteenth-century Kashmiri Sanskrit chronicler Jonaraja, "who rarely acknowledges the sanctity of any Muslim, describes him [Nund Rishi] the greatest sage of the time."[23] Even though there is just one contemporaneous reference to Nund Rishi in Jonaraja's *Rajātaranginī*, it is in the *tarīkh*s and *tadhkirā*s of the different Persian Sufi orders of Kashmir where we come across not only the first detailed accounts of Nund Rishi but also examples from his mystical poetry.[24]

The history and memory of the Rishi Order are inseparable from its founder, Nund Rishi, and his mystical poetry. Nund Rishi, or Shaikh Nūr al-Dīn Nūrānī, is one of the most significant figures in the history of religion and literature in Kashmir.[25] Many relatively recent historical and political commentators on Kashmir consider Nund Rishi to be Kashmir's "patron saint" or even "national saint," even as "patron saint" and "national saint" remain hard, if not impossible, to translate into Kashmiri.[26] For Kashmiris themselves, Nund Rishi is simply *'alamdār* (the standard-bearer, or flag bearer) of Kashmir or *shaikh al-'ālam* (the teacher of the worlds). The Hindus of Kashmir remember Nund Rishi with the honorific Sahajānanda (Innately Blissful One).[27] We shall discuss the significance of this epithet in more detail toward the end of Chapter 1. The word *rishī* itself is Sanskrit and means an ascetic or a sage. By choosing a Sanskrit word for Hindu ascetics to name an Islamic Sufi Order, Nund Rishi stressed continuities between Kashmir's past and present in politically turbulent times.[28] The popular culture that still surrounds Rishi shrines such as *bhānd pāṭhu'r* (Kashmiri folk theatre), *zūl* (a festival of lights), and *dambāḷ* (dervish dance) is also associated with pre-Islamic religious culture in Kashmir. Nund Rishi resisted the sectarian atmosphere created by Sultan Sikandar's chief minister Sūha Bhaṭṭa's violent persecution of Kashmiri Hindus and opened up a philosophical path to thinking, and negotiating, interreligious difference and, in doing so, laid the foundations of a new Kashmiri political spirituality grounded in the lifeworlds of the Kashmiri language.

The historian Chitralekha Zutshi writes that the mystical poetry of Nund Rishi contributed "to the development of the Kashmiri language, and later to the articulation of a self-consciously Kashmiri culture."[29] From the medieval sultanate to the modern Indian state, the rulers of Kashmir have attempted to capitalize on the popularity of the Rishis among Kashmiri masses.[30] But the discourse on the Rishis has acquired more of a centrality in Kashmiri public life with the rise of Kashmiri nationalism in the twentieth century. Nund Rishi became a central figure to what Zutshi has elsewhere called the "Kashmiri narrative public" that emerged in the nineteenth century.[31] The discourse on the Rishis intensified even more in the late twentieth century with the rise of a political conflict around Kashmir. It is against the background of these more recent circumstances that the Jammu and Kashmir Academy of Art, Culture and Languages prepared two editions of Nund Rishi's mystical poetry edited by Amin Kamil and Moti Lal Saqi.[32] The new administration of the Kashmiri nationalist leader Sheikh Abdullah celebrated the six-hundredth anniversary of Nund Rishi's birth in 1978 soon after Abdullah's release from prison and his landmark victory in the 1977 elections, which followed an accord between the Kashmiri nationalists and the Indian leadership.[33] In 1998, as an insurgency which began in 1990 still raged, the University of Kashmir in Srinagar established an independent research center devoted to the study of Nund Rishi called the Centre for Shaikh al-ʿĀlam Studies, or Markaz-e Nūr (Centre of Light), with its own dedicated journal in English and Kashmiri called *ʿAlamdār*.

The centrality of Nund Rishi (and his older contemporary Śaiva saint, Lal Ded) to Kashmiri cultural memory has never been in question. If the Muslim nationalist poet Muhammad Iqbal has dominated the political idiom of Kashmiri Muslim nationalism in the twentieth century, it is the Rishi thought which has been central to cultural and historical narratives of Kashmir's shared pasts.[34] But the politico-spiritual legacy of Nund Rishi is deeply contested in Kashmir in the present between such reformist and revivalist Islamic groups as the Ahl-e Ḥadīth, Deobandīs, and the Jamāt-e Islami and the new Sufi-leaning Barelvī groups such as Kārvān-e Islām and the traditional devotees of the Suhrawardī, Kubrāwiyyā, and Rishi shrines. If, for the Ahl-e Ḥadith, Nund Rishi is one of the early reformers of Islam, the Barelvīs see Nund Rishi as an early exemplar of a distinctively South Asian Sufi practice.[35]

Nund Rishi was born in 1378 in Kaimoh to a family of recent Hindu converts to Islam and died in 1440 at Chrar in central Kashmir. Nund Rishi's father, Salar Sanz, had converted to Islam (according to some accounts at the hands of the Kubrāwiyyā Sufi Sayyid Husayn Simnānī).[36] Pandit Anand Koul writes that the name Nūr al-Dīn (literally the Light of Faith) was conferred on him by Mīr Muḥammad Hamadānī, the son of Sayyid ʿAlī Hamadānī, who had settled many of the first immigrant Sufis in Kashmir.[37] Koul also writes that Nund Rishi's father was a disciple of Yasmān Rishi, who had converted him to Islam.[38] But some other scholars have written that both of his parents were the disciples of Sayyid Husayn Simnānī, a Kubrāwiyyā Sufi and a cousin of Mīr Sayyid ʿAlī Hamadānī, who lived near Nund Rishi's native Kaimoh in south Kashmir (Sayyid Husayn Simnānī is also connected by popular legends to the Śaiva saint Lal Ded).[39] According to popular hagiographical and biographical accounts, Nund Rishi retreated at the age of thirty to a complete withdrawal from social life.[40] But in 1420, Nund Rishi returned from twelve years of solitary meditation to establish a new Sufi order at a time of deepening crisis in Kashmir.[41] The remaining two decades of his life were spent in intense involvement in the spiritual and political life of Kashmiris.

Nund Rishi traveled all across Kashmir, and Amin Kamil suggests that he took up residence in Drobgam for twelve years, Devsar for one year, Beerwah for seven years, and Rupawan for seven years (the locations circumscribe an arc along south and central Kashmir).[42] Nund Rishi's disciples including Bābā Bām al-Dīn, Bābā Zain al-Dīn, Bābā Latīf al-Dīn, and Bābā Nāṣir al-Dīn – many of them recent converts to Islam – helped popularize and spread the Rishi Order to remote corners of Kashmir. But the Rishi Order faced a crisis of legitimacy as Nund Rishi could not trace his lineage back to either the family of Prophet Muhammad or any of the great Sufi masters, a *sine qua non* for Sufi teaching. Nund Rishi resolved this crisis of legitimation by claiming an Uwaysī initiation, that is, a direct spiritual initiation by Prophet Muhammad (we discuss Nund Rishi's claims of an Uwaysī initiation in more detail in Chapter 1). But it is the relationship of Nund Rishi to the Śaivite saint Lal Ded, who also composed mystical verse in Kashmiri, that has endured in the Kashmiri tradition.[43] The spiritual relation between Nund Rishi and Lal Ded is best expressed in the Kashmiri legend about the infant Nund Rishi's refusal to suckle at his mother's breast. Lal Ded is supposed to have taken the infant Nund Rishi into her arms and asked: *Yinu' mandchōkh nu' tu' chanu' chukh mandchān* (You were not ashamed of being born but you are ashamed of being breast-fed).[44] Dean Accardi, in a recent essay on Lal Ded and Nund Rishi, writes:

> Lal Ded and Nund Rishi are two saints who have been venerated in conjunction with each other in Kashmir for nearly five centuries. In fact, these two mystic saints are so significant to notions of Kashmiri identity that poems attributed to them are often recited to begin Kashmiri cultural events and festivals, and a plethora of institutions in Kashmir have been named after them – from schools and colleges to a maternity hospital and even the Srinagar International Airport, officially named the "Sheikh ul Alam Airport."[45]

Accardi further claims that these two saints were written by the earliest Kashmiri historical sources "into the fabric of Kashmir itself."[46] The beginnings of a new Kashmiri literary and religious culture in Kashmir at its moment of "origin" turn out to be the dissemination of the spiritual vitality of a Śaivite ascetic tradition into the idiom of Islamic mysticism.[47] Many historical accounts also mention that Nund Rishi's mother was known to Lal Ded.[48] Koul writes that Lal Ded said to Nund Rishi's mother, Ṣadru' Mōj, whose first name meant "ocean" in Kashmiri: *Sodras hay chu mokhtu' nýrān* (Pearls come only out of the ocean).[49] The beginnings of a new Kashmiri literary and religious culture in fourteenth- and fifteenth-century Kashmir is interwoven with the cultural memory of a relation between Lal Ded and Nund Rishi.

Even though many studies have been published on Lal Ded, there have been few serious attempts to address the poetry and thinking of Nund Rishi.[50] Jaishree Kak Odin's *Lallā to Nūruddīn: Rishī-Sufi Poetry of Kashmir* is an exception. The studies in English, Urdu, or Kashmiri published on Nund Rishi in the last few decades offer us Nund Rishi's poetry (with approximate translations into English or Urdu if the book is not in Kashmiri) along with some religious exposition and attempts to situate Nund Rishi in relation to the religious and political history of Kashmir.[51] Some isolated efforts do take on a more interpretive task but the thinking of this saint-poet remains largely unexplored.[52] In the earliest English-language study of Nund Rishi by a Kashmiri (which I have quoted earlier), Pandit Anand Koul, writing as early as 1929 in the *Indian Antiquary*, bemoans that the older works of literature in the Kashmiri language have been neglected.[53] Koul calls Nund Rishi "a hermit of the highest order" and adds that "despite six centuries having rolled by since he lived, his name is held in profound respect and veneration by both Muhammadans and Hindus throughout Kashmir."[54] Koul writes about the poetry of the great sages which shaped the religious history of Kashmir, in particular, the aphoristic style of Nund Rishi: "The Kashmiri repeats such aphoristic lines again and again in his every-day life as current coins of quotation."[55] The aphoristic also bears a relation to the thinking that irrupted across north India in the fourteenth and fifteenth centuries, which we now know by the name of *bhaktī*.[56] Koul also points out the difficulties involved in reading Nund Rishi and Lal Ded from the available manuscripts:

> What they had to say they taught orally to their disciples, and their sayings were written after their date in the Persian character, without punctuation or diacritical marks. Thus defectively recorded, they have become inextricably confused and full of interpolations by disciples, imitators and rhapsodists. Whatever was noted by any one person in the margin of his treasured private copy by way of interpretation, was regarded by the next owner or copyist as part of the text: there was no means of distinguishing *addenda* from mere *marginalia*, for they knew not that it was impossible to alter a word in such sayings without altering it for the worse.[57]

In this book, I avoid some of these notorious difficulties of studying Nund Rishi's mystical verse by turning to two excellent critical editions of the collected works of Nund Rishi supplemented by another collection by the Chrar-based independent researcher Asadullah Afaqi. The first two (*Nūrnāmu'* by Amin Kamil and *Kulliyāt-e Shaikh al-'Ālam* by Moti Lal Saqi) were commissioned by the Jammu and Kashmir Academy of Art, Culture and Languages in 1966 and 1985.[58] I have also consulted the more expanded collection of Asadullah Afaqi to include those popular verses (or variants of verses) that had not found a place in the Kamil and Saqi editions.[59] These collections are based on the earliest sources of Nund Rishi's mystical poetry that became available from the sixteenth and seventeenth centuries.[60] These Persian texts – *rishīnāmā*s and *nūrnāmā*s – give a biographical account of Nund Rishi's life. Amin Kamil writes that because the primary purpose of the *rishīnāmā*s and *nūrnāmā*s was not to record the mystical poetry of Nund Rishi, the authors of these texts have not been meticulous in writing down the *shruk*s (sometimes they have quoted the *shruk*s in a truncated form, and often the text of a particular *shruk* varies from *nūrnāmā* to *nūrnāmā*).[61] Kamil divides Nund Rishi's poetic corpus into three genres: *shruk*, *vatsun*, and *bāṭu'*.[62] *Vatsun* is a poem made up of quatrains where every fourth line repeats a refrain and *bāṭu'*, literally song, means a didactic poem in the context of Kamil's classification.[63] But often the word *shruk* is used singularly in common usage for the mystical poetry of Nund Rishi. Yet the *shruk* is a distinct form: a *shruk* is a quatrain that expresses a single thought.[64] The rhyme scheme is *abab*.[65] Sometimes a *shruk* is also recorded as a sestet, in which case, the rhyme scheme is *ababab*. The *shruk*s also sometimes make an even longer poem, but the pattern of the rhyme scheme remains the same. The *shruk*s have been composed in a simple syllabic meter, which T. N. Ganjoo elsewhere traces to older Kashmiri *pada* forms.[66] Kamil also writes that many of the *shruk*s consist of more than four lines, and this shows that the older quatrain form the *shruk* must have been based on had evolved by the time Nund Rishi turns to it.[67] It is mostly the *shruk*s that are going to form the basis of this study.

The word *shruk* appears to be derived from the Sanskrit *śloka* (a frequently used poetic form in classical Sanskrit).[68] In contemporary Kashmiri, *shruk* literally means a "knot," and an alternative reading could take this to be the meaning of *shruk*. The *shruk* deploys the force of the aphoristic and is often read from what it leaves unsaid. It also bears family resemblance to riddle-like genres, even though *shruk*s are different from riddles (it is the mood of the riddle which one sometimes encounters in the *shruk*). The resemblance is more striking in those *shruk*s that reveal "an excluded cosmos, a non-world or topsy-turvy world lurking just beneath or within our properly ordered and familiar one."[69] The *shruk* is also close to such modes of expression as prophecy and the proverb. Many lines from Nund Rishi's *shruk*s have passed into the Kashmiri language as proverbs, such as *an pōshi teli yeli van pōshi* (food shall last as long as forests last), cited by the environmentalist Sunderlal Bahuguna in an article in the *Times of India* in 1985.[70]

The *shruk* in vernacular Kashmiri emerged as a form at a time when two cosmopolitan languages were competing for ascendancy at the Kashmiri court: Sanskrit was still the language of the court but was to be soon replaced by Persian.[71] The *shruk*s are also the site where we detect a gradual shift in the Kashmiri vernacular from its connection to linguistic resources of Sanskrit to that of Persian and Arabic (this dynamic is not so visible in the *vākh,* Lal Ded's chosen form of poetic expression). The Kashmiri poet and literary critic Rahman Rahi writes that T. N. Ganjoo, the Kashmiri Sanskritist, has argued that both Lal Ded's *vākh*s and Nund Rishi's *shruk*s owe their origin to the *pada* form of poetry.[72] According to Ganjoo, *pada*, *vākh*, and *shruk* are three separate moments in the history of a particular genre.[73] Ganjoo traces the history of the *pada* form of poetry to as early as the eighth and ninth centuries and writes that the great tenth-century Śaivite Kashmiri philosopher Abhinavagupta mentions *chumma pada* in his classic *Tantrāloka*.[74] But Rahman Rahi contends that if there is no difference between these genres, how did the different names for *vākh* and *shruk* come about?[75] Rahi also asks the intriguing question why the *shruk*s are only associated with the name of Nund Rishi when *vākh*s are used by other Kashmiri poets (such as Rupa Bhawani in the seventeenth century).[76] Rahi also writes that the Sanskrit dictionaries give similar meanings for *vākh* and *shruk* (read as *śloka*) but also register differences.[77] For the contemporary Kashmiri reader, the *shruk*s have a synoptic, gnomic quality to them like proverbs, but *vākh*s develop a single thought to its extreme possibilities. But, for Rahi, the most significant difference is that the *vākh* is a call of the gods.[78] The *shruk*s, on the other hand, deal with the transitoriness of human life.[79] According to Rahi, the *vākh*s are revelatory and the *shruk*s an expression of the human situation. Rahi, however, stretches this interpretation to its limits when he suggests that the contemporary progressive poetry can be seen in philosophical continuity with the *shruk*s and the modernist/existential poetry in continuity with the *vākh*s (this is a none-too-subtle way of declaring allegiance to Lal Ded as well as claiming the superiority of "modernist/existential" poetry over Left-leaning 'progressive' poetry).[80] The *shruk*s are typified by compressions and omissions, and the relations of the *shruk* to such early Indo-Aryan forms such as *pada*, *dohā*, and *chaupāī* need investigation.[81] In many of Nund Rishi's longer poems (*vatsun* in Kamil's classification) made up of clusters of *shruk*s, for instance, the last line is presented as the refrain signaling their use in an oral performance tradition continuous with similar genres in medieval north India.[82]

Even though Rupa Bhawani wrote *vākh*s in the seventeenth century, and Bimla Raina has revived the genre in our own times, the question as to why the *shruk* has been ascribed to none other than Nund Rishi remains unanswered.[83] To imitate the poetic form used by the greatest Sufi exemplar of Kashmir was to risk being compared to Nund Rishi. This was increasingly untenable in an atmosphere of excessive devotional piety and appropriations of Nund Rishi by powerful Kashmiri Sufi orders such as the Kubrāwiyyā and the Suharwardīyya. The powerful currents in Nund Rishi's poetry belong as much to Tantric, Yoga, Nātha spiritual movements, Kashmir Śaivism and Mahayana Buddhism, as they do to early Islamic asceticism, medieval dervish traditions, and Sufi theology.[84] If the middle path between asceticism and worldliness that Nund Rishi advocates in many of his *shruk*s can be seen in relation to Abu Ḥāmid al-Ghazālī's synthesis between the sober and ecstatic tendencies in medieval Sufism, it resonates as powerfully with the attitudes of north Indian *siddhā*s. This tension is internal to Nund Rishi and shapes the *shruk* as a form.

Following Ranjit Hoskote's approach to Lal Ded, I am inclined to approach the body of mystical poetry that circulates in the name of Nund Rishi as the "Nund Rishi corpus" with multiple authors, rather than as the work of a single individual.[85] This intensifies, rather than lessens, our interest in the figure of Nund Rishi as a poet. The *shruk*s of Nund Rishi passed through what Ranjit Hoskote, discussing Lal Ded, calls "the informal editorial attention" of "reciters, scribes and votaries" from the fifteenth century to the present.[86] But I have taken care to privilege only those *shruk*s in my readings that are either more widely cited in twentieth-century scholarship on Nund Rishi or are more popularly invoked in everyday speech. Hoskote also cites Karin Schomer's excellent essay on *dōhā* to claim that the *vākh* belongs to the family of forms which are "grouped under the generic title of the *dōhā*."[87] *Shruk* also belongs to the same family of forms and reveals two of the major functions of the *dōhā*: compressed aphoristic statement and lyrical intensity.[88]

Even though the *vākh* and *shruk* differ in their thematic, their effects on the listeners are not dissimilar: these poems, as Hoskote writes of the *vākh*, "strike us like brief and blinding bursts of light: epiphanic, provocative, they shuttle between the vulnerability of doubt and the assurance of an insight gained through resilience and reflection."[89] What is unique about the *shruk* as a form is that it infuses new Islamic ideas into these north Indian genres steeped in Tantric and Yogic ideas at a time when the meaning of Islam was being contested between Kashmir's new Muslim rulers and the different Sufi orders of Kashmir.

The contestations over the meanings of Islam at the peripheries have been a major force shaping the Muslim world in the medieval period and inform some of the most central debates within the Islamic tradition. The Rishis were new Muslim converts to Islam, and it is their intervention in the thinking of religion and politics at the margins of the worlds of medieval Islam that has attracted the attention of historians. The contemporary histories of South Asian Islam, as pointed out by Bruce Lawrence in an early essay, have neglected regional Sufi orders such as those which emerged around Sayyid 'Alī Hamadānī and Nund Rishi in Kashmir.[90] It is in this context that the mystical poetry of Nund Rishi acquires even more significance, especially because, as Chitralekha Zutshi reminds us, he "contributed to the production of a regional culture on the site of the development of the new religious culture" after the advent of Islam in Kashmir.[91] The Kashmiri tradition remembers Nund Rishi's mystical poetry as the Koshur Qu'rān, or the Kashmiri Qur'ān, just as the Persians remember the poetry of Jalāl al-Dīn Rūmī as the Persian Qur'ān. Ronit Ricci, in an influential study on the spread of Islam in South East Asia, has highlighted the role played by "literary networks" that shaped regional and trans-regional Islamic histories.[92] This was a context in which "orally transmitted materials as well as performative traditions complemented and enriched written literatures" and a large number of people, whom some would call illiterate by contemporary standards, could recite texts for a whole number of occasions.[93] Texts like *shruk*s in Kashmir or *kāfī*s in Punjab had a similar function in pre-modern Islamic north India. The *shruk*s of Nund Rishi were widely disseminated among such audiences rather than "readers" and shaped the history of Islam in Kashmir. As Ricci puts it: "Texts written in metrical verse and meant to be recited, often in public, were central to conveying and shaping cultural codes, religious doctrines, and political agendas."[94] However, this conveying and shaping of "cultural codes, religious doctrines and political agendas" unfolded in a dynamic environment in fourteenth–fifteenth-century Kashmir and involved multiple acts of translating, and provincializing, Islam.[95]

What do we mean when we call Nund Rishi's mystical poetry the work of translating Islam? Nund Rishi grounds his thinking in Qur'ānic technical language but complicates our understanding of Islam by translating its conceptual vocabulary into the everyday language and lifeworld of an ordinary Kashmiri. It is in this act of translation and political deconstruction that Nund Rishi finds his own voice as a thinker and a poet at the cusp of the Hindu–Muslim encounter in medieval Kashmir. In her introduction to *A Multilingual Nation: Translation and Language Dynamic in India*, Rita Kothari writes: "It is largely (not entirely) in the devotional and the mystical that the mixed languages of premodern India have stayed with us, reminding us of the monolingual imagination of our own times."[96] Such monolingualism marks most translations of Nund Rishi into Urdu or English but is absent in the source text.[97] The saint-poets such as Nund Rishi instead "tell stories of multiplicities inadequately captured in the term 'multilingual.'"[98] But it is not only in this sense that we inherit Nund Rishi as always already translated. It is useful to remember that Nund Rishi was not addressing a monolithic Muslim audience in the modern sense but a heterogeneous Kashmiri audience with fluid religious boundaries. We also cannot ignore the fact that the mystical verses of Nund Rishi have come down to us in a living oral tradition (Lal Ded and Nund Rishi are both sung) which mediates our reading of the mystical verses in the *nūrnāmu'* and the *rishīnamu'*. I have often compared different versions and chosen mostly either Saqi or Kamil's renderings of the *shruk*s.

The cultural memory of the Rishi Order is inextricably connected to the historical and political imaginings of Kashmir as a region. The Rishi Order is the only regional Sufi Order to have emerged in Kashmir, and it is with the Rishis that a local articulation of Kashmir gets instituted (unlike the imperial articulations of early medieval Kashmiri rulers).[99] Most of the Rishis were Kashmiri, and Nund Rishi used the Kashmiri language to reach out to his Kashmiri audiences (primarily comprising the peasantry) as centers of Rishi thought and practice were gradually established all over Kashmir.[100] Even though the Kubrāwiyyā Order flourished in Kashmir, and was strongly associated in South Asia with Kashmir, it was a Persianate Sufi Order.[101] The Kubrāwiyyā, fueled by a pan-Islamic concern with the Sharī'ah in its early years in Kashmir, was to also eventually become intimately connected with the Muslim regional sentiment in Kashmir.[102] But the Kubrāwiyyā remained in its early years in an uneasy relationship with the local population which practiced a hybrid form of Islam.[103] We will explore the tensions between the Kubrāwiyyā and the Rishis in Chapter 1. But both Sayyid 'Alī Hamadānī and Nund Rishi came to be revered as Sufi exemplars by Kashmiri Muslims in the long run, and the Kashmiri tradition gradually smoothed out any historical memory of differences between the two orders (on questions such as the Sharī'ah and the relations of new Kashmiri Muslim converts to pre-Islamic religious culture of Kashmir). Yet the tensions persisted as a salient ingredient in Kashmiri social and political life and were further complicated by questions of caste and class. The regional problems of caste and class come under severe indictment in the *vākh*s and *shruk*s of Lal Ded and Nund Rishi but are largely absent from concerns expressed in the pan-Islamic mystical theology of Sayyid 'Alī Hamadānī. But one thing common between the Kubrāwiyyā and the Rishi Order was their strong regional identification with Kashmir. Bruce Lawrence raises a question as valid for Nund Rishi as it is for Sayyid 'Alī Hamadānī: "Is it not possible, however, that the too focused regional loyalties of his followers might restrict a saint whose contemporary reputation, *silsilā* affiliation and tomb-cult qualified him for pan-Indian fame?"[104] The question Lawrence raises about the limited pan-India fame of Sayyid 'Alī Hamadānī and Nund Rishi could also be rearticulated as a question about the limited influence of a pan-Indian Sufi Order like the Chishtiyyā in Kashmir. According to Lawrence, the reason that the Kubrāwiyyā remained a regional Kashmiri phenomenon in South Asia, and the Rishis also emerged as a powerful local order, is because Kashmiris "yield to non-indigenous cultural forms slowly, grudgingly, in most cases by transforming them into something identified as 'Kashmiri.'"[105] It is in this strong regional sentiment that we must locate the appeal of not only Nund Rishi but also Sayyid 'Alī Hamadānī and Lal Ded. As Chitralekha Zutshi writes, the Persianate literary and religious tradition in Kashmir eventually "attempted to localize Islam by associating it with the indigenous mystical sect of the Rishis in Kashmir."[106]

A regional sentiment has played a significant role in Kashmir's history since the medieval times. Kashmir could not be assimilated into the Delhi Sultanate and entered the powerful Mughal Empire only after a long struggle that ended as late as 1586. Bruce Lawrence writes that the "proprietary zest of Kashmiri devotionalism is further confirmed in the Rishi order."[107]

I would add that not only does the Rishi Order confirm the proprietary zest of Kashmiri devotionalism, it also exemplifies that devotionalism as a site of translation between the Islamic, Hindu, and Buddhist linguistic and social registers.[108] Vegetarianism on the death anniversaries (*vọrus* or *'urs*) of the Rishi saints, rituals such as distributing rice cooked with turmeric (*tạhạr*), offerings made at shrines (*niyāz*), and loud recitations of supplications after prayers (*awrād* and *manājāt* recitations) bear witness to the continuing influence of Hinduism and Buddhism on the social life of Islam in Kashmir.[109] According to G. N. Gauhar, Nund Rishi even composed a poem about the Buddha at the end of his twelve years of meditation called *Buddha Carita* (now believed to be lost).[110] But this could also be an allusion to a manuscript of Aśvagoṣha's *Buddhācharita* in possession of Nund Rishi (it is unclear on what evidence Gauhar based such a serious claim). D. J. F. Newall, in one of the earliest English-language writings on the hermits of Kashmir in 1870, writes of the Rishis that "the tendency to seclusion so characteristic of Buddhism may have also influenced these solitaries."[111] Many of these developments in the field of Kashmiri literary and religious culture emerged at the same time as the intensification of the regional sentiment in Kashmir.[112] The Rishi movement was a popular religious one because, as David Lorenzen suggests, like many pre-modern South Asian religious movements, most of its followers (if not the leaders) came "from middle- and lower-class groups and not from elite sections of the population."[113] According to Mohammad Ishaq Khan, the social classes most involved with the Rishi movement were "petty tradesmen, artisans, sweepers, tanners, *dombs*, *dambel-maets* and men belonging to other down-trodden castes...."[114] One of the central characteristics of the Rishi thought and practice was, according to Khan, their belief in the "dignity and fundamental equality of man."[115] Khan further writes that Nund Rishi's role was "undoubtedly marked off from most Sufis by his social concerns, over and above his spiritual pre-occupations."[116] The questions of caste and class are the ones that most troubled Nund Rishi, and he regarded hunger as "the most degrading of adversities."[117] Baba Ali Raina, a later Suharwardī Sufi, on a visit to the Chrar shrine, dreams of Nund Rishi, who draws his attention to the poverty of the caretakers of the tomb complex.[118] The condition of Kashmiri peasantry remained central to Nund Rishi's political concerns. For Khan, what was unique about Nund Rishi was that he could engage Kashmiris on "matters ranging from ontology to immediate social concerns."[119] Not only did the Rishi Order forcefully express a concern for Kashmir's poor, it also remained open to women. Among Nund Rishi's female disciples were Behat Bībī, Dehat Bībī, Shām Dẏd, and Shangu' Bībī.[120] Nund Rishi, much like Ḥamid al-Dīn Nāgorī of the Chishtī Order, embraced poverty and regional commitment. The function of the Rishis in Kashmir as such appears to be similar to those of the Chishtīs in north India and the Deccan.[121]

The Rishis were more popular in rural Kashmir than the city of Srinagar. There are shrines associated with all the major Sufi orders in Kashmir, but the Rishi centers in rural Kashmir far outweigh the number of shrines belonging to other Sufi orders, signaling a wider popularity of the Rishis in the countryside.[122] There are few Rishi shrines in the capital city of Srinagar, which is otherwise dominated by the shrines of the Kubrāwiyyā, Suharwardīyya, and Naqshbandīyya Sufis. Bruce Lawrence speaks of a double profile – high and low – for Sufi *silsilā*s (orders) in the subcontinent.[123] Such a classification has the same limits as that of the conceptual opposition between the Great Tradition and the Little Tradition, deployed, for instance, in the study of Islam in the region by the historian Aziz Ahmad, but it is nonetheless helpful as a heuristic tool in situating the tension between the Kubrāwiyyā and the Rishi Orders.[124] The Kubrāwiyyā and the Rishi Orders can be seen as expressions of this high and low profile for Sufi *silsilā*s in Kashmir. The multicreedal participation in the Rishi movement, which has persisted to the present, could also have played a role in the rapid development of Rishi shrines in rural Kashmir because the population of Kashmir in the early fifteenth century was still largely Hindu.[125] For the Hindus and Buddhists of Kashmir, the Rishis were hardly distinguishable from the *siddha*s and *yogi*s who had traversed the Kashmiri landscape for centuries. According to Mohammad Ishaq Khan, the Rishis did not marry, abstained from eating meat, and subsisted on wild vegetables (*vọpalhākh*, in particular), which were freely available in the forest.[126] Some of the Rishis even dressed like *yogi*s.[127] As Patton E. Burchett points out in relation to the Sufis and the *bhakta*s of the sultanate and Mughal periods, the Rishis of Kashmir were also operating in a historical context of

> the demise of mainstream, institutional tantra (alongside the rise of the Nāth *yogi*s, *haṭha yoga*, and Vedānta); an encounter between the cosmopolitan literary-political cultures of Persian and Sanskrit; the emergence of a transsectarian religious culture centered on charismatic ascetics possessing occult powers; and the rise of vernacular-literary composition and performance.[128]

Or, in other words, medieval *bhaktī* influenced north Indian Sufism as much as north Indian Sufism influenced medieval *bhaktī*. It is in the light of this fact that we should understand why Kashmiri tradition continues to remember Nund Rishi almost always in a relation to Lal Ded.

It remains unclear to what degree the Rishi *silsilā* (order) was like the other Sufi *silsilā*s. Sufism arrived in Kashmir when it had already passed from its classical to an institutional phase (and reached the historical development in which *khānqah*s, a physical residence for Sufi communities, and *ṭarīqā*s, Sufi orders, were established): it was no longer confined to ascetic protest groups but involved hierarchical organization, charismatic leaders (*pīr*s, *shaykh*s, or *murshid*s), and territories of spiritual jurisdiction (*wilāyat*). In other words, Sufism itself had been looking for fresh ground, especially those strands of it that were in competition with each other. The geographical spread of the network of Rishi *mazār*s (tombs) and the hagiographical accounts of its charismatic leaders suggest that the Rishis functioned like other medieval Sufi orders but also shared much in common with medieval dervish groups.[129] But more significantly, the Rishi Order emerged in fifteenth-century Kashmir not as a quietistic mystical order but as a popular religiopolitical movement that intervened in debates about the meanings of Islam at a time when Sufi rivalries in Kashmir had acquired unusual intensity over the relation of the new Muslim sultanate to the question of the Sharīʿah (or Islamic Law).

Aziz Ahmad writes, in a seminal essay on conversions in Kashmir, that at that early stage, "Islam in Kashmir was as tolerant and eclectic as the Hinduism of Kashmir," where it had been brought by soldiers and merchants from as early as the ninth century.[130] Even before the rise of the Rishis, "the basic Islamic model was the travelling or immigrant Ṣūfī of the 'little tradition,' the Qalandar and the dervish."[131] The conversions to Islam in Kashmir were gradual and started at the end of a long and turbulent period of internal instability made worse by the Mongol invasions.[132] Aziz Ahmad hints that caste appears to have played a significant role in conversions and consolidation of Muslim power in the fourteenth century.[133] The eight-month-long occupation of Kashmir by the Mongol commander Zulju in 1321 had ravaged the valley, and many Kashmiris were captured to be sold in the slave markets.[134] Zulju's was the third and the most severe of the Mongol invasions of Kashmir.[135] Even though Zulju perished on his return from Kashmir, there was a deep crisis of legitimacy amongst Kashmiris, who had organized themselves into communal self-help groups. The state of affairs in the early fourteenth century is best described in a Sanskrit chronicle from the fifteenth century: "When even the king cowered concealed like an owl from sheer fear, what need one say of all the other people?"[136] The small Muslim warbands in Kashmir slowly acquired positions of power, and a combination of circumstances pushed a fugitive prince from Ladakh, Rinchen, to the throne of Kashmir.[137] The rule of Rinchen, who converted to Islam and ruled as Sultan Ṣadr al-Dīn, lasted only three years, and Hindu rule was soon restored. But the Muslim nobles like Shāh Mīr had consolidated their power at the Kashmiri court. The resistance of Shāh Mīr to late Mongol threats in Kashmir made him even more popular, as the Hindu King Udayanadeva had fled to Ladakh during one such invasion.[138] Shāh Mīr's defense of Kashmir against other Muslim invaders such as Achala and Urdil also made him acceptable to Kashmir's Hindu political and military elite as a ruler.[139] But it was only after years of uncertainty and intrigue that Shāh Mīr finally ascended to the throne in 1339 AD under the title of Sultan Shams al-Dīn and founded the Shāhmīrī dynasty. Many groups of Muslim immigrants from Iran and Central Asia now began to arrive in Kashmir, who saw it as a land of opportunity just beyond the realm of Ilkhanid Mongols. It was at this time that the Kubrāwiyyā – a highly trained and professional class of immigrant Sufis from Iran – started missionary work in Kashmir and insisted on the strict implementation of the Sharīʿah. But it was not until the reign of Sultan Sikandar (1389–1413) that Islam began to impact state policy.[140] Even then the iconoclastic sultan had Hindu wives, and the atmosphere at the court still was, as Aziz Ahmad calls it, one of "highly symbiotic syncretism."[141] Yet Sultan Sikandar persecuted many of his Hindu subjects, which led to their migration to other regions of South Asia.[142] These were decades of rapid social transformation in Kashmir, which have been interpreted in retrospect along sectarian lines. The Sanskrit chronicler Jonaraja characterizes these changes in the following way: "As the wind destroyed the trees, and locusts the shali crop, so did the Yavanas destroy the usages of Kashmira."[143] Sultan Sikandar also destroyed the colossal Buddha image which had been spared destruction by Sultan Shihāb al-Dīn.[144] Even as Mohammad Ishaq Khan dismisses the anxieties of Jonaraja and Srivara, two Sanskrit chroniclers of the early sultanate period, as merely a concern for the preservation of Brahmin hegemony, it is more likely that the tensions between the Hindu and the Muslim communities had escalated by the end of the fourteenth century. It is against this background that Nund Rishi started the Rishi movement, which approached Islam from the standpoint of local, and non-elite, concerns of its new Kashmiri converts and the non-Muslim majority.[145] Even though Khan argues that Nund Rishi, and Lal Ded, helped connect the Little (peasant) tradition of Kashmir to the Great (Islamic) tradition, he concedes that Lal Ded and Nund Rishi's "verses of 'dissent' and 'protest' gradually created a sense of awareness in the common man against social and political discrimination."[146] It does not occur to Khan that this political rebellion may have nothing to do with the presumed desire in peasant society (which he calls, following Robert Redfield, a half-society) to connect with what he calls "the Great tradition of the reflective few...."[147] Rather, it may articulate a Kashmiri view from below at a time of political transitions.

The entry of the Kubrāwiyyā Sufis in Kashmir as immigrants, including for missionary work, had a clear consequence: an assertion of the superiority of Muslim rule and an assumption of the inferiority of the non-Muslim population.[148] For Aziz Ahmad, the purpose of the mission of Sayyid 'Alī Hamadānī "was not the 'conversion' of non-Muslims, but rather the 'Islamization' of the ruling dynasty and the nominally Muslim element of the ruling elite."[149] Hamadānī began by reforming the small Muslim minority in Srinagar and insisted that the ruler, Sultan Qutb al-Dīn, adopt Muslim dress and customs as well as distance himself from the prevailing Hindu–Buddhist culture in Kashmir.[150] Sayyid 'Alī Hamadānī also championed "a pietistic political concept of monarchy" best expressed in his treatise *Dhakhīrat al-mulūk*.[151] The move to "Islamization" and Sharī'ah-based rule by the Kubrāwiyyā gained momentum later under Sultan Sikandar, who ruled from 1389 to 1413, and the arrival of Sayyid 'Alī Hamadānī's son, Mīr Muḥammad Hamadānī, in Kashmir. The Kubrāwiyyā mantle was taken up later in the fifteenth century by the Nūrbakshīya, who also played a role in the gradual Islamization of Kashmir.[152] Sayyid 'Alī Hamadānī was more concerned about the state of the Sharī'ah in Kashmir than gaining new converts. As Mohammad Ishaq Khan writes:

> It would appear that the subsequent missionary activities of Saiyid 'Ali, his son, and their followers in the Valley need to be studied not only in the context of their missionary zeal to spread the true message of Islam but also in the context of their deep concern for the enforcement of the Islamic law in a land where the norms of the sharī'a were violated by the new converts; thus, their aim was not only to reconvert, but to consolidate the foothold already gained.[153]

According to Abdul Qaiyum Rafiqi, the fact that Sayyid 'Alī Hamadānī left Kashmir when Sultan Qutb al-Dīn did not implement the Sharī'ah is corroborated by four different sources.[154] Rafiqi argues that the conflict between Sayyid 'Alī Hamadānī and Sultan Qutb al-Dīn emerged "in their different attitudes regarding the implementation of the *Shari'a* which made it impossible for the Sayyīd to be reconciled with the policies of Sultan Qutbud'Dīn."[155] Sayyid 'Alī Hamadānī may have left Kashmir after disagreements with Sultan Qutb al-Dīn over the question of Sharī'ah but he always commanded the respect of the Shāhmīrī sultans.[156] The Shāhmīrī rulers of Kashmir wore the cap of Sayyid 'Alī Hamadānī, which he had given to Sultan Qutb al-Dīn before he left Kashmir, until the death of Sultan Fateh Shah in 1493.[157] Later, Muhammad Hamadānī, the son of Sayyid 'Alī Hamadānī, became the leader of the Kubrāwiyyā community in Kashmir and converted Sūha Bhaṭṭa, the sultan's chief minister and commander-in-chief, to Islam. Sūha Bhaṭṭa (who took the Muslim name of Saif al-Dīn) pursued a policy of persecution toward Kashmir's Hindu population. It was Sūha Bhaṭṭa (Saif al-Dīn) who placed restrictions on Nund Rishi.[158] The tensions between the Kubrāwiyyā and the Rishis did not, however, escalate in the subsequent rule of Sultan Zayn al-'Ābidīn even though one of Nund Rishi's closest disciples, Bābā Zain al-Dīn Rishi, was sent into exile by the sultanate authorities.[159]

Mohammad Ishaq Khan emphasizes that Nund Rishi made no conscious effort to convert people to Islam, even though some prominent non-Muslims did convert to join the Rishi Order.[160] Rafiqi concurs when he writes that the Rishis "did not concern themselves with missionary activities or the establishment of *madrasa*s, and kept themselves aloof from the ruling classes."[161] But elsewhere Khan reads in the asceticism of the Rishis a method and "mode of conversion."[162] Khan's anxiety about the Rishis is best betrayed by his own words: "... the beliefs of the Rishis were not incompatible with Islam."[163] This is something with which he struggles in his historical study as elements in Nund Rishi's thinking bear a strong relation to Hindu and Buddhist thought. The eventual popularity of the Rishis also hints at the reinstatement of the fluid exchange between the Hindu and Muslim traditions at the beginning of Sultan Zayn al-'Ābidīn's rule (revered in Kashmir as the Buḍ Shāh, or the Great King) in 1420. Nund Rishi had launched his religiopolitical movement under Sultan Sikandar's reign (1389–1413) and was even arrested under the subsequent rule of Sultan Ali Shah (1413–20).[164] But the Rishi Order gathered momentum during the egalitarian reign of Sultan Zayn al 'Ābidīn, who was among the mourners at his funeral in Chrar.[165] But not even half a century's rule of Zayn al-ʿĀbidīn (who even allowed the new Muslim converts to return to their old faith) could fully reverse the impact of Sultan Sikandar's policies.[166] Even though historians such as Mohammad Ishaq Khan place the Rishis at the heart of Kashmir's transition to Islam, Aziz Ahmad argues that the influence of the Rishis on conversion was comparatively small:

> ... the 'little tradition' of the Rishīs was ascetic: they lived away from urban areas either in little villages or forests. Though by the end of the fifteenth and during the sixteenth centuries they came to have a *khānqāh* with their own living saints: the influence of their order on conversion to Islam was comparatively small, compared to the ongoing conversion in the Great Tradition represented by the Hamadānī mosque and *khānqāh* and the efforts of Bayhaqi sayyids who had very soon become a militant elite.[167]

The tension between the Persianate Sufis and the Kashmiri Rishis was to have an enduring impact on Kashmiri society. Rafiqi asserts that the opposing approaches to Sufism among the Persian Sufis and the Kashmiri Rishis became "a latent ingredient of the Kashmiri social pattern."[168] What is it that the Rishis opposed? The involvement with political power of the Persian Sufis appeared to the Rishis to contradict the principles of Sufism; and for the Persian Sufis, the Rishi practices appeared to contradict the principles of Islam.[169] The Rishi–Kubrāwiyyā tensions evolved into the more muted Rishi –Suhrawardī tensions by the sixteenth century (even though there appears to have been more accommodation between the Rishis and the Suhrawardī Sufis).[170] There was another consequence of the control of the Persian Sufi orders over the Kashmiri court: the Persianization of Kashmir that Rafiqi contends "ushered in an era of cultural conquest" leading to changes in food, dress, and diet of Kashmiris.[171] Perhaps the situation was more fluid and complex. Yet these cataclysmic changes are echoed in the mood of anxiety that we often come across in the *shruk*s. The Rishis appear to have been working toward building an alternative spiritual and political community in Kashmir. It is for this reason that Nund Rishi traveled through the length and breadth of Kashmir and Rishi centers emerged in remote corners of Kashmir. Charles Ramsey reminds us that the Rishis had "emphasized solidarity through local governance, and warned of the consequences of inviting foreign rule."[172] The spirituo-political movement of the Rishis expressed nothing less than the Kashmiri political unconscious at a moment of difficult transitions.

The Rishis may have failed to achieve a secure and self-reliant Kashmiri political future, but their struggle for a pan-Kashmiri political spirituality endures in Kashmiri cultural memory.

Even though it is necessary to situate Nund Rishi's poetic thinking in its historical context, I will, however, not be dealing any more with the history of the Rishi movement in this book.[173] I restrict myself in this book to Nund Rishi's thinking on the themes of Islam, death, the Nothing, and the apocalyptic. I contend that Nund Rishi's thinking of Islam, death, the Nothing, and the apocalyptic are the elements of a vernacular Islamic negative theology – a negative political theology.[174] We have so far seen that the mystical poetry of Nund Rishi (and Lal Ded) inaugurated a vernacular literary culture in the Kashmiri language in a region dominated by Sanskrit and Persian literary cultures and, in doing so, challenged the new political order of medieval Kashmir in which the Persian Sufi orders and the urban elite remained dominant. But this vernacular literary culture also gave expression to a negative political theology. Let me state clearly that I do not think that the thinking of Nund Rishi must, or can, be read solely as a negative theology. The moments of negative theology in Nund Rishi are many but are also put into question by the other more cataphatic (God-affirming) moments. Nund Rishi's mystical poetry can certainly be read in the traditional register (that is, a devotional register which points toward the immense unnamable and unmarkable greatness of the divine), but there are moments where another register intrudes, and those are the moments that are of interest to me. These are the moments of sudden encounters that the *shruk*s set up with the questions of faith, death, the Nothing, and the apocalyptic: the signature of all negative theology.

Negative theology is nothing less than the name saved for a long inheritance of a shared understanding of the negative path, *via negativa*, across faiths from ancient Asia and the Near East, Greco-Roman Late Antiquity to the Islam of the medieval Indo-Persian worlds. Negative theology eludes attempts to approach its meaning because it is precisely in escaping such a determination that it establishes its field and boundaries. But minimally, let us begin with an understanding of negative theology as a discourse on the transcendent which turns on negations rather than affirmations by approaching the question of what God is from the standpoint of what God is not. Even though the historical legacy of negative theology is difficult to disregard in relation to Nund Rishi, I not only define negative theology historically but, following Michael Sells, consider it formally as a term that could designate any text that meets the requirements of its discourse.[175] The thinking of faith, death, the Nothing, and the apocalyptic; the critique of theological knowledge and absolutist power; and the turn to the everyday and an ecological ethic in Nund Rishi's mystical poetry – all bring us up against aporias that resemble those of negative theology. Negative theology is always this resemblance to negative theology.[176]

Let us also briefly consider a serious charge that has often been leveled against negative theology. Negative theology (in its Neoplatonic, Christian, Judaic, and Islamic moments) has been accused of being invested in a Being beyond being. The accusation is that it is impossible in the end for negative theology not to posit God as a Being. This is the accusation that the philosophers Michel Foucault and Jacques Derrida bring against negative theology.[177] As Derrida himself points out in his essay "How to Avoid Speaking: Denials," one is always accused of, never congratulated for, negative theology.[178] Yet, for Derrida, negative theology "seems to reserve, beyond all positive predication, beyond all negation, even beyond Being, some hyperessentiality, a being beyond being ... God as without Being."[179] Jean-Luc Marion too has cautioned that it is perhaps better to speak of a "negative way" rather than a negative theology because "it is inseparable from the 'affirmative way' that precedes it...."[180] Yet it is difficult to isolate with any degree of certainty a rule or measure in this move to reserve a "being beyond being" which is not at the same time slipping away from all predication. For the Neoplatonists, the question of being before or beyond difference is fundamental, but the question of being (and the Nothing) does not necessarily appear in the same way in Christian and Islamic negative theology. One needs to approach the discontinuities and denials which rend the "affirmations" of negative theology in order to decide about the accusation that negative theology seeks to conserve a hyperessential being beyond Being. Such an accusation runs the risk of foreclosing a serious consideration of the traditions of negative theology at the margins of multiple linguistic and religious traditions. Derrida too is also not entirely pessimistic and writes: "Perhaps there is within it [negative theology], hidden, restless, diverse, and itself heterogeneous, a massive and indistinct multiplicity of possibles for which the single expression 'negative theology' still remains inadequate."[181] This study of Nund Rishi's mystical poetry is a way of exploring a heterogeneous and nebulous multiplicity within the single field of a Kashmiri mystic's thought. Needless to add, such a heterogeneous and nebulous multiplicity is also at work even in such mystics taken up by Jacques Derrida as Meister Eckhart or Angelus Silesius.[182]

Why insist on reading the poetic thinking of Nund Rishi as a form of negative theology? Why persist with the name of negative theology? One way in which Nund Rishi's thinking belongs to the legacy of negative theology is, without doubt, its explicit connection to Sufism, Neoplatonism, and the thinking of the Nothing in the Hindu and Buddhist traditions. Indeed, it is not one negative theology which we see at play in the negative theology of Nund Rishi but many.[183] Even within the Islamic tradition, as Aydogan Kars has persuasively argued, there is not one negative theology but many negative theologies.[184] Derrida's remarks on negative theology in a late essay on the German mystic Angelus Silesius further clarify the stakes of risking the name of negative theology for the thinking of Nund Rishi:

> How would what still comes to us under the domestic, European, Greek, and Christian term of negative theology, of negative way, of apophatic discourse, be the chance of an incomparable translatability in principle without limit? Not of a universal tongue, of an ecumenism or of some consensus, but of a tongue to come that can be shared more than ever?[185]

Negative theology is this possibility of "a tongue to come that can be shared more than ever": it is the chance or risk of a translatability without limit[186] – of singularity and difference rather than oneness and universality. It is, of course, much easier to approach Nund Rishi's thinking, and the politico-religious movement from which it is inseparable, as mysticism (a universal term, which despite its complex trajectory, I sometimes do use interchangeably with negative theology because there is no absolutely cataphatic mysticism), but it is the work of negative theology in Nund Rishi's mysticism which concerns me the most. For at stake is the chance of "a tongue that can be shared more than ever."

Michael Sells points out that mysticism is often concerned with the extraordinary, transcendent, and the unimaginable, but in apophatic mysticism or negative theology, the extraordinary, transcendent, and the unimaginable appear in a relation to the common and the everyday.[187] There is almost an existential turn in the Islamic negative theology of Nund Rishi which situates God in relation to the common and the everyday in rural Kashmir. A negative theology irrupts in Nund Rishi's *shruks* on Islam, death, the Nothing, the apocalyptic and settles over his entire corpus. The moments of negative theology emerge in the mystical poetry of Nund Rishi in such a way that everything else seems to depend on it. Or to put it more simply, negative theology is the most powerful strand in Nund Rishi's mystical poetry. The slightness of the reference corpus (a few hundred *shruk*s of Nund Rishi) also should not pose a serious problem: Derrida reminds us that in negative theology, "the essential tendency is to formalizing rarefaction."[188] We cannot think of Nund Rishi without the knots (*shruki̱*), crossings (*tār*), and the winter (*pōh tu' māg*) of negative theology.

The negative theology of the Rishis in Kashmir, and I would go so far as to claim that the trajectory of negative theology in Kashmir and not merely in Rishism, emerges in a relation to moments of political crises.[189] Gershom Scholem, the Jewish philosopher, has pointed out that the great moments of mysticism "can be identified with great moments of crisis."[190] The trajectory of mystical saying and unsaying in Kashmir emerges in a relation to certain persistent political themes such as contestations over the meanings of Kashmir as a place, of religious law and political power, and controversies over the question of Islam. There is undoubtedly an intensification in the discourses of negative theology in times of political crisis in Kashmir. The fundamental manner in which negative theology marks Sufi poetry in Kashmir is in the way it seeks to collapse the idea of total transcendence of God into the experience of total immanence.[191] The Rishi Order emerged in the early fifteenth century in a Kashmir weakened by Mongol attacks and in a state of transition marked not only by the creation and consolidation of a new Muslim sultanate but also by religious conversions to Islam and immigration from Central Asia. As William Franke reminds us in relation to the Neoplatonic philosophy of the One (the Greek, pre-monotheistic moment of negative theology):

> Negative theology arises at a very advanced stage in the development of rational reflection in any given culture, a stage where the founding myths of that culture, and lastly language itself as the foundation of all culture, come into question.[192]

The late fourteenth and early fifteenth centuries in Kashmir's history were a time when the founding myths of Kashmiri culture had come into question. What were the political and cultural implications of the rise of an Islamic negative theology that affirmed a relation with Hindu and Buddhist negative theology at the frontiers of Islam? In the end, it is not very useful to approach this question by tracing the influence of this or that tradition of negative theology on Nund Rishi; instead, it is perhaps more productive to see the unfolding tradition of apophasis in Kashmir as informed by competing trajectories of mystical and negative theology. Michael Sells argues that even if apophatic discourse is grounded in particular traditions, it often opens onto interreligious conversation.[193] The sudden flowering of negative theology in medieval Kashmir also opens out to an interreligious conversation which the Kashmiri tradition has inherited as the cultural memory of a relation between Lal Ded and Nund Rishi and the promise of "a tongue that can be shared," a Kashmiri language to come. Such an "interreligious conversation" could not have taken place without risks or even courage. The practice of the mystics to go beyond what is permissible, or even accessible (often to return empty-handed), Jacques Derrida has called "apophatic boldness."[194] Derrida writes:

> ... apophatic boldness always consists in going further than is reasonably permitted. That is one of the essential traits of all negative theology: passing to the limit, then crossing a frontier, including that of a community, thus of a sociopolitical, institutional, ecclesial reason or *raison d'être*.[195]

The negative theology of Nund Rishi crosses the borders between Islam, Hinduism, and Buddhism with striking ingenuity and boldness. Does this thinking of crossing frontiers open on to the vision of a new, and possible, political community? This is the question the Rishi movement, and its thinking, poses for us.

Michel de Certeau ventures a fascinating hypothesis about the upsurge of mysticism in sixteenth- and seventeenth-century France: "Just as the massive adoption of German culture by the Jews in the nineteenth century made possible theoretic innovations and an exceptional intellectual productivity, the upsurge of *mystics* in the sixteenth and seventeenth centuries was often the effect of the Jewish difference in the usage of a Catholic idiom."[196] I venture that the upsurge of mysticism in fourteenth- and fifteenth-century Kashmir owed much to the effect of a Hindu difference in an Islamic idiom. This is certainly suggested by the very name *rishī* of the Sufi order founded by Nund Rishi. My proposition then is that it is the Rishi thinking of the negative that grounds the relation between Islamic negative theology and its others in medieval Kashmir, and drives the rise of the Kashmiri vernacular from the language of the everyday to a language of poetic and religious expression. This way of thinking need not be construed as a neo-syncretist impulse: an openness to interreligious conversation is a potential that inheres in negative theology within any mystical tradition.[197] It is rather a forceful expression of the essential unknowability of God that has the potential to transform the conflicting claims of theological knowledge in different religious traditions into an ethical concern about the limits, and dangers, of such theological knowledge.

I approach the Rishi thought in general and Nund Rishi's negative theology in particular as a mode of understanding the world which never formalized itself into a body of doctrine but instead founded in the Kashmiri tradition a mode of what Michael Sells has called "mystical saying and unsaying."[198] Such a tradition is incapable of formalizing a doctrine. This is perhaps the reason we find few traces of the order's historical trajectory except through and in the history of the other Sufi orders such as the Suharwardīyya and the Kubrāwiyyā with a relatively more stable archive. The Rishi Order did not attain the formalization and institutionalization which are typical of other Sufi orders because it never systematized its teachings or surrendered its tendency toward asceticism.[199] It was also more or less invisibilized by a gradual absorption into Persianate Sufi orders such as the Suharwardīyya.[200] Negative theology has, in any case, always appeared only as a possibility within different traditions without typically forming or congealing into schools.[201]

As soon as we speak of a Christian negative theology in medieval Germany or Islamic negative theology in medieval Kashmir, we are tempted to ask the question: Is negative theology one or many? Jacques Derrida concedes that the unity of the legacy of negative theology is difficult to delimit.[202] The emergence of negative theologies across geographical and religious boundaries in medieval Eurasia also poses a difficult question about the time and place of negative theology. Many radical exponents of negative theology across Eurasia flourished at a time of vernacularization and the transition from the pre-modern to early modern ways of life.[203] If Nund Rishi's negative theology was part of a larger discourse of Islamic mysticism in South Asia, it also emerged at a time when the Sufi–*bhaktī* movement was gaining ground in north India. The Indian poet and scholar A. K. Ramanujan reads such moments in the history of medieval South Asia as "anti-contextual" movements: as movements which think new universals that are not context-specific.[204] But the Rishi movement was contextualizing, or vernacularizing, the new universalism of Islam as a local, and anti-imperial, universalism.

We witness across medieval South Asia attempts to challenge political power in the name of a new thinking grounded in a personal relation to the transcendent which opens up the political to the demands of the subaltern. The negative theology of Nund Rishi must then be read not merely as one articulation among others of the "negative path" across regions in medieval

Europe and Asia but as a mode of approaching the question of the political from the standpoint of "the negative determination of God."[205] We must also keep in mind yet another helpful elucidation by Michel de Certeau: "There is a rural and urban register of mystical experience"[206] – an elite and subaltern register of mystical experience. And what he says about the mystics of sixteenth- and seventeenth-century France is as true of the Rishi movement in fourteenth- and fifteenth-century Kashmir: "A subterranean organization was brought to light, unveiling and multiplying the resources of a peasant tradition within the very mystical experience that sprang from it."[207] What does "mystical experience" mean outside the elite, urban register? What is the relation of "mystical experience" to vernacular proto-modernity? What is the religion of the subaltern? These are some of the questions that Nund Rishi's mystical poetry entrusts to us.

Negative theology pushes language to its limits only to remain open to that about which it cannot say anything. There is a wide range of texts that share in this condition, and the recent renewal of interest in these texts in Kashmir reflects the situation of a deep crisis in the contemporary political field. In Chapters 2 and 4, I trace the relations that a thinking of death and the apocalyptic bears to the language of a spiritual and political crisis. The thinking of death which I develop in Chapter 2 is unique to Nund Rishi in the Kashmiri mystical tradition, and I also interpret it through the lens of two early essays on Nund Rishi by the Kashmiri poet and critic Rahman Rahi. Chapter 4 explores the tensions between ontology and eschatology in Nund Rishi's thought. In Chapter 3, I take up the theme of the Nothing, and negation, in the *shruks*, especially in relation to the Sufi call to "die before you die." We see in Chapters 1 and 3 that this was not merely a call to an ethical self-transformation but also a call to political transformation that sought to open up the collective life of the new Muslim sultanate to radical forms of equality and social coexistence. I begin in Chapter 1 by situating Nund Rishi's negative theology in relation to the debates about Sufism and the Sharīʿah where Nund Rishi's Islam emerges in relation to a Ḥallājian, or Sufi, negative theology. The existential and political charge of this negative theology is explicit in Chapter 1 and developed in subsequent chapters in relation to some of the most dominant themes in Nund Rishi's mystical poetry.

Notes

1. John F. Burns, "Muslim Shrine in Kashmir Is Destroyed," *New York Times*, May 12, 1995, http://www.nytimes.com/1995/05/12/world/muslim-shrine-in-kashmir-is-destroyed.html (accessed August 19, 2020).
2. It was in Chrar that hundreds of thousands of Kashmiri nationalists gathered in March 1990 in response to a call given by the separatist Jammu and Kashmir Liberation Front (JKLF) to demand self-determination and vow to struggle for *azādi* (freedom) – a demonstration that also cost many Kashmiri lives.
3. I do not consider here the significance of the Chrar shrine for the Islamists with transnational commitments because of the latter's negligible impact on Kashmiri social and political life.
4. Some of the erstwhile territory of the State of Jammu and Kashmir, a princely state in British India, is controlled by China.
5. Mohammad Ishaq Khan, *Kashmir's Transition to Islam: The Role of Muslim Rishis* (Delhi: Manohar, 2002).
6. The two of the more influential of such commentaries are by Asadullah Afaqi and G. N.Gauhar. See Asadullah Afaqi, *Ā'īnā-e ḥaq: Kulliyāt-e Shaikh al-'Ālam* (Srinagar: Life Foundation, 2008), and G. N. Gauhar, *Kashmir Mystic Thought* (Srinagar: Gulshan Books, 2009).
7. For more on the origins and history of this conflict, see Sumantra Bose, *Kashmir: Roots of Conflict, Paths to Peace* (Cambridge: Harvard University Press, 2005); Alastair Lamb, *Kashmir: A Disputed Legacy* (Karachi: Oxford University Press, 1992); and A. G. Noorani, *The Kashmir Dispute 1947–2012, Volumes 1 and 2* (New Delhi: Tulika Books, 2013).
8. A. G. Noorani, *The Kashmir Dispute 1947–2012, Volume 1* (New Delhi: Tulika Books, 2013), 4–5.
9. For more on post-Partition developments, and the persistence of ideas of freedom, in Kashmir, see Shahla Hussain, *Kashmir in the Aftermath of Partition* (New Delhi: Cambridge University Press, 2021).
10. The official estimates of the Indian government about the loss of life in Jammu and Kashmir are substantially lower than the figures cited by rights groups. The figure that I cite here is taken from a new book on the Kashmir conflict by Sumantra Bose. See Sumantra Bose, *Kashmir at the Crossroads: Inside a 21st-Century Conflict* (New Delhi: Picador India, 2022), xii.
11. Saiba Varma writes in a recent article:

> In addition to being the site of ongoing violence and political unrest ... Kashmir has also emerged as a zone of mass psychological suffering. Media reports highlight the fact that Kashmir has one of the highest rates of post-traumatic stress disorder (PTSD) in the world, with approximately one-third of the population exhibiting traumatic symptoms.... Similarly, a

2006 report by Human Rights Watch entitled, "Everyone Lives in Fear," describes an "epidemic of trauma" underway because of sustained human rights abuses.

Saiba Varma, "Where There Are Only Doctors: Counselors as Psychiatrists in Indian-Administered Kashmir," *Ethos* 40, no. 4 (December 2012): 520.

12. For an anthropological study of the forced migration of Kashmiri Pandits, Kashmir's Hindu minority, see Ankur Datta, *On Uncertain Ground: A Study of Displaced Kashmiri Pandits in Jammu and Kashmir* (New Delhi: Oxford University Press, 2016). For a selection of personal accounts of the displacement of Kashmiri Pandits, see Siddhartha Gigoo and Varad Sharma (eds.), *A Long Dream of Home: The Persecution, Exile and Exodus of Kashmiri Pandits* (New Delhi: Bloomsbury, 2016). Also see Rahul Pandita, *Our Moon Has Blood Clots: A Memoir of a Lost Home in Kashmir* (New Delhi: Penguin, 2014).
13. Such imaginings of Pakistan as harbinger of Islam's renewal in South Asia were crucial to the campaign for its achievement. See Venkat Dhulipala, *State Power, Islam and the Quest for Pakistan in Late Colonial North India* (Cambridge: Cambridge University Press, 2015).
14. General Muhammad Zia-ul-Haq, "Inaugural Address" in *Shah-e-Hamadan: Amir Kabir Sayyid Ali Hamadani (AH 714–786)*, ed. M Sarwar Abbasi (Muzaffrabad: Institute of Kashmir Studies, 1991), 19. Azad Jammu and Kashmir is the official Pakistani name for the territory of the erstwhile state of Jammu and Kashmir now under the control of the state of Pakistan. General Zia-ul-Haq said in his inaugural address about the Kubrāwiyyā Sufi missionary: "...today when we are free and independent and we hold our head high ... it is primarily due to the wonderful achievements of great men like Shah-e-Hamadan." Ibid.
15. Ibid., 20.
16. See Mohibbul Hasan, *Kashmir under the Sulṭāns* (Calcutta: Iran Society, 1959), 55–57; Khan, *Kashmir's Transition to Islam*, 64–70; Abdul Qaiyum Rafiqi, *Sufism in Kashmir: Fourteenth to the Sixteenth Century* (Sydney: Goodword Media, 2003), 40–50; and Aziz Ahmad, "Conversions to Islam in the Valley of Kashmir," *Central Asiatic Journal* 23, nos. 1/2 (1979): 12–16.
17. Faheem Aslam, "After Weilding Gun, President talks Kashmiriyat," *Greater Kashmir*, May 27, 2008, 1.
18. During the "signature campaign" by the pro-independence JKLF, a campaign launched by the group in June 2003 to collect signatures in support of the inclusion of Kashmiris in any future talks on Kashmir between India and Pakistan, JKLF leader Yasin Malik often began his speeches with a few lines from Nund Rishi's mystical poetry.

19. For a survey of some of these accounts, see Khan, *Kashmir's Transition to Islam*, 2–14. Also see Rafiqi, *Sufism in Kashmir*, xxxiv–lxxxiii.
20. Sufism arrived in Kashmir at a time of intense rivalries between different Sufi orders that had become institutionalized by the fourteenth century. For a history of the rise and development of Sufi orders in the medieval period, see J. Spencer Trimingham, *The Sufi Orders in Islam* (New York: Oxford University Press, 1998).
21. Quoted in Rafiqi, *Sufism in Kashmir*, 236–37.
22. *The Jahangirnama: Memoirs of Jahangir, Emperor of India*, translated, edited, and annotated by Wheeler M. Thackston (New York: Oxford University Press, 1999), 334. The memoirs of Jahangir are commonly referred to as *Tuzūk-i-Jahāngīrī*, but Jahangir himself refers to his memoirs as *Jahangīrnama*. Ibid., ix.
23. Quoted in Rafiqi, *Sufism in Kashmir*, 174. The term that Jonaraja actually uses, *paramaguru*, can be translated as the supreme teacher rather than the "greatest sage of the time."
24. It is also in these *tarīkh*s and *tadhkirā*s that we first encounter the biography and poetry of the Śaiva *yoginī* Lal Ded, who inaugurates (with Nund Rishi) a vernacular literary culture in the Kashmiri language in the late fourteenth and early fifteenth centuries. There is, however, evidence of compositions in Kashmiri before the fourteenth century.
25. The *Encyclopedia of Islam* refers to Nund Rishi as Baba Nūr al-Dīn Rishī. Mohibbul Hasan, "Bābā Nūr al-Dīn Rishī," in *Encyclopaedia of Islam, Second Edition*, ed. P. Bearman, Th. Bianquis, C. E. Bosworth, E. van Donzel, and W. P. Heinrichs, http://dx.doi.org.ezp3.lib.umn.edu/10.1163/1573-3912_islam_SIM_8382 (accessed June 19, 2016). Hasan writes:

> Although a Muslim, he has been called *rishī*, because he was more influenced by the ideas and practices of the Hindu Sadhūs and Rishīs than by those of Muslim Ṣūfīs and saints. From the age of thirty, Nūr al-Dīn began to withdraw to caves for meditation and prayers. He finally renounced the world and its pleasures and left his wife and children. In his last days he subsisted only on one cup of milk, and towards the end he took nothing except water, dying at the age of 63 in 842/1438. He is the patron saint of the Valley, and is greatly revered by its people. His sayings and mystical verses, like those of Lallā Ded, are sung and recited all over Kashmīr. His tomb in Črār, 20 miles south-west of Srīnagar, attracts thousands of people, both Muslims and Hindus, every year.

Ibid. Rafiqi gives 1440 as the year of Nund Rishi's death. Most scholars accept the dates 1378 for Nund Rishi's birth and 1440 for Nund Rishi's death, even if there is some disagreement about 1377 or 1378 as the year of Nund Rishi's birth.

26. See, for instance, Walter Lawrence, *The Valley of Kashmir* (London: Henry Frowde, 1895), 295.
27. G. N. Gauhar claims that the Hindus of Kashmir gave this epithet to Nund Rishi because he was believed by some to be an incarnation of the Buddha. But the term was also in use in north Indian Tantric and Nāth-yogī traditions. See G. N. Gauhar, *Sheikh Noor-ud-Din Wali (Nund Rishi)* (New Delhi: Sahitya Akademi, 1988), 61–62.
28. Amin Kamil claims that just as the Rishi Order was open to women, it was also open to Hindus. Amin Kamil, "*Zān*," in Amin Kamil, *Nūrnāmu'* (Srinagar: Jammu and Kashmir Academy of Art, Culture and Languages, 1966), 28.
29. Chitralekha Zutshi, *Languages of Belonging: Islam, Regional Identity, and the Making of Kashmir* (Ranikhet: Permanent Black, 2015), 25. Zutshi adds: "Nooruddin was able to create a framework for a regional culture through his use of the Kashmiri language to propogate a devotional religion, which was significantly, outside the purview of the state." Ibid., 25–26.
30. The Rishis were so popular in Kashmir that the Afghan governor of Kashmir, 'Atā Muhammad Khan, struck coins in the name of Nund Rishi in the early nineteenth century. Rafiqi, *Sufism in Kashmir*, 174–75. Amin Kamil is right in stressing that this happened at a time when 'Atā Muhammad Khan declared Kashmir's autonomy from Afghan rule. Some of these coins are to be found in Lahore Museum. See Amin Kamil, *Nūrnāmu'* (Srinagar: Jammu and Kashmir Academy of Art, Culture and Languages, 1966), 28.
31. Chitralekha Zutshi, *Kashmir's Contested Pasts: Narratives, Sacred Geographies, and the Historical Imagination* (Delhi: Oxford University Press, 2014), 12.
32. See Kamil, *Nūrnāmu'*, and Moti Lal Saqi, *Kulliyāt-e Shaikh al-'Ālam* (Srinagar: Jammu and Kashmir Academy of Art, Culture and Languages, 1985).
33. The roots of the armed insurgency in Kashmir go back to the 1975 accord which lacked the popular support that political initiatives by Sheikh Abdullah (1905–82), Kashmir's popular nationalist leader, had received in the past from most Kashmiris. Many of the leaders of Kashmir's secessionist movement were former members of the Plebiscite Front, a party floated by a Sheikh Abdullah loyalist, which was dissolved after the 1975 accord. For more on the Plebiscite Front, see Hussain, *Kashmir in the aftermath of Partition.*
34. For more on Iqbal and Kashmir, see Jagannath Azad, *Iqbāl aur Kashmīr* (Srinagar: Ali Muhammad and Sons, 1977).
35. These are not, however, straightforward contestations: the Indian state mediates, and complicates, the relations between these old and new Islamic religious and political formations. We must also heed the warning of Hans Harder: "... it seems misleading to think of the orthodox/reformist and Sufi/shrine/popular clusters as separate and always clearly distinguishable modes of religiosity.

They should be thought of rather as polarities in a field of phenomena that allow for manifold intersections and discursive overlaps." Hans Harder, *Sufism and Saint Veneration in Contemporary Bangladesh: The Maijbhandaris of Chittagong* (Routledge: New York, 2011), 318–19.

36. Khan, *Kashmir's Transition to Islam*, 64.
37. Anand Koul, "A Life of Nand Ṛishi," *The Indian Antiquary* 58 (October 1929): 195.
38. Ibid.
39. Khan, *Kashmir's Transition to Islam*, 70.
40. Jaishree Kak Odin, *Lallā to Nūruddīn: Rishī-Sufī Poetry of Kashmir* (Delhi: Motilal Banarsidass, 2013), 17–18.
41. The traditional period of a *mahātapa* (period of great asceticism) for a Hindu ascetic is twelve years, and it is curious that the hagiographical tradition ascribes twelve years of meditation to Nund Rishi. Hugh van Skyhawk, *Well Articulated Better Paths* (Islamabad: Friedrich Naumann Foundation for Freedom, 2014), 7.
42. Kamil, "*Zān*," 32.
43. David Lorenzen, in the introduction to his *Religious Movements in South Asia 600–1800*, argues that we are yet to pose an important question about the Rishi movement: "What possible relation existed between the iconoclastic social and religious ideas of Lal Ded and Shaikh Nuruddin Rishi and those of later nirguni poet saints, particularly Kabir? To what extent were Muslim Sufis able to use Hindu texts and ideas for their own purposes?" See David Lorenzen, "Introduction," in *Religious Movements in South Asia 600–1800*, ed. David Lorenzen (Delhi: Oxford University Press, 2004), 4.
44. Koul, "A Life of Nand Ṛishi," 196. I have altered the transliteration for consistency. Jaishree Kak Odin writes: "This legend has been interpreted as Lallā acknowledging Nūruddīn as her spiritual heir." See Kak Odin, *Lallā to Nūruddīn*, 18. See also Rafiqi, *Sufism in Kashmir*, 162–63.
45. Dean Accardi, "Embedded Mystics: Writing Lal Ded and Nund Rishi into the Kashmiri Landscape," in *Kashmir: History, Politics, Representation*, ed. Chitralekha Zutshi (New Delhi: Cambridge University Press, 2018), 248.
46. Ibid.
47. In an essay on the Rishi movement, Charles Ramsey writes: "The underlying narrative of the Kashmiri transition to Islam is that Lal Ded was Nooruddīn's first nurse, or surrogate mother." See Charles M. Ramsey, "Rishīwaer: Kashmir, the Garden of Saints," in *South Asian Sufis: Devotion, Deviation, and Destiny*, ed. Clinton Bennett and Charles M. Ramsey (New York: Continuum, 2012), 198. Amin Kamil writes: "*Ḥaẓrat Shaikh al 'Ālam*, in establishing the Rishi

movement, created a *bhaktī* wave in Kashmir, which was steered before him by Lal Ded." Kamil, "*Zān*," 26.

48. Kak Odin, *Lallā to Nūruddīn*, 18.
49. Koul, "A Life of Nand Ṛishi," 196. I have altered the transliteration for consistency.
50. See, for instance, J. L. Kaul, *Lal Ded* (New Delhi: Sahitya Akademi, 1973), and Richard Carnac Temple, *The Religion and Teachings of Lalla* (New Delhi: Vintage, 1990). The study by Temple was originally published in 1924 by Cambridge University Press. Lal Ded has also been widely translated, among others, by Ranjit Hoskote, A. K. Ramanujan, and Coleman Barks.
51. See, for instance, Asadullah Afaqi, *Ta'līmāt-e Shaikh al-'Ālam, Volumes 1 and 2* (Tsrār: self-published, 1998), and Gauhar, *Kashmir Mystic Thought*. See also Gauhar's earlier study published by the Sahitya Akademi, India's National Academy of Letters: Gauhar, *Sheikh Noor-ud-Din Wali (Nund Rishi).*
52. I have here in mind, in particular, studies of Nund Rishi's poetry by Rahman Rahi, Shafi Shauq, and Hamidi Kashmiri. See Rahman Rahi, "Shaikh al 'Ālam sạnz shạ̄'irānā ḥạsiyath," in *Kahvat: Tanqīdī maẓmūnan hạnz sombran* (Srinagar: self-published, 1979); Shafi Shauq, *Shaikh-ul-Ālam tu' tasund zamānu'* (Srinagar: Bazm-e Adab Kaprin, 1978); and Hamidi Kashmiri, *Shaikh al-'Ālam: Ḥayāt aur shāyarī* (Srinagar: Idara-e Adab, 1997).
53. Koul, "A Life of Nand Ṛishi," 194.
54. Ibid.
55. Ibid., 195.
56. Andrew Hui, in a recent study of aphorism as a form, writes that "the history of aphorisms can be narrated as an animadversion, a turning away from grand systems through the construction of literary fragments." See Andrew Hui, *A Theory of the Aphorism: From Confucius to Twitter* (Princeton: Princeton University Press, 2019), 2.
57. Koul, "A Life of Nand Ṛishi," 195.
58. See Saqi, *Kulliyāt-e Shaikh al-'Ālam*, and Kamil, *Nūrnāmu'*. The controversial decision of the Academy to supersede Kamil's collection has been discussed by Kamil in his book of essays, *Javāban chu 'arẓ*. See Amin Kamil, *Javāban chu 'arẓ* (Srinagar: self-published, 2000).
59. See, in particular, Afaqi, *Ā'īnā-e ḥaq*.
60. Dean Accardi reminds us: "Since neither Lal Ded nor Nund Rishi wrote for themselves and the oral traditions about them cannot be reliably dated and authenticated, it is impossible to say who these saints were in the past and are in the present in isolation from the people and texts that memorialize them." Accardi, "Embedded Mystics," 253. According to Dean Accardi, *Tarīkh-e Sayyīd Ali* (1579), a Persian history of Kashmir, is the earliest source which

mentions Nund Rishi. This implies that the earliest written account of Nund Rishi's life emerges only about a century and a half after his death. Accardi also hints that the privilege accorded to the Rishis in this text could have something to do with the *Kubrāwiyyā* effort to enlist the Rishis in their dispute with the Nūrbakshīya. Ibid., 253. The other important historical source that Accardi mentions is Muhammad Ali Raina's *Tadhkirāt al-'ārifīn* (1587). The *rishīnāmā*s and *nūrnāmā*s were composed from the sixteenth century to the nineteenth century. For more on historical sources on the Rishis, see Khan, *Kashmir's Transition to Islam*, 2–16.

61. Kamil, "*Zān*," 11.
62. Ibid., 12.
63. Ibid., 13.
64. Ibid.
65. There are, however, ocassional inconsistencies in the rhyme scheme which could point to errors in transcription.
66. T. N. Ganjoo, "Kạshur adab tu' 'arūz," *Anhār*, 3, no. 1 (1979): 7–15. I must thank Mr. Muneebur Rahman for sharing his thoughts and valuable insights on this subject in a personal conversation about meter in early Kashmiri poetry.
67. Kamil, "*Zān*," 13.
68. *Śloka* literally means "song," from *śru*, to hear. See Arthur A. Macdonell, *A Sanskrit Grammar for Students* (London: Oxford University Press, 1927), 232–233.
69. Galit Hasan-Rokem and David Shulman, "Introduction," in Galit Hasan-Rokem and David Shulman, *Untying the Knot: On Riddles and Other Enigmatic Modes* (New York: Oxford University Press, 1996), 4.
70. Sunderlal Bahuguna, "Life Depends on Forests," *Times of India*, October 16, 1985, 8.
71. Chitralekha Zutshi writes that "Sanskrit and Persian coexisted on Kashmir's intellectual landscape through the sixteenth centrury, drawing copiously on each other's literary repertoires." Chitralekha Zutshi, *Kashmir* (New Delhi: Oxford University Press, 2019), 16.
72. Rahman Rahi, "Vākh tu' shruki̱: Akh ḥayạtī muṭạllu' tu' sām," in "Mashriqī shạ'irī jamāliyāt," special issue, *Anhār* (1997), 124.
73. Ibid.
74. T. N. Ganjoo, "Lallu' vākh lisạni zạvijār," in *Shīrazu'*, *Lal Ded Number,* 16, no. 6 (2002): 131.
75. Rahman Rahi, "Vākh tu' shruki̱: Akh ḥayạtī muṭạllu' tu' sām," 129.
76. Ibid.
77. Ibid.

78. Ibid., 130. For Rahi, this call of gods resonates in an *andrūnuk ʿālam* (an inner world).
79. Ibid.
80. Ibid., 134.
81. Imre Bangha, in a study of vernacularization in an early Hindi epic by the fifteenth-century poet Vishnudas of Gwalior, writes that many of *bhaktī* poet Kabir's poems are *chaupāī* compositions reworked as *pada*s with their first line presented as the refrain. See Imre Bangha, "Early Hindi Epic Poetry in Gwalior: Beginnings and Continuities in the Rāmāyan of Vishnudas," in *After Timur Left: Culture and Circulation in Fifteenth-Century North India*, ed. Francesca Orsini and Samira Sheikh (Delhi: Oxford University Press, 2014), 392. In the same essay, Imre Bangha speaks of the friendly relations between the Gwalior ruler Dungar Singh and Sultan Zayn al-ʿĀbidīn of Kashmir, the Shāhmīrī ruler during the last two decades of Nund Rishi's life.
82. There are still professional singers who sing the *shruk*s. One such singer was filmed by the author and Meenu Gaur in our 2002 documentary film, *Paradise on a River of Hell*. See *Paradise on a River of Hell*, directed by Meenu Gaur and Abir Bazaz (New Delhi, India: PSBT, 2002), DVD.
83. See S. L. Sadhu, *Rupa Bhavani* (New Delhi: Sahitya Akademi, 2003), and A. N. Dhar, *Country of the Soul: An English Translation of Bimla Raina's Kashmiri verses* (New Delhi: Atlantic Publishers, 2009).
84. Abdul Qaiyum Rafiqi notes a strong parallel between the Rishi movement and Nātha *yogi*s: "All they (Rishīs) seem to have added to the *Nātha* framework was the name of Allah or *huwa*." Cited in Ramsey, "Rishīwaer," 199.
85. Even a cursory examination of the popular collections of Nund Rishi's mystical verse suggests that the situation is no different from the Lal Ded corpus.
86. Ranjit Hoskote, *I, Lalla: The Poems of Lal Děd* (New Delhi: Penguin Books, 2011), xii.
87. Ibid., l.
88. Ibid., liii.
89. Ibid., ix.
90. Bruce Lawrence, "Islam in India: The Function of Institutional Sufism in the Islamization of Rajasthan, Gujarat and Kashmir," *Contributions to Asian Studies* 17 (January 1, 1982): 27.
91. Zutshi, *Languages of Belonging*, 26. Elsewhere Chitralekha Zutshi has pointed out that Islamic universalism in Kashmir "combined seamlessly with Sanskrit cosmopolitanism and Kashmiri localism to produce a clearly defined sense of Kashmir as a place." See Zutshi, *Kashmir's Contested Pasts*, 11.
92. Ronit Ricci, *Islam Translated: Literature, Conversion and the Arabic Cosmopolis of South and Southeast Asia* (Chicago: University of Chicago Press, 2012), 1.

93. Ibid., 2.
94. Ibid., 3.
95. I use the term "provincializing" here in the sense Dipesh Chakrabarty uses it in his *Provincializing Europe: Postcolonial Thought and Historical Difference* to suggest not only a decentering but also the opening out of universalizing histories (of Islam, in this case) to "the diversity of the human life-worlds" and a renewal from the margins. See Dipesh Chakrabarty, *Provincializing Europe: Postcolonial Thought and Historical Difference* (Princeton: Princeton University Press, 2000), 16–18.
96. Rita Kothari, "Introduction," in *A Multilingual Nation: Translation and Language Dynamic in India*, ed. Rita Kothari (New Delhi: Oxford University Press, 2018), 17.
97. There are multiple translations of Nund Rishi from Kashmiri into Urdu. But only a few from Kashmiri into English or Hindi. Many of these translations are by independent scholars or religious followers of Nund Rishi. For an English translation of the *shruks*, see B. N. Parimoo, *Unity in Diversity* (Srinagar: Jammu and Kashmir Academy of Art, Culture and Languages, 1984). For another English translation, see Rashid Afaque, *The Ark: Transcreation of Sheikh Noor-u-din Wali* (Sopore: Rabani Book Stall, 2003). Also see K. N. Dhar, *A Rosary of Hundred Beads* (Srinagar: Jammu and Kashmir Academy of Art, Culture and Languages, 1981); Badruddin Muqeem, *Kashmir Bliss* (Srinagar: Gulshan Books, 2008); G. N. Adfar, *Alchemy of Light: Selected Verses of Sheikh Noor-u-din, Volumes 1 and 2* (Srinagar: privately published, 2011); and Abu Nayeem Ullah and Ali Mohammad, *The Garden of Mystic Rose: Selected Poems of Sheikh Noor-ud-din Noorani* (Srinagar: Gulshan Books, 2016). For an Urdu translation, see Abu Na'īm, *Nūrnamu' ya'ni kulliyāt-e Shaikh al-'Ālam* (Srinagar: Sheikh Muhammad Usman and Sons, 2012). For a Hindi translation, see Shashi Shekhar Toshakhani, *Kahā thā Rishī ne* (Jammu: Jammu and Kashmir Academy of Art, Culture and Languages, n.d.).
98. Kothari, "Introduction," 17.
99. The Kubrāwiyyā and Nūrbakhshīya had a strong presence in Kashmir but these were essentially trans-regional Sufi orders. The influence of the Rishi Order was largely restricted to the Kashmir Valley. On the imperial articulations of early medieval Kashmiri rulers, Ronald Inden writes:

> Kashmir seems to have emerged as a privileged locale in the first or second century in the reign of the Kuṣāṇa imperial ruler Kaniṣka (78–102).... So far as Hindus – Vaiṣṇavas and Śaivas – were concerned, Kashmir remained a marginal "barbarian" country until the Post-Gupta period, the fifth to seventh centuries. Kashmir's kings then turned it into the "middle province" of an imperial kingdom, one consisting of the Valley of Kashmir

> and the surrounding countries or kingdoms. They and the scholars around them even claimed it was the place from which India originated, a sort of Indian "homeland."

Ronald Inden, "Kashmir as Paradise on Earth," in *The Valley of Kashmir: The Making and Unmaking of a Composite Culture?* ed. Aparna Rao (New Delhi: Manohar, 2008), 523.

100. Sheldon Pollock, in an essay in 1995 for a special issue of the Indian journal *Social Scientist* on "Literary History, Region and Nation in South Asia," connects the rise of vernacular literatures in medieval India to new social movements: "It is particular social groups seeking a voice that create new languages, texts, and definitions of the 'literary,' and social groups that, in writing the histories of how all this happens, are writing the histories of themselves." See Sheldon Pollock, "Literary History, Region, and Nation in South Asia," *Social Scientist* 23, no. 269–71 (October–December 1995): 1.
101. Mohammad Ishaq Khan writes:

> That Nur al-Din wielded greater influence than the Sufis from Persia and Central Asia is shown by the fact that Rishi folk literature remained in many ways the most significant medium of instruction in the values of Kashmiri society; it has had a deeper impact than mosques, *madrasas* and *maktabs*, where formal teaching was carried on.

See Mohammad Ishaq Khan, "The Impact of Islam in the Sultanate Period (1320–1586)," in *India's Islamic Traditions 711–1750,* ed. Richard Eaton (New Delhi: Oxford University Press, 2003), 354.

102. As late as the early twentieth century, the *khānqāh* (Sufi hospice) of Sayyid 'Ali Hamadānī in Srinagar played a pivotal role in the anti-Dogra movement in Kashmir in the 1930s and 1940s. For the significance of the *khānqāh*, and disputes over sacred space in Kashmir, see Chapter 3 in Zutshi, *Languages of Belonging*, 118–68.
103. The disagreements about the implementation of the Sharī'ah was the primary reason that Sayyid 'Alī Hamadānī decided to leave Kashmir. Rafiqi, *Sufism in Kashmir*, 47.
104. Lawrence, "Islam in India," 40.
105. Ibid. In his note about Kashmir, Alberuni writes in his *Kitab al-Hind*:

> They are particularly anxious about the natural strength of their country, and therefore take always much care to keep a strong hold upon the entrances and roads leading into it. In consequence it is very difficult to have any commerce with them. In former times they used to allow one or two foreigners to enter their country, particularly Jews, but at present

> they do not allow any Hindu whom they do not know personally to enter, much less other people.

See Edward C. Sachau (ed.), *Alberuni's India, Volume I* (London: Kegan Paul, Trench, Trübner & Co. Ltd., 1914), 206.

106. Zutshi, *Kashmir*, 20. Here Zutshi is alluding not only to the rapproachment between the Kubrāwiyyā and the Rishi Orders but also the strong association between the Suharwardiyyā and the Rishis in the sixteenth and seventeenth centuries. See, for instance, how the Rishis not only influenced but also transformed the attitudes of the Suharwardiyyā toward the Shī'a adherents of Islam in Kashmir: Khan, *Kashmir's Transition to Islam*, 150–51.
107. Lawrence, "Islam in India," 41.
108. Following Tony K. Stewart's work on the Hindu–Muslim encounter in medieval Bengal, I use translation here as a way of seeking equivalence between two different traditions, avoiding the twin pitfalls of syncretism on the one hand and measuring Nund Rishi's Islam against some essentialized ideal on the other. See Tony. K. Stewart, "In Search of Equivalence: Conceiving Muslim-Hindu Encounter through Translation Theory," *History of Religions* 40, no. 3 (February 2001): 263. Stewart writes of the Bengali situation:

> In contrast to the model of syncretism that proposes to describe the new amalgam created by these Sufi texts, I would propose that we can re-construct a process by which the premodern Sufi or other Muslim writer, working within the constraints of a Bengali language whose extant technical vocabulary was conditioned largely by Hindu ideational constructs, attempted to imagine an Islamic ideal in a new literary environment.

Ibid., 273.

109. The vegetarianism of the Rishis appeared as a problem to the Persianate Sufi orders who considered vegetarianism against the *sunnah* (the established traditions of the Prophet Muhammad). Mohammad Ishaq Khan writes that "the so-called low-born like the village dancers and acrobats (*bhands*, *dambael maets* or *faqirs*), played a significant role as transmitters of the values of the Rishis in the traditional rural society." Khan, *Kashmir's Transition to Islam*, 181. Akhtar Mohi-ud-din explores the relation between language, region, and religion in Kashmir in his thought-provoking set of reflections in *A Fresh Approach to the History of Kashmir*. See Akhtar Mohi-ud-din, *A Fresh Approach to the History of Kashmir* (Srinagar: Book Bank, 1998).
110. Gauhar, *Sheikh Noor-ud-din Wali (Nund Rishi)*, 61–62.
111. D. J. F. Newall, "Some Account of the Rishis or Hermits of Kashmir," *Journal of the Asiatic Society of Bengal* XXXIX (1870): 265.

112. Shahzad Bashir has characterized this situation in medieval Kashmir as that of a "relatively open religious marketplace…." Shahzad Bashir, *Messianic Hopes and Mystical Visions: The Nūrbakhsiyā between Medieval and Modern Islam* (Columbia, SC: University of South Carolina Press, 2003), 201.
113. It is also useful to bear in mind what David Lorenzen says about the social origins of religious movements such as the Rishi movement:

> Among Hindus and Sikhs, as well as most South Asian Muslims, caste is in most contexts a more useful measure of social status than economic class, although caste and class boundaries do of course roughly coincide. In a South Asian context, then, a "popular" religious movement is one whose followers mostly come from middle and low castes. The leaders of the movements, on the other hand, may come from either lower or higher castes. The religious movements in which the leaders come from non-Brahmin castes tend to embody social ideologies opposed to the religious and worldly dominance of upper castes, while movements with leaders from Brahmin castes tend to accept or reinforce such dominance.

David Lorenzen, "Introduction," in *Religious Movements in South Asia 600–1800*, ed. David Lorenzen (Delhi: Oxford University Press, 2004), 4.
114. Khan, *Kashmir's Transition to Islam*, 49.
115. Ibid., 73.
116. Ibid., 120.
117. Ibid., 125–26.
118. Ibid., 146.
119. Ibid., 28.
120. Ibid., 190.
121. For an introduction to the Chishtī Order, see Carl W. Ernst and Bruce Lawrence, *Sufi Martyrs of Love: Chishti Sufism in South Asia and Beyond* (New York: Palgrave Macmillan, 2002). For Chishtī attitudes to Hindus, in particular, see K. A. Nizami, *Tarīkh-e Mashāikh-e Chisht* (Karachi: Oxford University Press, 2007), 357–62.
122. Elsewhere Mohammad Ishaq Khan writes that Nund Rishi "seems to have visited almost every part of the Valley…. There are a number of villages in Kashmir that still preserve the tradition of his visit or sojourn in one form or the other." See Khan, "The Impact of Islam in the Sultanate Period (1320–1586)," 352. Nund Rishi speaks of his extensive travels in the Kashmir Valley in one of his *shruks*: *Kashīri phyūrus ạndī ạndī* (I have been to every end of Kashmir). See Saqi, *Kulliyāt-e Shaikh al-ʿĀlam*, 75.
123. Lawrence, "Islam in India," 36.
124. Mohammad Ishaq Khan also finds this distinction useful but traces it to the work of the American anthropologist Robert Redfield. Khan writes:

> In any civilization there is a Great tradition of the reflective few, and a Little Tradition of the unreflective many. The societal dimensions of these two traditions are the great community and the little community.... Viewed in the context of Redfield's definition, the Little Tradition of Kashmiri peasant society seems to have linked itself with the Great Tradition of Islam through Nuruddin, who, in his numerous verses, seems to have established channels of communication between the two traditions and set up standards of mutual reference and influence.

Khan, *Kashmir's Transition to Islam*, 43.

125. This situation was no different at the Kashmiri court in the early decades of the Muslim sultanate. The historian Aziz Ahmad writes:

> Until then the Muslim Sultans and their newly-converted Muslim nobility which had been growing in numbers were indistinguishable from the largely Hindu nobility in dress, manners and customs, and often even in proper names. These early Muslim Sultans married Hindu women, the preferential marriages being with Dogra Rajput princess [*sic*] from Jammu, who retained their Hindu names and probably their Hindu religion. Thus Shihāb al-dīn's (1356–74) favourite was a Hindu, Lakshmī. Even the iconoclast Sikandar's wives had Hindu names, Mīrā and Śobha.

Ahmad, "Conversions to Islam in the Valley of Kashmir," 10.

126. Khan, "The Impact of Islam in the Sultanate Period (1320–1586)," 353.
127. Ibid.
128. Patton E. Burchett, *A Genealogy of Devotion: Bhakti, Tantra, Yoga and Sufism in North India* (New York: Columbia University Press, 2019), 276–77.
129. *Dervish*, literally, means a poor, indigent ascetic. The Persian term seems to be of Zoroastrian origin. In the Islamic period in Iran, "dervish" came to be used for those who possess "the virtue of spiritual poverty, that is, nonattachment, often in conjunction with deliberately chosen or passively accepted material poverty" but also more generally for "practitioners of Sufism, especially its undisciplined or antinomian forms; and mendicants with pretensions to sanctity." Hamid Algar, "Darvīš," *Encyclopædia Iranica*, Vol. VII, Fasc. 1, pp. 72–76, available at https://www.iranicaonline.org/articles/darvis (accessed February 20, 2023). *Qalandar* came to be often used synonymously with dervish at times in the South Asian context. The term *qalandar* appears first in Sufi literature in the eleventh century and came to connote a figure "who defies the conventions of social order." See Katherine Pratt Ewing and Ilona Gerbakher, "The Qalandariyya: From the Mosque to the Ruin in Poetry, Place and Practice," in *Routledge Handbook of Sufism*, ed. Lloyd Ridgeon (New York: Routledge, 2021), 252. I use the term *dervish* here for itinerant, antinomian Sufis in South Asia who could trace their origins to similar dervish groups of

the Middle East but were transformed by their encounters with the Indian ascetic traditions. For more on libertines and antinomians of medieval Sufism, see Ahmet T. Karamustafa, "Antinomian Sufis," in *The Cambridge Companion to Sufism*, ed. Lloyd Ridgeon (New York: Cambridge University Press, 2015), 101–24. For a more detailed study of the dervish groups of medieval times, see Ahmet T. Karamustafa, *God's Unruly Friends: Dervish Groups in the Islamic Middle Period 1200–1550* (Oxford: Oneworld Publications, 2013).

130. Ahmad, "Conversions to Islam in the Valley of Kashmir," 8.
131. Ibid.
132. The transition in power is likely to have promoted conversions at the court. Such low castes as *dombas*, for instance, could only convert by joining the army of the new Muslim state. Ahmad, "Conversions to Islam in the Valley of Kashmir," 11.
133. Ibid., 5.
134. Simon Digby, "Between Ancient and Modern Kashmir: The Rule and Role of Sultans and Sufis (1200/1300–1600)," in *The Arts of Kashmir*, ed. Pratapaditya Pal (New York: Asia Society, 2007), 116. I use the spelling "Zulju" even though Aziz Ahmad uses the spelling "Zalacha." Abdul Qaiyum Rafiqi claims that the real name of Zulju was Zulqadr Khan and that he was a Muslim (a claim he pitches against Mohibbul Hassan's contention that he was not a Muslim). See Rafiqi, *Sufism in Kashmir*, 7–8.
135. Ahmad, "Conversions to Islam in the Valley of Kashmir," 4.
136. Walter Slaje, *Brahmā's curse: Facets of Political and Social Violence in Premodern Kashmir* (Halle an der Saale: Universitatsverlag Halle-Wittenberg, 2019), 13.
137. It is possible that Rinchen's precarious situation as a refugee from Ladakh fleeing internecine strife had led to his conversion. The Kashmiri tradition attributes this to the saintly powers of the Suhrawardī saint Bulbul Shah. The history of Islam in Kashmir appears entangled from the beginning with the interventions of Persian Sufis. On the Sufi Bulbul Shah, see Yoginder Sikand, "Hazrat Bulbul Shah: The First Known Muslim Missionary in Kashmir," *Journal of Muslim Minority Affairs* 20, no. 2 (2000): 361–67.
138. Hasan, *Kashmir under the Sulṭāns*, 41–42.
139. Ahmad, "Conversions to Islam in the Valley of Kashmir," 9.
140. Ibid., 10.
141. Ibid., 11.
142. Satoshi Ogura traces this persecution to the influence of the Kubrāwiyyā Sufis on the Kashmiri court: "A group of Muslim immigrants led by a Kobravi Sufi Mohammad Hamadāni, son of ʿAli Hamadāni (d. 1385), reached Kashmir, owing to the sultanate's close commercial relationship with Central Asia. The group convinced Sekandar to oppress Brahmins, to burn Sanskrit books on Brahmanism, and to break idol-temples." See Satoshi Ogura, "In this Corner of

the Entangled Cosmopolises: Political Legitimacies in the Multilingual Society of Sultanate and Early Mughal Kashmir," *Journal of Persianate Studies* 12 (2019): 244.

143. *Shali* is the paddy crop. Khan, "The Impact of Islam in the Sultanate Period (1320–1586)," 345.
144. Slaje, *Brahmā's Curse*, 33.
145. Even though scholars remain divided along sectarian lines about whether the conversions to Islam in Kashmir were peaceful or not (some attribute it to the missionary work of the Sufis and others to the persecution of the Muslim sultans), the contemporary sources are silent on the processes of religious conversion. See Rafiqi, *Sufism in Kashmir*, 253. Richard Eaton has suggested that the Islamization at the periphery of Indo-Muslim states was a dual process of accretion and reform, and the religious change was often connected to ecological change. See Richard Eaton, "Approaches to the Study of Conversion to Islam in India" in *Approaches to Islam in Religious Studies,* ed. Richard C. Martin (Oxford: Oneworld Publications, 2001), 122–23.
146. Khan, "The Impact of Islam in the Sultanate Period (1320–1586)," 348.
147. Ibid.
148. Ahmad, "Conversions to Islam in the Valley of Kashmir," 11. According to one of the biographers of Sayyid 'Alī Hamadānī, Prophet Muhammad had commanded the saint in a dream to visit Kashmir to convert the people of Kashmir to Islam. See Rafiqi, *Sufism in Kashmir*, lxxi.
149. Ahmad, "Conversions to Islam in the Valley of Kashmir," 12.
150. Khan, *Kashmir's Transition to Islam*, 65.
151. Ahmad, "Conversions to Islam in the Valley of Kashmir," 12. See also Muzaffar Alam, *The Languages of Political Islam in India* (Delhi: Permanent Black, 2004), 43–46.
152. Bashir, *Messianic Hopes and Mystical Visions*, 201.
153. Khan, "The Impact of Islam in the Sultanate Period (1320–1586)," 343.
154. Rafiqi, *Sufism in Kashmir*, fn78, li.
155. Ibid., 47.
156. Sayyid 'Alī Hamadānī had urged the ruler to adhere to the Sharī'ah and annulled a marriage between the sultan and his sister-in-law (deemed illegal under Islamic Law). Khan, *Kashmir's Transition to Islam*, 65. Also see Mohibbul Hasan, *Kashmir under the Sulṭāns*, 56–57.
157. Khan, *Kashmir's Transition to Islam*, 68.
158. Rafiqi, *Sufism in Kashmir*, lxv.
159. Ibid., 197.
160. Khan, "The Impact of Islam in the Sultanate Period (1320–1586)," 352.
161. Rafiqi, *Sufism in Kashmir*, xxxii.

162. Khan, *Kashmir's Transition to Islam*, 15.
163. Ibid., 167.
164. Zutshi, *Languages of Belonging*, 26.
165. Writing about the rule of Sultan Zayn al-ʿĀbidīn, the Sanskritist Walter Slaje concludes an essay about history in medieval Kashmir with the following remark: "I think that for the outstanding services Zayn has rendered to both religious parties as a Muslim ruler, he deserves to be held up posthumously as an example for integrationist politics of which Kashmir is so urgently in need, torn as it is by the tensions of today." See Walter Slaje, *Medieval Kashmir and the Science of History* (Austin: South Asia Institute, The University of Texas at Austin, 2004), 24.
166. Ahmad, "Conversion to Islam in the Valley of Kashmir," 16.
167. Ibid., 18.
168. Rafiqi, *Sufism in Kashmir*, 248. Amin Kamil writes: "The poetic compositions of Nund Rishi, and the circumstances of his life that we find in the *Rishīnāmu'*, show that the Persian immigrants were opposed to him and troubled him in so many different ways." Kamil, "*Zān*," 27.
169. Rafiqi, *Sufism in Kashmir*, 248.
170. Charles.M.Ramsey writes: "Despite this facile unity, one can trace an uneasy tension between the urban missionary Suharwardis and the rural ascetic Rishīs." Ramsey, "Rishīwaer," 200.
171. Rafiqi, *Sufism in Kashmir*, 257.
172. Ramsey, "Rishīwaer," 199. Ramsey also claims, based on his interviews, that it is a common belief that the Rishis fought on the side of Yusuf Shah Chak against the Mughal emperor Akbar. Ibid. fn. 31.
173. For more on the historical context, one can profitably turn to Rafiqi's survey of Kashmir's Sufi history. See Rafiqi, *Sufism in Kashmir*.
174. Aydogan Kars points out that Western scholarship identified an Islamic negative theology with the Muʿtazilites, a rationalist school of Islamic theology. Kars adds: "Western representations of Muʿtazilite negative theology were fundamentally shaped by the sustained image of Islam as a Semitic monotheistic religion that overemphasizes divine transcendence." Aydogan Kars, "What Is 'Negative Theology'? Lessons from the Encounter of Two Sufis," *Journal of the American Academy of Religion* 86, no. 1 (March 2018): 182. But after the 1970s, "a new, ethicalized divine transcendence associated with Sufism emerged with the rise of the concept 'apophasis,' commonly translated as 'negative speech,' or 'unsaying.'" Rūmī and Ibn al-ʿArabī were taken to be "the foremost representatives of Islamic apophasis or negative theology." Ibid. Manṣūr al-Ḥallāj came to represent a more radical Islamic negative theology, a political negative theology. By explicitly invoking Rūmī and Ḥallāj, and the political

conditions of his times, Nund Rishi's mystical poetry declared an allegiance to this tradition of Islamic negative theology (Islamic negative political theology, to be precise!).

175. Michael Sells argues in *Mystical Languages of Unsaying*, his comparative study of negative theology in Judaism, Christianity, and Islam, that the mode of discourse on the transcendent in negative theology begins in an aporia which he characterizes as an "unresolvable dilemma." The aporia is that one must name the transcendent in order to even make the claim that the transcendent is beyond names. Sells envisages three possible responses to such a dilemma: (*a*) silence, (*b*) to see how the transcendent is beyond names and not beyond names, and (*c*) the refusal to solve the dilemma and instead accept it as a genuine aporia, that is, as unresolvable. All of these discourses are, for Sells, negative theology. Michael A. Sells, *Mystical Languages of Unsaying* (Chicago: University of Chicago Press, 1994), 2.
176. More so when we bear in mind what Jacques Derrida reminds us of about the history of negative theology: "Whatever the translations, analogies, transpositions, transferences, metaphors, never has any discourse expressly given itself this title (negative theology, apophatic method, *via negativa*) in the thoughts of Jewish, Muslim, Buddhist culture." See Jacques Derrida, *On the Name* (Stanford: Stanford University Press, 1995), 49. The designation "negative theology" is given to a discourse but not chosen by it.
177. Arthur Bradley, "Thinking the Outside: Foucault, Derrida and Negative Theology," *Textual Practice* 16, no. 1 (2002): 59.
178. Jacques Derrida, "How to Avoid Speaking: Denials," in *Psyche: Inventions of the Other, Volume II*, ed. Peggy Kamuf and Elizabeth Rottenberg (Stanford: Stanford University Press, 2008), 144.
179. Ibid.,147. For Derrida, the privileging of mysticism as a path to radical transcendence, a being beyond being, remains a phase of positive ontotheology (in its Heideggerian sense, ontotheology is a metaphysics that seeks the mastery of reality through a combination of ontology and theology, that is, it connects the thinking of being, ontology, to the thinking of a higher being, theology). Also see Jacques Derrida, *Writing and Difference* (London: Routledge, 2001), 440, n.37.
180. Jean Luc Marion, "What Do We Mean by 'Mystic'," in *Mystics: Presence and Aporia*, ed. Michael Kessler and Christian Sheppard (Chicago: University of Chicago Press, 2003), 6.
181. Derrida, "How to Avoid Speaking," 151.
182. See Jacques Derrida, "Postscriptum: Aporias, Ways and Voices," tr. John P. Leavey, in *Derrida and Negative Theology*, ed. Harold Coward and Toby Foshay (Albany, NY: State University of New York Press, 1992).

183. Jacob Taubes, for instance, suggests that the Gnostic *via negativa* is a link between Christian and Indian negative theology (Islam is a link in that chain which he misses). Taubes considers the Neoplatonic teacher of Plotinus, Ammonios Sakkas, to have been a Buddhist: "Ammonios Sakkas presents the Alexandrian link between Indian (Buddhist) theology and Christian and pagan neo-Platonism and this connection explains *why* we are 'forcibly reminded' of Hindu and Buddhist terminology in neo-Platonic theology." See Jacob Taubes, "The Realm of Paradox," *Review of Metaphysics* 7, no. 3 (March 1954): 485–86.
184. Aydogan Kars, *Unsaying God: Negative Theology in Medieval Islam* (New York: Oxford University Press, 2019), 13.
185. Derrida, *On the Name*, 47. But Michel de Certeau warns us of the risks: "One would not therefore know how to sanction the fiction of a universal discourse about mysticism, thereby forgetting that the East Indian, the African, or the Indonesian have neither the same conception of nor the same practices for what we call mysticism." See Michel de Certeau, "Mysticism," *Diacritics* 22, no. 2. (Summer, 1992): 13.
186. Jacques Derrida speaks of translation as something fundamental to deconstruction in his letter to the Japanese scholar of Qur'ān and Islamic Studies, Toshihiko Izutsu. See Jacques Derrida, "Letter to a Japanese Friend," in *Psyche: Inventions of the Other, Volume II*, ed. Peggy Kamuf and Elizabeth Rottenberg (Stanford: Stanford University Press, 2008), 1–6.
187. Sells, *Mystical Languages of Unsaying*, 7. Annemarie Schimmel considers Sufism to be a form of Islamic mysticism and claims that mysticism "contains something mysterious, not to be reached by ordinary means or by intellectual effort" and "is understood from the common root to the words *mystic* and *mystery*, the Greek *myein*, 'to close the eyes.'" Annemarie Schimmel, *Mystical Dimensions of Islam* (Chapel Hill: University of North Carolina Press, 2011), 3. Admittedly, mysticism as a term has been worn by excessive usage, and it is seldom clear if it invokes the domain of knowledge, experience, language, literature, culture, or social being. It often carries the meaning of "hidden" or "secret" and is derived from the Latin word *mysticus* (which, in turn, is derived from the Greek *mustikos*). However, Richard H. Jones reminds us:

> The nouns "mystic" and "mysticism" were only invented in the seventeenth century when spirituality was becoming separated from general theology. In the modern era, mystical interpretations of the Bible dropped away in favor of literal readings. At that time, modernity's focus on the individual also arose. Religion began to become privatized in terms of the primacy of individuals, their beliefs, and their experiences rather than being seen in terms of rituals and institutions.

See Richard H. Jones, *Philosophy of Mysticism: Raids on the Ineffable* (Stony Brook: State University of New York Press, 2016), 1. Jones adds: "But this is not to deny that there were mystics in the modern sense earlier or in other cultures. Simply because the term 'mysticism' did not refer explicitly to experiences before the modern era does not mean that 'mystical theology' was not informed by mystical experiences." Ibid., 2.

188. Derrida, *On the Name*, 49.
189. I have here in mind the sudden irruption of negative theology in the late-nineteenth- and early-twentieth-century Kashmiri poetry.
190. Michael Kessler and Christian Sheppard, "Preface," in *Mystics: Presence and Aporia*, ed. Michael Kessler and Christian Sheppard (Chicago: University of Chicago Press, 2003), xii. William Franke, the comparative literature scholar, echoes this in the introduction to his seminal anthology of apophatic texts: "... apophatic reflection belongs particularly to periods of crisis, when confidence in established discourses crumbles, when the authoritative voice of orthodoxies and their official affirmations – and even affirmative, assertive discourse per se – begin to ring hollow." William Franke, "Introduction," in *On What Cannot Be Said: Apophatic Discourses in Philosophy, Religion, Literature and the Arts, Volume 1. Classical Formulations*, ed. William Franke (Notre Dame: University of Notre Dame Press, 2014), 31.
191. Clearly medieval Kashmir – a hotbed of Kubrāwiyyā missionary activity – was well versed with the works of Ibn al-ʿArabī (1165–1240) as disseminated through the teachings of Sayyid ʿAlī Hamadānī. William Franke writes:

    > In apophasis, which empties language of all positive content, absolute difference cannot be positively distinguished from absolute unity, even though the respective discourses of difference and unity nominally stand at the antipodes. Both configurations, unity and difference, are exposed as relatively arbitrary and, in the end, equally inadequate schemas for articulating what cannot be said.

    Franke, "Introduction," 33.
192. William Franke, "Apophasis and the Turn of Philosophy to Religion: From Neoplatonic Theology to Postmodern Negation of Theology," in "Self and Other: Essays in Continental Philosophy of Religion," *International Journal for Philosophy of Religion* 60, nos. 1/3 (December, 2006): 64.
193. Sells, *Mystical Languages of Unsaying*, 13.
194. Derrida, *On the Name*, 36.
195. Ibid.
196. Michel de Certeau, *The Mystic Fable* (Chicago: University of Chicago Press, 1992), 23.

197. I am thinking here, for instance, of Sri Ramakrishna Parmahamsa. For more on Sri Ramakrishna Parmahamsa, see Ayon Maharaj, *Infinite Paths to Infinite Reality: Sri Ramakrishna and Cross-cultural Philosophy of Religion* (New York: Oxford University Press, 2018).
198. Sells, *Mystical Languages of Unsaying*, 3.
199. Nund Rishi is often critical of extreme forms of asceticism but never fully repudiates it. The *shruks* suggest he embraced a form of political asceticism.
200. A reading against the grain of Mohammad Ishaq Khan's chapter about the attitudes of other Sufi orders toward the Rishis in *Kashmir's Transition to Islam: The Role of Muslim Rishis* makes this clear. See Khan, *Kashmir's Transition to Islam*, 144–61.
201. Sells, *Mystical Languages of Unsaying*, 3.
202. Derrida, "How to Avoid Speaking," 143.
203. Ilse N. Bulhof and Laurens ten Kate, "Echoes of an Embarrassment: Philosophical Perspectives on Negative Theology – An Introduction," in *Flight of the Gods: Philosophical Perspectives on Negative Theology*, ed. Ilse N. Bulhof and Laurens ten Kate (New York: Fordham University Press, 2000), 6–7.
204. A. K. Ramanujan, "Is there an Indian Way of thinking? An Informal Essay," *Contributions to Indian Sociology* 23, no. 41 (1989): 54. Sudipta Kaviraj has suggested that we must consider the moments of vernacularization in medieval India as the beginning of "something like European modernity." See Sudipta Kaviraj, "The Sudden Death of Sanskrit Knowledge," *Journal of Indian Philosophy* 33 (2005): 120.
205. Derrida, "How to Avoid Speaking," 74.
206. de Certeau, "Mysticism," 21.
207. Ibid.

1

The *Sahaja* Islam of Nund Rishi

> My son, may God hide from you the apparent meaning of the Law and reveal to you the truth of impiety! Because the apparent meaning of the Law is hidden impiety and the truth of impiety is manifest knowledge. Now therefore: praise to God, who manifests Himself upon the point of a needle to whomsoever He will and who hides Himself in the heavens and on the earth from whomsoever He will, with the result that one attests that "He is not" and the other attests that "There is only Him." Neither is he who professes the negation of God rejected, nor is he who confesses his existence praised. The intent of this letter is that you explain nothing by God, that you extract not a single argumentation from him, that you desire neither to love him nor to not love him, that you do not confess his existence and that you are not inclined to deny it. And above all, refrain from proclaiming his Unity![1]: Manṣūr al-Ḥallaj, cited by Michel de Certeau.

The contemporary discourses on Kashmir turn often to the idea of Kashmiri Islam as being unique and distinctive in South Asia.[2] Such notions have appealed to Kashmiris themselves and inform articulations of Islam and Muslim nationalism in contemporary Kashmir.[3] Even Kashmiri historians such as Mohammad Ishaq Khan who are critical of an understanding of Kashmir's pasts as "syncretic," and not unqualifyingly Islamic, have found it difficult to reject the idea of an exclusive, even exceptional, Islam in Kashmir.[4] The Rishi Order of Kashmiri Sufism is fundamental to these debates about a distinctive history of Islam in Kashmir. The *shruk*s of Nund Rishi in the Kashmiri vernacular not only turn to metaphors, symbols, and events from the Qur'ān but also rely on pre-Islamic Kashmiri cultural memory at a time (the late fourteenth and early fifteenth centuries) when Islam was still a minority religion in Kashmir after the establishment of a Muslim ruling dynasty in the fourteenth century. The Rishi Order is recognized by most scholars of religion, history, and literature in Kashmir to have played a significant role in Kashmir's transition to Islam.[5] The Rishi Order is also considered central to the claims of a distinctive Kashmiri Islam because of its retention of such pre-Islamic ascetic practices as vegetarianism and celibacy. As we have already discussed in the Introduction, the scriptural reference to pre-Islamic texts and concepts and the admission of women to the Rishi Order of Kashmiri Sufism also make the Rishi Order distinct from Sharīʿah-oriented Persianate Sufi orders of Kashmir as do such practices as *bhānd pāthu'r* (Kashmiri folk theatre), *zūl* (a festival of lights), and *dambāl* (dervish dance).

Many of the Rishi practices are, by no means, particular to Kashmir. The dervish dance, *dambāl*, is strikingly similar to the practice of *dhamāl* around the Sufi shrines of Punjab and Sindh.[6] The connections between vernacularization and Sufism are also not particular to Kashmir. The early Chishtī Sufis such as Bābā Farīd in Punjab and Gīsū Darāz in the Deccan are known to have composed verse in Old Punjabi and Deccani. I am not here concerned with the question of the legitimacy or illegitimacy of the notion of a distinctive Kashmiri Islam or the exceptionalism of the Rishis. Instead, I want to explore the thinking of Islam as it is articulated in the mystical poetry of Nund Rishi. Does Nund Rishi's thought and practice inaugurate, or contribute to, a Kashmiri iteration of Islamic thinking? Does Nund Rishi provincialize Islamic thinking?[7] This question assumes even more relevance in the present where the notion of a distinctive Kashmiri Islam is invoked in competing, and unfailingly contentious, political claims about the future of Kashmir. For many contemporary Islamic reformist and revivalist movements in Kashmir, such as the Ahl-e Hadīth and Jamāt-e Islāmī, Islam is universal (the first and the last universal), and Nund Rishi merely articulates the meanings of this universalism in a Kashmiri setting. This in a nutshell is also the position of the historian Mohammad Ishaq Khan, who in his *Kashmir's Transition to Islam: The Role of Muslim Rishis* calls the Rishi movement the force of change that created "conditions for the total assimilation of Kashmiris in Islam."[8] This seems to be a rather uncomplicated reading of a fairly complex cultural and historical phenomenon.

Ahl-e Hadīth and Jamāt-e Islāmī may have differing ideas on the future of Kashmir (even within these organizations there is a wide range of political positions), but both seem to be in agreement about the beginnings of Islam in Kashmir. Both Nund Rishi and Mir Sayyid ʿAlī Hamadānī are seen in their narratives to have engaged in missionary activity to secure Kashmir to the fold of Islam. The historians Mohammad Ishaq Khan and Abdul Qaiyum Rafiqi complicate this understanding in their influential books (*Kashmir's Transition to Islam: The Role of Muslim Rishis* and *Sufism in Kashmir: Fourteenth Century to the Sixteenth Century*) but never challenge it. However, this traditional Islamic reading of Nund Rishi as an Islamic missionary struggles to make sense of those moments in Nund Rishi's thinking and practice which exceed the bounds of canonical Islam. The *shruk*s give us a point of entry into those moments and make possible an alternative thinking of Islam in Nund Rishi (and Kashmiri negative theology, more generally) that otherwise remains obscure.

The Jamāt-e Islāmī, Ahl-e Hadīth, and Deobandi scholars of Kashmir do not share the same approach to problems posed by the influence of pre-Islamic modes on local Sufi practices, but nonetheless anything that deviates from their revivalist Islamic understanding has come in for sharp criticism. The Ahl-e Hadīth (Salafi reformists) reject anything that does not conform to their understanding of Islam in the light of the Qur'ān and the six canonical books of *hadīth* (collections of Prophet Muhammad's sayings), arguing that the former should be interpreted along the terms suggested by the latter. But even the Ahl-e Hadīth have published posters in recent years in Kashmir that combine traditional Islamic teachings from the Qur'ān and the *hadith* with examples from the Kashmiri *shruk*s of Nund Rishi.[9] Even after more than half a millennium, Nund Rishi's poetry in vernacular Kashmiri has an appeal which remains undiminished beyond sectarian and religious denominations. Not only have phrases and idioms from his mystical poetry become a part of everyday Kashmiri, but new editions of his mystical poetry appear almost every year. But the Ahl-e Hadīth in Kashmir deploy only those of Nund Rishi's *shruk*s that conform to their understanding of the *sunnah* (the way, or practice, of Prophet Muhammad). Jamāt-e-Islāmī in Kashmir does not approach Sufism with the same degree of severity but remains critical of tomb shrine cults and local practices at odds with the Sharī'ah. Jamāt-e-Islāmī also favors a non-confrontational approach to Sufi belief and practice and has had space for an understanding of classical, and pietistic, Sufism. A senior leader of Jamāt-e-Islāmī, Qāri Saif al-Dīn, has even published a book on Nund Rishi in which he presents him as a leading Islamic thinker (*mufakkir*) of Kashmir.[10] It is significant to note that the polemic against the Sufis, common to some of these modern Islamic revivalist movements, is more restrained in Kashmir, because it is the Sufis who are seen locally as being responsible for the large-scale conversions to Islam in the region. Even though conversions to Islam by Nund Rishi figure prominently in the hagiographical literature, there is very little understanding, or evidence, of the missionary work of the Rishis themselves. If the Islamic revivalist movements are anxious to situate Nund Rishi as an early reformer of Islam and a missionary in Kashmir, some Sufi-oriented Barelvī groups see Nund Rishi not only as opposed to forms of Islamic orthodoxy and orthopraxy but also as an early exemplar of a local, devotional Islam. These groups are not at all anxious about shrine veneration and other practices associated with Sufism in Kashmir, and do not consider these to be pre-Islamic. For example, the Barelvī theology connects shrine veneration in South Asia to Sunni theology.[11] But the political stakes of reading Nund Rishi are not restricted to Islamic groups. The Kashmiri nationalists, for instance, see Nund Rishi as one of the first Kashmiri spiritual leaders to express the national sentiment of the oppressed in Kashmir. The Indian state, in turn, promotes Nund Rishi's Sufism as an instance of what it calls *Kashmīriyat*, an ethos of tolerance and coexistence, which in its ideological expressions bears a striking resemblance to the official Indian ideology of secularism.[12]

Reading Nund Rishi in the present then is nothing less than reading Islam in a regional setting at a time when contestations over Sufism and Islam are no longer confined to academic debates but involve critical stakes in relation to an understanding of Muslim societies from the Middle East and North Africa to South and South East Asia. The shrine at the Chrar tomb complex of Nund Rishi remains the focal point of devotion to Nund Rishi in Kashmir and attracts not only Muslims but also Hindus and Sikhs. The heterodox appeal of Nund Rishi across different Islamic and non-Islamic traditions in Kashmir partly owes to the historical memory of the saint but also to the way different religious traditions are gathered together in the mystical poetry that circulates in his name. As we briefly discussed in the Introduction, Nund Rishi remains connected in Kashmiri folklore, oral history, and cultural memory at large to his older contemporary Śaiva *yoginī*, Lal Ded. Nund Rishi invokes the spiritual station of Lal Ded as the one to which he himself aspires in the following *shruk*:

Tas Padmānpōr chi Lalay
Tami galay amrÿth pivō
Tami Shiv vuch thalay thalay
Tyuth me var ditō divō[13]

That Lalla of Padmanpore
The one who drank the nectar

The one who kept gazing at Śiva
God, give me a gift like that!

Here in this *shruk*, from a longer poem which invokes Kashmir's legendary spiritual masters, Nund Rishi remarkably addresses God in Kashmiri as *divō*, from the Indo-Aryan *deiwos* (Sanskrit, *deva*). The spiritual attainment of Lal Ded (gazing at the countenance of Lord Śiva) is likened by Nund Rishi to drinking the *amrita* (nectar) which, in the Hindu tradition, conferred immortality to the gods. In many of Nund Rishi's *shruk*s, God himself is used interchangeably with Śiva, one of the main gods of the Hindu pantheon. Not only does this *shruk* then involve an act of translation from Hinduism to Islam in the religious register but also a vernacularization of both the classical Hindu and Islamic traditions at the margins.

The way Nund Rishi engages with the pre-Islamic Hindu and Buddhist traditions of Kashmir gives us an unusual access to the thinking of faith and politics in medieval Kashmir. It also complicates our understanding of Islam in contemporary Kashmiri discourses about identity and nation. These discourses include the public discourses of secularism in Indian and Kashmiri nationalism and the discourses of an inherently tolerant Kashmiri Islam, or the discourses of an inherently tolerant Islam, which inform variants of Kashmiri nationalism and Kashmiri Islamism. Even though a concept of a faith that is universal informs the contemporary discourses on Islam in Kashmir (which includes the contemporary reception of the mystical poetry of Nund Rishi), we do not come across any clear articulation of a universal faith at the imagined "origin" of these discourses in either Nund Rishi or Lal Ded. Rather, there is an interweaving of translations and movements between the Hindu, Buddhist, and Islamic linguistic and religious registers.

What then does Islam mean for Nund Rishi? This question is particularly significant because nowhere does a notion of "Kashmiri Islam" appear in Nund Rishi's *shruk*s. I will read the thinking of Islam in Nund Rishi from his negotiations of the question of the Sharīʿah, his approach toward controversies around such Sufi martyrs as Manṣūr al-Ḥallāj, his invocation of the legendary early Islamic ascetic (and a contemporary of Prophet Muhammad) 'Uways al-Qaranī, and his attitude toward Hinduism and Buddhism. I will begin with the long poem that has the refrain *Suy dupze Musalmān* (He alone is a true Muslim) for the reason that it explicitly addresses the question of who is or is not a Muslim. My reading of this poem situates Nund Rishi in relation to the politics of questioning the name (and naming) of the Muslim – in medieval South Asia – not just by Muslim theologians and Sufis but also by such figures as the founder of Sikhism, Guru Nanak, and the Indian saint-poet Kabir. The poem is an answer to the following question: who is a Muslim? The poem hints at contestations around this question which seem to be common around fourteenth- and fifteenth-century north India. The trope of a true Muslim, or a true Sufi, persists across religious traditions in South Asia against orthodox approaches to Islam that could also function in the past as a political challenge to Muslim rulers of South Asia. The binary of Sufism and Sharīʿah that we often come across in the scholarship on Islam in South Asia, even though at times reductive, is a useful intellectual device to help clarify the stakes of a poem such as *Suy dupze Musalmān*.

The new Sultanate of Kashmir had to deal with the pressures from immigrant Sufis and the *ʿulamā* to implement the Sharīʿah and press the cause of Islam in Kashmir's predominantly non-Muslim environment. It is against this background that Nund Rishi approaches Islam from the emotional and political registers of the Kashmiri vernacular by putting the idea of what it is to be a Muslim itself into question. This is a move the Rishi movement shared with the Sufis and *bhaktī* saints of north India who were then negotiating the rule of another Muslim sultanate. Not only does Islam, in the Rishi iteration, resemble the revolution of early Islam, but it is also held in a relation to pre-Islamic Kashmiri spirituality.

The "true Muslim" is a trope in South Asian vernacular Sufi poetry just as the "true Sufi" is a trope in Sufism signaling the terms "Muslim" and "Sufi" as sites of contestation in the medieval period. From its beginning, the history of Islam is marked by this struggle over "true Islam" and "true Sufism." What is at stake in these struggles over the "true" is the truth of spirituality. To what degree is the truth of spirituality connected to political possibility? This history of questioning spills over into other spiritual movements in north India and the question of a "true Muslim" also marks its appearance in the Sikh religious tradition. The Islamic tradition makes a distinction between a Muslim (the one who surrenders to God) and a *momin* (a believer). A *momin* need not be a Muslim, but a Muslim must be a *momin*. The "true Muslim," which stands in for "true Islam," becomes the idea that establishes equivalences between competing claims about Islam, politics, and power in the new Muslim sultanates of medieval north India. Not only did these contestations influence imperial attitudes to Sufism and Islamic theology, but they also shaped the relation of the new Muslim ruling elites in north India to the new Indian Muslim converts and, more significantly, the non-Muslim majority.

Even though Nund Rishi unambiguously situates himself within the Islamic tradition (this is the fundamental argument made by the historian Mohammad Ishaq Khan in his influential study on the Rishis), consistent with the Sunni orthodoxy which he often affirms in his *shruk*s, he nonetheless repeatedly turns to Islam in the spirit of questioning. My point is that the thinking and practice of Islam in Kashmir is distinctive because of these acts of translating Islam as a question which neither begins nor ends with Nund Rishi. But Nund Rishi along with his mystical poetry is a figure around which coheres an idea of Islam as a question and its multiple translations. It is the translatability of Islam that enables Nund Rishi to found the Rishi movement against all odds as a Kashmiri Sufi order and why it still endures in Kashmiri cultural memory. The *shruk*s of Nund Rishi inherit an unfolding tradition of thinking on Islam in Sufism, of its political failures and its eschatological promise, but in a language which is in a relation to its own historicality. The *shruk* as a fragment is the site of an encounter which allows the rupture between the pre-Islamic and Islamic pasts of Kashmir to flash up.[14]

Let us turn now more explicitly to the question of Islam as Nund Rishi addresses it in his long poem *Suy dupze Musalmān*. B. N. Parimoo writes that the Kashmiri *tazkirāh*s (a genre of texts that collects biographies of poets and Sufis with some examples from their works) suggest that Nund Rishi's poem answered a direct question posed to him about his idea of a Muslim.[15] The question was apparently addressed to Nund Rishi by a Brahmin convert to Islam who also became the scribe of Nund Rishi.[16] I quote here the complete poem from the Moti Lal Saqi edition of the collected poems of Nund Rishi:

Angu' yas khọsh bọe mọkhu' zan vudē
Nishi vudỳn bạḍ gath hỳth ās mān
Sọstū' kreyi tu' rostuy krodē
Suy dupze Musalmān

Dū'thchi kāmi kar vuḍāli
Āsỳs nanzaru'ch sakal kāmān
Tsỳth kisaru' yavu' madu' vāli
Tsāli gob vacun tu' avmān
Yi paras paru'ni tu' pānas pāli
Suy dupze Musalmān

Su purọshah swọrgas pravē
Yas ahar chuy beyan sān
Ru'tӯn dọhan yus rozu' thāvē
Āsi yavu' vạsith navi namān
Krōd lōb mad ahankār travē
Suy dupze Musalmān

Pānas mọl kari nu' hāre
Sū't beyis kari nu' mānas mān
Dọrzan trạvith sọzan gāre
Rātas dohas dāre dyān
Par tu' pān yus sodras tāre
Suy dupze Musalmān

Beyis dọpsham vakhnī
Pānas brōnth ani īmān
Beyis nazar kari nu' hạnī
Āsi nu' danu' dīshith bramān
Vāre paki tu' shara' zānī
Suy dupze Musalmān

Andvan nīrith pand yem hyetsu'y
Sạtsu'e logun panun jān
Yami̱ yad gạnḍ tu' tsӯḍ tạmi̱ hyetsu'y
Metsē vyondun panun pān
Andkun ru'hith bari yemi̱ phyetsu'y
Suy dupze Musalmān[17]

His body and mind fragrant
Meditating on the wise sayings of the awakened
He who is of right action and free of anger
He alone is a Muslim

One who does not turn his back on everyday labor
One who desires to work for an honest living
One who controls his ego and mad passions
One who is tolerant of harsh speech and humiliation
One who practices what he preaches to others
He alone is a Muslim

That person will attain heaven
Who shares his food with the others
And fasts on holy days
He who bends low in prayer
He who abandons anger, greed, self-love and pride
He alone is a Muslim

One who does not value himself at a cowrie
One who does not compete with the others
One who searches for the good and abandons evil
One who is mindful day and night
One who ferries the self and the other across the ocean
He alone is a Muslim

One who gives discourses to the others
Only about that which he himself practices
One who does not look down upon the others
One who never gets tempted by wealth
One who walks steadfastly and knows the path of the Sharī'ah
He alone is a Muslim

The one who leaves the forest for the village
The one who commits to the search for truth
The one who controls his appetites and acts with patience
The one who reduces himself to dust
The one who retreats to an inward calm and reflects on past forgetfulness
He alone is a Muslim

The ideas expressed in this poem are strikingly similar to those of the Sikh guru Guru Nanak (1469–1539), who was born in neighboring Punjab within thirty years of Nund Rishi's death in the realm of the Chishtī saints. If one reads the above poem in parallel with Guru Nanak's hymns about being a "true Muslim," there is a striking similarity between the two approaches to the question of a "true Muslim."[18] In Nund Rishi's poem, the Muslim is the subject of a difficult self-transformation and not merely a member of a particular religious community: he or she meditates on the sayings of the wise and is free of anger. There is a strong stress on honest living and patience when confronted with aggression. A Muslim is also one who practices what he preaches: he shares his food and resources with others and turns his back on anger, greed, attachment, and pride. We also see the development of similar ideas in Muslim north India with the rise of the Chishtī Sufi Order in the twelfth century. But what is significant about Nund Rishi is that he does not use any of the Sufi technical terms for expressing his idea of a Muslim but instead turns to Sanskrit concepts of *krodha* (anger), *lobha* (greed), *moh* (attachment), *ahankār* (pride), and *mad* (intoxication). The terms are significant in the Sikh tradition and are also used by the Chishtī Sufi of the Punjab, Bābā Farīd, also venerated in the Sikh tradition. But Nund Rishi significantly also emphasizes the Sharī'ah and considers a Muslim as someone who has turned his back on the path to the forest, and hence of total renunciation, and returns to the village, a public community. Yet this is not a complete rejection of asceticism. Nund Rishi ends the poem by calling a Muslim someone who retreats inward to strive for the truth in patience and through constant remembrance of one's mortality. A distinction is made between an asceticism that involves turning inward and the one that involves a turn to the forest.

The poem is striking as it foregrounds the question of who is and is not a Muslim (or a good Muslim) as a concern in fourteenth- and fifteenth-century Kashmir. The question also appears in an Indo-Persian cultural climate where the question of who is or is not a Sufi was also significant as tensions emerged between different Sufi orders in Kashmir. From its beginning, Sufism emerges entangled with the question of its relation to the Sharī'ah and political power. But these developments had acquired, as we have already noted, an unusual intensity with the deepening of the crisis in the Muslim world after the Mongol attacks on eastern and central Islamic lands as well as such traumatic events as the hanging of Manṣūr al-Ḥallāj by the Caliphate in 922 AD. Even though the question of the Sharī'ah was at stake in the Manṣūr affair, the developments were also tied to questions of political power, which we will discuss in greater detail later. Nothing less than the meaning of Islam was at stake, and it is in this atmosphere that Ḥallāj's martyrdom is supposed to have, as the Sufis often assert, renewed the Islamic faith.

The line "Suy dupze Musalmān" can also be translated as "Only such a person is a Muslim." Nund Rishi connects Islam to a necessary askesis marked by a lack of anger (*krōd*, or *krodha*) and the possession of right thoughts combined with right action. There is also a strong insistence on depending on one's own labor. Much like the Chishtī Sufi Ḥamīd al-Dīn Nāgorī, Nund Rishi advocated and practiced farming. The Kubrāwiyyā Sufis in Kashmir had also educated people in different arts, crafts, and skills for livelihood.

But they differed from the Rishis in their approach to non-Muslims (the Kubrāwiyyā practiced Shafi'i school of Islamic jurisprudence which, unlike the Hanafi school, is slightly stricter on the question of the relations to non-Muslims).[19] For Nund Rishi, the ideal Muslim is someone in control of the passions of the ego who practices only what he or she preaches. The stress is on *'amal* (practice, or meaningful action).

In the third stanza of the poem, Nund Rishi warns that only such a Muslim shall attain Paradise who shares his food with others and who prays and fasts night and day (combines generosity with Muslim ritual prayer). A Muslim gives up *krōd* (rage), *lōb* (greed), *mad* (intoxication with the ego), and *ahankār* (pride). A Muslim does not think much of himself or herself and avoids competing with others. Rather, in constant search of the good, in *dyān, or dhyāna* (mindfulness), day and night, a Muslim must help self and the other cross the ocean of life. A Muslim must only preach what he practices himself, and he or she should never covet the other's property. A Muslim is not tempted by wealth and steadfastly moves on the straight path of the Sharī'ah. A Muslim does not isolate himself or herself from community, searches for the truth without abandoning community, controls the appetites of the *nafs* (ego), and never forgets his mortality. But despite living in the community, Nund Rishi's Muslim retains an inwardness which is not at the same time a retreat from the world outside. What is remarkable about this poem is that Nund Rishi finds cognates such as *mad* (intoxication) or *ahankār* (pride) for the workings of the Qur'ānic *nafs* (blameworthy ego) and attempts a translation of Sufi technical terminology into the Sanskrit-inflected vernacular Kashmiri.[20] A Muslim that Nund Rishi speaks of here not only resembles the figure of the Sufi in a Kashmiri regional setting (like the Chishtīs and Suhrawardis of the Hind and Sindh) but also such early God-fearing Islamic mystics as Ḥasan al-Baṣrī and Sahl b. 'Abdullah Tūstārī.

Even though we sense the fear of God, and the fear of encountering God in death, as the dominant strain in Nund Rishi's mystical poetry (as we will discuss in Chapter 2), he also invokes the figures of Manṣūr al-Ḥallāj, Jalāl al-Dīn Rumi, and 'Uways al-Qaranī from the Islamic tradition. The ecstatic Sufism of al-Ḥallāj is not as unrestrained here. Nor is the asceticism of 'Uways al-Qaranī as extreme. Even though there is an affirmation of the legacy of al-Ḥallāj, and of his discomfort with political power, in Nund Rishi, there are also a few *shruks* which are almost at the borders of Ḥallājian ecstatic utterances (*shaṭḥ*). Rather, the tone and tenor of Nund Rishi's mystical poetry is strikingly similar to that of early Chishtī Sufis such as Bābā Farīd.[21] The approach to political power in Nund Rishi is also cautious like that of the Chishtīs. It is beyond the scope of this book to speculate on the relationship between the Sufis of the Delhi Sultanate under the Tughlaqs and the Sufis of the new Kashmir Sultanate, but the attitudes of the Rishis to the Kashmiri Sultanate do bear a resemblance to those of the Chishtīs to the Delhi Sultanate. Even though there is no consistent pattern to this relationship, both the Chishtīs and the Rishis laid stress on independence from the sultans and their court. The retreat to an inner experience in Islamic mysticism at its beginnings cannot be isolated from the political failures of the Abbasid Caliphate (750–1258 CE).[22] Nund Rishi searched for a new language that could help circumvent the tension between a Sharī'ah-oriented Sufism and Hindu–Buddhist elements in the thinking and practice of Islam in Kashmir. The situation was similar to that of the Delhi Sultanate where the sultans adopted a pragmatic approach to governance but failed to check the influence of theologians demanding a strict implementation of the Sharī'ah. Sultan Iltutmish, for instance, had to defer the demands for the implementation of the Sharī'ah in the thirteenth-century Delhi Sultanate.[23] As we have seen in the Introduction, it is these tensions which would force the celebrated Kubrāwiyyā saint Mīr Sayyid Alī Hamadānī to leave Kashmir only after a short stay of three to four years.[24] A reading of the correspondence of Mīr Sayyid 'Alī Hamadānī to the Kashmiri sultan after his departure from Kashmir clearly reveals the differences in their approach to the question of the Sharī'ah.[25] The Kashmiri sultans venerated Mīr Sayyid Alī Hamadānī but they could do little about his demand to implement the Sharī'ah. What Nund Rishi does is that he complicates our understanding of the Sharī'ah by approaching the question in the vernacular from the loci of the everyday.

For more than 500 years after the advent of Islam in seventh-century Arabia, the Sufis of the Middle East, Central Asia and South Asia had evolved a language Qur'ānic in origin but concerned with the practices of self-transformation which resembled pre-Islamic religious practices in all of these regions (Christianity in the Middle East, Buddhism in Central Asia, and Hinduism in South Asia). Nund Rishi shifts effortlessly between Islamic and Hindu–Buddhist registers in speaking of these processes of self-transformation. He grounds his thinking in the Qur'ānic technical language but by first translating it into the vernacular. It is in this act of translation that Nund Rishi finds his own voice as a thinker and a poet on the cusp of the Hindu–Muslim encounter in medieval Kashmir. Such an act of translation is obvious in a line like *Nafsu'ī myōn chuy madu'h hostuy* (My *nafs* is like a mad elephant).[26] Here Nund Rishi speaks of the condition of the desiring self (*an-nafs al-'ammārah*, the inciting self, in Qur'ānic terms) as that of an elephant in a state of must which invokes the legend of the Buddha's encounter with a mad elephant. Nund Rishi calls the *nafs* the tortured, mad elephant that the Buddha tames in a single glance of compassion. A Qur'ānic term infused into a Buddhist milieu gives many other *shruk*s their unique flavor in a similar manner.

Let us return to the aforementioned poem which deals with the question of who is and is not a Muslim. A striking thing about the poem is that Nund Rishi considers the Muslim as someone who knows the Sharī'ah. Yet Nund Rishi is quick to complicate this understanding of the Sharī'ah by comparing it to a pathway. Nund Rishi uses the Kashmiri idiom *Vāru'pakun*, to walk well (or to stay on the good path), to invoke the etymological meaning of the Sharī'ah as the simple and the straight path.[27] The Sharī'ah belongs to the same root which gives us words like *shāra'* (or road) in Arabic and *shāhrāh* (highway) in Urdu. The walking path also emerges in another *shruk* by Nund Rishi: *Pakān pakān pakān gos* (I kept on, kept on, walking). The world of medieval Hindu and Muslim mysticism in South Asia had a unique term for the simple yet blissful: *sahaja*. Nund Rishi returns us to the origins of the meaning of the Sharī'ah by speaking of it as the *sahaja* path.[28] Nund Rishi does not use the term *sahaja vath* (*sahaja* path) but he does call the Qur'ān the "*sahaja* Qur'ān" and Islam as the *sahaja gyān* (*sahaja* knowledge, or knowledge of the *sahaja*).[29] I will return to the meanings and implications of this key term, *sahaja*, for Nund Rishi toward the end of this chapter.

How are we to understand the tensions between the Sharī'ah and Sufism? The figure of Abū Ḥamīd al-Ghazālī (1058–1111), who reconciled Sufi ideas with theological Islam, helps us situate these tensions to an uneasy truce he pioneered between what has sometimes been called the ecstatic and sober approaches to Sufism which are, in turn, related to a less and more orthodox approach to the Sharī'ah.[30] Such Sufis as Bāyazīd Besṭāmī (804–874 AD) and Manṣūr al-Ḥallāj (858–922 AD) had come under severe criticism for those of their ecstatic utterances (*shaṭḥ*) that appeared to challenge the Sharī'ah. By the fifteenth century in Kashmir and elsewhere, much after the tragic denouement of these tensions in the martyrdom of Manṣūr al-Ḥallāj, the Sufis generally reiterated their commitment to the Sharī'ah and the ecstatic approaches were pushed to the margins of Sufism. Nonetheless, it is interesting how

Nund Rishi reads the Sharīʿah as a *vath* (path) and in another of his *shruks* as *soth* (the embankment). Nund Rishi accuses Manṣūr of endangering the river embankment (*soth*): *Sharahkis sothis sīrah wạ̄jin* (He hurled a brick at the embankment of the Sharīʿah).[31] It is not only dangerous to breach the banks, but a river without banks is unthinkable. In his *Studies in Islamic Culture in the Indian Environment*, Aziz Ahmad argues that nowhere was the tension between Sufism and Sharīʿah as resolved as it was in medieval South Asia:

> In Islamic religious history the tension between the religious assertion of the transcendence of God and the mystical aspiration for His immanence was perhaps nowhere more thoroughly resolved to a middle of the road position than in India where Islam was propagated mainly by Sufis with a firm emphasis on the observance of the tenets of the *shari'at*.[32]

Yet India too had its Sufi martyrs who challenged the Sharīʿah in the Chishtī Sufi Masʿud Bakk (executed by Firoz Shah Tughlaq in 1378) and in the Jewish Armenian Sufi Sarmad (executed on the orders of the Mughal Emperor Aurangzeb in 1661).[33] We might at first discern a middle of the road position in the *shruks* but we soon come up against a barely disguised insurgent spirit in a strong identification with the ecstasies of Manṣūr al-Ḥallāj that we shall soon examine in greater detail.

Nund Rishi unambiguously declares that the Sharīʿah is fundamental to the possibility of a spiritual transformation that he calls becoming a Muslim. But at the same time, he complicates our understanding of the Sharīʿah as that which is the condition of possibility of this process of self-transformation, a *soth* (bank) to the river of *ʿamal* (human action). This is an approach to the Sharīʿah–Sufism question which has had an enduring and powerful impact on Islam in Kashmir (a seemingly middle of the road position which nonetheless conserves an ecstatic mysticism). The Sharīʿah–Sufism debate has such a long history in the intellectual history of South Asian Islam that it reemerges as a problem as late as the twentieth century in the Deobandī school of Islamic theology.[34] But back in fourteenth-century Kashmir, Sharīʿah and Sufism were no longer seen in opposition but as complementing each other in ways which are not always apparent (there are differences in the ways Sufis of different orders approach the relationship between Sharīʿah and Sufism but the relation remains fundamental to their thinking). A radical departure from this approach had to wait until the rise of the so-called Wahhabi movement in nineteenth-century India (and the beginnings of the scripturalist

Ahl-e Hadīth movement), which exhibits less and less tolerance for Hindu influences on Sufism, and increasingly lays stress on the Sharī'ah.[35] The Sufi tendencies that contravened the Sharī'ah found themselves pushed to the space of dervish traditions in South Asia which had evolved in a heterodox environment (for instance, the shrine of the dervish Lāl Shāhbāz Qalandar in Sindh emerged close to a Śaiva site where annual celebrations involved Śaiva practices).[36] But even in the dervish traditions at the margins of Sufism in South Asia, a distinction was made between the *bā shara'* (with Sharī'ah) and *be shara'* (without Sharī'ah) dervishes.

The tension in fifteenth-century Kashmir is not only one between Sharī'ah and Sufism but also between different approaches to the Sharī'ah in Sufi orders such as the Kubrāwiyya and the Rishi Orders. The historian Abdul Qaiyum Rafiqi gives us a detailed account of these tensions in his influential *Sufism in Kashmir: Fourteenth to the Sixteenth Century*.[37] Rafiqi writes: "The political activities of immigrant Sufis and their Kashmiri followers appeared to the Rishīs essentially contradictory to Sufism as they understood it."[38] Even though Mohammad Ishaq Khan resists this interpretation of Sufi history in the early days of the sultanate, it is largely because he refuses to admit any possibility of tensions between the different Sufi orders of the time. But even in the account of the history of Sufism in Kashmir that we get in Khan's work, we can discern signs of tension between the Kubrāwiyyā and the Rishis in the fifteenth century and the Suharwardīyya and the Rishis in the sixteenth century. A case in point are also the tensions between the Kubrāwiyyā and the Nūrbakhshīya in Kashmir which emerged later in the sixteenth century.[39] These tensions were quite widespread among different Sufi orders in medieval South Asia. The Chishtīs, for instance, differed with the Suharwardīyya not only on the question of Sufi relations to political power and accumulation of wealth but also on such sensitive Sharī'ah-related questions as the permissibility of the use of music in Sufi gatherings.

The Rishis, unlike other Kashmiri Sufi orders, remained open to disciples regardless of caste, class, or gender. It is also clear from the Rishi *tadhkirāhs* that they were uneasy about any ties to political power. The question of their reconciliation with the Kubrāwiyyā and Suhrawardīs, and the ways in which Nund Rishi speaks of the Sharī'ah, suggest that these tensions were not only about the role of the Sharī'ah but also about approaches to the Sharī'ah itself. This recalls the attitude of the Chishtī Sufis who did not oppose the Sharī'ah in relation to such practices as the *sama'* (listening to music) but interpreted the Sharīʿah in a way that deemed the *samaʿ* practice as legal. More than the tensions between different Sufi orders in medieval South Asia, it was the differences between the Sharīʿah-minded *ʿulamā* and the Sufis as such that shaped the trajectory of Islam in South Asia. For instance, Nund Rishi endorses the Sharīʿah but he is also at the same time unsparing and relentless in his criticism of the *mullāhs*, the religious clergy. The critique of the *mullāhs* is a common trope of Persian Sufi poetry that persists in Muslim literary culture in South Asia as late as the twentieth century (the seventeenth-century Mughal prince Dara Shikoh calls Paradise a place free of the *mullāhs*).[40] But a critique of the figure of the *mullāh* in Nund Rishi emerges in relation to tensions between the new Persian immigrants (Sufis, theologians, noblemen) and the new Kashmiri converts to Islam: it reveals a tension between the settler Sufis and Kashmiri Rishis. Let us return to a *shruk* that I have already cited:

Nÿbray shūbu'li̱ andru'h shūmī
Minbaran khasan tu' kạri̱ kạri̱ kār
Mallay dapzih tu' Mōlvī Rūmī
Natu' mallu' dīshith istig̱hfār.[41]

Pleasing on the outside, rotten on the inside
They sermonize from the pulpit after evil deeds
If you want to speak of a true *mullāh*, it is Maulana Rūmī
Or else seek God's refuge if you sight a *mullāh*.

The example of Rūmī here is not merely incidental. There is a sharp critique of the fake *mullāhs* in Rūmī who stressed the inner dimensions of Islam over ceremonial observance. Rūmī himself had trained in Islamic sciences such as the study of the *hadīth* and the *fiqh* (jurisprudence) but distrusted the privileging of theological knowledge as opposed to the Sufi path of love.[42] Even though there emerged a consensus on the relation between inner or esoteric Sufism and the outer or exoteric Sharīʿah among the Sufis, the tensions between the Sufis and the orthodox *ʿulamā* persisted in history. One consequence of these tensions was the assertion of Sunni orthodoxy in Central Asian and South Asian Sufism, which reached its apogee in the sixteenth century with the Naqshbandī Sufi Shaykh Aḥmad Sirhindī writing a treatise against Shiʿīsm.[43] We see Nund Rishi affirm Sunni orthodoxy in many of his *shruks*, but he never takes an anti-Shiʿī stand. Let us take, for instance, the following *shruk*:

Ḥaẓrat Ṣiddīqas tas durdānas
Yus avval hyot sāhiban pānas sạ̄t
Umari Kh̲attāb-as pahalvānas
Yem jang kor shaitānas sạ̄t
Ḥaẓrat Us̱mānas ibni 'Affānas
Yem kathu' kạri furqānas sạ̄t
Ḥaẓrat Shāhas sher-e yazdānas
Yem tsọt kheyi mahmānas sạ̄t
Rasūli khudāyas shāh-e sult̲ānas
Yus 'ummat panin heyi pānas sạ̄t
Nund Ryosh 'arz kari Shah-e Hamdānas
Tatiy janatas hy̆tam pānas sạ̄t[44]

To the Siddīq, the Truthful One, that Pearl
The One who the Master took along as his first friend
To Umar ibn al-Khattab, the Strong One
The One who fought the Satan
To Uthman ibn al-Affan
The One who spoke to the Qur'ān
To the King, the lion of God
The one who broke bread with the stranger
To the Prophet of God, the king of kings
The one who will shield his community
Nund Rishi appeals to Shāh-e Hamadān
In heaven, keep me by your side

Here Nund Rishi offers salutations and praise to the first caliph of Islam (Abū Bakr) followed by the second ('Umar ibn al-Khattāb), the third (Uthmān ibn al-'Affān), and the fourth caliph (Alī ibn Abī Ṭālib) and then praise to Prophet Muhammad. Nund Rishi ends with an appeal to Shāh-e Hamadān ("the King of Hamadan"), Mīr Sayyid 'Alī Hamadānī, the Kubrāwiyyā saint from Hamadān, who visited Kashmir with hundreds of his followers (seven hundred, according to popular Kashmiri belief), and whose son, Mīr Muḥammad Hamādanī, as we have already discussed, played a significant role in the consolidation of Islam in Kashmir. Nund Rishi prays for the company of Shāh-e Hamādān in Paradise. Regardless of whether this is a later interpolation to ease the differences between the two orders (the local Rishi and the foreign Kubrāwiyyā) and affirm Sunni orthodoxy or a *shruk* by Nund Rishi himself, it nonetheless points to a certain asymmetry between the cultural power of the Rishis and the Persian Sufis. The affirmation of the early Caliphate situates Nund Rishi within orthodox Sunni pietism that considers the rule of all the first four caliphs as rightly guided and legitimate. The presence of this and similar *shruk*s in the Nund Rishi corpus indicates a general anxiety about Shiʿīsm in the region which developed into a serious concern by the sixteenth century and led key Naqshbandī and Suharwardī Sufis of Kashmir to turn to Mughal imperial power in the hopes of an intervention in a Kashmir ruled by the Shiʿī Chak dynasty. Let us turn to another *shruk* reinforcing this allegiance to Sunni orthodoxy:

Muhammad tu' tsōr yār bar haq gạnzrakh
Timan nish andī dīnuk nyāy
Jān pān panun timan path bạnzrakh
Sọy chay tōr kits bạḍ rahkāy
Anis athu' wāl pāy kÿth sạyzrakh
Yāmāthnu' varzakh pīru' su'nz jāy[45]

If you take the path of Muhammad and the four friends as true
You will be able to seek an end to your spiritual search
If you sacrifice your life and wealth for them
This is the only true investment for the future
You will not be able to find the right path
Like a blind man without a walking stick
As long as you don't understand the station of your teacher

Yet again we see Nund Rishi affirm the leadership of all the four rightly guided caliphs. The *shruk* also strongly endorses tradition by urging the spiritual seeker to abide by one's teacher. It is striking then that such advice about the relation between a *pīr* (Sufi teacher) and a disciple is preceded by a call to give allegiance to not just the Prophet but the four rightly guided caliphs. On an alternative reading, the *pīr*s of the *shruk* could be read as the Prophet and the four rightly guided caliphs. Even though Nund Rishi's attitude is far from anti-Shiʿī, it nonetheless affirms Sunni orthodoxy. It is easier to see now why Nund Rishi is spared the anti-Sufi polemical attacks from such Islamic revivalists in Kashmir as the Jamāt-e Islāmī, Ahl-e Hadīth, and Deobandīs. Most of these revivalist movements are accommodating of pietistic Sufism as long as the latter does not contradict the Sharīʿah or deviate from core Sunni doctrine.

Even though there is little that is controversial in Nund Rishi from the standpoint of Sunni orthodoxy, there is a strategic ambiguity in the *shruk*s in relation to the Sharīʿah and Shiʿīsm. This is not entirely unexpected in a climate where even Kubrāwiyyā attitudes to the *ahl al-bayt* (family of the Prophet) came to be seen as pro-Shiʿī and at the same time the Nūrbakhshīya Order (the only Shiʿī Sufi Order) came to prominence in Kashmir a century after Nund Rishi's death.[46] How does then one read Nund Rishi's affirmation of the Sunni consensus? There are, for instance, other Nund Rishi *shruks* which invoke only members of Prophet Muhammad's family, such as his beloved daughter, Fāṭimāh:

Pạ̄r pạ̄r lạg zi tas pạ̄ghambaras
Yihindis dōras raḥmat che jạ̄rī
Kạ̄l yali haq lagi rōz-e maḥsharas
Tas kun vọmedvār āsan sạ̄rī
Sạmith ʿarzā karan jabāras
Dōstas pananis ghōssu' vani sạ̄rī
Vuch tu' kū'tsu' nyāmạts ditsam samsāras
Kạ̄nsi nu' karạm shukar guzạ̄rī
Ti bōzi Faṭimā nishi khandu'kāras
Dapi rabbanā bābas gham kās sạ̄rī
Tōru' adu' bar vuchran rahmatu'kis garas
Yāras pananis sū't diyi sạ̄rī[47]

Each part of my body I wish I could sacrifice for the Prophet
In his age, God's mercy still shelters us
A time shall come of the Final Judgment
That day everyone shall place his hopes in the Prophet
And together will pray for God's forgiveness
God that day shall complain to his friend
That He put no limit on his blessings in the world
Yet could not find anyone giving thanks
This Fatima too shall hear from God
And pray that God end all her father's worries
It is then that the doors of the house of mercy shall open
And God will accept everyone in Paradise along with his friend

This is a simple poem steeped in traditional Muslim piety, but the vision it reveals of end times is quite striking. It foregrounds the intercessory powers of Prophet Muhammad on the Day of Judgment (*yawm al-qiyāmah*). The love of Muhammad (*ʿishq-e muḥammadī*) is fundamental to most Sufi movements, but the *'ulamā* were cautious about excesses in expressions of Sufi love for the Prophet. In this *shruk*, Muhammad's intercession with God on the Day of Judgment is turned into nothing less than a final, dramatic encounter between the human species and its Creator. God complains to his friend about the heedlessness of human beings, who received freely but did not offer any thanks. It is not only Muḥammad but also his daughter Fāṭimāh who is involved in these events and prays that God ease her father's worries about the fate of the human species. It is only then that God throws open the doors of the house of mercy, Paradise, for everyone. Here the human species attains salvation because of the intercession of Prophet Muhammad in which his beloved daughter Fāṭimāh also plays a significant role. The Islamic tradition highlights Prophet Muhammad's anxiety for the future of his new community and about the way they will fare on the Day of Judgment. The intercession (*shafā'a*) is a controversial subject in traditional Muslim theology, but there is general agreement that Prophet Muhammad would have powers of intercession on the Day of Judgment when the anxiety of human beings, burdened with a difficult questioning of their actions in the world, crosses all limits.[48] Only Prophet Muhammad takes up this task of intercession (the Islamic tradition alludes to the Prophet saving up the power of his prayer for this day).[49]

Prophet Muhammad's daughter, Fāṭimāh, also plays a role in the events of intercession in the Shi'ī tradition, and the *shruk* by Nund Rishi suggests porous borders between the Shi'ī and Sunni traditions in the early years of Kashmiri Sufism. In Islamic theology, it is not very clear if every human being is or is not going to eventually end up in Paradise. But this *shruk* makes Prophet Muhammad's intercession a universal prayer for humanity and assures all human beings of glad tidings about the end. But there were far more controversial issues than intercession at stake in the larger debate about Sharī'ah and Sufism in the Indo-Persian world. The Sharī'ah–Sufism debate never disappeared from Muslim South Asia, acquiring a centrality in Mughal India, and persisted even after the collapse of Muslim sovereignty over north India and the emergence of British colonial rule. One could even argue that these debates intensified in colonial India as Muslims negotiated the loss of political power in north India.

The Sharī'ah–Sufism debates in north India can be traced all the way back to similar debates among the Sufis of Baghdad in the ninth and tenth centuries which precipitated events that ended in the tragic martyrdom of

Manṣūr al-Ḥallāj. Manṣūr al-Ḥallāj remains a controversial figure in the history of Islam, but, quite paradoxically, his legacy in South Asia is affirmed not only by the Sufis but also by such modernist Islamic thinkers as Iqbal and even such Deobandī theologians as Maulana Ashraf 'Alī Thānvī. Reading the *shruk*s, one cannot help but think of the struggle between Junayd al-Baghdādī's "sober" Sufism and his student Manṣūr al-Ḥallāj's "ecstatic" Sufism as a dialectic internal to Nund Rishi's poetry. Nund Rishi is difficult to read precisely because of this extreme caution he exercises toward Sunni, and Sufi, orthodoxy. It is for this reason that he continues to appeal not just to the Sufis but also to reformist and revivalist Islamic movements in Kashmir. Even though Nund Rishi never really openly challenges the Sharī'ah like Manṣūr al-Ḥallāj, he often ridicules the figure of the *mullāh* (a figure synonymous in Islamic culture with the calls for a strict adherence to the Sharī'ah) and their public displays of knowledge and piety. This critique of the *mullāh* is difficult to separate from a critique of theological knowledge and imperial power. Indeed, the attack on the figure of the *mullāh* is unusually strident in Nund Rishi:

Mallav cholukh tu' mallav chokukh
Mallav dyūnthumay nu' ạliṃuk nāv
Mallav tatu' bọnu' bar tal dōlukh
Mallō lạzrāvruth mallu' nāv[50]

The *mullāh*s washed you out
The *mullāh*s haven't even heard the name of true knowledge
The *mullāh*s waylaid you from the doors of heaven
O *mullāh*, you have truly endangered the boat

In this *shruk*, Nund Rishi sarcastically addresses his reader as someone who has been washed out of all virtue by the *mullāh*. The metaphor of washing here also appears to satirize the obsession of the *mullāh*s with ritual purity and clean clothing. Nund Rishi draws attention to the ordinary clothing of the Kashmiri peasants in many of the *shruk*s. Nund Rishi reminds his reader that he was very close to entering the sacred space of divine presence on his own but the *mullāh* has waylaid him right from the doorstep to the path. In a pun on the words *mallu'* (which could also be read in Kashmiri as "the boatman") and *nāv* (which could also be read as "name"), Nund Rishi in the last line of the *shruk* addresses the *mullāh*s directly in the vocative and bemoans the way the *mullāh* endangers the boat and the name of true Islamic scholars.

The boat, in the last line of the *shruk*, can also be read as a metaphor for the self or faith. As we shall see, Nund Rishi does not attack the Sharīʿah (law, or an embankment, which makes life, or the river, possible) but rather its misuse by the *mullāh*. Nund Rishi then warns not only his reader about the danger the *mullāh* poses to his spiritual journey but also the *mullāh* himself about the danger he poses to Islam. In another of his *shruk*s, Nund Rishi again praises Maulana Rūmī as a true *mullah*:

Mallay ạs zi tu' Mōlāy Rūmī
Natu' kạr zi rumu' rumu' istighfār
Sodras tār dituy tạmi
Pānay sapun pānas yār[51]

If you have to be a *mullāh*, then be a *mullāh* like Maulana Rumi
Or else seek refuge from being a *mullāh*
He is the one who crossed the ocean
And he became his own true friend

Crossing the ocean appears in both Nund Rishi and Lal Ded (*āmi panu' sodras nāvi chhas lamān*) as a metaphor for the task of a spiritual life.[52] This seems to be a variant of the *shruk* about Maulana Rūmī quoted above. Here Maulana Rūmī is praised not only as someone who is a true *mullāh* but also as the courageous one who crosses the sea of ignorance to recognize himself as his own true friend. There are many ways we can read this *shruk* as the "true friend" does also allude to one of the names of God in the Islamic tradition, that is, *al-walī*, the friend (the Sufis are also often called *'awliyā*, or the friends of God). There is a gnostic strain in this *shruk*: one must make a return journey through stages to one's true friend. In yet another of his *shruk*s, Nund Rishi reserves this bitter advice for the *mullāh*:

'Ālim chuy bod tu' mallu' chukh dānā
Khabar yeti sanā kihō
Āru' ros dyūnthmakh tōr-i ros chānā
Varhol arkhạli ginā hihō
Asi yeti racāv dayi sund panāh
Myvu' ros dyūnthmakh vanā hihō
Sahyb pānay yeti ladi khānā
Panu' khọtu' byākh zān dānā hihō[53]

You have great knowledge and you are a big *mullāh*
But what on earth are you doing here?
I saw you as a carpenter without a saw and chisel
I saw you as the hard wood that cannot be cut
We had taken here refuge in God
I saw you as a forest without any fruits
The Friend will set up house here out of his own liking
But you must first consider others better than you

Nund Rishi castigates the *mullāh* for his vanity and compares his state to someone who has scholastic knowledge but lacks any real skill. He then advises the *mullāh* to respect the other more than his own self, and not to think of himself as someone who mediates the relations between the human and the divine realms. Nund Rishi urges the *mullāh* not to arrogate to himself the right to take God's affairs in his own hands and at the same time reminds him that Kashmiris have always sought refuge in divinity. The lack of a skill becomes a metaphor for the limits of abstract knowledge: it is a forest without any fruits. Nund Rishi does not hesitate to reprimand the *mullāh* for claiming that he is doing God's work. For Nund Rishi, the first task of the *mullāh* should have been to consider others as wiser than himself. In yet another of his *shruk*s, he almost gives up on the *mullāh*s as shallow, irritable, and irredeemable:

Mallu' chivu' tọh tu' manzu' kam dọsu'
Tshalas chivu' zāgān ạkis akh
'Ilm chivu' parān ma'āshiki hāvasu'
Mahmān dīshith yivān tsakh
Yiti chuvu' gumanu' ạs chi khāsu'
Tati no mọkliv sāsu' manzu' akh[54]

If you are preachers, then why these walls between you?
You are just waiting to jump at each other's throat
You study the scripture only to earn a living
But if you see a guest, you become irritable
And then you consider yourselves the chosen ones
Not even one in thousand will attain salvation over there

The competition among religious scholars is derided here as charlatanry and deception. Nund Rishi accuses the *mullah*s of acquiring knowledge for the sake of securing their livelihood. Such knowledge is condemned by

Nund Rishi when it fails to create even a sense of hospitality for the stranger in the *mullāh*.[55] In the name of the there and then of end times, the here and now of the *mullāh* is condemned. The critique of the figure of the *mullāh* also hinges here on the gap between a "false Muslim" and the "true Muslim." There is no salvation for the congregation of such a *mullāh*.

The most obvious form the critique of the *mullāh* takes in Nund Rishi's mystical poetry is of the *mullāh* as the local religious scholar, mosque leader, or *madrassa* teacher. Let us, for instance, consider the following *shruk*:

Mallu' āsi soṇats waqtas halān
Mallan tsīrī nýrun phọlān āsi
Mallu' chī sāl būzith balān
Tavay mạshidi kun tsalān āsi[56]

The *mullāh* wakes up when it is late for the morning prayer
The *mullāh* is happiest putting off the start to his day
The *mullāh* only feels better at an invitation to a feast
The *mullāh* only runs to the mosque for such an invitation

In this *shruk*, Nund Rishi attacks the *mullāh* for his negligence of the prescribed religious duties. The *mullāh* who is late for the pre-dawn prayers is always on time when there is a feast to be served at the mosque. Such biting satire is missing from much of medieval Kashmiri poetry and is characteristic of Nund Rishi's attack on the figure of the *mullāh*. Rahman Rahi ends his seminal essay on Nund Rishi, which I have discussed in detail in the chapters to come, with the following words:

> This brief survey of *Shaikh-ul-Ālam*'s poetry would remain incomplete if we also do not speak of the satire and humour of the Shaikh because it is this specialty which sets him apart from Lal Ded and other Sufi poets. The way Nund Rishi relentlessly satirizes the *makkār mullahs* and fake Rishis of his time almost mirrors the characters of Chaucer's *Prologue*.[57]

But despite his biting satire, Nund Rishi extends the critique of the *mullāh* into a more general critique of positive theological knowledge. The Sufis often not only occupied the margins of imperial Islam but also laid claim to the wilds beyond the frontiers of theological knowledge. This critique was not only made possible by the Qur'ānic message about the limits of human knowledge but also the image of Prophet Muhammad himself as *al-nabī al-ummi*, the unlettered prophet.[58] Such a critique of theological knowledge acquires a deeper meaning in medieval Kashmir where the prestige of immigrant Persian Sufis largely rested upon their membership in learned networks of Sufis across Central and South Asia. Shahzad Bashir reminds us that when the Nūrbakhshīya Sufi Shams al-Dīn Irāqī left Kashmir in 1490–91, he wondered if the Kashmiris were at all capable of leading a Sufi practice.[59] The Rishis as a religious group were neither Muslim immigrants from Persia or Central Asia nor members of the local elite. Additionally, Nund Rishi's attacks on the *mullāh* must be situated in the intellectual history of Sufism itself, which developed with a view of corruption at the heart of Muslim political centers, and the concomitant idea that a reversal could be effected from the periphery. The Rishi Order emerged in a period of Kashmir's history when the *'ulamā* (religious scholars) and the Sufis were increasingly opposed to each other through much of the Islamic world, even though such an opposition was absent at the time of such early figures of Islamic history as Ḥasan al-Baṣrī (642–728), who was considered both a great *'ālim* and a great Sufi. The tensions emerged around the ninth and tenth centuries and were brought under control by the time of Imam al-Ghazālī (1058–1111). The uneasy truce between the *'ulamā* and the Sufis that prevailed in most of South Asia for about 900 years owes much to the intervention of al-Ghazālī and his precursors. There might no longer have been an open opposition after Ghazālī between Sharī'ah and Sufism, but the Sufi critique of theological knowledge and the unease toward Sufism among the *'ulamā* persisted. Rarely did the Sufi challenge to the political influence exercised by the *'ulamā* break out into open rebellion. The move from both sides was to affirm the true Sufi or the true *'ālim* and to attack the pretenders. The Sufis continued to warn against a one-sided approach to Islam that would neglect questions of ethics and politics, and the Sharī'ah appeared in their understanding as a condition of possibility of spiritual transformation but not as an end in itself. For the *'ulamā*, an increasing focus on inner states, will, and motivation made it impossible to legislate in a meaningful way: for them, the Sharī'ah was both the means and the end. But what made the stance of the *'ulamā* suspect for the Sufis was their proximity to imperial power.

Both these stances played out against a climate of fierce struggles for political power, and the situation was not the same in the different regions of Islamic South Asia. The trope of an inauthentic *mullāh*, however, emerges early in Islamic mystical poetry and persists even in such twentieth-century Urdu poets as Muhammad Iqbal (1877–1938). One way we can read the severe indictment of the *mullāh* by Nund Rishi is by treating the figure to be a local *madrassa* (religious school) teacher or mosque leader who is ignorant of and indifferent to the demands of Islamic spirituality and not the learned Islamic theologian. But it is also clear that Nund Rishi extends his critique of the *mullāh* from the sociological to the ethical and the political. The *mullāhs* Nund Rishi severely castigates in his *shruks* are often the ones who lay claim to superior knowledge. A similar attitude is exemplified in the Sufi tradition by al-Ghazālī, who in his famous *Letter to a Disciple* writes:

> This conceited fool does not know that when he acquires knowledge, if he does not act on the strength of it, the evidence against him will become decisive, as the Messenger of God ... said, "The man most severely punished on the Day of Resurrection is a scholar whom God did not benefit by his knowledge."[60]

But even for al-Ghazālī, the challenge was to reconcile scholastic knowledge with Sufism. Nund Rishi echoes this attitude of the Sufis when he speaks of the state of the scholar as a beast of burden: *'Ạlimuk bōr lọdahakh kharan* (This knowledge is a burden to them like a huge weight loaded on an ass).[61] Nund Rishi does celebrate *'ilm* (knowledge) in his *shruks*, but he makes a distinction between the *'ilm* of the Real and the *'ilm* of the theologian.

Why this discomfort with the *'ilm* of the theologian? The problem with theological knowledge is that it reproduces social hierarchies. In one of his *shruks*, Nund Rishi compares the knowledge which leads one to pretend that one is better than the others as nothing less than the way of Iblīs (the Devil, or Satan, who rebels against the command of God in the Qur'ānic creation story):[62]

> *Yimay parith lāgan kalān*
> *Timan Iblīs ralān āsi*
> *Tōbu' chuy davā tavay chi balān*
> *Tōbu' ros vath dalān āsi*[63]
>
> Those who study to pretend to be Elders
> They step into the shadow of Iblīs, the Satan
> Repentance is the only way to cure and return
> If you don't repent, you lose your way

In the Islamic tradition, Iblīs is the angel (or a *djinn*) who refused to bow before Adam when God created Adam and whispers temptations (*waswas*) into the hearts of men. The reason for his own downfall is that he considered himself as superior to Adam. Iblīs epitomizes pride and disobedience in the Islamic tradition.[64] But this pride and disobedience has its origins in his claim to superiority in knowledge. Nund Rishi considers those *'ulamā* who develop a sense of pride because of their knowledge as associates of Iblīs. There is nothing short of a complete reevaluation, a revolution, in the way Nund Rishi makes the figure of the illiterate, the lover, and the minor central to his sustained critique of knowledge. Unlike these impostors (the fake *mullahs*), for Nund Rishi, there are true seekers of knowledge who will shine on the Day of Judgment:

Haq lagī ạkhạr cāk gatshi palan
Ạliman ruh prazlān ạsiy
Sạd āsi tsalān tsūr āsi lāran
Teli kīlak akreyi pholān āsiy[65]

There will be a Day of Reckoning, the rocks shall be sundered
The souls of the thinkers will be glowing
The pretenders will run and the thieves escape
The dancing boy shall rejoice in inaction

The true seekers of knowledge for Nund Rishi are the Sufis and saints (not always Muslim as in the case of Lal Ded) that he invokes in countless *shruks*. Nund Rishi takes poetic license in this *shruk*, which invokes conventional metaphors of apocalyptic reversals at end times, to declare that only the true Islamic thinkers shall be at peace on the Day of Judgment. According to Islamic theology, the Day of Judgment is a horrific end that does not spare anyone (not even the prophets). But the term he uses for pretender, as opposed to the thinker, is *sạd*, which is also used in medieval Kashmiri for the immigrant Muslims (*sạd makkār*, for instance, in contemporary Kashmiri, carries the meaning of hypocrite even though it was originally used for those immigrants who pretended to be Syeds, that is, belonging to the family of Prophet Muhammad).[66] The new immigrant Muslims in Kashmir could establish a claim to their share in political power and a role in the new sultanate by claiming to be better Muslims than local Kashmiris in matters of adherence to the Sharī'ah or by claiming association with the family of Prophet Muhammad. It is this situation which Nund Rishi repeatedly castigates in the *shruks*.

The relations between Sufism and theology were complex throughout the Muslim world, but the emphasis on religious law in Kashmir was strong from the beginning and found expression in the insistence of the Kubrāwiyyā missionary Sayyid 'Alī Hamadānī and his son, Mīr Muḥammad Hamadānī, on a strong Sharī'ah-based state during their missions to Kashmir. But the Kubrāwiyyā could not persuade the Kashmiri sultans to implement a strict rule of the Sharī'ah and Sayyid 'Alī Hamadānī left Kashmir only after a brief stay of around three to four years.[67] The conflicts between the sultans and the Sufi *shaikhs* in the medieval period were by no means confined to the Kashmir Sultanate. Such conflicts were to recur in the sultanates of north India and the Deccan. But the reasons which contributed to Chishtī success in the Delhi Sultanate worked against the Rishis in Kashmir. The rise of the Chishtīs happened in a city which was also the capital of the Delhi Sultanate when it controlled a vast empire, but the rise of the Rishis appears to have been halted in Srinagar where the Kubrāwiyyā (and then Suharwardiyyā and Naqshbandiyyā) Persian Sufi orders gained ground. The Persian Sufi orders could rely on a transnational network as opposed to the Rishis, whose influence remained largely confined to rural Kashmir. Let us turn to a description of the political situation of the new immigrants to the Delhi Sultanate by the historian Muzaffar Alam:

> While on the one hand they were surrounded by a hostile population in India, on the other the Mongols had torn apart the fabric of Muslim power in Central Asia. Many members of ruined ruling dynasties – noblemen, saints and scholars – now looked to north India as the place where they might settle in peace. Rulers in such newly gained lands could not, thus, afford policies or actions which might reinforce opposition to their conquest.[68]

The situation was similar in fourteenth-century Kashmir where elite immigrants from Central Asia were accommodated after the Mongol plunder of their lands. The immigrant members of the ruling class in both the Delhi and the Kashmir Sultanates insisted on the Sharī'ah to secure their position in the new political dispensation. Yet the rulers of both the Delhi and the Kashmir Sultanate (notwithstanding certain exceptions, such as the reign of Sultan Sikandar in Kashmir) largely refused to pursue policies that might alienate their Hindu populations. Like the Muslim rulers of the Delhi Sultanate, the rulers of the Muslim Shahmīrī dynasty in Kashmir nonetheless "looked for legitimacy from the Sufis, who had by then amply demonstrated that truth – the Islamic truth – was not confined to the pages of a book on *sharī'a*."[69] The stage was set for an atmosphere of competitive spirituality, not only between the Persian and the Kashmiri Sufis, but also between the Muslims and the Hindus. It is in this atmosphere of competitive spirituality (in particular, between the immigrant Sufis and the local Rishis) that Nund Rishi affirmed a "learned ignorance" against theological knowledge.[70] But we already encounter this idea in the transformations of medieval Sufism by figures such as Manṣūr al-Ḥallāj, Ibn al-'Arabī, and Maulana Jalāl al-Dīn Rūmī who privileged love over law.

The tensions between Sufism and theology go back to the early centuries of Islam as Sufism emerged as a tendency opposed to the growth of Islamic imperial power under the Ummayad and Abbasid dynasties. In its early years, however, Sufism was nothing but a tendency toward asceticism as Muslim conquests brought wealth to the central Islamic lands. But, as Ayman Shihadeh suggests, by the fifth century of Islam (eleventh century of the Common Era), Sufism had consolidated from the ascetical-mystical milieu of early Islam to "a systematic and well-structured path to knowing God (*ma'rifa*) through a process of internal transformation, which attempts to transcend the ordinary human condition, usually by means of ethico-spiritual discipline."[71] It is unclear to what degree external stimuli such as encounters with Christianity, Buddhism, or Hinduism at the borders of Islam precipitated this internal transformation.[72] Most contemporary scholars of Sufism are in agreement that the transformation depended upon elements internal to Islamic intellectual and spiritual history and the technical language of Islamic mysticism emerges from the Qur'ān.[73] But from the eighth to the eleventh centuries, Islam also developed theological and legalistic forms of inquiry which attempted "to know God, through an exposition which reasons from evidence, whether rational or scriptural."[74] The Sufis did not possess a systematic theology, nor did they develop jurisprudence (even though Sufis were often also trained in both theology and jurisprudence). This situation was peculiar before al-Ghazālī attempted his synthesis of theology and Sufism. Shihadeh writes:

> Even by the 5th/11th centuries, Sufis, *qua* Sufis, had relatively little of their own to offer by way of formal or systematic theology or theosophy. The learned, formal and reasoned exposition of the nature and acts of God continued to be the mainstay of the theologians. Jurists dealt with practice; theologians took care of creed. And in theology, as in jurisprudence, dialectical fault-lines were defined purely in relation to the epistemological dichotomy of scripture

> and reason, mystical intuition (*ilhām*) or vision (*kashf*) almost never making an appearance.[75]

There were indeed tensions between the rational and scriptural approaches to theology, but it was the tension between Sufism and theology that evolved into a serious crisis. The Sufis denounced excessive concern with formal or systematic theology. They were not in search of a new epistemology and stressed reflection on the relations between knowledge and action. Nund Rishi himself often invokes the idea of *'amal* (action), or practices of the self, and connects ontology to ethics by stressing the accountability of all human action. In Arabic, the same three-letter root gives us both *'ilm* (knowledge) and *'amal* (action). But the tensions between Sufism and theology were as much about politics as they were about doctrinal or legalistic issues. Moreover, the relations between Sufism and theology were seldom mutually exclusive: the examples of Ḥārith al-Muḥasibī, Abū al-Qāsim al-Qushayrī, and 'Abdullāh al-Anṣārī should suffice. The early Sufis engaged with theology: al-Qushayrī, for instance, studied both Sufism and scholastic theology (*kalām*).[76] 'Abdullah al-Anṣārī, a Ḥanbalī traditionalist and a Sufi, made an effort to reconcile the traditionalist Ḥanbalī legalistic position with Sufism.[77] The situation, in other words, was far from simple. Even such traditionalists as Ibn Taymiyya, considered a strong opponent of Sufism, sometimes turned to the Sufis to oppose scholastic theology (*kalām*).[78] Shihadeh writes:

> As Sufism consolidated its position as a distinct and increasingly learned and intellectual tradition, and given both the shared noetic concerns of both the Sufi and theological traditions, and the significant overlap in their constituencies, it was inevitable that tension and interaction between the two currents would increase. Political circumstances were, furthermore, often contributing factors, subtly or overtly intertwined with religious and intellectual concerns.[79]

These political circumstances were often about attitudes to imperial power and the fate of those at the margins in new Muslim societies (the Zanj slave labor, for instance, in the case of Manṣūr al-Ḥallāj; or the situation of peasants and lower-caste Kashmiris as well as a large non-Muslim majority in the case of Nund Rishi). Even as 'Ayn al-Quḍāt al-Hamadāni (1098–1131) and Shihāb al-Dīn Yaḥyā al-Suhrawardī (1155–1191) developed a theosophical form of Sufism, and paid for it with their lives (such were the risks involved in straying too far from mainstream Islamic teachings), al-Ghazāli and Maybudī synthesized Ash'arite theology with Sufism.[80] The attempts to reconcile Sufism and theology, in particular, culminated in the voluminous writings of Abū Ḥamīd al-Ghazālī, which brought together Ash'ari theology and Sufi teaching. But about a century prior to this moment of synthesis, the tensions between Sufism and theology had exploded with the torture and hanging of Manṣūr al-Ḥallāj. Even though post-Ghazālī synthesis of theology and Sufism left a strong impact on Sufism in South Asia, the secret love for Manṣūr flowed unrestrained in South Asian Muslim vernacular poetry.

What was the situation in medieval South Asia in relation to these debates and polemics? A Sunni orthodoxy and Sufi heresy found a middle ground where the task of Sufi hermeneutics often revolved around narrowing the gap between the Sharī'ah and Sufism. The situation between Sufis and non-Sufis in medieval South Asia was neither too polarized nor binary.[81] The controversies around the position of the Sharī'ah on the use of music and ecstatic utterances persisted, however, from the early centuries of Muslim rule in South Asia. Even though there was legal sanction to the practice of *samā'* (Sufi practice of listening to music) under the Delhi Sultanate and al-Ghazālī too had made the use of music permissible under special circumstances, the use of music by the Sufis remained a matter of controversy.[82] The conditions in Kashmir were slightly different because the tenor of Sufi rivalry there had more to do with the Kubrāwiyyā insistence on the norms of the Sharī'ah in matters of governance. A powerful Kubrāwiyyā Sufi like Mīr Sayyid 'Alī Hamadānī had appealed to the Shahmīrī Sultan to strictly adhere to the norms of the Sharī'ah, which in turn put pressure on the relations between Kashmir's Muslim ruling classes and the largely non-Muslim population. As we have already discussed, the practices of local Rishis were seen by the Persian Sufis as a challenge to the Sharī'ah as the Sharī'ah mediated their understanding of such issues as the relations between Muslims and non-Muslims, the permissibility of women joining Sufi orders, and such practices as vegetarianism and celibacy. Nund Rishi unhesitatingly drew on Hindu and Buddhist religious culture in his *shruks*, admitted women into the Rishi Order (such as Shām Bībī and Dehat Bībī), and ordained vegetarianism and celibacy for the members of the Rishi Order. Yet the Rishi line of attack was rarely against the Sharī'ah but against its misuse toward worldly ends. The question then often turned around the idea of an authentic *faqīh* (jurist), an authentic *'ālim* (scholar), and an authentic Sufi. The categories such as Muslim, Sufi, and *'ālim* became sites of contestation, as is powerfully attested in Nund Rishi's mystical poetry.

The Rishi Order appeared at a time of theoretical consolidation of Sufism but also the weakening of Muslim power in central Islamic lands. The Persian Sufi orders were keenly aware of the political failures of the Caliphate and sought an Islamic renewal from the periphery that involved strict spiritual and political regimens and stressed the teacher–student relationship. The students were trained in modes of obedience that resembled modes of servitude considered best only in one's relationship to God. Even though the Rishi Order was unique for its adherence to vegetarianism, celibacy, and other ascetic practices unfamiliar to the Persian orders, the Rishis also relied on a mode of training that depended upon a strong teacher–student relationship. But, as we have already discussed, the most fundamental difference between the Persian orders and the Rishis was in their attitudes to political power. The Rishis in the Kashmir Sultanate and the Chishtīs in the Delhi Sultanate, on the whole, kept a careful distance from political power. But the Kubrāwiyyā in Kashmir and the Suharwardiyyā in Multan and Delhi endeavored to influence imperial policy. The attitude of the Rishis (and the Chishtīs in the Delhi Sultanate) is akin to those of the early Islamic mystics, or *zuhhād*, who retreated from worldly power and did not challenge their political opponents. As Gerhard Böwering observes:

> The Muslim mystics of classical Sufism – from the beginnings of Islamic asceticism to the time of al-Ghazzali – did not challenge their opponents with an agenda of the just society, a blueprint of political reform or a call for an Islamic State. Instead, they saw this world, Allah's creation, as a transitory home, a theater of trial and tribulation, a situation to overcome rather than to organize and enjoy. Fully aware of the injustices of this world, they were intent on reaching God, the sole source and goal of justice and the only ruler and lord of the world to come. They identified the root and cause of injustice as within man and devised ways to conquer evil by spiritual renewal, termed *tawba*, "repentance and inner conversion."[83]

It is this tendency of medieval Sufism that was overturned by the Naqshbandīs in Central Asia and the Suhrawardīs in South Asia. The Rishis and the Chishtīs retained a distrust of worldly power but also developed a vision for a just society. If the early Islamic mystics did not actively challenge their opponents, it was in equal measure due to the lack of political space available to them. But the concern for questions of social and economic justice was rarely abandoned. The Rishis, on the other hand, are unambiguous and relentless in their concern about the fate of the poor, lower castes, non-Muslims, and women. The Rishis made a very different attempt at intervention in Kashmiri politics than the Kubrāwiyyā Sufis. If, following Talal Asad, we concur with Bruce Lawrence that "orthodoxy is always the product of a network of power," then we can claim that the Rishis challenged the rise of an Islamic orthodoxy in medieval Kashmir by refusing to collude with either the sultanate or the Kubrāwiyyā Sufis.[84] We must, therefore, understand the Rishi challenge in medieval Kashmir in relation to the networks of political power, which included the politically ascendant new immigrants, the *'ulamā*, and the ruling classes of the new sultanate.

Nund Rishi explicitly invokes three figures from the history of Sufism in his mystical poetry: 'Uways al-Qaranī, Manṣūr al-Ḥallāj, and Jalāl al-Dīn Rūmī. The turn to these figures allows Nund Rishi to challenge the limits of Sufi theology. We have briefly discussed Nund Rishi's turn to Rūmī in order to critique theological power. 'Uways al-Qaranī, as we shall see later, is invoked to secure the legitimacy of a Sufi order with no chains of transmission going back either to other Sufi masters or to 'Ali ibn Abī Ṭālib or 'Abū Bakr. A chain of transmission that goes back to a recognized Sufi saint or to 'Ali ibn Abī Ṭālib or 'Abū Bakr is the *sine qua non* for Sufi teaching. But it is with the figure of Manṣūr al-Ḥallāj that Nund Rishi engages more than any other figure in Sufi history. Manṣūr al-Ḥallāj appears in the history of Sufism as the epitome of an "ecstatic" Sufism at odds with the Sharī'ah. But even though Nund Rishi celebrates the life, rebellion, and martyrdom of Manṣūr al-Ḥallāj, he is cautious in his approach to Sunni orthodoxy.

Manṣūr al-Ḥallāj, the first martyr of Sufism, was brutally tortured and hanged for openly challenging Islamic theology. It is significant, as we shall see in our discussion of a *shruk* about this subject, that Nund Rishi situates himself in relation not only to the legendary ascetics of Kashmir such as Palās Rishi and Mīrān Rishi but also to the legacy of such Sufi martyrs as Manṣūr al-Ḥallāj. Manṣūr al-Ḥallāj (with the possible exception of Rūmī) is the only prominent Sufi that Nund Rishi invokes repeatedly in the *shruk*s to align himself with a Ḥallājian rebellion against orthodox Islamic theology. Ḥallāj is a key figure in Nund Rishi's poetry and allows us deeper access to Nund Rishi's thinking on the question of the Sharī'ah and the relations between Sufism and politics in medieval Kashmir. Yet Nund Rishi approaches the controversy around Manṣūr al-Ḥallāj obliquely so as not to stir up a controversy.

For generations of Sufis in South Asia, speaking about Manṣūr al-Ḥallāj became a way of speaking about the meanings of Sufism and its relations to the Sharī'ah. Nund Rishi is unequivocal in his affirmation of the Sharī'ah but at the same time he does not hesitate to affiliate himself with the controversial legacy of Manṣūr al-Ḥallāj. This seemingly paradoxical strategy was effectively pursued by the Chishtī and Qādirī Sufis of South Asia. Muzaffar Alam discusses the case of 'Abd al-Razzaq Bansawi, an eighteenth-century Qādirī Sufi of Awadh, who not only was the teacher of Mullah Niẓām al-Dīn Sihalwī, the compiler of the *dars-e nizāmī* curriculum still in use in Muslim *madrassa*s in South Asia, but also encouraged accommodation of Hindu ideas and practices.[85] Even though Bansawi participated in many Hindu practices that may have been considered dubious from the standpoint of the Sharī'ah, he took care to be cautious in any public avowal of these heterodox ideas and practices.[86] It is clear from the tone and tenor of the *shruk*s that celebrate Manṣūr al-Ḥallāj and others that attack the *mullāh*s that Nund Rishi had a more expansive idea of the Sharī'ah which could accommodate Manṣūr al-Ḥallāj's controversial *shaṭḥiyāt* (ecstatic sayings). Even though a few of Nund Rishi's own ecstatic utterances are inadmissible from the standpoint of the Sharī'ah, he is by no means the only Kashmiri mystic who turns to such *shaṭḥiyāt* (ecstatic sayings). The sixteenth-century Kashmiri Suhrawardī Sufi Shaikh Ḥamza Makhdūm was also known for his ecstatic utterances.[87]

It is by exploring Nund Rishi's thinking on Manṣūr al-Ḥallāj that we get a better sense of his position on what we have called here the Sharī'ah–Sufism debate. But there could possibly be another reason why Nund Rishi turns to Manṣūr al-Ḥallāj in a familiar and intimate tone: Manṣūr al-Ḥallāj had visited Kashmir around 896 AD, and it is plausible that the cultural memory of that visit had endured in Kashmir and circulated in transimperial Sufi networks.[88] Nund Rishi addresses Manṣūr al-Ḥallāj affectionately as "Kāk," which is a term sometimes used for an elder of the community but often means "uncle" or even "father" or "brother" (it is usually a term of address for a respected elder male relative). In its challenge of Islamic orthodoxy, Manṣūr al-Ḥallāj's martyrdom is seen as a moment of great renewal even by some modernist Muslim thinkers such as Iqbal, who are otherwise critical of the excesses of Sufism.[89] The martyrdom of Ḥallāj was seen by some Sufis as an epochal event in the spiritual history of Islam, which was to resonate in the Muslim world because of its striking resemblance to the martyrdom of Ḥusayn, the grandson of Prophet Muhammad, who challenged the authority of the corrupt Ummayad ruler Yazīd. The tragedy at Karbala, where Ḥusayn and many of his family members were brutally massacred by Yazīd's army, and the martyrdom of one of the greatest Sufis in the Islamic tradition are two of the most traumatic events in Islamic history. These two moments still shape the contours of Islamic intellectual and cultural life. We have already noted that Nund Rishi steers clear of any controversy in relation to the Sunni–Shi'ī split in Islam but it is not so easy for him to keep a clear distance from Manṣūr al-Ḥallāj.

Manṣūr al-Ḥallāj is seen in some Sufi scholarship as representing an ecstatic tendency within Sufism in opposition to some of his own teachers such as Junayd al-Baghdādī who are supposed to have advocated a more sober Sufism.[90] It is useful to remember that the debate about Ḥallāj is not an ordinary one: nothing less than the meaning of Islam is at stake. No less a figure than the theologian Ibn Taymiyya (often invoked by radical Muslim theologians in our own times) writes explicitly in opposition to Manṣūr al-Ḥallāj.[91] But it is Sufis such as Ḥallāj and Ibn al-'Arabī and their philosophy of love that dominated South Asian Sufism until the nineteenth century rather than the theology of figures like Ibn Taymiyya. Nowhere in South Asia is the influence of a figure like Ḥallāj as strong as it is in Kashmir, Punjab, and Sindh. Louis Massignon points out that Kashmir is "the only, sure point on Ḥallāj's itinerary" in India.[92] The Kashmiri scholar Hamid Naseem Rafiabadi adds: "... it seems likely that Ḥallāj was quite well-known in Kashmir as he had visited Kashmir in A.D. 895."[93] Let us briefly turn to the life of Manṣūr al-Ḥallāj before taking up Nund Rishi's *shruk*s about Ḥallāj's martyrdom. Despite his having a huge following (which included the early Ahl al-Hadīth), Manṣūr al-Ḥallāj was put to a gruesome death in Baghdad by the Caliphate. Born into an Arabicized Fars in 858 AD, Manṣūr took up his father's profession as a wool carder. His first name was also, quite surprisingly, Ḥusayn.[94] His grandfather was a Zoroastrian convert to Islam just as Nund Rishi's grandfather was a convert from Hinduism. Ḥallāj learned the Qur'ān from the great mystic Sahl bin 'Abdullah al-Tūstārī, who followed the esoteric and interiorizing Islam of Ḥasan al-Baṣri.[95] His early training was as a strict Sunni Ḥanbalite traditionalist in Tūstār (a town in the Persian province of Ahwaz) but against a background of the revival of Hellenistic thought around the same time in the caliphal capital of Baghdad.[96] From Tūstār, Ḥallāj moved to Basra, where he came into touch with the circle of Junayd al-Baghdādī.[97] It is in Basra that Manṣūr al-Ḥallāj developed a deep awareness of social injustices, and it is his early rejection of political quietism which would distinguish him from a purely ascetic Sufi stance.[98] Herbert W. Mason writes:

> Basra had become in the third Islamic century a center also of social crisis, prompted by the revolt of black slaves, the Zanj, imported from the Sudan and East Africa to dig in the salt mines of lower Iraq. As a result of gross mistreatment by the 'Abbasid Sunnite masters ruling from Baghdad and aroused by opposition from Shi'ite propagandists using the issue to undermine the authority of the dynasty's central government, the banner was raised as an outcry for justice in a religious community that professed equality among all members.[99]

The failure of the Zanj revolt made Ḥallāj increasingly dissatisfied with the political quietism of the Sufis of his time. He not only protested against the Caliphate authorities for Zanj salt field laborers but would also support the starving Bedouins when they stormed Basra and Baghdad in search of food.[100] He also contested the control of Baghdad's elites over public resources and funds.[101] Annemarie Schimmel writes about these larger political circumstances against which the Ḥallāj controversy unraveled:

> Aside from the problem of mystical love, political and social problems were at stake. Hallaj was a friend of the chamberlain Naṣr al-Qushūrī, who favored better administration and juster taxation, dangerous ideas in a time when the caliph was almost powerless and the viziers, though all-powerful for a short period, changed frequently. The Shia groups who supported the vizier Ibn al-Furāt considered Ḥallāj as dangerous as did the Sunni orthodox wing surrounding the "pious vizier" 'Ali ibn 'Isā. All of them were afraid that the effect on the people of spiritual revival might have repercussions on the social organization and even on the political structure.[102]

Manṣūr al-Ḥallāj stressed the cultivation of love (*maḥabba*) which could lead to a union with God, but he was attacked by Ibn Dawūd, a leading expert on Zahiri Law, and a *fatwā* of denunciation was proposed to the caliph against Ḥallāj.[103] Though spared an inquest by a Shāfi'ī jurist, Ibn Surayj, who countered the *fatwā* with his own *fatwā* declaring the matter to be outside the purview of canonical law, Ḥallāj retreated to Mecca.[104] The involvement of such a prominent Shāfi'ī jurist as Ibn Surayj in not assenting to Ḥallāj's persecution indicates that the affair was complex and cannot be reduced to a simple opposition between the Sharī'ah and Sufism. After two years in Mecca, Ḥallāj returned to Baghdad and built a miniature Ka'aba followed by the assertion

> that it was permitted to substitute it for the pilgrimage itself if one was unable for financial or health reasons to visit the Holy City according to the legal prescription for which he was accused of trying to overthrow the Islamic law, which makes Hajj, or the pilgrimage to Mecca, mandatory for every believer.[105]

He was arrested and given three days of public exposure in the pillory as a sentence. The next nine years were spent by Manṣūr in the royal palace in protective custody, where he composed many of his works. It is in these years that he wrote *Tā' Sīn al-Azal*, a work that considers Iblīs (Satan) as a pure monotheist because of his refusal to bow down to Adam.[106] A victim of court intrigues and corrupt ministers of the caliph, al-Ḥallāj was eventually again brought to trial amidst many public demonstrations in his favor by Ḥanbalite traditionalists, and his idea of the symbolic pilgrimage that contravened the Sharī'ah was used as evidence against him.[107] In March 922 AD, after a trial that lasted for about seven months, Manṣūr al-Ḥallāj was sentenced to death as a heretic.[108] He was flogged in public, his limbs cut off, his head put on a pole, and his body burned as the city was thrown into tumult.[109] Despite this gruesome death, Manṣūr al-Ḥallāj survived in cultural memory and literary culture as the first of Sufi martyrs and a great poet.

We already find in Manṣūr al-Ḥallāj the use of the short, pithy observational poem that reveals the intransience of this world, which resembles such Kashmiri genres as the *vākh*s of Lal Ded and the *shruk*s of Nund Rishi. Manṣūr al-Ḥallāj's *qiṭ'a* are only one or two lines long but resemble the popular Persian quatrain (*rubā'ī*). The *qiṭ'a*, much like the *shruk* and the *vākh*, is restricted to a single theme and is often riddle-like. The effect elicited by the practice of such poetry (and music) in Sufi gatherings was for the listener to enter into a state of *tawajjud* (being ecstatic).[110] The psychological impact of Sufi poetry was an essential component of its aesthetic dimension. Let us take, for example, the following poems by Manṣūr al-Ḥallāj, Lal Ded, and Nund Rishi which suggest a deep interpenetration of Sufi and Hindu themes:

> Manṣūr al-Ḥallāj:
>
> One moment I'm a shaykh
> Who holds the highest rank,
>
> And then I am a little child
> Dependent on a nurse

Or sleeping in a box
Within the brackish earth[111]

Lal Ded:

Damī dīthu'm nad vahvạnī
Damī dyūthum sum na tu' tār
Damī dīthu'm thạr phọlu'vu'nī
Damī dyūthum gul na tu' k̲h̲ār[112]

Now I see a flowing stream,
now a flood that's drowned all bridges,
now I see a bush flaming with flowers,
now a skeleton of twigs.[113]

Nund Rishi:

Damī dyūnthum shabnam pẏvān
Damī dyūnthum pẏvān sūr
Damī dyūnthum gatu' pach hẏvāṉ
Damī dyūnthum phọlvun nūr[114]

In an instant, I see dew on earth
In an instant, I see ashes on earth
In an instant, I see a dark moonless night
In an instant, I see the bright light of dawn

There is a striking similarity of thematics in these short poems: a quasi-cinematic montage, with its rapid cut-like reversals, creates a sudden awareness of temporal finitude. But Nund Rishi invokes Manṣūr al-Ḥallāj directly in the *shruk*s with a cautious dismissal of his decision to disclose Sufi secrets (the allusion could be to Manṣūr al-Ḥallāj's purported declaration, '*Ana al-Ḥaq*, I am the Truth).[115] In one of his *shruk*s, Nund Rishi speaks of how Manṣūr abandoned the fragrance of his spiritual truth by revealing hidden secrets and got himself stoned to death:

Pānay ạ̄sith pānay bōvun
Pānay khọshbọy krăvun latshē
Pānay pān kani kani krōvun
Shara'uk soth byūth adu' patshe

Dariyāvu' patu' yeli mojā hōvun
Lāl tu' ru'tu'n prāvin dọtshe[116]

He revealed the secret of his being
He crushed the fragrance of his secret to dust
He got himself stoned to death
To restore faith in the Sharīʿah
He got scattered in the river as a wave divine
But gathered rubies and jewels in his empty hands

Ḥallāj gets himself stoned to death (which was only part of the torture he faced) in the manner of Majnūn, the mad lover of the Arabic romance *Majnūn Laylā*.[117] Ḥallāj is accused by the poet of revealing the secret of the self. The perfume of the secret is scattered by his revelation into the dust and is in turn mirrored in the scattering of his ashes in the Tigris. But it is this sacrifice which secures the embankment of the Sharīʿah. Yet Nund Rishi praises Manṣūr's courage because his open declaration of Sufi secrets bore witness to divine unity and cleared the path to his martyrdom. It is only when Ḥallāj's ashes are scattered in the Tigris that the rubies and jewels he has gathered in his empty hands flash up in the image of an ecstatic wave. *Mojā hovun* means to show something beautiful like the surge of a wave. But Nund Rishi also claims that Ḥallāj's martyrdom reinforced the embankments of the Sharʿiah. Manṣūr's ecstatic revelations are seen as nothing short of a surging, even flood, that had to be contained through his martyrdom. In yet another *shruk* in a similar vein, Nund Rishi is more explicit:

Ārifan tu' āshiqan shūbā lājin
Āndric āvāz nÿbar kavu' gạy
Shara'kis sothis sīrah vājin
Adu' kāthis khorukh khabar gạy[118]

He honoured the gnostics and lovers with his courage
But why did his inner voice travel outside?
He hurled a brick at the embankment of the Sharīʿah
And he was made to climb the gallows
The news spread

Here Nund Rishi goes as far as to say that Manṣūr had hurled a brick at the embankment of the Sharīʿah, an embankment that makes possible the flow of human existence. He did this because he wanted to glorify the gnostics and the lovers. Yet the revelation of divine secrets about which Nund Rishi almost speaks in code could not go unpunished and he had to climb the gallows. Nund Rishi considers Iblīs and Manṣūr to have been two figures that were not only aware of the divine secret but also chose to disclose it. Manṣūr paid with his life for this disclosure, just as Iblīs (Satan) paid for it with his banishment. But Manṣūr's disclosure is defended by Nund Rishi: even if the universe of meaning was threatened by Manṣūr's disclosure of the secret, nonetheless he also appears to have sheltered the Sharī'ah by accepting his punishment. Hamid Naseem Rafiabadi argues that Nund Rishi makes it clear that Manṣūr had uttered *'Ana al-Ḥaq* in a state of ecstasy whereas Iblīs had willfully chosen to disobey God.[119] The theme of Iblīs as a friend of Manṣūr is already there in Manṣūr al-Ḥallāj's *Ṭawāsīn* (in the sixth chapter, *Ṭā Sīn al-azal wa al iltibās*).[120]

For the Sufis, the transformation of the heart was a far more fundamental concern than the disagreements about the Sharī'ah. Nund Rishi insists that a Sufi does not learn what he learns by means of "it is said" (*qīl wa qāl*), or theology, but through a transformation of the state of the heart:

Su chunu' wuchān qīlas tu' qālas
Su chuy wuchān hālas kun
Zikrē haq par zyv dith tālas
Razu' hōnz yīy zālas kun[121]

He does not look at "it is said"
He looks at the state of your heart
Remember the One, chant His name
You can then trap the royal swan

Qīl tu' qāl can also be translated as "idle chatter," and, in this *shruk*, Nund Rishi privileges the state of the heart over idle talk about theology. One can approach the royal swan of one's true self through one's experience (*hāl*, literally "state") and not knowledge. Love, or *'ishq*, plays a fundamental role in the transformation of the seeker's heart.[122] But there are slight differences in approaches to love to be found among the Sufis. For instance, take the example of what Ḥallāj's friend Shiblī has to say of his martyrdom:

Ours were the acts of lovers
Mad with love.

Only my madness saved me,
While his reason brought him death.[123]

According to Shibli, Ḥallāj refused the contradiction of love's madness. A similar sentiment is to be found in Nund Rishi, who is cautious with his praise of Ḥallāj but also draws attention to the element of excess in the latter's ecstatic utterances. For Nund Rishi, Manṣūr revealed the secrets of Sufism and paid a price for it with his life:

Māshūqan yeli darshun hōvun
Darshun dyōvun Mansūr say
Shauquk sharāb su yali tsōvun
Qatl krōvunas zan tsūr say
Kọngu' tu' kostūru' tatu' yeli nōvun
Man manvovun tạmi̠ dār say
Āshiqan ārifan vathā hăvu'n
Kathā thăvu'n samsārsay[124]

The moment the Beloved revealed a glimpse to the lovers
A vision was revealed to Manṣūr
He drank the wine of yearning
And got himself killed like a thief
He cleaned his body with musk and saffron
And prepared his heart for the gibbet
He showed a new path to lovers and gnostics
And left behind something enduring in the world

In this *shruk*, the relationship of the self to God is approached as a difficult love, which ends in the annihilation of the lover. In terms of Kashmiri Sufi poetry, Nund Rishi inaugurated a new binary between the *'ārif* (the gnostic) and the *'āshiq* (lover). The way of the *'ārif* is gnosis and the way of the *'āshiq* is love. It is often the moments at which Nund Rishi speaks of love (*'ishq*) that he also turns to Manṣūr al-Ḥallāj. One way of approaching the theory of love in medieval South Asian Sufism is to turn to one of its foundational texts, *Kashf al-maḥjūb* (Revelations of the Unseen), composed in Lahore by the Sufi 'Alī al-Hujwīrī (Dātā Ganj Bakhsh). The Sufi psychologist Ḥārith al-Muḥasibī is quoted in the *Kashf* as saying "Love is the vision of Him in hearts," and Manṣūr al-Ḥallāj's friend Shibli is quoted thus on love: "Love obliterates from the heart all but the Beloved."[125] It is this vision of love which leaves nothing intact, or in place, which is epitomized in Sufi poetry by the image of a moth that chooses passionate self-annihilation in the flame of a candle. This image of a moth's self-immolation which first appears in Ḥallāj as a symbol of *via negativa* is also taken up by ʻAyn al-Quḍāt Hamadānī.[126] It is such an annihilation (*fanā*) that Nund Rishi invokes in relation to Manṣūr as a reader of the Qur'ān in a *shruk*, which we will also discuss in Chapter 2:

Qur'ān parān kōnō mūdukh
Qur'ān parān goy nō sūr
Qur'ān parān zindu' kÿthu' rūdukh
Qur'ān parān dod Manṣūr

Did you not die after reading the Qur'ān?
Did you not burn to ashes after reading the Qur'ān?
How did you survive after reading the Qur'ān?
Manṣūr set himself on fire after reading the Qur'ān[127]

The esoteric secret Manṣūr divulges is connected by Nund Rishi to a reading of the Qur'ān. It is the secret of the Qur'ān that sets Manṣūr on fire and reduces him to ashes. It is not possible to survive such a reading. The obvious implication is that the *mullāh*s, even though they invoke the authority of the Qur'ān, do not have the true courage to read it. Here the only possible reading of the Qur'ān is apocalyptic.

The charge brought against Manṣūr was the way he blurred the distinctions between the lawful and the unlawful, Islam and apostasy, Kaʻaba and the home. Carl W. Ernst catalogues the charges against Manṣūr in his introduction to his selection and translation of Manṣūr's poems:

> Hallaj was denounced as a sorcerer and praised as a saint. He was accused of claiming to be the incarnation of God or possibly the Messiah, and he was also charged with being an agent of the Shiʻi revolutionary movement of the Qarmatis. He was imprisoned off and on and subjected to interrogations by viziers and their legal advisers. His trials took place at a time when the ʻAbbasid Empire was experiencing a crisis of major proportions and the government was in serious financial, political and military disarray. The final trial, dominated by political factionalism and questionable procedures, condemned Hallaj as an apostate on a technicality; the last straw was his reported opinion that those lacking the means to undertake the hajj, the pilgrimage to Mecca, could create a symbolic Ka'ba in their homes, which would fulfill this religious duty.[128]

A nephew of Manṣūr al-Ḥallāj found this note: "One who makes difference between kufr and iman he has committed infidelity and one who does not make difference between believer and non-believer he also commits infidelity."[129] It appears Ḥallāj seeks to both destroy and affirm the Sharīʿah. It is quite clear which tendency wins out in the end. This paradox is carried over into the way Ḥallāj first challenges the Sharīʿah and then surrenders his life in a state of bewilderment and love. Love is a witnessing, *shuhūd*, which is connected in the Islamic tradition to not only the *shahādah*, the first article of the Muslim faith proclaiming the unity of God, but also to *shahādah*, martyrdom. A true reader of the Qur'ān can only be love's martyr (*shahīd*).

The martyrdom of Manṣūr is no ordinary event in the history of Islam. It became a turning point in the history of Sufism. The legend of Ḥallāj, as told by Farīd al-Dīn 'Aṭṭār, was well known among the Sufis of India in the thirteenth and fourteenth centuries. As Carl Ernst reminds us, "the folklore and vernacular songs of northwest India are full of references to Mansur (Hallaj) and his fate."[130] Kashmir is no exception to this. What Schimmel writes in the context of Ḥallāj's visit to Sindh is as true of Kashmir: "The country through which Ḥallāj had wandered once has received his message gladly in later times; his name is used here, as everywhere, as a symbol of suffering love and self-sacrifice at the one, of a measureless pantheistic feeling on the other hand."[131] Manṣūr al-Ḥallāj does not merely figure in Nund Rishi's poetry but remains a significant figure in vernacular Kashmiri Sufi poetry and folk music into the present.[132] The South Asian Sufis, however, remained internally divided about the fate of Ḥallāj. Yet most such Sufis, and even some theologians, were quick to recognize the spiritual attainments of Ḥallāj even if they considered it best to avoid the subject in public. A case in point is the Deoband theologian Maulana Zafar Aḥmad Usmānī, who, in the early twentieth century, expressed his thinking about the subject in a biography of Manṣūr prepared under the guidance of his teacher and uncle, Maulana Ashraf 'Alī Thānvī.[133] The reason why Ḥallāj was avoided as a subject even in Sufi texts was the "potentially revolutionary implications of martyrdom."[134] The martyrdom of Ḥallāj echoed the martyrdom of Ḥusayn and threatened to open old wounds in Muslim politics. Carl Ernst reminds us that the Bengali Chishtī saint Ḥusam al-Dīn Mānikpūrī (d. 1418), a contemporary of Nund Rishi, warned that Ḥallāj was not the best model for novices to follow.[135] A prominent Suhrawardī Sufi such as Jalāl al-Dīn Bukhārī Makhdūm-i-Jahāniyān considered Ḥallāj's execution as "justified both externally as an affront to the religious law and internally as a deliberate self-sacrifice."[136] Soon after Ḥallāj, his disciples Ibn "Aṭā" Aḥmad and Shākir bin Aḥmad Baghdādī were executed for their support of Ḥallāj.[137] South Asian Chishtīs also had their own martyrs in the Ḥallājian tradition: Mas'ud Bakk and Sarmad. When the Chishtī Sufi Mas'ud Bakk was put to death in Delhi by Firoz Shah Tughlaq, he too was hung from the gibbet and then burned like Manṣūr al-Ḥallāj.[138] Sarmad, a friend of the Sufi-inclined Mughal prince Dārā Shikoh, was executed on the orders of Dārā Shikoh's younger brother, Aurangzeb, after the latter's ascension to the Mughal throne, on charges of apostasy.[139]

What was at stake in Manṣūr al-Ḥallāj's martyrdom? Or what were the uses to which it was put in Sufi poetry? Carl Ernst writes: "Martyrdom is the final resort of the weak against the powerful. It is an act of truth performed without regard for one's life."[140] The whole question of Sufi martyrdom was connected to the question of speaking truth in the public realm. Ernst adds: "The Islamic world has also had martyrs who resisted tyranny and injustice at any cost, from Muhammad's grandson Husayn to the self-sacrificing warriors who sought paradise through battle."[141] Manṣūr al-Ḥallāj is a figure who not only had an extraordinary influence on the development of a Sufi martyrology but who also began to represent the embodiment of a Sufi reworking of death as the affirmation of an abiding life. Death appears here as the Beloved, or as a threshold that opens the gate to the Beloved. For many Sufis, Manṣūr remained a model of the lover and the martyr because he had actively courted martyrdom at the hands of fellow Muslims and cried "Kill me, my trustworthy friends, for in my killing is my life."[142] But this martyrdom conferred eternal life on Manṣūr. As Nund Rishi puts it:

Dāras lodukh kọnu' sanu' mūdō
Nāras loyukh tu' rūd mō
Ārifo tu' āshiqo tavay vodō
Manṣūru'y ōs tu' mūd mō[143]

They pushed him to the gallows: he did not die
They threw him into the fire: he did not die
The gnostics and lovers mourn for Manṣūr
But it is Manṣūr who did not die

This *shruk* plays on the meaning of Manṣūr's name as the victorious one. It is not the people who hanged Manṣūr, quartered his body, and set it on fire who emerge victorious. But it is Manṣūr's tortured and quartered body, which fearlessly bore witness to the truth of love that emerges victorious.

Ḥallāj's spiritual stature and "cruel death earned him the respect of many moderate Sufis, nonetheless his position remained ambiguous."[144] Many Sufis supported his execution, because "he had revealed the secret of divine lordship."[145] This is how the Persian poet Hafiz puts it: "That friend by whom the gibbet's peak was ennobled – his crime was this, that he made secrets public."[146] Nund Rishi puts it in more or less the same words:

Charā peyāyas kau' sanu' tsājin
Manṣūr Kākas vuhu'nājin gạy
Shanti hạnz kray kÿth sodu' vājin
Ándric ās tu' khabar nÿbar kath pey[147]

Why did Manṣūr not bear the blow of the Divine flash?
Why did he get his windpipe shattered?
Why did he go astray from the path of peace?
How did the inner secret get revealed?

Nund Rishi raises the question of why Manṣūr could not just bear the burn of the divine flash of truth, and why the encounter with truth left him shattered. There is a striking parallel that the *shruk* builds between the divine flash and the shatter of the windpipe. As God is as near to us as our windpipe, its sudden shattering by the divine flash can only mean the collapse of the distance between human beings (Manṣūr in this case!) and God. In her study of the figure of Ḥallāj in the mystical poetry of Sachal Sarmast, Annemarie Schimmel writes that the public proclamation of Ḥallāj, the revelation of the secret, is to be "likened to the sound of the great kettle-drum: proclaiming by kettle-drum means 'to announce publicly', and it was just Hallaj's greatest disadvantage in the eyes of his fellow-mystics that he had disclosed the highest secret of loving unity."[148] Ḥallāj not only disclosed the Sufi secret but he did so publicly. His ecstatic utterances had not just threatened the Sharī'ah but also endangered Sufi lives. This was also the attitude inherited by Kashmiri Sufis. Those who speak openly of spiritual secrets must also be prepared to pay a heavy price. The Islamic path of peace (*shanti hạnz kray*) here is abandoned for a direct encounter with divinity which poses a great threat to social and political order. Despite declaring his allegiance to Manṣūr, Nund Rishi approaches Islam as a *sahaja* path (a simple, blissful path not necessarily in conflict with the Sharī'ah-grounded path of Islam).

Annemarie Schimmel writes that she was surprised when traveling in Sindh in 1961 to find out "that everybody in the remotest corners of the Indus valley" seemed to know of Manṣūr al-Ḥallāj.[149] The reason Schimmel gives for the popularity of Manṣūr's ideas in Sindh could hold just as true for Kashmir albeit for a different historical period (fourteenth–fifteenth-century Kashmir):[150]

> A certain interest in mystical speculations is likely to have grown there rather early – a large part of the population were Hindu, and there was also a deeper layer of Buddhist elements; the ideas of Buddhism and – a quite unorthodox – Hinduism may have acted as a ferment in the development of religious thought in the country during the early Islamic period....[151]

The popularity of Manṣūr al-Ḥallāj was not restricted to Sindh, and he was popular in regions as far away from Sindh as Chittagong. The Ḥallāj legend found its way into Persian, Pashto, Sindhi, Urdu, Bengali, and Kashmiri. Schimmel adds:

> ... it would be wrong to assume that mystical poetry of this kind is found only in the lower parts of the Indus valley: Panjabi folk-poetry and mystical literature contains outstanding examples which mention Hallaj and his fate, and poetical references to his death on the gibbet trace in this area at least as far back as Kabir (d. 1495). Already Hujwiri (d. after 1073), one of the first mystics who settled in Lahore, has composed, besides his famous *kashf al-maḥjūb*, a separate book on Ḥallāj so that the continuity of the tradition in this part of the subcontinent is given. In Pashto literature the name of Hallaj is also popular.... Muslim Bengali poetry will surely contain numerous verses on the martyr mystic – a "magnifique éloge" on Hallaj under the name *Maharshi Manṣūr* has been signalized by L. Massignon.[152]

The mystical poems of Nund Rishi and other Kashmiri Sufi poets also belong to the same corpus of regional Sufi poetry on Ḥallāj. This influence could be traced to the dissemination of Sufi texts such as Farīd al-Dīn 'Aṭṭār's *Tadhkirāt al-Awliyā*. According to Schimmel, 'Aṭṭār's allegories of love from *Manṭiq uṭ-ṭayr* (Conference of Birds) were well known all the way up to Kashmir.[153] If Maulana Rūmī compared Ḥallāj's state to that of "iron in fire," Maḥmūd Shabistārī compared Ḥallāj's state to that of the Burning Bush from which God spoke to Moses.[154] It was not Muslims alone who wrote about Ḥallāj:

a *Qiṣṣa-e Manṣūr* in Urdu was written by Shivarajpuri (d. 1750) in Lucknow.[155] Dervishes like Lāl Shāhbāz Qalandar of Sehwan composed verses that invoked Manṣūr al-Ḥallāj and his martyrdom. The Sindhi mystic and poet Sachal Sarmast calls himself "the Mansur of this last time who utters the cry I am the Truth openly (*āshikār*)."[156] We also see that Sindhi Sufi poets like Sachal Sarmast connect this martyrdom, the voluntary dying on the gibbet, with the Sufi call to "die before you die":

> Thou hast not yet passed away from self,
> Hast not mounted on the gallows-tree,
> Hast not died before dying –
> How canst thou be called lover,
> How canst thou say I am the Truth?[157]

Such ideas are also to be found in the *bhaktī* poet Kabir:

> That death which the world fears so much is my happiness
> When shall I die and when shall I contemplate Him who is highest bliss?[158]

The idea of love is connected to the Sufi idea of a dying before death and the lovers are supposed to be always inclined toward the gibbet. It is the gallows that is declared to be the place proper for loving people.[159] Dara Shikoh's Sufi friend, Sarmad, who had also fallen in love with a Hindu boy in Thatta, Sindh, compared himself to Ḥallāj in one of his last verses:

> It is a life long that the voice of Mansur became old –
> I'll give anew the manifestation of gallows and rope![160]

But it is one of the most popular Urdu poets of the nineteenth century, Ghalib, who finds the right words for the Ḥallāj controversy: "You can say it on the gallows, but not from the pulpit."[161] The gallows and the gibbet are often opposed to the preacher's pulpit in Islamic mystical poetry. As another Sindhi mystical poet, Shah Abdul Latif Bhittai, puts it: "Those who are from Mansur, those necks were cut."[162] Schimmel adds:

> In the moment that Hallaj gives his head to the impaling stake he realizes the highest mystery of the ascension, that of the prophetical hadith *lī ma'a Allāh*.... "I have a time with God" which points to the immediate nearness of man and God where not even Gabriel can interfere, and has been one of the key-words of Sufism through the ages.[163]

The nearness of man and God is the secret Manṣūr al-Ḥallāj is accused of having divulged. This recalls the Qur'ānic verse, oft-quoted by the Sufis: *wa naḥnū aqrab ilay-hi min al-ḥabl al-warīd* (We are closer to him than his jugular vein).[164] The divine flash that Nund Rishi speaks of in relation to Ḥallāj does claim his windpipe (and plausibly the jugular vein) eliminating all distinction between the self and the other. The Sufis also posed the question of God's silence on Ḥallāj's martyrdom and expressed despair about the killing of love's martyrs. When Ḥallāj's friend, Shiblī, asked God why and how long were God's lovers to be killed, the answer he received was: "Those whom I kill their blood money is upon me and I (or 'My Beauty') am their blood money."[165] God himself is the recompense for the blood of Sufi martyrs.

The resolute yet also love-intoxicated martyrdom of Manṣūr is seen by the Sufis as the true measure of commitment in the path of God. Love is the wine which Ḥallāj, headless (*bē sar*), was seen holding in his hand in a dream by someone after his execution.[166] Nund Rishi also speaks of Manṣūr's fatal intoxication with love:

Saras manz vatshāv pav kōh trōvun
Chon mu'ynạe chu vatu' viy
Qarb ās bod tu' dāras hōvun
Bōvun sir rūd adu' paviy[167]

He entered the lake
Why did he abandon the simple, navigable path?
He drank openly at the crossroads
He thirsted for nearness and revealed it to the gibbet
He uttered the secret and found an easy way out

Manṣūr enters the lake but he does not stay on the simple, navigable path (*pav*, literally, the boat path). He openly drinks the wine of intoxication with the Beloved. A Sufi could possibly drink the wine of intoxication in secret but to drink it at the city crossroads could only invite danger. As Schimmel puts it, Ḥallāj's is "the goblet of martyrdom from the winestore of Not-Being which the lover is asked to drink."[168] Wine leads to *be khudī*, a state of selflessness or non-awareness, in which the Beloved may even get you killed.[169] This wine makes Manṣūr thirst for the nearness to the Beloved and he ends up revealing the secret on the gibbet. The price of this revelation is his own life. As Carl Ernst puts it, in a 1992 Festschrift essay in honor of Schimmel, Ḥallāj's position "is one of the boldest formulations of Islamic mysticism."[170] But the problem with Ḥallāj's approach to the thinking of God as Love is the lack of a scriptural basis in the Qur'ān.[171] According to the tenth-century Sufi and philosopher al-Daylamī, Ḥallāj was isolated among the Sufis for holding that love is the divine essence.[172] Yet it is this idea of love as the divine essence which becomes the Sufi leitmotif in the centuries to come.

Nund Rishi does not go as far as Manṣūr, but he also does not hesitate to declare his fidelity to him. Yet Nund Rishi's insistence on the Shar'īah, in some of the same *shruks* in which he invokes Manṣūr, reveals that this is a cautious declaration during politically turbulent times. The other Sufis whom Nund Rishi invokes in his *shruks* such as Rūmī are also exemplars of what William C. Chittick calls "the Sufi path of love."[173] Vernacular Sufism in Punjab, Kashmir, and Sindh appears to have turned more often to the "Sufi path of love" than the "Sufi path of knowledge." The latter is, in William C. Chittick's studies of Sufism as much as elsewhere, often associated with Ibn al-'Arabī.[174] Ibn al-'Arabī's ideas were disseminated in Kashmir through the writings of the Kubrāwiyyā Sufis. Yet Nund Rishi unambiguously affirms the Sufi path of love, especially in his *shruks* which explicitly deal with *'ishq* (love). For Nund Rishi, however, *'ishq* does not come into an opposition with the Sharī'ah and, if it does, the Sharī'ah must take precedence. Nund Rishi never abandons his commitment to Manṣūr's path. This conserves Nund Rishi's Manṣūr for both the traditional "sober" Sufis and the radical "ecstatic" Sufis. But little is revealed of Manṣūr's secret for which he pays with his own life. It is only hinted that the secret is the same as the mystery of *'ishq*.

There was more than one way in which *'ishq* (love) posed a problem for Sufi theology.[175] The claim to a personal relation to God through *'ishq* was troubling for theologians who remained committed to the idea of God's absolute transcendence. Yet there were enough verses in the Qur'ān that supported Sufi speculations on the relations between man and God.[176] But what do we know of the meaning of *'ishq* from Nund Rishi's mystical poetry? The idea of a Ḥallājian *'ishq* clearly influenced the development of the theme of love in Nund Rishi and survives as late as the poems of Ahad Zargar in the twentieth century. Here is Nund Rishi directly addressing the question of *'ishq*:

'Āshiq suy yus pāk rachi badan
Lā shaq hūru' chas khadmu'tsī

Āh vọshi sū't yus lyadrāvih badan
Mọkhu' mọkhu' vuchi tas prŷth soru'tsī
Sārinu'ī bronth pāvi̱ janatas ladan
Tim yim yati lolu' vudnis yạtsū'ī[177]

A lover is the one who keeps his body pure
There is no doubt that houris will attend him in Paradise
The lover is the one who turns pale with laments and sighs
The lover sees the Beloved in every face
The lovers shall enter Paradise before everyone else
The lovers are those who keep vigil at night

Even though there is an affirmation of the reward in the Islamic afterlife that awaits the lover, the lover here is someone who has gone pale in separation and searches for the Beloved in the face of every human being. Nund Rishi connects the figure of the *'āshiq* to traditional Islamic piety, or *zuhd*, which is rewarded in Paradise. The tension is palpable between a *zuhdiyyā* (ascetic) approach to an absent God in this *shruk* and the more Ḥallājian ecstatic declarations in the other *shruk*s. There is little that separates the believer (*zāhid*) from the lover (*'āshiq*) in this *shruk*. But the Sufi idea of love as a difficult trial by fire appears in the following *shruk*:

'Āshiq suy yus 'ashqu' nāru' dazē
Sọn zan prazlŷs panunuy pān
'Ashqun dod yas vālinji sazē
Su adu' vatē lā makān[178]

The lover is the one who burns in the fire of love
Only to shine like pure gold
The one with the pain of love deep in his heart
He is the one who shall reach the placeless place

Love is seen here as suffering, without which one can never hope to reach the *lā makān* (the No Place, or the Placeless Place). It is only by burning in the fire of love that the true self of an individual shines. It is the pain of separation from the Beloved that brings the self to the threshold of the *lā makān*. In a *shruk* we will discuss in more detail in Chapter 3, Nund Rishi connects the experience of the love of God to the kenosis of asceticism (as in the *shruk* on *'ishq* which begins with the line *'Āshiq su yus pāk rachi badan*):

La Illāhā ṣahib korum
Vaḥi korum panun pān
Vojūd travith mūjūd myūlum
Adu' bu' vōtus lā makān[179]

I decided on "There is no god"
And made of myself a site of revelation
Abandoning existence, I found presence
Thus have I reached the placeless place

Love is a decision which turns you into a site of revelation. It makes you abandon your existence for a more abiding Presence in the placeless place, *lā makān*. Yet Nund Rishi complicates his idea of *'ishq* by speaking of it elsewhere in a sequence of violent metaphors and bringing it closer to the Ḥallājian idea of love:

'Ishq chuy māji kun pothur marun
Sọy zọlu' karay tu' kạhi̠
'Ishq chuy gunu' tularih bỳob barun
Su hay sọkh bare tu' kạhi̠
'Ishq chuy tez kartaji chanci darun
Su' hay chọkh zaray tu' kạhi̠[180]

Love is the loss of a mother's only son
If she wants to sleep, how will she?
Love is taking in a beehive into your coat
If he wants to be happy, how can he?
Love is withstanding the blow of a sharp sword
If he wants to bear the wound, how can he?

There is little that separates love here from a sudden, and violent, experience of loss, pain, and suffering. A strange vision of love unfolds here as a difficult, even impossible, commitment. But this difficult commitment is made possible by a surrender. In another *shruk*, Nund Rishi returns to the relation between love and kenosis:

Lōlaki vọkhalu' vānij pishim
Kọkal chạjim tu' byūthus rasu'
Pishim tu' pishim pānas tsu'shim
Kovu' zānu' tavu'h sāt maru'h kinu' lasu'[181]

The violent stirrings of love have battered my heart
I abandoned evil and am just sitting
I got crushed and ground, and sunk into my self
I don't know now if I'll live or die

Yet again we see that love demands a self-emptying which is not a self-destruction. This is how Nund Rishi transforms the Ḥallājian idea of love. Here love is a slow emptying out of the self (Nund Rishi) as opposed to a violent surrender or self-sacrifice (Ḥallāj). Yet the border between these positions in Nund Rishi is porous. Rather, we can claim that Nund Rishi's thinking of love is constituted by the tension between the experience of an ascetic withdrawal and the hope of an ecstatic union. By turning to love, ascetic or Ḥallājian, Nund Rishi situates himself in the *madhhab-i 'ishq* (the religion of love) within the Islamic tradition – a path associated with such Sufi poets as Ḥallāj and Rūmī. Shahab Ahmed reminds us: "The word *madhhab* means, literally, 'way of going' ... love is *a way of going about being Muslim* – a mode of being with God, of identifying, experiencing and living with the values and meaning of Divine Truth."[182] For Nund Rishi, *the way of going about being Muslim* is the commitment to a difficult love.

The relation claimed by Nund Rishi to Ḥallāj is by no means unique. Such mystics as 'Aṭṭār and Ruzbihan Baqli also claimed a special relationship with Ḥallāj, and so did the Sufis of Sindh. The claim to such a relationship was often also a claim to a special – and even secret – spiritual initiation which did not need the stamp of approval from the theologian. The claims on special relationships and secret initiations were not only made by those who considered themselves the intellectual and spiritual heirs of mystic rebels such as Ḥallāj. Nor were such claims restricted to Ḥallāj. They were also sometimes invoked in relation to 'Uways al-Qaranī (a contemporary of Prophet Muhammad) from the margins of Islam's central and eastern lands by Sufis who could not trace their spiritual lineage either to 'Ali, the son-in-law of Prophet Muhammad and the fourth caliph of Islam, Abū Bakr, the first caliph of Islam, or any other Sufi saint – a *sine qua non* for Sufi teaching. Nund Rishi invokes this idea of a secret initiation; but, as with many other such concepts formative of the Islamic tradition, he often interprets it in a unique way. Carl Ernst and Bruce Lawrence suggest that an 'Uwaysī initiation is the "non-physical binding of two like-minded Sufis" but it also involves claims to direct initiation from Prophet Muhammad regardless of separation in time and distance.

Nund Rishi's 'Uwaysī initiation involved the claim of a direct initiation from Prophet Muhammad.[183]

The asceticism, sexual celibacy, and vegetarianism of the Rishi Order posed a challenge for Nund Rishi's new movement within a religious tradition where the formula *Lā rahbāniyya fī al-Islām* (There is no asceticism in Islam) had become popular.[184] The way Nund Rishi approaches the problem of asceticism in the Rishi Order is by securing its legitimacy through tracing its genealogy to early Islam and 'Uways al-Qaranī, one of the first ascetics of Islam, who was praised for his piety by none other than Prophet Muhammad. This made it possible for Nund Rishi to ally himself to early *zuhd* (asceticism) and counter the accusations against the Rishis about their lack of conformity with the Sharīʿah (even on such questions as vegetarianism, the Rishis could always make a strong case). An affiliation with 'Uways al-Qaranī also allowed Nund Rishi to circumvent any questions about the legitimacy of the Rishi Order by Persian Sufis who could trace their lineage back to either 'Ali, Abū Bakr, or other Sufi saints in Islamic history.

Nund Rishi not only connects the Rishis to the early history of Islam by turning to 'Uways al-Qaranī, but he also places Muḥammad at the beginning of all Rishis as the first Rishi (as we shall see in the *shruk* discussed below). Nund Rishi addresses the anxieties that Persian Sufis expressed over the influence of Hindu and Buddhist ascetic practices on the Rishi Order by calling Prophet Muhammad the first Rishi (*avval Rishī*) and inviting a serious reflection on his use of the term *rishī* for figures in Islamic and Kashmiri spiritual history. The Sanskrit term *rishī* for a seer, or a sage, thus acquires a new meaning in the Kashmiri vernacular and situates Rishism as the site of a double translation between the technical languages of Sufism and the prevailing modes of Hindu and Buddhist spirituality. Nund Rishi posits the term *rishī* as a universal term for a spiritual practitioner on the path of self-transformation. This paradox of a Kashmiri order of Muslim Rishis (many of them new converts) laying claim to the whole spiritual history of Islam in utter disregard of established hierarchies and theological discourse is reflected in the following *shruk* where Nund Rishi addresses the question of his spiritual lineage:

Avval Rishī Aḥmad Rishī
Dōyum Uways Qarnī āv
Treyum Rishi Zalk Rishī
Tsūryum Ḥaẓrat Palās āv

Pūntsyum Rishī Rumē Rishī
Shayum Ḥaẓrat Mīrān āv
Saṭim kạru'm du'shnā hishī
Bu' nu' kunh tu' me kyā nāv?[185]

The first Rishi is Aḥmad Rishī (Muḥammad)
The second Rishi is 'Uways
The third Rishi is Zalku' Rishī
The fourth Rishi is Palās Rishī
The fifth Rishi is Rumu' Rishī
The sixth Rishi is Mīrān Rishī
The seventh they thought a Rishi
What Rishi am I? What is my name?

Why does Nund Rishi propose such a genealogy? We have already discussed why Nund Rishi invokes 'Uways al-Qaranī. But why are Muḥammad and 'Uways al-Qaranī followed by the legendary Rishis of Kashmir? Why is Kashyapa Rishi, the Vedic *ṛṣi*, associated with the myths of origin in Kashmir in such texts as *Nīlamata Purāṇa* (composed between the sixth and the eighth century of the Common Era), missing from this genealogy?[186] These are not easy questions to answer. But the major question of lineage, which Nund Rishi foregrounds here, indicates the degree to which tensions over caste, race, and ethnicity marked Kashmiri society. By calling Muḥammad the first *rishī*, Nund Rishi sends the roots of the Rishi movement into the originary moment of Islamic revelation, and at the same time places Muḥammad among the first of the legendary seers and sages of Kashmir.[187] He gives the Kashmiri Rishis an Islamic prehistory and Islam a Kashmiri home. But he does so in order to stress continuity rather than rupture in Kashmir's religious history. Nund Rishi turns to the unknowability of God to translate Islam's new universalism into a language shared with Kashmir's pre-Islamic traditions laying the ground for Kashmiri language as the site of a new, and possible, Kashmiri universalism. Nund Rishi's new universalism gives us a clue for thinking about the relations between Sufism, *bhaktī*, vernacularization and the rise of a South Asian proto-modernity in medieval north India. The enduring appeal of Nund Rishi's new universalism is that it not only circumvents any threat of violence between Kashmir's different religious traditions but also approaches religious life as the impending task of a spiritual self-transformation. But, more significantly, it commits Nund Rishi to a political vision that he does not hesitate to express as a radical democracy. The paradox is that Nund Rishi expresses his vision of a new universalism in violent and turbulent times first and foremost as a Kashmiri. Perhaps it is for this reason that the tradition remembers him as the 'Alamdār-e Kashmir, or the flag-bearer of Kashmir. This can easily be forgotten if we choose to read him only as a spiritual exemplar. Yet the fusion of the prehistory of the Rishis with the history of Islam is made possible by the authority that Nund Rishi exercises in claiming to speak for Islam (it is this authority which was put into question by the Persian Sufis).

Nund Rishi considered himself an Uwaysī because 'Uways al-Qaranī, a Yemeni Sufi, had claimed direct spiritual initiation by Prophet Muhammad. Such a direct initiation, as we discussed earlier, came to be known as an Uwaysī initiation in the history of Sufism. By invoking 'Uways al-Qaranī, Nund Rishi not only lays claim to a similar initiation but also legitimizes a Sufi order which traces its genealogy to legendary Rishis of Kashmir such as Zalku' Rishi, Palās Rishi, Rumu' Rishi, and Mīrān Rishi. The reason the turn to 'Uways al-Qaranī is critical is because he is one of the early Islamic ascetics most praised by Prophet Muhammad for his devotion in reports from one of the canonical books of *hadīth*. The invocation of 'Uways allows Nund Rishi to bridge the gap between the universal history of early Islam with the regional history of Kashmiri Islam. But invoking 'Uways also nullifies the mediation of any temporal authority (including that of the Sufis) in the relation between an individual and God. The claim to an 'Uwaysī initiation allowed Nund Rishi to strike out on an autonomous path to inaugurate a regional thinking of Islam in the Kashmiri environment which has had an enduring impact on all aspects of Kashmiri life.

Even though Nund Rishi considered himself an Uwaysī, he also explicitly invokes the Śaiva *yoginī* Lal Ded as one of his *gurus* (teachers).[188] By tracing the genealogy of the Rishis to Prophet Muhammad, and proclaiming the Śaiva woman saint-poet Lal Ded and other Kashmiri Rishis as his gurus, Nund Rishi not only secures the foundation of the Rishi Order but also provincializes Islam. Nund Rishi achieves this not only through the use of the Kashmiri vernacular, his strong critique of caste, race, and the social conditions of the Kashmiri peasantry, but also by invoking the *zuhd* (asceticism) of early Islam against the mystical theology of the immigrant Sufis. There is a circular movement between the moment Nund Rishi claims the anti-imperial stance that was found among the early ascetics and mystics of Islam and the moment he lays the groundwork for a distinctive history of Islam in sultanate Kashmir which does not repudiate pre-Islamic Kashmiri culture. An affirmation of Islam's political universality becomes at the same time an affirmation of Kashmir's pluralist singularity.

If, with the figure of Manṣūr al-Ḥallāj, we are right at the heart of controversies over Sufism and theology in medieval Islam, the figure of 'Uways al-Qaranī opens up a different set of questions about religion and politics. 'Uways al-Qaranī had accepted Islam at the time of the Prophet's life but without himself ever having seen the Prophet. Thus the figure of 'Uways al-Qaranī anticipates all the problems which one would encounter in the study of a figure like Nund Rishi. A. S. Hussanini writes in his essay about 'Uways al-Qaranī that many biographers of the Prophet, such as Ibn Isḥāq and Wāqidī, do not mention 'Uways at all.[189] Imam Mālik went so far as to reject his existence.[190] Even as Imam Bukhārī mentions 'Uways, he considers those traditions as "weak."[191] But another prominent traditionist, Muslim ibn al-Ḥajjaj, mentions 'Uways. Let us look at the tradition from Muslim ibn al-Ḥajjaj in more detail:

> Muslim mentions ... 'Umar asked them: "Is there any person among you called Uways, for, I heard the Prophet saying, "There will come unto you (i.e., 'Umar) a person from Yaman called Uways, leaving behind his mother. He will have suffered from leprosy (*barṣ*), but, after praying to God, he was cured except for a white spot equal to a dinar or a dirham. When you meet him request him to ask forgiveness for you from God."[192]

The caliph 'Umar also quoted the Prophet as saying that 'Uways will be the best of the Tabi'ūn (the generation born after the Prophet but contemporary with his Companions).[193] It is written that 'Uways preferred to live in obscurity and died in a battle most likely fought on the side of 'Alī at Siffīn.[194] But why exactly is this obscure figure from the days of early Islam so central to the Sufis? 'Uways was a renowned ascetic (*zāhid*) of his time, and his appearance with 'Alīds at the battle of Siffīn hints at the massive political significance of the 'Uways legend. We must keep this in mind as we assess the significance of Nund Rishi's 'Uwaysī initiation. It is with Hujwīrī, the author of the famous Sufi treatise *Kashf al-maḥjūb*, which we discussed earlier, that the legend of 'Uways "soars to tremendous heights."[195] The centrality of both Ḥallāj and 'Uways to Nund Rishi may also owe to the popularity of *Kashf al-maḥjūb* in medieval north India. Hujwīrī mentions that the people of Kufa said about 'Uways: "He is a madman, who dwells in solitude and associates with no one.

He does not eat what others eat, and feels no joy or sorrow. When others smile, he weeps, and when others weep, he smiles."[196] According to Farīd al-Dīn 'Attar, 'Umar and 'Ali were both commissioned by the Prophet to deliver his mantle to 'Uways as a gift.[197] Hussanini concludes:

> It seems to me that such a person as Uways really existed and that he embraced Islam without learning its tenets from anyone. Although he lived during the lifetime of the Prophet he was prevented from meeting the Prophet, according to Hujwīrī, "firstly by the ecstasy which overmastered him and secondly by the duty to his mother." There is no doubt, however, that the Prophet and his Companions knew about him.[198]

Nund Rishi's turn to 'Uways al-Qaranī and his self-insertion into the chain which goes back to Prophet Muhammad depends on the love of Prophet Muhammad, which is a significant element of 'Uwaysī ideas.[199] The genealogy Nund Rishi speaks of for the Rishis is imaginary and bears a resemblance to similar genealogies not far from Kashmir in ex-Soviet Central Asia. Julian Baldick has done a detailed study of the history of the Uwaysīs in Central Asia that develops our understanding of the Uwaysī phenomenon at the fringes of the mainstream Islamic mystical tradition.[200] Baldick writes: "The words of the Qur'an are extremely hard to understand, and Arabic is not the native tongue of most Muslims ... the Uwaysi method had the advantages of overcoming barriers of time, space and language."[201] In the medieval period, Sufism insisted on a spiritual director, an elder (*shaykh* or *pīr*), for the aspiring mystic. Baldick writes:

> According to a well-known adage, "He who has no elder has Satan for his elder." The elder is the indispensable physician of the soul. However, there always had been some mystics outside the pale of Sufism and the usual elder-disciple relationship. These mystics would often fall under the general heading of "dervishes", a word which literally just means "poor people" (Persian *darwishan*), but came to mean "people of the spiritual life". Sufis also fall under this heading, but not all dervishes are Sufis. An Uwaysi, then, is a dervish who apparently has no elder or instructor, but claims to receive guidance from Muhammad or some other invisible teacher.[202]

The *Tadhkirāt al-Awliyā*, a text by Farīd al-Dīn 'Attar, which was also very popular in South Asian Sufism, already mandates that there is a class of people who call themselves the 'Uwaysīs and "do not need an 'elder' because they acquire their instruction from Muḥammad directly."[203] According to Baldick, the tendency came to India, where one of the greatest mystics and theologians of medieval times, Shaykh Aḥmad Sirhindī (1564–1624), claimed initiation through Prophet Muhammad) via Naqshbandi intermediaries.[204] But we find the Uwaysī content among the Rishis of Kashmir as early as the early fifteenth century. The appeal to an 'Uwaysī initiation also appears to have gone hand in hand with a critique of imperial conditions.[205] Even Ibn al-'Arabī, who clearly is one of the greatest of the Sufi thinkers, had no clear masters and speaks of "mysterious encounters with hidden 'friends of God' and the enigmatic prophet Khidr."[206] The role of Shī'īte influences on these schemas in the context of revolutionary political activity is obvious but beyond the scope of this study.

In all the reports about 'Uways, it is clear that he embraced Islam without knowing about Islam. This returns us to our fundamental question in relation to Nund Rishi: is it possible to arrive at an understanding of Islam unmediated by theological knowledge? Can there be a direct experience of Islam? The question has obvious connections to our discussion of Manṣūr al-Ḥallāj. The legend of 'Uways clearly suggests the possibility of an Islam beyond doctrine and universal in its appeal. It opens up Islam to the political demands of the subaltern and makes the question of lineage (race, caste, class, or ethnicity) irrelevant to living and experiencing Islam. It is this mystical-political idea of Islam that I call Nund Rishi's negative political theology. Nund Rishi often uses the Sanskrit term *sahaja* to name such an Islam. He explicitly calls the Qur'ān the *sahaja* Qur'ān:

Haẓ-i Rasūlas kāmat tsājī
Tsý tas sūzuth sahaz Qur'ān
Bhugih su yami̱ riyāẓat pājī
Chuham tsýtas tsu' meharbān[207]

You freed the Prophet from all evil
You revealed to him the *sahaja* Qur'ān
To the one, my God, who followed all the spiritual exercises
I remember how gracious you are!

According to this *shruk*, the *sahaja* Qur'ān is revealed to Prophet Muhammad on the path of *riyāẓat* (spiritual exercises), and Prophet Muhammad is addressed as someone who has taken care of a certain ascetic practice which is here just named as *riyāẕat* (spiritual exercise). Nund Rishi addresses God as *bhugih* (or *bhugi*, in a variant spelling), which is a derivative of the Sanskrit noun *bhaga* for wealth that gives us the word *bhagavān* for the divine in Sanskrit and modern Hindi.[208] *Sahaja* was used as an adjective in the Buddhist tantric tradition (in terms such as *sahajānanda*), and Nund Rishi's use of *sahaja* as an adjective for the Qur'ān reads Islam in relation to pre-Islamic Kashmiri spiritual traditions.

From Buddhist and Vaiṣnava *sahajiyā*s, Gorakhnāth, Kabir, Raidās, Nund Rishi, and Guru Nanak, *sahaja* has been a key term in multiple Indian spiritual traditions. *Sahaja* appears in the *Bhagvadgīta* to mean "inborn" or "innate," but it became a critical term for esoteric Buddhism in early medieval north India.[209] This term had moved into Sufi, *bhaktī*, and Sikh environments by the late medieval period.[210] If the term appears often in Nund Rishi, it is also found in the Guru Granth Sahib and *Gorakh Bāni* of Gorakhnāth.[211] Ronald S. McGregor discusses *sahaja* in relation to the exchanges between Sufis and Nātha yogīs in post-Sultanate north India: "The *sahaja* state is not that of union of the self with the ultimate brahman as described in the Upaniṣads, but rather a supraconscious state of 'void' (*śūnya*)."[212] Ronald Davidson writes that *sahaja* "was a preclassical word that became employed in scholastic, particularly Yogacāra, literature as an adjective describing conditions natural, or less frequently, essential with respect to circumstances encountered in an embodied state."[213] Joseph T. O'Connell demonstrates that the meaning of *sahaja* as "natural" persists as late as the sixteenth-century Chaitanya Vaiṣnavite tradition.[214] In his *An Introduction to Tantric Buddhism*, Ronald Davidson quotes an early description of Sahajiyā Buddhism by Shashi Bhushan Dasgupta, which helps unpack some of the meanings of the term:

> … its aim is to realize the ultimate innate nature (*sahaja*) or the self as well as of the dharmas, and it is Sahaja-yana also because of the fact that instead of suppressing and thereby inflicting undue strain on the human nature it makes man realize the truth in the most natural way, i.e., by adopting the path through which the human nature itself leads him.[215]

It is easy to see here that the term *sahaja* could lend itself to translating Islam's self-understanding as an innate religion, which takes care to avoid the extremes of excessive worldliness and asceticism, and does not inflict any undue strain on human nature. The Sufis, in turn, radicalized this self-understanding of

Islam by suggesting that there is nothing more *sahaja*, more innate, than our capacity for love.

Sahaja has often been translated as "innate," "spontaneous," or "natural." Yet *sahaja* is not an easy term to translate. As Kabir puts it: "Sahaj sahaj sab koi kāhe sahaj na cinhen koi/Jinhe sahaje Harijī mile sahaj kahije soi" (Everyone speaks of *sahaja*, *sahaja* but nobody knows *sahaja*/Those who find God through *sahaja* are the ones who know *sahaja*).[216] *Sahaja* has also been discussed in the context of Prakrit and Apabrhaṃśa poetry, and it is not without significance that the term appears often in the medieval *dohā* tradition.[217] Per Kværne writes that *sahaja* "literally signifies "being born (-ja) together with (saha-)."[218] According to H. V. Guenther, *sahaja* means "'co-emergent' (it can be read as a noun or adjective) where emergence (ja) is a spontaneous and uncaused manifestation of what we might call the principle of 'complementarity' (saha).... A precise translation of the term would therefore have to be something like 'complementarity-in-spontaneity'...."[219] Quoting Guenther, Charlotte Vaudeville in her study of Kabir writes that the term refers to "Transcendence and Immanence, Subject and Object, indivisibly blend."[220] Gordan Djurdjevic and Shukdev Singh in their translation of the *Gorakh Bānī* write: "It [sahaja] refers to the natural spontaneity that emerges as a behavioral concomitant to the state of an accomplished adept (*siddha*)."[221] For the *bhaktī* saint Raidās, *sahaja* refers "to the supreme state in which duality is dispelled and union with God is attained."[222] It gradually came to denote "an absolute level of reality or its cognitive component, nondual gnosis."[223] The term was abstracted from its ritual context in Buddhist tantra and came to acquire new associations "precipitated by the Buddhist support of a discourse on naturalness as the *siň qua non* of correct realization."[224] Not only did *sahaja* mean "natural" or "spontaneous" but also "uncontrived." Davidson calls it the spiritual path of least resistance.[225] It is this discourse on naturalness that allows Nund Rishi to contemplate Islam as a religion of the *sahaja*.

The term *sahaja* also appeared in esoteric Buddhism in the context of sociopolitical fragmentation in early medieval India and the concomitant critique of excessive ritualism.[226] Much like Rishism, the *sahajiyā* tendency in medieval Indian thought appears connected to the search for an alternative politics in the face of social fragmentation and political chaos. Let us consider the following *shruk*:

Yi sād vọpal hākas tu' handē
Sọzan sahazas grande zāv

Dọd trạ̄vith poni̱ yus mandē
Su samsāras kandē zāv[227]

The one who has found taste in wild vegetables
He is counted among the *Sahaja*
The one who abandons milk for water
He is born again into the world

Yet again Nund Rishi connects *sahaja* to a simple and ascetic lifestyle not indistinguishable from Prophet Muhammad's insistence on *faqr*, or voluntary poverty. The path to a spiritual transformation could be as simple as a turn away from the wealth of the world. Even in the Vaiṣnava Sahajiyā tradition, *sahaja* had come to mean an equilibrium between the self and the world.[228] Davidson poses this problem in the context of Mahāyāna in the following manner: if "all humans are already possessed of human awakening, then is there nothing that actually needs to be done?"[229] But that which is innate is not easily accessible, and this is why Nund Rishi speaks of the turn to *sahaja* as a rebirth (*Su samsāras kandē zāv*). The simple turns out to be the most difficult. That which is more near than our jugular vein (*Wa naḥnū aqrab ilay-hi min al-ḥabl al-warīd*) is also at the same time at an impossible distance. The spiritual task of narrowing this distance turns out to be a political task connected to the search for truth and justice in the present.

Sahaja was a key term in the tantrico-yogic and *bhaktī* milieu of medieval north India. It is quite clear that Nund Rishi identified the Qur'ān, and, therefore, Islam, with the *sahaja*. This was made easier by Islam's self-representation as an "innate" or "natural" religion (*dīn al-fiṭrī*) which came to be corrupted over time. Nund Rishi turned to the anti-ritualistic resonance of *sahaja* to articulate his understanding of Islam in a predominantly Hindu–Buddhist environment. Hans Harder has argued that in pre-eighteenth-century Bengali Islamic writings, for instance, "Islamic religious ideas integrating yogico-tantric practices were the rule rather than the exception...."[230] Hans Harder further claims that the texts of pre-modern Bengali Islam show a striking affinity with mysticism of yogico-tantric descent and with popular strands of Buddhism.[231] This is as true of medieval Kashmir as it is of medieval Bengal. In his study of the Buddhist and Vaiṣnava Sahajiyā movements as well as the influence of Nātha and Dharma "cults" on Bengali literature, Shashi Bhushan Dasgupta writes: "The word 'Sahaja' literally means that which is born or which originates with the birth or origination of any entity (*saha jāyate iti sahajaḥ*). It is, therefore, what all the Dharmas possess by virtue of their very existence, and is thus the quintessence of all the Dharmas."[232] *Sahaja* is a trans-religious idea.[233] For instance, Raidās speaks of *sahaja* in relation to an abandonment of the duality of the Hindu name of God, Rām, and the Muslim name of God, Khudā: "I renounced both in the *sahaj śūnya*/I call on neither Rām nor Khudā."[234] Nund Rishi also uses the term *sahaja* as a way of translating the political universalism of Islam into the Kashmiri vernacular at a time when the Persian Sufis in Kashmir articulated a Sufi metaphysics inaccessible and alien to the local population. A practical implication of the move was that it created space within the practice of Islam in Kashmir for forms of asceticism that had their origins in Buddhism and Hinduism. Or, in other words, *sahaja* and similar terms became sites of translation and inter-religious conversation.

Sahaja had also been "a reference point for the siddhas' criticism of Buddhist ritualism, scholastic involvement, and excessive yogic obsession, so that it occupied a soteriological, moral high ground excluding the artificial."[235] These meanings of *sahaja* were also deployed against Islamic and Hindu ritualism by Nund Rishi to evolve a shared Kashmiri religious vocabulary. Nund Rishi, at one point, addresses Muslim ascetics of Kashmir as siddhas:

Poz yod bōzakh pantsh nomūrakh
Natu' māz nomūrakh sọy chay namāz
Shivas tu' Shunịyahas myul yod karakh
Sidō sọy chay danthra namāz[236]

If you are true, you'll bend the five senses
Or else you'll be bending only your frame
You must unite Shiva with the Nothing
That Siddha is tantra *namāz*

Nund Rishi urges a Muslim to train in spiritual exercises lest his prayers are reduced to merely bending his body. He calls ascetic practices of exercising control over the senses as the true *namāz*, the Muslim prayer (*ṣalāh*). But the actual phrase he uses is *danthra namāz*, the tantric *namāz*. The presence of the term "tantra" here is strongly indicative of the Śaiva milieu in which Nund Rishi composed his mystical verse. For Nund Rishi, the Muslim prayer involves a detachment from the world the purpose of which is to unite Śiva (Being) with the Śunya (Nothing). What is involved in uniting Śiva with the Śunya? This is not a knowledge which can be communicated but a practice to which one is invited. This is the practice he calls *danthra namāz*, the tantric *namāz*. It is also suggested that this practice is the core around which multiple religious traditions constitute themselves. For Nund Rishi, Islam is one of the many frameworks for such a practice (one of the reasons he counts both Śaivas and Sufis as his teachers) and the site of an active invitation.

It is useful to remember that the Kashmiri tradition remembers Nund Rishi as Sahajānanda: the one who had tasted the ecstasy of *sahaja*. *Sahaja* as a condition is innate inasmuch as it names our being in its natural state. Nund Rishi translates Islam as a *sahaja* way of life (*dīn*) foregrounding the Sufi message of "the unity of being," *waḥdat al-wujūd*, and love, *'ishq*, as a powerful mode of its realization in our lives.[237] What connects Nund Rishi's *sahaja* Islam to the *sahaja* of Gorakh Nāth, Kabir, Raidās, and Guru Nanak? We can better approach these questions only after a more thorough understanding of the history of Sufism, *bhaktī*, and tantra in Kashmir.[238] For now, we can conclude that Nund Rishi, in his critique of the *mullāh*s, cautious avowal of Manṣūr al-Ḥallāj's challenges to the Shar'īah, and the claim to a direct spiritual initiation from Prophet Muhammad, is translating Islam into Kashmir's local Sufi–*bhaktī*–tantric environment as one of the many *sahaja* paths of spiritual self-transformation. For Nund Rishi, *sahaja* is the key that unlocks the promise of Islamic spirituality. Both Lal Ded and Nund Rishi inaugurate Kashmir's Sufi–*bhaktī* literature and open up the possibility of a *sahaja vath* (*sahaja* path) in Kashmir's turbulent religious and political history.[239] The search for the *sahaja vath* in these two saint-poets – Hindu and Muslim – is not merely a search for the truth and a call to justice but also a powerful vision of being-with-others. One could call Lal Ded and Nund Rishi, borrowing a phrase from Marcel Detienne, the masters of truth (*sachiar*s in Guru Nanak's terminology) in medieval Kashmir.[240]

Notes

1. Manṣūr al-Ḥallaj, cited in de Certeau, "Mysticism," 19.
2. See, for several essays which touch upon this theme, Aparna Rao and T. N. Madan (eds.), *The Valley of Kashmir: The Making and Unmaking of a Composite Culture?* (New Delhi: Manohar, 2008). See also Yoginder Sikand, *The Role of Kashmiri Sufis in the Promotion of Social Reform and Communal Harmony, 14th–16th century* (Mumbai: Centre for Study of Society and Secularism, 1999).

3. See, for instance, the essays on *Kashmīriyat*, Kashmiriness, in G. M. Khawaja and Gulshan Majeed, *Approaches to Kashmir Studies* (Srinagar: Gulshan Books, 2011). See also Muhammad Ishaq Khan, *Crisis of a Kashmiri Muslim: Spiritual and Intellectual* (Srinagar: Gulshan Books, 2008).
4. See Khan, *Kashmir's Transition to Islam*. Khan died in Srinagar in 2013 soon after publishing a comprehensive biographical dictionary of Sufism.
5. See, for instance, Muhammad Ashraf Wani, *Islam in Kashmir: Fourteenth to Sixteenth century* (Srinagar: Oriental Publishing House, 2004).
6. See Jürgen Wasim Frembgen, "Dhamāl and the Performing Body: Trance Dance in the Devotional Sufi Practice of Pakistan," *Journal of Sufi Studies* 1 (2012): 77–113.
7. As already discussed in the Introduction, I use the term "provincialize," following Dipesh Chakrabarty, to suggest a decentring and opening out of universal histories as well as to stress how "universalistic thought was always and already modified by particular histories, whether or not we could excavate such pasts fully." See Chakrabarty, *Provincializing Europe*, xiv.
8. Khan, *Kashmir's Transition to Islam*, 32.
9. Personal collection. The Jami'at-e Ahl-e Hadīth in Kashmir claims hundreds of thousands of members all over Kashmir and is a strong religio-political movement even though it maintains a distance from contemporary Kashmiri politics. This has been a reason for dissension within the ranks of the Ahl-e Hadīth in Kashmir and the rise of smaller groups like the Ṣawt al-Ḥaq. One of the senior leaders of the movement, Maulana Showkat Ahmad Shah, was assassinated in Srinagar in 2011.
10. The Jamāt-e Islāmī Kashmir has a history separate from the Jamāt-e Islāmī Hind of India and the Jamāt-e Islāmī Pakistan of Pakistan even though the thinking and politics of the Jamāt-e Islāmī Pakistan has had a greater influence over the Jamāt-e Islāmī Kashmir. For a wider history of the Jamāt-e Islāmī and its revivalist politics in South Asia, see Irfan Ahmad, *Islamism and Democracy in India: The Transformation of Jamaat-e-Islami* (Princeton: Princeton University Press, 2009). For a history of the Jamāt-e Islāmī in Kashmir, see Yoginder Sikand, "The Emergence and Development of the Jamaʿat-i Islami of Jammu and Kashmir (1940s–1990s)," *Modern Asian Studies* 36, no. 3 (2002). See also Mushtaq Ahmad Wani, *Muslim Religious Trends in Kashmir in Modern Times* (Patna: Khuda Baksh Oriental Public Library, 1997).
11. See, for a discussion of the ideas of the founder of the Barelvī movement in South Asia, Usha Sanyal, *Ahmad Riza Khan Barelwi: In the Path of the Prophet* (Oxford: Oneworld Publications, 2005).
12. See Balraj Puri, "Kashmīriyat: The Vitality of Kashmiri Identity," *Contemporary South Asia* 4, no. 1 (1995): 55–63. See also Neil Aggarwal, "Kashmiriyat as

Empty Signifier," *Interventions* 10, no. 2 (2008): 222–35. See also Chitralekha Zutshi, "Kashmir and Kashmiriyat: The Politics of Diversity in South Asia," in *Heterotopias: Nationalism and the Possibility of History in South Asia*, ed. Manu Bhagavan (New Delhi: Oxford University Press, 2010). For the debates on Indian secularism, see Rajeev Bhargava, *Secularism and Its Critics* (New Delhi: Oxford University Press, 1999). For a trenchant critique of secularism as Indian ideology, see Perry Anderson, *The Indian Ideology* (London: Verso, 2013).

13. Saqi, *Kulliyāt-e Shaikh al-'Ālam*, 148. I have slightly corrected Saqi's transcription of *pivō*.
14. "To articulate the past historically does not mean to recognize 'the way it really was' (Ranke). It means to sieze hold of a memory as it flashes up at a moment of danger." See Walter Benjamin, *Illuminations: Essays and Reflections*, tr. Harry Zohn, edited with an introduction by Hannah Arendt (New York: Schocken Books, 1968), 255.
15. Parimoo, *Unity in Diversity*, 161.
16. Ibid., 167.
17. Saqi, *Kulliyāt-e Shaikh al-'Ālam*, 175–76. In stanza 5, line 1, the word *dọpsham* appears to be an incorrect transcription of *wọpshun*, or religious discourse. I have gone with the Moti Lal Saqi version despite some inaccurate transcriptions and variations in the poem which we encounter in different editions of Nund Rishi's poetry. I have taken these inaccuracies and variations into account in my translation of the poem. The words *vakhnī*, *haṇī*, *zānī*, *hyetsu'y*, and *phyetsu'y* in the last two stanzas must be pronounced as *vakhnē*, *haṇē*, *zānē*, *hyetsē* and *phyetsē* to maintain rhyme.
18. A good example is the following *shloka* from *Vār Mājh*:

    Make mercy your mosque and devotion your prayer mat,
    righteousness your Qur'an;
    Meekness your circumcising, goodness your fasting,
    for thus the true Muslim expresses his faith.
    Make good works your Ka'bah, take truth as your pir,
    compassion your creed and your prayer.
    Let service to God be the beads which you tell
    and God will exalt you to glory

    See W. H. McLeod, *The Sikhs: History, Religion, and Society* (New York: Columbia University Press, 1989), 28.
19. See Susanne Olson, *Minority Jurisprudence in Islam: Muslim Communities in the West* (London: I.B. Tauris, 2016), 36–37. See also Khan, *Kashmir's Transition to Islam*, 4.
20. There is a gap between the Qur'ānic meanings of this term (*nafs*) and its use in Sufi technical terminology.

21. It perhaps comes as no surprise then that the Kashmiri literary critic Rahman Rahi, who has written two of the most influential essays on Nund Rishi, also translated Bābā Farīd from Punjabi to Kashmiri.
22. Some of the political failures of the Caliphate had to do with its struggles with the centralization of power and the relations between Arabs and non-Arabs, hereditary basis of political power, abandonment of Shi'ī revolutionary ideals and the inability to control growing internal unrest. For a more detailed political history of the Abbasid Caliphate, see Tayeb El-Hibri, *The Abbasid Caliphate: A History* (Cambridge, UK: Cambridge University Press, 2021).
23. Alam, *The Languages of Political Islam in India*, 42.
24. Rafiqi, *Sufism in Kashmir*, 44, 49.
25. Ibid., 48–49. See also Letter no. 7 addressed to Sultan 'Alau'd-Din in Abdul Qaiyum Rafiqi, *Letters of Mir Saiyid Ali Hamadani* (Srinagar: Gulshan Books, 2007), 60–61.
26. Kamil, *Nūrnāmu'*, 173.
27. See Fazlur Rahman, *Islam* (Chicago: University of Chicago Press, 1979). Rahman writes:

> This word originally means "the path or the road leading to the water", i.e. a way to the very source of life. The verb *shara'a* means literally 'to chalk out or mark out a clear road to water. In its religious usage from the earliest period, it has meant "the highway of good life, i.e. religious values, expressed functionally and in concrete terms, to direct man's life.

Ibid.

28. Interestingly, Moti Lal Saqi, who edited the second most influential collection of *shruks* by Nund Rishi and spent the last years of his life away from Kashmir in forced exile, called his autobiography *Sahaja vath* (The Sahaja Path).
29. Kamil, *Nūrnāmu'*, 63. See also Saqi, *Kulliyāt-e Shaikh al-'Ālam*, 38.
30. For more on Abū Ḥamīd al-Ghazālī, see Ebrahim Moosa, *Ghazālī and the Poetics of Imagination* (Chapel Hill: University of North Carolina Press, 2005). For Ghazālī, as he is popularly called in South Asia, "if God is utterly unique then it follows that He is utterly unknowable." Fadlou Shehadi, *Ghazali's Unique Unknowable God* (Leiden: Brill, 1964), 98.
31. We shall examine the whole *shruk* later. Saqi, *Kulliyāt-e Shaikh al-'Ālam*, 90.
32. Aziz Ahmad, *Studies in Islamic Culture in the Indian Environment* (London: Oxford University Press, 1964), 131. Ahmad turns to the Sufi text *Kashf al-maḥjūb* by al-Hujwīrī to trace this "integration of religious law and mysticism in India" to the eleventh century which is also the time al-Ghazālī addresses these tensions in his *Iḥyā' 'ulūm al-dīn*: "The exoteric aspect of Truth without the esoteric is hypocrisy, and the esoteric without the exoteric is heresy.

So with regard to the Law mere formality is defective, while mere spirituality is vain." Ibid.

33. See Ernst and Lawrence, *Sufi Martyrs of Love*, 41. See also Gandhi, *The Emperor Who Never Was*, 183, 247.
34. See, for instance, Ashraf Ali Thanvi, *Sharī'at va ṭarīqat* (Mumbai: Maktabah al-ḥaq, n.d.).
35. For more on the Wahhabi movement in India, see Qeyamuddin Ahmad, *The Wahhabi Movement in India* (New Delhi: Routledge, 2020). This book was originally published in 1966.
36. Anna Suvorova, *Muslim Saints of South Asia: The Eleventh to Fifteenth Centuries* (New York: RoutledgeCurzon, 2004), 18, 186–87.
37. Rafiqi, *Sufism in Kashmir*, 247–48.
38. Ibid.
39. For a detailed study of the tensions between the Kubrāwiyyā and Nūrbakhshīya, see Bashir, *Messianic Hopes and Mystical Visions*, 198–243.
40. Annemarie Schimmel, *Islam in the Indian Subcontinent* (Leiden: Brill, 1980), 99.
41. Kamil, *Nūrnāmu'*, 183.
42. For more on Rumi's Sufi path of love, see William Chittick, *The Sufi Path of Love: The Spiritual Teachings of Rumi* (Albany: State University of New York Press, 1984).
43. J. G. J ter Haar, *Follower and Heir of the Prophet: Shaykh Aḥmad Sirhindī (1564–1624) as a Mystic* (Leiden: Het Oosters Instituut, 1992), 25. Julian Baldick claims that Sirhindī's strident views on Shi'ism are from a time before his turn to Sufism. Julian Baldick, *Mystical Islam: An Introduction to Sufism* (London: Bloomsbury, 2012), 120. For a more detailed analysis of the life and thought of Shaykh Aḥmad Sirhindī, see Yohanan Friedmann, *Shaykh Aḥmad Sirhindī: An Outline of His Thought and a Study of His Image in the Eyes of Posterity* (New Delhi: Oxford University Press, 2002).
44. Moti Lal Saqi, *Kulliyāt-e Shaikh al-'Ālam*, 36.
45. Ibid., 30. It should be *vezrukh* (to acquire full knowledge of something) instead of *varzukh* (to abandon). Asadullah Afaqi transcribes the *shruk* correctly. Also see Afaqi, *Ā'īnā-e ḥaq*, 95.
46. Devin DeWeese suggests that the ascription of Shi'īte tendencies to Mīr Sayyid 'Alī Hamadānī have been overstated in the early scholarship on the Kubrāwiyyā saint. See Devin DeWeese, "Sayyid 'Ali Hamadānī and Kubrawī Hagiographical Traditions," in *The Heritage of Sufism, Volume II: The Legacy of Medieval Persian Sufism (1150–1500)*, ed. Leonard Lewisohn (Oxford: Oneworld Publications, 1999), 121–22.
47. Saqi, *Kulliyāt-e Shaikh al-'Ālam*, 30.

48. See Valerie J. Hoffman, "Intercession," *Encyclopaedia of the Qur'an, Volume II, E–I* (Leiden: Brill, 2002), 551–55.
49. Ibid., 553.
50. Saqi, *Kulliyāt-e Shaikh al-'Ālam*, 126.
51. Ibid., 128–29.
52. "I tow a boat across the ocean with a loose thread." See *Lal Ded*, edited by Jia Lal Kaul (Srinagar: Jammu and Kashmir Academy of Art, Culture and Languages, 1984), 62.
53. Saqi, *Kulliyāt-e Shaikh al-'Ālam*, 129.
54. Ibid., 127.
55. For more on the notion of hospitality in the Abrahamic and other traditions, see Richard Kearney and James Taylor (eds.), *Hosting the Stranger: Between Religions* (New York: Continuum, 2011). Also see Mona Siddiqui, *Hospitality and Islam: Welcoming in God's Name* (New Haven: Yale University Press, 2015).
56. Afaqi, *Ā'īnā-e ḥaq*, 320. This *shruk* is a part of a longer poem with similar *shruks*. This *shruk* is also given in the collection by B. N. Parimoo. See Parimoo, *Unity in Diversity*, 243.
57. Rahi, "Shaikh al 'Ālam sạnz shạ'irānā ḥaṣiyath," 167. *Makkār mullah* means a deceitful or cunning preacher.
58. The Arabic word *ummi* carries meanings such as the "mother" or the "unlettered."
59. Bashir, *Messianic Hopes and Mystical Visions*, 216. Bashir writes that even though Mir Shams al-Dīn Irāqī chose 'Ismā'īl Kubrāvī as the leader of the spiritual community he had established in Kashmir, he believed that "no one among the Kashmiris possessed the fortitude and self-control to become a full-fledged Sufi guide." Ibid. Even a Kashmiri historian like Mohammad Ishaq Khan wonders if the ordinary Kashmiri was capable of understanding Islam: "It is, in fact, open to question whether the more intellectual version of Islam, when propounded by a Sufi scholar like Saiyid 'Ali Hamadani, could have been understood by the common man." See Khan, "The Impact of Islam in the Sultanate Period (1320–1586)," 347.
60. Al-Ghazali, *Letter to a Disciple*, tr. Tobias Mayer (Cambridge: The Islamic Texts Society, 2005), 6.
61. Kak Odin, *Lallā to Nūruddīn*, 113.
62. *Al-Qur'ān* 7:10–18. See *Al-Qur'ān: A Contemporary Translation*, tr. Ahmed Ali (Princeton, Princeton University Press, 1984), 133–34.
63. Parimoo, *Unity in Diversity*, 240–41. This and the following *shruk* are not included either by Amin Kamil or Moti Lal Saqi. Parimoo claims to have had

access to manuscripts in private collections. I have modified the transliteration for consistency.

64. In Sufi poetry, Iblīs is also sometimes considered a true lover because of his refusal to bow before Adam because Iblīs is seen to have a deep, and jealous, love of God. See, for instance, Michael Sells, *Early Islamic Mysticism: Sufi, Qur'an, Mi'raj, Poetic and Theological Writings* (Mahwah, NJ: Paulist Press, 1996), 271.
65. Parimoo, *Unity in Diversity*, 241. I have modified the transliteration for consistency.
66. Mohi-ud-Din, *A Fresh Approach to the History of Kashmir*, 75. Mohi-ud-Din adds that fake *'ulamā* were called *kete peers* [*sic*]. Ibid.
67. See Rafiqi, *Sufism in Kashmir*, 49.
68. Alam, *The Languages of Political Islam in India*, 87.
69. Ibid., 84.
70. I have borrowed the term "learned ignorance" from the Christian-Neoplatonic philosopher Nicholas de Cusa. See Nicholas of Cusa, *Nicholas of Cusa: Selected Spiritual Writings*, tr. H. Lawrence Bond (Mahwah, NJ: Paulist Press, 1997), 19–22.
71. Ayman Shihadeh, "Introduction," in *Sufism and Theology*, ed. Ayman Shihadeh (Edinburgh: Edinburgh University Press, 2007), 1.
72. The early Orientalist scholarship on Sufism often traced the rise of Sufism to the influence of either Christianity, Neoplatonism, Buddhism, or Hinduism. A good example of this is Reynold A. Nicholson's *The Mystics of Islam*. See Reynold A. Nicholson, *The Mystics of Islam* (London: G. Bell and Sons Ltd., 1914), 1–27. But most contemporary scholarship on Islam considers Sufism as a movement internal to the growth of the Islamic tradition which may understandably have absorbed influences from different traditions.
73. See, for instance, Louis Massignon, *Essays on the Origins of the Technical Language of Islamic Mysticism* (Notre Dame: University of Notre Dame Press, 1992).
74. Shihadeh, "Introduction," 1.
75. Ibid., 2.
76. Saeko Yazaki, "Morality in Early Sufi Literature," in *The Cambridge Companion to Sufism*, ed. Lloyd Ridgeon (Cambridge: Cambridge University Press, 2015), 82.
77. The Ḥanbalī school is one of the four schools of jurisprudence in Sunni Islam. Shihadeh, "Introduction," 3.
78. Ibid., 4–5.
79. Ibid., 3.
80. Ash'arite theology, a synthesis between rationalist Mu'tazalite theology and revelationist traditionalist theology, was a school of Islamic theology founded

by Imām Abū al-Ḥasan al-'Ash'ari (874–936). Ibid., 3. Ira M. Lapidus provides a useful summary of the Ash'ari position in his *A History of Islamic Societies*: "Religious truths, according to the Ash'ari position, can only be known through revelation, though reason may play a subordinate role in defending the truth and persuading others." Ira M. Lapidus, *A History of Islamic Societies* (Cambridge: Cambridge University Press, 2002).

81. F. de Jong and Bernd Radtke, "Introduction," in *Islamic Mysticism Contested: Thirteen Centuries of Controversies and Polemics*, ed. F. de Jong and Bernd Radtke (Leiden: Brill, 1999), 11.
82. See Abu Hāmid al-Ghazzālī, *Al-Ghazzali on Listening to Music*, tr. Muhammad Nur Abdus Salam (Chicago: Great Books of the Islamic World, 2003). The Kubrāwiyyā Sufis allowed the chanting of *Awrād al-Fātaḥiyya*, an invocatory prayer composed by Mīr Sayyid 'Alī Hamadānī, as a concession to Islamic practice in Kashmir.
83. Gerhard Böwering, "Early Sufism between Persecution and Heresy," in *Islamic Mysticism Contested: Thirteen Centuries of Controversies and Polemics*, ed. F. de Jong and Bernd Radtke (Leiden: Brill, 1999), 45.
84. Bruce Lawrence, "Veiled Opposition to Sufis in Muslim South Asia: Dynastic Manipulation of Mystical Brotherhoods by the Great Mughal," in *Islamic Mysticism Contested: Thirteen Centuries of Controversies and Polemics*, ed. F. de Jong and Bernd Radtke (Leiden: Brill, 1999), 436.
85. Alam, *The Languages of Political Islam in India*, 98–112.
86. Ibid., 106.
87. Hamid Naseem Rafiabadi, *Sufism and Rishism in Kashmir: The Lesser Known Aspects of Some Sufi Orders* (Srinagar: City Book Centre, 2011), 122.
88. Louis Massignon, *The Passion of al-Hallāj: Mystic and Martyr of Islam, Volume I* (Princeton: Princeton University Press, 1982), 178.
89. See Iqbal, *Javid-Nama*, tr. Arthur J. Arberry (London: George Allen & Unwin, 1966), 90–105.
90. William Chittick, the preeminent scholar of Sufism, offers a good summary of these two positions in the history of Sufi literature, that is, the sober and the ecstatic, or drunk, tendency:

> The contrast between sober and drunk, or between the vision of differentiated multiplicity and the experience of all-embracing unity, reverberates throughout Sufi writing and is reflected in the hagiographical accounts of the Sufi masters. Those who experience intimate oneness are boldly confident of God's mercy, and those who experience awe-inspiring distance remain wary of His wrath. By and large, drunken Sufis tend to de-emphasise the Sharia, and declare union with God openly, whereas the sober Sufis observe the courtesy (*adab*) of a servant's relationship with

> his Lord. The sober fault the drunk for disregarding the Sunnah, and the drunk fault the sober for forgetting the overriding reality of God's mercy.

See William C. Chittick, *Sufism: A Beginner's Guide* (Oxford: Oneworld Publications, 2000), 32–33.

91. See also Yahya Michot, "Ibn Taymiyya's Commentary on the Creed of al-Ḥallāj," in *Sufism and Theology*, ed. Ayman Shihadeh (Edinburgh: Edinburgh University Press, 2007), 123–36.
92. Massignon, *The Passion of al-Hallāj*, 178.
93. Rafiabadi, *Sufism and Rishism in Kashmir*, 121.
94. Herbert Mason, *Al-Hallaj* (Richmond, Surrey: Curzon Press, 1995), 1.
95. Ibid., 2. Sahl bin 'Abdullah al-Tūstārī also wrote a classical Sufi commentary (*tafsīr*) on the Qur'ān.
96. Ibid., 6. The century saw the founding of the Bayt al-ḥikma translation center for the dissemination of Greek learning in Baghdad. Tūstār is the Arabicized form of the Persian Shūshtar.
97. Ibid., 2–3.
98. Ibid., 8.
99. Ibid., 5.
100. Ibid., 79.
101. Ibid.
102. Schimmel, *Mystical Dimensions of Islam*, 68.
103. Mason, *Al-Hallaj*, 15–16. Ibn Dawūd opposed the Sufis but was also a thinker of love who collected poetic meditations on love in his *Kitāb al-Zahra* (The Book of the Flower). Also see Abū Bakr Muḥammad Ibn Abi Sulaiman Dawud Al-Isfahani, *Kitab al-Zahra: The Book of the Flower* (Chicago: University of Chicago Press, 1932).
104. Mason, *Al-Hallaj*, 16.
105. Ibid, 18.
106. Ibid., 21.
107. Ibid.
108. De Lacy O'Leary, "Al-Hallaj," *Philosophy East and West* 1, no. 1 (April 1951): 61–62.
109. Ibid.
110. Carl Ernst and Bruce Lawrence in their book on the Chishtī Sufis translate *tawajjud* as "empathetic ecstasy." Ernst and Lawrence, *Sufi Martyrs of Love*, 37.
111. Mason, *Al-Hallaj*, 74.
112. Kaul (ed.), *Lal Ded*, 72.
113. This translation of the Lal Ded *vākh* is by Ranjit Hoskote. See Hoskote, *I, Lalla*, 34–35. This *vākh* is sometimes included as a *shruk*. The boundaries between

the Lal Ded and the Nund Rishi corpora are porous, and this has sometimes led to contentious debate about whether a poem is a Lal Ded *vākh* or a Nund Rishi *shruk*.

114. Kamil, *Nūrnāmu'*, 257.

115. Manṣūr al-Ḥallāj is also known as *Ḥallāj-i asrār* (Ḥallāj of the secrets) in the Sufi tradition. As to his purported declaration, '*Ana al-Ḥaq*, I am the Truth (a claim to divinity as al-Ḥaq is one of the divine names of God), it is found in Farīd al-Dīn 'Aṭṭār's *Tadhkirāt al-Awliyā* (Memoir of the Saints). See "Introduction," in *Hallaj: Poems of a Sufi Master*, tr. Carl Ernst (Evanston: Northwestern University Press, 2018), 5. Ernst adds:

> … 'Attar provides the gripping detail that the death verdict was delivered by Hallaj's own teacher, the respected Sufi master Junayd, who nevertheless had to remove his Sufi garb and don the costume of a judge before he gave the judicial decree (*fatwa*); 'Attar's powerful narrative is marred here by the contradictory fact that Junayd had actually died twelve years before the execution of Hallaj.

Ibid.

116. Saqi, *Kulliyāt-e Shaikh al-'Ālam*, 90.

117. This old story of Arabic origin is also the subject of the Persian poet Nezami Ganjavi's *masnavi*, *Laylī va majnūn*. See Nezami Ganjavi, *Layli and Majnun*, tr. Dick Davis (New York: Penguin Classics, 2021).

118. Saqi, *Kulliyāt-e Shaikh al-'Ālam*, 90.

119. Rafiabadi, *Sufism and Rishism in Kashmir*, 129.

120. Ibid., 132.

121. Kamil, *Nūrnāmu'*, 238. I have heard many people recite the second line with the following slight variation: *Su chu wuchān dil kis hālas* (He looks at the state of your heart).

122. Love is also a strong theme in Ḥanbalite traditionalism. See Joseph Norment Bell, *Love Theory in Later Ḥanbalite Islam* (Albany: State University of New York Press, 1979).

123. Mason, *Al-Hallaj*, 91.

124. Saqi, *Kulliyāt-e Shaikh al-'Ālam*, 67.

125. Mason, *Al-Hallaj*, 82, 84. See also 'Ali ibn 'Usman al-Hujviri, *The Kashf al-Mahjub: The Oldest Persian Treatise on Sufism*, tr. R. A. Nicholson (Lahore: Islamic Book Foundation, 1976).

126. 'Ayn al-Quḍāt Hamadānī, a Sufi martyr of the twelfth century, writes in his *Tamhīdāt* (Preludes):

> The moth does not obtain life through fire until fire so completely transfigures him that he beholds the entire world to be fire.... When the

> moth hurls itself into the fire, it is totally consumed, becoming itself all fire. Of self what awareness could it possess? As long as the moth abided with its "self" it was fettered and "hung-up". Now, it beholds "love" and love possesses such an [attractive] power that when love is commingled with the Beloved, the Beloved draws the lover to herself and devours him. The fire of love gives both power and nutriment to the moth. The lover is the moth and the beloved is the candle which bestows such power and nutriment to it [the moth]. Seeking these things, the moth hurls itself upon the flame. The candle-flame, that is, the beloved, commences to bum the moth, until the entire candle becomes fire: neither love nor moth remains.

See Leonard Lewisohn, "In Quest of Annihilation: Imaginalization and Mystical Death in the *Tamhīdat* of 'Ayn al-Quḍāt Hamadhānī," in *The Heritage of Sufism, Volume I: Classical Persian Sufism from Its Origins to Rumi (700–1300)*, ed. Leonard Lewisohn (Oxford: Oneworld Publications, 1999), 311.

127. Saqi, *Kulliyāt-e Shaikh al-'Ālam*, 37.
128. Carl Ernst (tr.), *Hallaj: Poems of a Sufi Master* (Evanston: Northwestern University Press, 2018), 4.
129. Rafiabadi, *Sufism and Rishism in Kashmir*, 113. *Kufr* and *iman* [*sic*], which Rafiabadi leaves untranslated, mean unbelief and faith.
130. Carl Ernst, "From Hagiography to Martyrology: Conflicting Testimonies to a Sufi Martyr of the Delhi Sultanate," *History of Religions* 24, no. 4 (May 1985): 315.
131. Annemarie Schimmel, "The Martyr-Mystic Ḥallāj in Sindhi Folk Poetry: Notes on a Mystical Symbol," *Numen* 9, Fasc. 3 (November 1962): 166–67.
132. One example is Ghulam Safdar's song *Mot gov Manṣūr nūr-i anwāras* (Manṣūr was driven mad by the Divine Light) sung by the popular Kashmiri folk singer Abdul Rashid Hafiz. The other is Ahmad Batwār's song *Bahādūr bāhuzūr chhum Shaikh Manṣūr* (Courageous and present is my teacher Manṣūr).
133. See Zafar Aḥmad Usmānī, *Sīrat-e Manṣūr* (Karachi: Maktaba-e Dar al-'uloom Karachi, n.d.).
134. Ernst, "From Hagiography to Martyrology," 315.
135. Ibid, 317.
136. Ibid.
137. *Hallaj*, tr. Ernst, 16, 32.
138. Ernst, "From Hagiography to Martyrology," 321.
139. The historian Supriya Gandhi claims that Sarmad (Muhammad Said Sarmad Kashani) was "a Jewish convert to Islam, who had been a merchant in Baghdad before traveling across the Persian-speaking world to India." See Gandhi, *The Emperor Who Never Was*, 183, 247.

140. Ernst, "From Hagiography to Martyrology," 308. Many commentators have suggested that it is either the challenge his mystical poetry posed to the Sharī'ah or his association with Dārā Shikoh that was among the main reasons for bringing Sarmad to trial at the court of the Mughal emperor Aurangzeb. His decision to roam around naked (a violation of the Sharī'ah) was dismissed as insufficient grounds for execution but his recitation of only half the *kalimā*, or the first article of Muslim faith, was deemed to be a clear enough violation of the Sharī'ah to merit the most extreme punishment. Sarmad refused to repent and chose self-consciously to walk in the footsteps of Ḥallāj. Sarmad is also believed to have explicity invoked Ḥallāj at the time of his execution. Maulana Abul Kalam Azad discusses Sarmad's martyrdom in great detail in his *Ḥayāt-e Sarmad*. See Maulana Abul Kalam Azad, *Ḥayāt-e Sarmad* (Lucknow: Tanvir Publications, n.d.), 18–26.
141. Ernst, "From Hagiography to Martyrology," 308.
142. Ibid., 313.
143. Saqi, *Kulliyāt-e Shaikh al-'Ālam*, 90.
144. Ernst, "From Hagiography to Martyrology," 315.
145. Ibid.
146. Ibid.
147. Saqi, *Kulliyāt-e Shaikh al-'Ālam*, 76.
148. Schimmel, "The Martyr-Mystic Ḥallāj in Sindhi Folk Poetry," 189.
149. Ibid., 161.
150. The legend of Manṣūr was so popular in Kashmir that in an eighteenth-century Kashmiri *tarīkh*, the Kashmiri Śaiva *yoginī* Lal Ded is called a sister of Manṣūr al-Ḥallāj. R. L. Bhat, "Political Content in the Vaakhs of Lal Ded," in *Cultural Heritage of Kashmiri Pandits*, ed. S. S. Toshkhani and K. Warikoo (Delhi: Himalayan Research and Cultural Foundation, 2009), 193.
151. Schimmel, "The Martyr-Mystic Ḥallāj in Sindhi Folk Poetry," 162.
152. Ibid., 198. Annemarie Schimmel clearly did not have access to Nund Rishi's *shruk*s on Manṣūr al-Ḥallāj.
153. Ibid., 164.
154. Ibid.
155. Ibid., 165.
156. Ibid., 175.
157. Ibid.
158. Ibid., 181.
159. Ibid.
160. Ibid., 169. Annemarie Schimmel speculates that it was Ḥallāj's ideas that led the Mughal Prince Dara Shikoh to study the Upaniṣads and Vedānta.

161. Ibid., 181. The complete verse of Ghalib, which alludes to Manṣūr al-Ḥallāj's martyrdom in a manner similar to that of Nund Rishi, is: "The secret in your heart is not a sermon/You can say it on the gallows, but not from the pulpit."
162. Ibid., 182.
163. Ibid., 197.
164. Shahab Ahmed, *What Is Islam? The Importance of Being Islamic* (Princeton: Princeton University Press, 2016), 280.
165. Schimmel, "The Martyr-Mystic Ḥallāj in Sindhi Folk Poetry," 182.
166. Ibid., 186.
167. *Alchemy of Light: Selected Verses of Sheikh Noor-u-din (RA) (Volume 1)*, tr. Adfar, 466. The text of the original is from the book of translations by G. N. Adfar and the translation is my own. The transliteration has been modified for consistency.
168. Schimmel, "The Martyr-Mystic Ḥallāj in Sindhi Folk Poetry," 187.
169. Wine as a symbol of unitive experience is by no means restricted to Islamic mysticism. Shahab Ahmed writes:

> The *positive* valorization of wine is, of course, universally evident in the history of the poetical discourses of Muslim societies – that is, in the form of speech regarded as the highest register of human self-expression and social communication – where wine served as the pre-eminent and pivotal image for the deepest experience of the meaning of human existence in relation to the Divine.

Ahmed, *What Is Islam?* 62.

170. Carl Ernst, "Rūzbihān Baqlī on Love as Essential Desire," in *God Is Beautiful and He loves Beauty: Festschrift in Honour of Annemarie Schimmel Presented by Students, Friends and Colleagues on April 7, 1992*, ed. Alma Giese and J. Christoph Bürgel (New York: Peter Lang, 1994), 181.
171. Yet this idea persists in Islamicate cultures through the world. When K. Asif's long-awaited Hindi–Urdu film on the legend of *Majnūn Layla*, *Love and God*, was finally released about fifteen years after his death in 1986, one of the songs simply announced: *Muḥabbat khudā hai* (Love is God). This theme is recurrent in Bollywood film songs which draw upon an Urdu literary culture steeped in Islamic mysticism.
172. Ernst, "Rūzbihān Baqlī on Love as Essential Desire," 182. Al-Daylamī includes a major meditation on love as the essence of God by Ḥallāj in his comprehenseive treatise on love, *The Book of the Inclination of the Affectionate Alif towards the Inclined Lam*. See *Hallaj*, tr. Ernst, 9–10.
173. For Rūmī's poetry as the Sufi path of love, see Chittick, *The Sufi Path of Love*.

174. Shahab Ahmed approaches this opposition between the "Sufi path of love" and the "Sufi path of knowledge" in a slightly different manner:

> I suggest, however, that rather than to draw a sharp distinguishing line between "love" and "knowledge," it is more accurate to conceive of love as constructed and practiced by the *madhhab-i ʿishq* precisely as a register or *type of knowing*: the *experience* of love is a learning experience (or an experience of learning) that *teaches* the lover how to identify value (i.e., what is valuable) and to constitute the human being – both as individual and as society – accordingly, in terms of those values.

Ahmed, *What Is Islam?* 42.

175. Abū al-Haṣan al-Nūrī, in the early years of Sufism, speaks of *ʿishq* in ways suggestive of eroticism and anthropomorphism for which he was charged with heresy by the caliphal court. Al- Nūrī is supposed to have said: "I love (*aʿshaqu*) God and He loves (*yaʿshaqu*) me." Ernst, "Rūzbihān Baqlī on Love as Essential Desire," 188.
176. Carl W. Ernst has argued that there are two sources for this idea of *ʿishq* in Sufi poetry: pre-Socratic and the traditional sources of Islam, that is, Qur'ān and the Hadīth. Ibid., 189.
177. Kamil, *Nūrnāmu'*, 197.
178. Ibid., 198.
179. Saqi, *Kulliyāt-e Shaikh al-ʿĀlam*, 29. For a slight variation in the text of the *shruk*, see the footnote to the *shruk* in Chapter 3.
180. Kamil, *Nūrnāmu'*, 199. The word *chanci* given in Kamil's *Nūrnāmu'* is in a variant spelling of the word *chanji* ('of the blow', 'blows'). The last word in line 4 must be pronounced as *lasay* or the last word in line 2 must be pronounced as *rasu'* to maintain rhyme. The meaning remains unaltered even if the tone shifts slightly. I have here used the standard Arabic spelling for *ʿishq*.
181. Ibid., 200. I have corrected the spelling of *rasu'* here which must rhyme with *lasu'*.
182. Ahmed, *What Is Islam?* 38.
183. Khan, *Kashmir's Transition to Islam*, 46.
184. There is no precedence to vegetarianism in the early Islamic tradition, and this difference would often come up in the relations between the Rishis and the Sufis of other Persian orders in Kashmir. Nund Rishi approached these contradictions by problematizing the binaries between ascetic and orthodox Islam: for instance, he not only criticized a merely ritualistic adherence to the Sharīʿah but also rejected the idea of asceticism for its own sake. This hews close to an admonition against the extremes of asceticism in the Qu'rān. It is this double critique that enables Nund Rishi to open up a third

space without entering into a confrontation with Islamic theology and law. The Rishis practiced vegetarianism but did not criticize anyone who chose to eat meat. Prophet Muhammad had also warned against the extremes of asceticism and urged marriage as completion of half of the *dīn* (faith). On asceticism in the Qur'ān, see See Julian Baldick, "Asceticism," *Encyclopaedia of the Qur'an, Volume I, A–D* (Leiden: Brill, 2002), 181–84.

185. Saqi, *Kulliyāt-e Shaikh al-'Ālam*, 33. A variant of the last line reads: *Bu' nu' kunh rishī me kyā nāv* (I am no Rishi. Who am I?). Ibid. Elsewhere, we also come across *Bu' kus rishī me kyāh nāv* (What Rishi am I? What is my name?). The fifth line should read as *Pūntsyum Rishī Rumu' Rishī.*
186. Kashyapa Rishi appears in many of Kashmir's myths of origins and some commentators of Kashmir even trace the origins of the name, Kashmir, to him. These myths of origin are layered and require a more detailed investigation. See, for instance, Ved Kumari Ghai, *Nilamatapurana, Vol. I* (Srinagar: J&K Academy of Art, Culture and Languages, 1968).
187. The move to begin with Prophet Muhammad could also be considered an element of those Sufi discourses that put the creation of a Muhammadan light (*nūr-i Muḥammadī*) before the creation of Adam at the origins of human history. It is "the first creation (or emanation) of God, the self-manifestation of divine consciousness." See *The Oxford Dictionary of Islam*, ed. John L. Esposito (Oxford: Oxford University Press, 2003), s.v. "Nur Muhammadi."
188. For more about Lal Ded, see Jaishree Kak Odin, *Mystical Verses of Lalla: A Journey to Self-realization* (Delhi: Motilal Banarsidass, 2007).
189. A. S. Hussanini, "Uways al-Qaranī and the Uwaysī Ṣūfīs," *Muslim World* 57 (1967): 104.
190. Ibid.
191. Ibid.
192. Ibid.
193. Ibid.
194. Ibid., 105.
195. Ibid., 109.
196. Ibid.
197. Ibid.
198. Ibid., 111.
199. The element of the love of the Prophet in the Uwaysī phenomenon had a radical consequence. The subject of the love of the Prophet is also a political subject inasmuch as this love has the potential to challenge established religious and political authority in the name of an individual lover's agency. As Julian Baldick writes: "The position of the Uwaysi is really, as we have seen, the position of every Muslim with regard to Muhammad: like Uways himself, the believer has

not met the Prophet in the flesh." Julian Baldick, *Imaginary Muslims: The Uwaysi Sufis of Central Asia* (New York: New York University Press, 1993), 226–27.

200. Ibid., 1.
201. Ibid., 4.
202. Ibid., 6–7.
203. Ibid., 25.
204. Ibid., 26.
205. This is true not only of Sirhindi's critique of the Mughals but also of Üveys ibn Mehmed's critique of the Ottoman Empire. Ibid., 26–27.
206. Ibid., 29.
207. Kamil, *Nūrnāmu'*, 63. I have eliminated the additional vowel at the end of *Qur'ān* and *maharbān* given in the Kamil text for ease of reading.
208. *A Sanskrit-English Dictionary*, ed. Sir Monier Monier-Williams (Delhi: Motilal Banarsidass, 1986), s.v. *bhaga*, 743.
209. Ronald M. Davidson, "Reframing *Sahaja*: Genre, Representation, Ritual and Lineage," *Journal of Indian Philosophy* 30 (2002): 52–53. Kalidasa uses it in the sense of "innate" in *Raghuvaṃśa*. Ibid.
210. For a discussion of the use of the term *sahaja* in the Sikh tradition, see Niharranjan Ray, "The Concept of Sahaj in Guru Nanak's Theology – Its Antecedents," in *Perspectives on Guru Nanak*, ed. Harbans Singh (Patiala: Publications Bureau Punjabi University, 1999). Ray also points out that *sahaja* appears in *sant* traditions, Sahajayāna Buddhism, Nāthpanthis, and Guru Nanak in contexts that involved "(a) a sharp criticism and rejection of all external formalities in regard to religious practices and spiritual quests, and (b) a protest against and rejection of priestly and scriptural authority, celibacy, penances, austerities, and the like." Ibid., 62.
211. In *Gorakh Bāni*, *sahaja* is compared to *nirālambha sthithi* (supportless condition) and *nirati* (unattached state), 107. See Gordan Djurdjevic and Shukdev Singh, *Sayings of Gorakhnāth: Annotated Translation of the* Gorakh Bānī (New Delhi: Oxford University Press, 2019), 71, 107.
212. Ronald S. McGregor, *Hindi Literature from Its Beginnings to the Nineteenth Century* (New Delhi: Manohar, 2021), 22. McGregor has this to add about the *Gorakh Bānī*: "Suggestive of an age of cultural rapprochement is an occasional hint of sympathy for teachings of Islam; but such a hint can be coupled with the suggestion that Muslim lawmen and divines of the present day would do well not to despise the Hindu gods." Ibid.
213. Davidson, "Reframing *Sahaja*," 52–53.
214. Joseph T O'Connell, "Were Caitanya's Vaiṣṇavas Really Sahajiyas? The Case of Rāmānanda Rāya," in *Shaping Bengali Worlds, Public and Private*, ed.

Tony K. Stewart (East Lansing, MI: Asian Studies Center, 1989), 12–13. The term had also acquired connotations of friendship in the Chaitanya community. Ibid.

215. Quoted in Davidson, "Reframing *Sahaja*," 49.
216. Hazari Prasad Dwivedi, *Kabir* (New Delhi: Rajkamal Prakashan, 2008), 68.
217. Davidson, "Reframing *Sahaja*," 48.
218. Per Kværne, "On the Concept of Sahaja in Indian Buddhist Tantric Literature," *Temenos* 11 (1975): 88.
219. Quoted in Davidson, "Reframing *Sahaja*," 50.
220. Charlotte Vaudeville, *A Weaver Named Kabir: Selected Verses with a Detailed Biographical and Historical Introduction* (New Delhi: Oxford University Press, 1993), 115.
221. Djurdjevic and Singh, *Sayings of Gorakhnāth*, 45.
222. Winand M. Callewaert and Peter G. Friedlander, *The Life and Works of Raidās* (New Delhi: Manohar, 2020), 101.
223. Davidson, "Reframing *Sahaja*," 62.
224. Ibid., 52.
225. Ibid., 70.
226. Davidson writes: "It would therefore appear that *sahaja* operated as a point of intersection between the caustic disapprobation of excessive ritualism ever in the background of the Buddhist subculture, the iconoclasm of vernacular literary expressions, and the peripatetic behavior of wandering siddhas, for whom physical yoga was a waste of time." Ibid., 70.
227. Saqi, *Kulliyāt-e Shaikh al-'Ālam*, 62.
228. Edward C. Dimock, *The Place of the Hidden Moon: Erotic Mysticism in the Vaiṣnava-sahajiyā cult of Bengal* (Chicago: University of Chicago Press, 1989), 42.
229. Davidson, "Reframing *Sahaja*," 70.
230. Harder, *Sufism and Saint Veneration in Contemporary Bangladesh*, 325.
231. Ibid.
232. Shashibhushan Dasgupta, *Obscure Religious Cults as Background of Bengali Literature* (Calcutta: University of Calcutta, 1946), 90. Dasgupta reminds us: "The poets of the Sahajiyā school laid their whole emphasis on their protest against the formalities of life and religion." Ibid., 58.
233. In *Essential Postulates of Sikhism*, N. Muthumohan claims that the path to *sahaja* (which he treats as co-terminous with *nirvana* and *sunyata* in the Buddhist tradition) is through the rejection of *haumai* (individual pride) including the *haumai* (or pride) in one's religion. N. Muthumohan, *Essential Postulates of Sikhism* (Patiala: Punjabi University, 2003), 132.
234. Callewaert and Friedlander, *The Life and Works of Raidās*, 102.

235. Davidson, "Reframing *Sahaja*," 73.
236. Saqi, *Kulliyāt-e Shaikh al-'Ālam*, 32.
237. I use translation here in both the senses suggested by Ronit Ricci: "conveying a text of one language in another and in a wider, more flexible sense of striving for an 'equivalence' of meaning." See Ricci, *Islam Translated*, 33.
238. One possible site for exploring these questions is Kashmiri language and literature. See, for instance, Mohi-ud-Din, *A Fresh Approach to the History of Kashmir*, 83–87.
239. John Stratton Hawley offers an evocative understanding of *bhaktī* (often translated as 'devotion'), a pan-Indian historical phenomenon that lasted from about the sixth century to the eighteenth century, on its own terms as a "heart religion, sometimes cool and quiescent but sometimes hot – the religion of participation, community, enthusiasm, song, and often of personal challenge ... a widely shared religiosity for which institutional superstructures weren't all that relevant, and which, once activated, could be historically contagious – a glorious disease of the collective heart." John Stratton Hawley, *A Storm of Songs: India and the Idea of the Bhakti movement* (Cambridge, MA: Harvard University Press, 2015), 2.
240. A *sachiar* in the Japji Sahib of Guru Nanak is one who has attained the truth after seeking and striving for it and not someone who has mere abstract knowledge of the truth. The term also invokes a community of such truthful ones.

2

Practicing Death

Rōzi tạm sund nāv (Nothing shall remain: save His name).

—A Kashmiri saying

Everything will perish save His countenance

—*Qur'ān* 28:88

... these mystics are, I believe, those who have been true philosophers. And I in my life have, so far as I could, left nothing undone, and have striven in every way to make myself one of them.

—Socrates, *Phaedo*[1]

Death is the fundamental theme of Nund Rishi's poetry.[2] I take up this insight in this chapter from the Kashmiri poet and critic Rahman Rahi's seminal essay "Shaikh al ʿĀlam sạnz shạ̄ʿirānā ḥạsiyath" (The Poetic Personality of Shaikh al-ʿĀlam) in relation to Rahi's extended reading of Nund Rishi as well as my own reading of the thinking of death in the Islamic tradition and certain strands of existential–phenomenological thought. The reason I develop this reading of death in Nund Rishi's mystical poetry comparatively across different traditions is to better approach the stakes involved in reading Nund Rishi's negative theology as a powerful discourse on death. The moments of negative theology in Islamic mystical poetry often take the form of a discourse on death and infuse a crisis in positive Islamic theology. To borrow Rahman Rahi's title for the critical collection in which the essay on the thinking of death in Nund Rishi appears, death is the true *kahavạt* (touchstone) for Nund Rishi's thinking.

Let us recall Nund Rishi's prayer from one of his *shruk*s: *Yiman padan me vỳtsār gotshiy* (These verses call to thinking). Nund Rishi calls his readers to a thinking (*vỳetsār*) on his *pada*s (verses). Much has remained unthought in

Nund Rishi's *padas* (or *shruks*), but what remains inescapable for any reader of Nund Rishi is the sudden encounter that the *shruks* set up with death. Nund Rishi hurls his reader on a collision course with the inevitability of death that reaches out from everywhere on earth: the way the dry clay vessels instantaneously absorb water, shops are abandoned at closing time, or the suddenness with which lightning descends down the sky (as the domes that shudder or the thunder that strikes) reducing human being(s) to nothing. I invoke Rahman Rahi's reading right at the outset because his 1978 essay is the first to trace the path of an interpretation I develop here: the fundamental theme, the arche-theme, of Nund Rishi's poetry, is death. Let us turn to Rahi's own words:

> One can get a better idea of the extraordinary form of *Shaikh al-'Ālam*'s experience and his overwhelming truth from those of his verses which deal with death. Death is a universal truth and there is hardly any language in the world which does not illuminate one or the other of its aspects. Even many Kashmiri poets have expressed their own responses to death from different perspectives. The singularity of *Shaikh al-'Ālam* is in this that he does not limit himself to a speaking or narrating of death, or present it in a unique way as it appears to his solitary imagining, but rather recognizes death approach him in such a slow and calm manner that an awe-inspiring encounter appears before our eyes which eventually grips the reader in its tight embrace (*kọmu' rattān che*). This is neither an ordinary experience and nor is the expression of *Shaikh al-'Ālam* ordinary. It is a living possibility from which escape is impossible....[3]

Rahi speaks of the fear of the subject held captive by death in its sudden, intimate embrace. The uncanny encounter with death turns life into a ghostly existence. A sudden fog descends down on the light of the day, envelopes everything, paralyzes life, and all that remains is a waiting. Rahi approaches this encounter in a series of metaphors:

> My inner experience and I had been blessed with a light but something happened all of a sudden which shrouds the light in a soot of darkness. The darkness enveloped me all of a sudden from all sides, and pushed me deeper into its embrace, and then before my eyes moved the stealthy, calm and slow-moving shadow of a hesitant thief. And I who am already trapped in this dragnet, it does not really matter if I also now close my eyes. The one with the wolf-face who affects love for me, and yet waits for me in hunt, is a hungry lion whose embrace is unbearable and grip limitless.[4]

A darkness descends as a mood. The curtains of ordinary experience suddenly part to reveal the slow-moving, stealthy shadow of a thief. There is no escape for the living from the dragnet of death.

Rahi first introduces Nund Rishi as a spiritual practitioner (*'ạmil*), mystic (*'ạrif*), and a spiritual leader (*dīnī peshwā*) who makes manifest the life of a multilayered (*tahdār*) and a multi-hued (*rang bastu'*) culture.[5] One should not be distracted by such rhetorical strategies as Rahi moves fast between a conservative critical idiom and a devastating critique of tradition. The explicit task he sets himself in this essay is circumscribed to addressing a gap in the critical scholarship on Nund Rishi.[6] Rahi announces that he is going to restrict himself to the figure of Nund Rishi as a poet, or in his own words, to the poetic personality (*shạ'irānā shakhsiyath*) of Nund Rishi.[7] One of the reasons Rahi gives for the neglect that Nund Rishi has received in twentieth-century Kashmiri language scholarship is that it was only as late as 1968 that the first critical edition of a collection of Nund Rishi's poetry was edited and published by Amin Kamil for the Jammu and Kashmir Academy of Art, Culture and Languages.[8] Rahi begins his reading by tracing two critical interventions in the reception of Nund Rishi's poetry in the twentieth century: (*a*) in the literary history of the Marxist poet and critic Abdul Ahad Azad (*Kashmīrī Zabān aur Shā'irī*) and (*b*) in the collection of essays, *Studies in Kashmiri*, by the literary critic J. L. Kaul. By invoking the similarities and differences in these two early critical approaches to Nund Rishi, Rahi opens up a different path to reading Nund Rishi. Rahi begins by reminding us that Abdul Ahad Azad (1903–48) is the first critical commentator on Nund Rishi's poetry who attempts a reading of Nund Rishi in relation to the elements of poetry (*aṣnāf-e sukhan*) and its themes (*moẓū'*). According to Rahi, Azad expresses a pure literary judgment when, setting aside Nund Rishi's high mystical (*ārifānā*) station and religious provenance (*manṣab*), he suggests that when Nund Rishi speaks of pure religious principles in his *shruks*, poetry does not come to his aid. If poetry does come to the aid of Nund Rishi, it does so as the reason and rhetoric of an expert religious teacher (*mubaligh*) even as *au contraire* spontaneous emotion pours forth from his heart (*ath bar'aks chi farạrī jazbāth tihendi dilu' manzu' buka kạrith tshat divān*).[9] Rahi struggles in the rest of his essay to move beyond Azad's interpretation of Nund Rishi as a religious teacher even as he strives to follow Azad's advice of approaching Nund Rishi primarily as a poet. The difficulty of Rahi's task is that he does not always restrict himself to reading Nund Rishi's mystical poetry but also approaches Nund Rishi's mystical experience from the standpoint of his poetry. Rahi searches for a way to hold mysticism and poetry together in his reading under the signs of literature and death but in the end is unable to do so.

Maurice Blanchot could be expressing the inexpressible about the world of mystic experience that opens out to us in Nund Rishi's *shruk*s when he speaks of the relations between literary saying and death:

> My speech is a warning that at this very moment death is loose in the world, that it has suddenly appeared between me, as I speak, and the being I address: it is there between us as the distance that separates us, but this distance is also what prevents us from being separated, because it contains the condition for all understanding. Death alone allows me to grasp what I want to attain; it exists in words as the only way they can have meaning. Without death, everything would sink into absurdity and nothingness.[10]

It is this ontological primacy of death that we encounter in Rahman Rahi's reading of Nund Rishi. Rahman Rahi, in principle, affirms Abdul Ahad Azad's move of reading Nund Rishi first and foremost as a poet but hastens to add that Azad's reading of Nund Rishi remains provisional and leaves us with an extreme thirst for more.[11] Rahi then turns to yet another serious study of Nund Rishi's poetry by J. L. Kaul in his *Studies in Kashmiri*, where Kaul, a legendary teacher of English literature in post-1947 Srinagar, suggests that most of Nund Rishi's *shruk*s are thematically didactic and tonally admonitory, and the poetic utterance in these *shruk*s reveal those points of wisdom (*ḥakīmānā nọqtu'*) and such scaled and measured (*mīnith tu' tūlith*) sayings that have become proverbial in Kashmir and enriched the Kashmiri language.[12] For Kaul, this proverbial measure of Nund Rishi, nonetheless, is also the limit of his poetry. Kaul concedes that the Kashmiri language remains indebted to Nund Rishi but reserves a final aesthetic judgment. As I have already indicated earlier, Rahi compares these two early views of Azad and Kaul as a point of departure for his own attempt to retrieve Nund Rishi as a poet and a thinker beyond the preacher (*mubaligẖ*) of Azad and the sermonizer (*vā'iẓ*) of Kaul.[13] Do we read the *shruk*s as a testament to Nund Rishi's mystical height or as a literary work? Rahi argues that the limit Azad sets (that even in those *shruk*s which are religious but also aided by the poetic, Nund Rishi succumbs to the plan of a preacher) can in itself be a productive limit.[14] The *shruk*s can be approached as a form of religious lyric. Even as Kaul, according to Rahi, brings up the didactic thematic and admonitory tone of Nund Rishi and restricts himself to points of wisdom and the scaled and measured sayings that reveal the riches of Kashmiri language, Azad does pay attention to what he calls the sermonic brilliance (*vā'iẓānā shān*) of Shaikh's poetry.[15] But Rahi struggles to reconcile faith and poetry in Nund Rishi, which has some autobiographical resonance for Rahi that acquires dramatic tension in his own later collection of poems, *Siyāh rūdu' jaryn manz*.[16] The third important point (which emerges from these early assessments of Nund Rishi's poetry) is the following question: if at all the didactic themes and admonitory tone so overwhelms Nund Rishi's poetry, then do we need no longer keep anything else in mind while evaluating his whole oeuvre?[17] Rahi asks:

> Are there no *shruks* in Ḥaẓrat Shaikh's poetry which bear out the criterion of real poetic value? Or are such *shruks* so few in number that, even in a critical evaluation, these are taken to be exceptions or accidents, and therefore, neglected? I think only by finding an answer to this question can we satisfactorily attempt a critical evaluation of *Shaikh al-'Ālam*'s poetry and only by recognizing the poetic personality of Ḥaẓrat Shaikh in a real sense can we finally decide his true stature in the firmament of Kashmiri poetry.[18]

It is clear that, for Rahi, there are enough *shruks* in the Nund Rishi oeuvre of "real poetic value." Rahi then turns to Amin Kamil's 1968 edition of *Nūrnāmu'* – the first critical collection of verse by Shaikh al-'Ālam to be published – in the foreword to which Kamil divides Nund Rishi's poetry into three broad themes: Islamic, Sufi, and philosophical. In an unusually strident critique of Kamil, Rahi writes:

> Leaving aside the matter that these three divisions are not reliable because something can be Islamic, Sufi, philosophical and everything else at the same time, it calls our attention that some people turn to Islamic and unIslamic imaginations as the touchstone (*kahavạt*) for understanding and evaluating literature and thus estimating its position and value.[19]

Rahi further suggests that just because Nund Rishi's *shruks* reflect the examined faith and desire of a true Muslim (*pạzis Musalmān sạndi rasykh 'aqīdu'k*), it is not necessary that the *shruks* should also therefore count as an example of good poetry: "The conflict and depth of a poetic persona cannot be gauged from the security of the poet's faith or the heights of his or her ambition."[20] For Rahi, it is the aporias, or the knots, of the *shruks* that call our thinking.[21]

Or rather, the *shruk* is often an aporia. Rahi quotes two *shruks* with opposed meanings which taken together reveal a paradoxical approach to the question of Islam in relation to Hinduism in Kashmir in order to caution against too literal a reading of Nund Rishi (and also warn us about the difficulty of reading the question of faith in Nund Rishi's poetry). Rahi first quotes the following *shruk*:

Ȧkis mạ̄lis māji handẏn
Timan dạy trạ̄vith ti kyāy
Musalmānan kyāv hendẏn
Kar bandan tōshi khọdāy[22]

They are born of the same parents
Why would God abandon them?
To both the Muslims and the Hindus
May God send his blessings

Rahi then contrasts this with another *shruk* (there are slight variations of this *shruk* in different published collections):

Rindō hendẏn hạnz kāmi trạ̄vitō
Trạ̄vitō prạ̄vitō ḥaqu' su'nz vath
Ḥaẓrat Muḥammad matu' mạshrạ̄vitō
Asi nin nāras timan rōzi kath[23]

Friends, abandon the path of the Hindus
Abandon their path to find the path of truth
Don't forget *Ḥaẓrat Muḥammad*
For we will be hauled to Hell, but he will be embarrassed for us

The point is not whether either, or both, of the above *shruks* are later interpolations, or if literal readings of these verses are adequate, but that both now belong to the Nund Rishi corpus in ways that nonetheless offer clues to Nund Rishi's thinking on these questions as we become acquainted with similar paradoxes in the rest of the *shruks*. One way to read such a corpus is to not merely reduce it to an expression of this or that philosophical or religious outlook but judge it on the *kahavạt* (touchstone) of literature. Rahi quotes the two *shruks* to reveal the undecidability involved in reading them and insists on a paradoxical thinking at work in the internally differentiated thematic of the *shruk*s which makes it difficult to reduce Nund Rishi's poetic thinking into a belief-system.[24] Or, in other words, Rahi insists on reading the *shruk*s as poetry. He adds that critical decisions on literary texts must in the end also necessarily involve considerations other than literary but literature must first be judged on literature's touchstone.[25]

Even though Rahi refuses to engage with Nund Rishi's stature as one of Kashmir's greatest Sufi saints, he remains undecided about the place of Sufism in any critical evaluation of Nund Rishi's poetic oeuvre. The question remains then as to what might be involved in judging Nund Rishi solely on literature's touchstone. It is clear that Rahi is not calling for literary criticism or some other aesthetic or hermeneutic operation. Rahi proposes that we turn to the language of Nund Rishi in order to develop an understanding of his thinking:

> The fundamental potentiality of literature is in debt of its process of creation. The elements which give birth to this process, of these elements the most important is the miracle-working of language and the poetic saying which depends on the gift of the passion of creative imagination that makes possible the reappropriation of experience, and very nearly, the creation of experience itself and even its understanding.[26]

But Rahi also sounds a word of caution. There is no easy way into the language of Nund Rishi:

> Reading and judging Haẕrat-e Shaikh's poetry, it is important to bear in mind that Haẕrat-e Shaikh is fundamentally a Rishi and a Sufi of deep meanings because of which the overall air (*kulham fiẕā*) of his experience is extraordinary (*g̲h̲ār mōmūlī).* Like most poets, he does not array his poetry in human love, longing, or revenge. Nor does he clothe everyday experience in the garment of poetry. In his best moments, Haẕrat-e Shaikh, instead of desiring recognition for his self from you or us finds his self face-to-face before the Six Directions [the universe] and the creator of universe.[27]

Rahi has one more advice about reading Nund Rishi: we cannot pay attention to the language of Nund Rishi without taking into account the reality that continuously for four to five hundred years, much of Shaikh al-'Ālam's poetry has passed into the Kashmiri language:

> We must pay attention to the corpus of Nund Rishi's verses in a way that takes into account the reality that, because of our being dull of hearing and constant

> repetitions over four to five hundred years, much of Ḥaẓrat Shaikh's poetry has passed into the everyday idiom of Kashmiri language in ways in which the sense of life and attraction of its sounds and words, the allure and effect of the meaning-creation of its tones, and the potentiality of experience to retrieve hidden meanings which are embodied in it, has become difficult in much the same way that it is difficult to experience the originary potentiality for creation that lies dormant in any proverb which has become overworn by use in a language.[28]

Rahi trains the reader's ears for Nund Rishi's language so as to retrieve the force of the poetic utterance, which has become obscure from its being overworn through use in everyday life. As Rahi puts it: "The truth is that many of the Shaikh *shruk*s are like sleeping embers in the ash and until the soot that has settled on these embers is shaken off, we cannot have a proper estimate of their light or heat."[29] Rahi's alternative path to Nund Rishi is not to wait for the poet's "Alexandrian assault" (*sikandarānā sanjūn*) on meaning but in the following advice about reading from the nineteenth-century working-class Sufi poet Wahab Khār:

Shamā zajōm hati ke ratē
Su gahē ẓulmātu' pyōm
Tath ẓulmātas lāl kyāh chatē
Su kas patē gōm[30]

I lit the candle with the blood of my throat
Such was the darkness that enveloped me
The jewels do not fade in the darkness
Where has the Beloved gone?

By quoting Wahab Khār here, Rahman Rahi reminds us that the act of reading is a painful activity, a struggle, in which one must search for the scattered meaning even as its horizons recede into darkness. An act of reading must be like lighting a candle with the blood of your throat in the depths of the night of darkness. Despite the darkness, the jewels of meaning keep shining. But all creation of meaning is a speaking of the loss of the Beloved, a remembrance of the name of the absent God. Such courage of reading is also evoked in the first two lines of the following *shruk*:

Yath wāvu' hālay tsōng kus zālay
Tilu' kani zālhas 'ilm tu' dīn[31]

> Who would light a lamp in this storm?
> In place of oil, I would burn faith and knowledge

The question hidden in Rahi's insistence that we read Nund Rishi as a poet (even if not only as a poet) is the question of literature. Or, in other words, the relation of literature *qua* question to faith. But Rahi has barely posed this question before he turns to the thinking of death in Nund Rishi. This is perhaps inevitable. Rahi's rejection of an easy opposition between literature and mysticism, poetry and philosophy, brings us to the threshold of negative theology as a powerful discourse on death.

The question of Nund Rishi's stature as a poet remains. How does one approach Nund Rishi as a poet? Even though Rahi suggests that Lal Ded surpasses Nund Rishi as a poet, yet he finds himself deeply engaged with Nund Rishi's poetry.[32] This is not necessarily an impulse to conserve Nund Rishi but a provocation that we perhaps have as yet not learned to read Nund Rishi. Not knowing how to approach the singular event of Nund Rishi's poetry, Rahi is tempted to turn to a Sufi hermeneutic:

> It is not about narrating an idea nor is it about lending a feeling to a thought. This is about the reappropriation of an experience which is singular, untouched, and unspeakable. This is not the story of beholding a fairy-faced or a kohl-eyed person but rather it is the extraordinary experience of encountering the creator of the universe, of annihilating one's self in seeing the creator's unity.[33]

For Rahi, it is the mystic experience of Nund Rishi that makes the air and light of his poetry extraordinary. Rahi creates a vivid image of this mystic experience: "A limitless heat and light that human reason cannot even imagine: it is the experience of drinking the whole ocean in a single gulp."[34] The Sufi narrative about the self – its stages on a journey, its annihilation and revival – is one way we can approach Nund Rishi's mystic experience, but he himself rarely turns to spiritual autobiography. Nund Rishi even explicitly warns his reader: *Kạm māli chŷth hyok su dariyāv* (Who, my dear, could drink up the ocean?).[35] No doubt there are autobiographical elements in the *shruk*s, but these do not trace the contours of an inner experience as they do in Lal Ded.[36] Perhaps it is better to turn to this simple advice of Rahi:

> ... in order properly to get a measure of the real potential of Shaikh al-ʿĀlam's poetry, it is necessary to study it word for word, by time and again diving into it,

so that the world of thinking and emotion which lies dormant in the shadow of the words springs back to life.[37]

The image of a diver who does not swallow the ocean but jumps into it to retrieve jewels of meaning suggests that the proximity to this mystic experience offers us unfathomable gifts. Close reading can bring us nearer to the gifts of mystic experience that remain concealed behind the words. On a more practical note, this is great advice in a situation where some of Nund Rishi's language has become obscure for the modern Kashmiri reader. Rahi speaks of reading as a slow experience of touching:

> Poetry is like a snail and just like a snail perceives things by very slowly and carefully feeling its way and spreading its touch in the surroundings, much in the same way a poet brings words into play to seek the subject of his poetry, or the shape of his experience, of which, before composing his verses, he had only a faint or ambiguous perception. It is clear that to reach the spirit of such verses, the reader must touch every word of the poet with the fingertips of feeling, ponder over their meaning in the depths of thinking and raise them to the heights of creative imagination so that he too may discover the magic of the poet's fundamental experience as a unity.[38]

The end of reading mystical poetry is the experience of the poet's transcendence. Rahman Rahi then turns to just such a close reading of Nund Rishi's poetry to bring to life Nund Rishi's philosophical and affective worlds (*fikrī tu' jazbāṭi duniẏā*) and proceeds to give us powerful readings of some of the *shruks*.[39] Let us begin with one of these *shruks*:

Kyāh tagi mōtas tu' mōtu' kẏn kānan
Kaman javānan chhāngu'r peyi
Pōnị zan shrapay navẏn bānan
Vạnị dith vānan phālav gạyi[40]

What can Death or its arrows do?
Death that shattered our youth
The way water is absorbed by new clay vessels
The way shops are abandoned at closing time

Here Nund Rishi appears, in a way not entirely dissimilar from Lal Ded, to have cultivated an indifference to death. The *shruk* opens with an almost

Epicurean disinterest in death's power, but the second line recognizes the sheer helplessness of the self before the rain of arrows from death. The second line mourns the youth devoured by untimely death the way new and dry clay vessels absorb drops of water. A remorse rises to the surface here in the recognition of the death-work of life. The verb *chhāngu'r peyn* in the second line invokes the sudden scattering-shattering of the death of every "I" or "we." The image is that of a lightning falling on something that shatters and scatters everything. The youth on which such a lightning has fallen are recalled with love and melancholy. The last line conjures up the image of a deserted street where the iron crossbars (*phālav*) on the shops are the only trace of the shopkeepers who have left the bazaar. The overall effect of death is captured in this last line; it is the effect of death for the living: *Vạni̱ dith vānan phālav gạyi* (The way shops are abandoned at closing time). The haunting absence in the image voids the possibility of any return. The image of the iron, or wooden, crossbar (*phālav*) suggests a finality to the end and the unforeseen ways death suddenly, and without warning, interrupts life. The last line of the *shruk* reveals the world as a bazaar which is approaching closing time. The bazaar has become a staging ground for this new thinking of death.

The time-image of an abandoned bazaar on a desolate street also recollects a sense of waiting for all those who left never to return and are now not even remembered in the bustle of the everyday. For the living, death is a waiting, a ruin of time. One can only encounter death in the traces of its work: the violence of the arrows which strike down the youth, the absorption of the water droplets by a new and dry clay vessel, the desolation of the bazaar after closing time. Yet the becoming-death of life is paradoxically challenged by Nund Rishi when he suggests that death is blundering and it knows nothing (*kyāh tagi mōtas*). This is closer to Lal Ded, who in one of her *vākh*s says, *Māran kasū tu' māran kas?* (Who will they kill and who will die?) Both Nund Rishi and Lal Ded refuse the fear of death and avow an immortal eternity. For instance, Lal Ded declares: *ạsī ạ̄s tu'ạsī āsav* (We have been and we shall be). Nund Rishi affirms the reality of death but also that of an eternal afterlife. Even though Nund Rishi, hewing close to Islamic eschatology, paints a vivid and terrifying picture of physical death, he also reassures his reader of an Islamic afterlife:

Athu' zu' tuvith khọr zu' vahạ̄rith
Ninam duni̱yahich lolạr trạ̄vith kath
Garay ninam gīhe bār trạ̄vith

Yinam and mazār sạvith kath
Nundẏn ḥūru' thavan valu'lạvith
Dū'thẏen dozakhan nār tạvith kath[41]

My hands folded, my feet stretched out
I will be separated from worldly attachments and how?
They will carry me off from home and its burdens
To abandon me in the desolate graveyard
The good will be surrounded by the houris of Paradise
And for the evil, there will be a smoldering Fire

These are stock images of Islamic eschatology, of a Sufi *memento mori*, which also promise the believer that it is all going to turn out well after a horrific end. In many of his verses, Nund Rishi turns to classical Islamic themes of death and resurrection such as punishment in the grave, the encounter with the angels Nakīr and Munkar, the *barzakh*, the Day of Judgment, and the immortals of Heaven and Hell. But he keeps returning to the inevitability of death, its sheer inescapability, which is reinforced in the following *shruk* that emphasizes the point that death did not even spare the great saints:

Yas ōru' yāmun yōr vasay
Tas hay ālam vadī lasī mō
Ḍāyan gazan tal yus tsasay
Su hay valī āsi khasī mō[42]

If the Angel of Death descends on him
Even if the whole world mourns for him, will he live?
Anyone who sinks into his two and a half yards
Even if a saint, will he return from the grave?

Death is the great equalizer, the true universal. The use of the term *yāmun* is ambiguous: it invokes Yama, the Hindu god of death, but also hints at the angel 'Izrā'īl, who in the Islamic tradition is tasked by God to collect individual souls at death. This is one of the many moments of translation from the Islamic to the Hindu and Buddhist conceptual terminology and vice versa that we come across in Nund Rishi's oeuvre. The fundamental message is universal: death is inescapable for everyone and the only true certitude in life. Nund Rishi further bolsters this idea by speaking of the death of Prophet Muhammad:

Ḥaẕrat Muḥammad dayi sund pyārō
Damu' damu' Jibrīl yār tas
Taṃ yelī sakhar kaṛ tot pārō
Daphtu' duniyāh sōr chu kas[43]

Prophet Muhammad, the Beloved of God
The angel Gabriel, his friend, closer than his breath
If even he made preparations for his death
Tell me, for whom does the world never end?

The death of Prophet Muhammad was a traumatic event for early Muslims, and the *shruk* here reinforces the idea in the Islamic tradition that death is one inescapable truth about life and that it does not even spare prophets and saints. Rahi, however, turns to three different moments and moods of the saint-poet's thinking of death to caution against a simple reading of it as a rehearsal of Islamic themes on death and resurrection:

1. *Veshi dar yelī grezith yiyam*
   Adu' man tsalỳm sandānu'
   Bhugi'u' shọdi manu' lazi kū'ts gatshỳm
   Chuham tsỳtas tsu' meharbānu'[44]

   The poisonous one would pounce on me with a roar
   My soul shall abandon the sandalwood body
   God, I shall be humiliatingly reduced to heart's purity
   I do remember the Gracious One

2. *Kyāh tagi mōtas tu' mōtu' kỳn kānan*
   Kaman javānan chhāngu'r peyi
   Pōni zan shrapay navỳn bānan
   Vạni dith vānan phālav gạyi[45]

   What can Death or its arrows do?
   Death that shattered our youth
   The way water is absorbed by new clay vessels
   The way shops are abandoned at closing time

3. *Shōgu' tsali nīrith panzar mathỳm*
   Lọti lọti tulnam hā hā kār
   Āru'val pōsh zan badan shithỳm
   Bār khọdāyā pāp nivār[46]

The bird will fly away and the cage close in
Slowly there will be a hue and cry
My body will freeze like the flower *āru'val*
God, ease the burden of my soul

I have already introduced the second *shruk* but retain it here to consider it with the other two *shruks* Rahi interprets. Here is Rahman Rahi's interpretation of the three *shruks*:

1. To call the messenger of death the bearer of poison and then to hear the roar of his arrival and fearful that the time has come, and the heart which you spent your whole life indulging, to be abandoned by that cowardly heart to a helplessness, and then in this feeling of helplessness to appear before the Merciful presence of God, pure of intent and overwhelmed by shame, these allied feelings, shapes and forms turn Shaikh's poetic experience into an ecstatic situation.

2. In the second *shruk*, death appears in the form of a hunter who, at the height of the summer of youth, rains down arrows without mercy. They were such buoyant, joyful youth but in no time, shocked and bewildered, they were scattered and their state before death was like that of small droplets of water which are quickly absorbed by a new and dry clay pot. There are also those affluent youth, who before death cast its shadow over them, their shops were the pride and splendor of the bazaar, but now you truly see the whole world in a different light. There is nothing left here: the shopkeepers have disappeared, the shops are empty in the surrounding devastation, and neither can you hear a murmur nor a sound.

3. A similar graphic image is hidden in the third *shruk*. Please imagine a small child who truly cares for a strange bird of colorful plumage. He expects that there would be a time when the bird will regale him with its sweet speech. But when the time draws near, without even raising the slightest suspicion, suddenly the bird escapes. The child slowly becomes conscious of his sudden loss and starts crying and wailing loudly. But in the end the child's body becomes pale like an *āru'val* flower.[47]

Rahi develops some of Nund Rishi's metaphors in his interpretations, and indeed it is possible to forget here if one is on the trail of the poetic thinking of Nund Rishi or Rahman Rahi. But we certainly get a better sense of the world in which Nund Rishi's death is at work. If death has such a menacing countenance and there is no escape from it, it is also a healing. Life is a disease healed by the sweet gift of death:

Maru'g chuy su'h tu' kotū tsalizay
Kheli manzu' kadī tsārith kaṭh
Margu'c sharbath canu' ros nu' bạlịzay
Suli kýthu' gạyās mu'rith kath[48]

Death is a leopard which we never escape
It will sieze its prey from the herd
Death is a sweet drink without which we never heal
Why did I not understand this before?

We witness in Nund Rishi not merely a thinking of death but an experience of death as a healing: *marnu' ros bạlịzay nō* (You will not be cured without dying). Clearly this is not a death that takes place at the end of our life. Nund Rishi is, to borrow the phrase Ravinder Raj Singh uses for Socrates in his book about the thinking of death in Schopenhauer, a death-contemplator.[49] But the contemplation of death-in-life and life-in-death makes possible a new life. Socrates, as we read in Plato's *Phaedo*, had defined philosophy as *thanatos melete*, preparing for death.[50] But such a preparation begins with an ascetic turn away from the world. According to Rahi, the meaninglessness of the world (*gạ̄sil sombru'm vạ̄sil kyāt*: I collected blades of grass/Of what use was this life to me?) and the realization of its illusoriness and poisonousness give Nund Rishi's vision of reality and its capacity for truth-recognition a complete shape and final form.[51] Rahi insists that there is hardly a Kashmiri poet who insists so uncompromisingly on the impermanence of the world and its finitude:

Duniyahas āyey bạ̄j bạ̄j
Sạmith karō bạ̄j baṭh
Tsay brōnth gạyi mōl tu' mạ̄j
Kạ̄tsāh gamu'ts chay vạ̄nij vaṭh[52]

We came into the world as partners
To share our burdens in companionship
You lost even your father and mother
Yet your heart has turned to stone

The life in the family or community offers no shelter against death. Yet it is the companionship that one finds in the family and the community that also eases the burdens of a life that is on its way toward death. One way of ignoring the ubiquity of death that we witness all around us (in our families and communities) is to harden our hearts and turn away from any thinking of death. But that is the fate of death in the community. Rahi quotes another *shruk* that returns to the metaphor of shops at closing time:[53]

Laṛāh laẓu'm manz māḍānas
Ȧndi̠ ȧndi̠ kȧri̠mas taki̠yu' tu' gath
Laṛ rozi yeti̠ tu' bu' gatshu' pānas
Vāṇ gatshi vānas phālav dith[54]

I cast my residence in the middle of the earth
I circumambulate around it and pay obeisance
This dwelling will be left behind and I'll go my own separate way
The way one abandons shops at closing time

The building on earth around which one circumambulates in reverence is left behind much in the same manner that shopkeepers leave behind their shops at closing time.[55] Here we encounter an existential dread of human building with its roots in a traditional Islamic apocalyptic. A questioning of the community (*bāj bāj*, partners), the bazaar (*bāzar*), and the residence (*laṛ*) gathers force through the *shruks*. The longer *shruk* that follows in the Rahi text reveals that Nund Rishi turns to the thinking of death, and the impermanence of life, as the basis of a thoroughgoing social and political critique:

Khānan handẏn yiman rōb khānan
Jānan dapā̠n̠ apā̠ri̠ gatsh
Sọndru' vuchmakh harvakh nāvan
Tsamrō sā̠tẏn duvān latsh
Ṭath māli dīthu'm kapas bovan
Naṣru' me vuch tu' tsu' vuchni gatsh[56]

These intimidating residences of the rich
The moment they see you, they chase you away
I see beautiful women sing in those palaces
And dust being swept with chowries
I see people grow cotton over there
I have seen all this, Nasr, you go and see

In this *shruk*, Nund Rishi addresses his disciple Bābā Nāṣir al-Dīn on the impermanence of structure, power, wealth, and beauty in the world. This is a devastating critique of the Kashmiri elite, whose houses intimidate the poor and who are accused of turning the poor away the moment the latter cross the path to their houses. There is a tension here between the *khān*, a clear allusion to the ruling class, and the *jān* (literally, good), the Kashmiri masses (the use of *khān* here hints toward the new and powerful immigrant settlers who had moved into Kashmir from Iran and Central Asia). Even as the beautiful young women in these houses sing melodious songs and dust is being swept off with chowries, it is the land under the same palaces that, in a different time, is used to grow cotton (the Kashmiri *kapas* is derived from the Sanskrit *karpasam*). The palaces turn into ruins and are reclaimed for farming. The senselessness of the tension between the ruling class and the Kashmiri peasantry becomes all the more clear in the impermanence of the ground that sustains these divisions. The ground on which a palace stands is the same which is reclaimed by the farmlands or even the forest. Perhaps it is even necessary to reclaim it for farming. The earth yields different worlds, and a meditation on the transience of human existence returns us to a contemplation of mortality. But yet there is a political promise hidden in the *shruk*: the palaces of the rich give way to the farmland of the poor. Nund Rishi invites his disciple Bābā Nāṣir al-Dīn, and the reader, to go and examine this situation, and its promise, for themselves.

Rahi has a mode of reading Nund Rishi in which he arrives at the meaning of the *shruk* by filling in the missing metaphors. The meaning of the *shruk* cannot be properly understood unless one approaches it through this attention to what remains outside of it. This is a fundamental difficulty in reading the *shruk*s, which makes their interpretation a difficult task. In the above *shruk*, we see the *khān*s (the chiefs and the nobles) shoo away the poor. The women of these houses are beautiful and sing songs as dust is being swept off with chowries. But the same palace is in ruins with the passage of time, and a day comes when people reclaim the land to grow cotton. Here death not only is a way of thinking one's end(s) but also challenges us to rethink political equality from the standpoint of our existence as temporal beings and the ruination of things and beings.

Let us now turn to another aspect of Nund Rishi's *shruk*s that Rahi brings up in his essay: the asceticism of the poet. As Rahi puts it, in Nund Rishi's poetic universe it is not possible to be in the world and yet not of it.[57] Rahi suggests that asceticism is fundamental to Nund Rishi's thinking even though many recent revisionist accounts stress a final, and Islamic, repudiation of asceticism in Nund Rishi.[58] There are indeed *shruk*s in Nund Rishi that are critical of extreme asceticism, but a closer reading of the *shruk*s reveals that Nund Rishi never really ceased to be critical of a forgetful immersion in life. This attitude is consistent with traditional Sufi pietism and also resembles forms of Kashmiri Hindu and Buddhist asceticism. The overall theme of Nund Rishi's *shruk*s remains death, which he approaches through turning to metaphors of the impermanence of life. The impermanence of life is heightened in the following *shruk*, which Rahi compares, in its greatness, to the poetic experience of the classical Urdu poet Mirza Ghalib (1797–1869), which brings forth a frightful picture (*trahrāvan vōl taṣvīr*) of the ruination of life and leaves you trembling:

Ganbar prakat karān chum kāv
Tīr chanẏm anbar bāvu' kas
Sạri̲ gōm gur tu' wọkhu'li̲ gayạm nāv
Bōr gōm gob tu' trāvu' kas[59]

The crow reveals a serious word that makes it shed
All its feathers that are a heap of dust at its feet
My horse is drowning and my boat has run aground
This burden has become heavy and I cannot even pass it on

There are other variants of this *shruk*, but this is the one quoted by Amin Kamil and Rahman Rahi. For Rahi, Ghalib is the epitome of poetic expression, and in comparing this *shruk* to Ghalib, Rahi offers us his understanding of poetic expression in Nund Rishi.[60] Rahi writes:

> Leaving aside the symbolic meaning to one side (and those symbols which are to be found in this *shruk*, there is a long tradition of such symbols in Kashmiri poetry), the secret situation which is sculpted in this *shruk* appears as frightening, unquiet and helpless. The crow reveals a profound word and the self sheds all its plumage, which collects at its feet in a heap. Such a serious and heavy word that my horse instead of trotting on land drowns in water and my boat instead of floating on the water has run aground.[61]

Rahi misses the metaphorical correspondence that the *shruk* sets up between the metaphor of the horse drowning in waters and the boat that runs aground. It is the horse that should have been on the ground and the boat that should have been on the waters, but everything has been turned upside down. This is a language of crisis, and it persists through much of Nund Rishi's *shruks* except in certain places such as the *shruk* where he speaks of *Hōnzi pāṭhỳn lobmu's tār* (I crossed over like a royal swan). As we shall see in Chapter 4, this language of crisis gathers momentum in Nund Rishi to reveal an apocalyptic thinking at work.

Rahi returns to the tension between poetry and mysticism in Nund Rishi and mitigates it by refusing to draw a distinction between the experience of poetic creation and the experience of the mystical. He understands the relation between Nund Rishi's poetic thinking and Sufi mysticism by making explicit its political meaning:

> Much like the creative use of language in its search for the meaning of experience needs fire of creative imagination, extremes of emotion and the miracle-working of art, so does indeterminate thinking and vision need all of these things to give moving form and body to human situations. If these conditions are not there, even if the thoughts are deep and meaningful, they get paralysed. His personality was such a furnace in which a Prakritic overturning overwhelmed the old and modern springs of faith and thinking to give birth to that plural philosophy of which he himself was the greatest flag-bearer (*'Alamdār*). The stature of *Shaikh al-'Ālam* as a thinker is serious and his poetry is its living evidence. Whenever this philosophy acquires the warmth of feeling in Shaikh's poetry and becomes the vibration of the pulse of his thought, idea becomes movement and movement takes the form of a play and acquires drama's design and grip.[62]

Rahi situates Nund Rishi's mystical poetry in the milieu of north Indian *bhaktī* revolts against classical Hinduism. The task for future readers of Nund Rishi is to approach his philosophy in a relation with not only histories of asceticism in Islam, Hinduism, and Buddhism in Kashmir but also the thinking of such *bhaktī* and Sikh figures as Kabir and Guru Nanak – in other words, to try and make more explicit the relations between poetry, history, and politics in medieval South Asia. Rahi gives us an example of how poetry, history, and politics may appear together in a knot in one of Nund Rishi's most powerful *shruks*:

> *Duniyahkis ṭatis maṭis nāras*
> *Dīshith anāras ku'rim gath*
> *Shaitāṇ laṣhi̱ laj̱im petsi bāras*
> *Rāvu'm tsūras tāras vath*[63]

The fire of desire for this world
I circumambulate around a pomegranate tree
The mound of dry grass catches fire
The thief loses even the path back home

This is not an easy *shruk* to understand, or translate, but Rahi teaches us one way of approaching the *shruk*. In a private interview, Rahi suggested that he was quite surprised about how he had arrived at what is clearly a masterly act of interpretation.[64] Let us turn to Rahi's interpretation of the *shruk* at length in which he illustrates what he means by the hidden drama of ideas in Nund Rishi's poetry:

> A whole dramatic situation hides in this *shruk* as a simile. In Kashmir, in autumn, in the season of the pomegranates, the children slip away to orchards in order to steal fruit. Consider for a moment such a child who, without giving anyone even as much as a hint, leaves his home late in the evening and crosses a small stream to an orchard. He imagines the ripe, juicy pomegranates at the tip of the tree branches and many pleasurable ember-colors take flight in his heart. He is full of desire, overly exuberant and slowly circumambulates the tree. An accident takes place just as he moves a mound of dry grass right under the tree so that he can climb it and reach out to the farthest tips of the highest branches for juiciest pomegranates. As soon as he lifts the mound of grass, it suddenly catches fire. As the flames spread, the watchman and neighbouring residents raise a hue and cry. The child gets nervous and runs. But because of fear, he cannot even find the boat which he had used to cross the stream and his return is blocked by a fast-flowing stream. On the riverbank: the child's remorseful desperation and fear of punishment.[65]

The desire for pomegranates meets the confusion of a self suddenly abandoned by life to face up to a calling of accounts. The fate of human beings in the world is no different from the child in the *shruk* which begins with a mad desire for juicy pomegranates but ends in remorse at the end for the self which is helpless before a final crossing. But even in this *shruk*, the encounter with a final reckoning is a moment of decision. Death is always with you, but it sometimes rushes toward you like a fast-flowing stream. Rahi often resolves such paradoxes in the *shruk*s by turning to an interpretive unity of experience, which even though at times hinted at in Nund Rishi himself, lacks the aporetic force of the antinomies in the *shruk*s. Rahi writes:

> We get a proper sense of the potentiality of creative imagination when because of it consciousness crosses its limits to acquire impressions of different things in a way that despite being dissimilar in appearance, form, effect and manner are at their root a unity. This act matches the capacity of creation in modern painting. Its foundation is simile and wonder. The melting, the halting, arresting, pleasing pictures and collage created in the river of consciousness, you can discern all this here. This is the process because of which, according to Ghalib, the sleeping path awakens with the laughter of flowers and the becoming of trees and animals which take flight in the air of poetry.[66]

The way Rahi struggles with the nearness and distance between mysticism and poetry is at its most obvious in this passage where he explicitly compares Nund Rishi with the Urdu poet Ghalib. Rahi is by training a scholar of Persian poetry where this relation between mysticism and poetry receives an explicit formulation and development. Yet Rahi is quick to add that Nund Rishi's poetry does not have the warmth and flight of Ghalib's poetry but nevertheless it does come close.[67] Even though there isn't the warmth or the flight of Ghalib in the *shruks*, it is not as if Nund Rishi's poetry is totally bereft of it.[68] Rahi struggles to reserve the highest place for poetry, but he also does not abandon Nund Rishi's mysticism. This pushes Rahi to trace a different path to understanding Nund Rishi's poetic thinking:

> The singularity of poetry, its magical potentiality, its fabulous experience, are the essence of those known and unknown elements which together in one usage, we call form, style, or color and it is because of this it becomes easy to recognize the separate and unique voice of the poetic persona. The linguistic matrix matters as much as the elements of form, or the poet's search for meaning or theme; and additionally there is another element of form called syntax where the differences of sound, tone, pitch and accent come into consideration. These elements of poetry, in their different colors and forms, differentiate one poet's sense of reality (*pazar bāsh*) from another poet's sense of reality. Ḥaẕrat Shaikh, in his best moments, brings all these elements into play in his poetry. This is how Nund Rishi establishes the singularity of his poetic Saying and the peculiarity of his expression.[69]

We yet again witness Rahi struggle to elaborate on what he perceives to be the singularity of Nund Rishi's poetry. The only evidence Rahi has in support of this claim is that Nund Rishi's poetry reveals the use of those elements of poetry that were the subject of much reflection in the formalist school of

New Criticism in the history of English literary criticism. The poetry of Nund Rishi is approached by Rahman Rahi in his close readings as a flawed but equally self-contained aesthetic object as the Urdu poetry of Mirza Ghalib. There is hardly a better example from the *shruk*s than the one Rahi quotes to illustrate this:

Hāras nyendu'r payam yāmath poh gōm
Kāras doh ām nu' granz akh
Teli pyōm tsy̆tas yelī vothun koh gōm
Pata'e ām yāmun tu' dopnam pakh[70]

I slipped into deep slumber in early summer
until late autumn was on me
Not a single day of work I put in
I remembered my work only after awakening
had become as difficult as moving a mountain
The Yama came to me then and said: Come!

One of the reasons Rahi cites this *shruk* is for its sheer formal brilliance: the *shruk* maps a journey through life where the work of self-transformation never begins because of neglect until it is too late and death takes us by surprise. Rahi points out how the opposition between *hār* (early summer) and *poh* (late autumn) in the first line and the stress at the end of the second line on the word *akh* (one) deepen our sense of the loss of time.[71] The spiritual action is postponed by the self until the day it becomes as difficult as moving a mountain. Not even a day's work has been made to count before the angel of death (Yama) appears and demands the surrender of life. But the pace of crisis, anticipation of death, is quickened in the second and the last line of the *shruk*.[72] The self, paralyzed by spiritual neglect, can no longer act in the face of death. Yet again we learn from this *shruk* that the theme of death is the true subject of Nund Rishi's poetry.

Rahi also turns to the thinking of death in Nund Rishi in another essay from the same volume, "Lal Dy̆d tu' Shaikh al-'Ālam: Akh sarsarī taqobulī muṭālu'" (Lal Ded and Shaikh al-'Ālam: A Comparative Study), where he offers us a comparative reading of Lal Ded and Nund Rishi. The beginnings of Kashmiri literary culture in the fourteenth century have come down to us in the form of the memory of a relation: the relation of Lal Ded to Nund Rishi. In this later essay, Rahi suggests that Nund Rishi's poetry is imbued with a deep sense of the impermanence of the world: "The impermanence of the world and the inevitability of death, the fierce and deep realization of this, which is found in different places in Shaikh *shruk*s, appears as the life and ornament of his poetry."[73] But this sense of impermanence of the world is also bound up with a certain dread. Rahi begins this essay on Nund Rishi and Lal Ded by sketching out the challenges of such a comparative reading:

> To compare the poetry of Lal Ded and Shaikh al-'Ālam, by all means, remains a difficult task. This is first of all because even after about six hundred years, no basic research has been done on their poetry, which means that there is still much verse about which it is not evident in a reliable and clear way, if it is Shaikh's verse or Lal Ded's verse. The second problem is that so much of their oeuvre is recorded in different manuscripts and books with different diacritical marks. The third reason is that many researchers are still not satisfied that all of the work of these two saint-poets (especially Shaikh al-'Ālam) has become available because new *vākh*s and *shruk*s emerge every now and then. It is obvious then that any opinion under the circumstances about these poets of early Kashmiri would be tentative. The other difficulty for a comparative analysis of these two poets is that they have been very close to each other in certain fundamental beliefs and traces and, for hundreds of years, their verse has moved in history so close to each other that, much like folk poetry, it has most likely been revised to reflect a shared affective life. Quite apart from it, the other difficulty is that more than being poets, both of them have been great spiritual leaders of their time.[74]

There is no real explanation that we find in Rahi about why the two poets have moved so closely together in history that it is hard to definitively ascribe authorship to certain *vākh*s and *shruk*s. Even in this essay, Rahi returns to the question of the difference between mysticism and poetry by arguing that a high spiritual status does not necessarily confer great poetic skill:

> Just as it is not necessary that a Prophet must be a poet, much in the same way it is possible that someone may have acquired great status in the spiritual world but would not be able to express himself or herself in poetry and even if he or she turns to poetry, the expression is not very good. Or it can even be so that sometimes the poet brings forth good verse and sometimes struggles to even find the appropriate words.[75]

We are now familiar with this tension in Rahi's reading of Nund Rishi. The challenge for Rahi is to make sense of the unevenness in the esthetic quality of Nund Rishi's mystical verse. This is Rahi's assessment of Nund Rishi: "… sometimes the poet brings forth good verse and sometimes struggles to even find the appropriate words."[76] But to what degree is this a fair assessment of Nund Rishi? Rahi proposes that a comparative analysis between Nund Rishi and Lal Ded should be accomplished by thinking through the ways in which these two poets express a feeling or experience and then turn to the truth behind that feeling and experience in itself and in closer attention to the color of their expressions.[77] Rahi chooses a *vākh* and a *shruk* about which there is little doubt that one is largely attributed to Lal Ded and the other to Shaikh al-ʿĀlam. Both seem to be expressing a crisis but do so in different and unique ways. Let us take a look at the *vākh* and the *shruk* quoted by Rahi (we have already encountered the *shruk* earlier in this chapter):

Lal Ded:

Nābu'dị bāras atu' ganḍ ḍyol gōm
Deh kād hol gōm hỳku' kehyō
Gọru' sund vanun rāvan tyol pyōm
Pahli ros khyol gōm hỳku' kehyō[78]

I'm carrying this sack of candy, its knot gone slack on
my shoulder
I took a wrong turn and wasted my day, what's to be done?
I'm lost, my teacher's warning blisters me like a whiplash.
This flock has no shepherd, what's to be done?[79]

Shaikh al-ʿĀlam:

Ganbar prakat karān chum kāv
Tīr chanỳm anbar bāvu' kas
Sạri gōm gur tu' wọkhu'lị gayạm nāv
Bār gọbyōm tu' trāvu' kas[80]

The crow reveals a serious word that makes it shed
All its feathers that are a heap of dust at its feet
My horse is drowning and my boat has run aground
This burden has become heavy and I cannot even pass it on

Rahi offers us a detailed comparative reading of these two *shruk*s as a way of drawing attention to the difference and identity between Lal Ded and Nund Rishi:

> These examples reveal to us an identity of experience. Both deal with a burden which is heavy. Both reveal a feeling of loss and because of that a restlessness and helplessness becomes visible. The Saying of a guru becomes an ember of loss (*rāvan tyol*) in one and in the other the trembling crow reveals a body shorn of all feathers which lie at its feet in a heap. The anxiety in the one about the herd losing its shepherd and the bewilderment of a boat which has run aground in the other. The color of the metaphor of the sweet burden of rock-candy in the one and the ambiguity of the burden in the other. The difficulty of the loosening of the knot on the sweet burden in the one and the heaviness of the burden in the other as well as the crisis of the temptation to pass it on. The guru's unsaid words in the one and the silent speaking of the crow in the other. If the sweet burden of Lal Ded is the world in its everydayness, the burden of Ḥaẓrat Shaikh is the emptiness of human existence. If it is difficult to leave the world behind because of its sweetness, it is difficult to leave behind the burden because it is nothing other than one's existence. The experience and the expression of both is more or less the same. There is only one thing which does not appear to the eye in the same way and this can help take us from one level of interpretation (expression) to the other (ideas) and help us distinguish between Lal Ded and Shaikh al-ʿĀlam as poets. Let us call this unique matter inner strife. In Lal Ded's poetry, there is an important metaphor called the sweet burden which because of the loosening of the knot has become heavy and difficult and the reason for one's suffering is precisely because it is a sweet burden which Adam [*sic*] does not want to throw away. To leave it behind is to leave behind the sugar of the world. If we consider this sweet burden to be the world and reflect, a living and human situation appears before us. Contrary to this, Ḥaẓrat Shaikh's *shruk* only speaks of a difficult burden which he cannot pass on to anyone else. Or, in other words, this burden is his own. That means if he could pass it on to someone else, he would do so. But he cannot do so. His helplessness is in this that he alone must carry this burden. We come across a tragic situation in one and in the other a world of helplessness. One illuminates the human situation more than the other and as such may appear to be closer and appealing to us as readers.[81]

We see Rahi privilege Lal Ded's poetry as being more near to the human situation as it speaks of an ek-static existence: the *bār* (burden) in Lal Ded is a sweet, ecstatic burden. But the *bār* (burden) in Nund Rishi is *gob* (serious, heavy). One discloses a human, existential situation and the other the relation to an eschatological end. The human situation, according to Rahi, has the form of strife in Lal Ded. Rahi writes: "In Lal Ded, often instead of a mere inner conflict, a struggle emerges. A struggle to bring a difficulty in control, a struggle to attain a purpose, a life-to-death struggle to find a Beloved."[82] Rahi gives us more examples:

Ȧmi̱ panu' sodras nāvi chas lamān
Kati bōzi day myōn meti diy tār[83] (Lal Ded)

Look at me:
towing a boat over vast waters with such slender sewing-thread
Where will my shining one hear me?
If only he would ferry
even me.[84]

Shaikh al-'Ālam says:

Dū'this kalkī kālas manzu'y
Honzi pạthỳn lobmu's tār[85] (Shaikh al-'Ālam)

In this Dark Age
I crossed over to the other side
A royal swan

Rahi further explicates the distinction between Lal Ded and Nund Rishi by turning to the uniqueness of Lal Ded's poetic vision:

> Lalla holds her heart between her hands because of this inner struggle and subjects our love and loss to torture. The destining and the height in Ḥaẕrat Shaikh, his spiritual greatness and stature, reduces us to respect. The inner strife in Lal Ded and her struggle does not become the reason for her involvement in any idea or experience, and that's why in her poetry in different places there is a constant flare of feelings and the revolutions of emotion intensify and confer on her ideas and thinking, doubts and prayers (*sharan tu' dāyan*), faith and beliefs (*yatshan tu' patshan*), her words and Sayings (*lafẕan tu' kathan*), the form of great poetry.[86]

Rahi suggests that Nund Rishi's address is on the borders of *k̲hiṯāb* (lecture, preaching):[87] "Even then the truth is that compared to Lalla *vākh*, in Shaikh *shruk* there is more preaching than dialogue with the self; and because of the warmth of ownness (*pānnyār*) we see in Lal Ded, we miss its lack in the poetry of Shaikh al-'Ālam."[88] It is difficult to guess what Rahi implies by Lal Ded's ownness and how he can suddenly claim that Nund Rishi is often on the borders of *khiṭāb* when he himself has put so much effort in his other essay to claim Nund Rishi for the singularity of poetry as opposed to mere *khiṭāb*. Rahi also speaks of some other critical differences between Lal Ded and Nund Rishi:

> Lal reveals more of the different stages of her spiritual journey and the distance that separates the human from the divine and expresses her state and emotions about these stages on the way to union, the union of the part and the whole which she extols.
>
> Contrary to this, Ḥaẓrat Shaikh is deeply anxious about the weaknesses and faults of the human and appears to be trembling with the fear of death and this is true that in this affair no Kashmiri poet can measure up to Shaikh al-ʿĀlam.[89]

Rahi turns to an essay by the Kashmiri literary critic Shafi Shauq, who also draws a distinction between Lal Ded and Nund Rishi on the basis of their standpoint on the question of death:

> Shafi Shauq is right that the fear of death is there much more in Shaikh al-ʿĀlam than Lal Ded, but it would not be correct perhaps to go as far as saying that Shaikh al-ʿĀlam favors self-mortification to the degree of masochism. In the first place, Ḥaẓrat Shaikh's poetry is as free and pure of the sexual pleasure associated with masochism as Lal Ded's *kalām*. The practice which Shauq *Ṣāb* calls giving pain to the self is a way of controlling the *nafs*, the seat of the self, which is the same action which Lal Ded calls killing *lōbh, manmath, mad* etc.[90]

Rahi refuses to concede Shafi Shauq's point that for Nund Rishi there is just one path to salvation and that is to turn one's back on the world. Rahi writes: "The truth is that, much like Lal Ded, Ḥaẓrat Shaikh too believes that one can attain to a spiritual truth while being in the world and he too is a believer in *Yami yati vov tām tati lūnō* (The one who sows shall reap)."[91] The fear of death in Nund Rishi does appear, according to Rahi, to approach a form of necrophobia, but nevertheless this still does not justify calling Shaikh al-ʿĀlam's death dangerous and Lal Ded's death pleasing.[92] Rahi quotes a verse where Shaikh al-ʿĀlam appears closer to the thinking of death in Lal Ded:

> *Yādas taḥndis doh dyn barizi*
> *Zindu' āsith marizi nu' zānh*[93]

You should spend your day and night remembering Him
If you live, you'll never die

For Rahi, the inconsistency in Nund Rishi's thinking of death raises a question about its poetic value. But he never considers the possibility that such internal inconsistency is constitutive of Nund Rishi's discourse. Some of the reflections of Rahi on Nund Rishi appear excessive as Rahi advances a mode of reading in which the reader's creative imagination must enter the world of the poet's experience. Rahi even suggests that the insistence on death in Nund Rishi may be a spiritual strategy:

> The other point is that in stressing on death so much, the purpose of *Ḥaẓrat-e Shaikh* is not only to prepare a human being for death but also to make him or her realize that if the end of this life is ashes and dust then why this clamour of 'what should I do! what should I do!' and the hubris, hatred and violence.[94]

Here Rahi appears to touch upon the political implications of Nund Rishi's mystical poetry. Rahi's final word about the difference between Nund Rishi and Lal Ded's poetic thinking is this:

> If Lal roasts our heart on the fire of love, Shaikh does nothing less than move a mountain. Lal searches for herself in the fields of Nothingness. But Lal moves towards the inside from the outside. The Shaikh leaves behind the world and takes to the forest.[95]

Rahi is closer here to Shauq's criticism than he is prepared to concede. Nonetheless, Rahi, much like Azad, does recognize the unique aesthetic quality of Nund Rishi's mystical verse. Yet Rahi is unable to unequivocally express that unique aesthetic quality and hints that its origins are to be found in Nund Rishi's mystical experience. The point Rahi is trying to make is that this mystical experience is not inaccessible to language and that one draws near to it in poetry. For Rahi, poetic creations and mystic experience appear in a relation which does not acquire a clear formulation. Perhaps what Rahi misses is that Nund Rishi's mysticism is not merely an aesthetic experience but aims at the spiritual and political transformation of the world. It is in the end in their thinking of the world that differences appear between Lal Ded and Nund Rishi's poetic and political thinking. The question of death is not only a way of thinking the political in Lal Ded and Nund Rishi but also a way of approaching the distinctions in the thinking of these two saint-poets.

One way of approaching Nund Rishi's existential thinking of death is to approach it in relation to Martin Heidegger's existential thinking of death. I am not here trying to suggest that we read Nund Rishi in Heideggerian terms but that we arrive at an understanding of the existential thinking of death in Nund Rishi that Rahi is at pains to develop (like that "giant negative, black/and white, still undeveloped" that Agha Shahid Ali speaks of in his poem "Postcard from Kashmir").[96] For both Nund Rishi and Heidegger, the question of death appears in relation to the possibility of an authentic existence in which we are not in the fallenness of the they-self (in Heideggerian terms) or a state of forgetfulness (in Nund Rishi's terms). Heidegger develops his thinking of death between sections 46 and 53 of *Being and Time* (and here I restrict myself to Heidegger's thinking of death in *Being and Time*). For Heidegger, the question that turns us to the thinking of death is the possibility of our own death.[97] Nund Rishi repeatedly brings us up against this possibility in the *shruks*. The *shruks* bring our death into sharp focus by putting our lives and their meaning into question. The face-to-face encounter that Nund Rishi sets up with death reveals the ideal reader of Nund Rishi to be someone who is contemplating his or her own death. We should first of all eliminate any misunderstanding that may arise from the fact that Nund Rishi often also speaks of a life-beyond-death. Heidegger, as we know, refuses to address the question of a life-beyond-death: "As long as I have not asked about Dasein in its structure and as long as I have not defined death in what it is, I cannot even rightly ask what would come after Dasein in connection with its death."[98] We would here elide the differences between Heidegger's Dasein and Nund Rishi's forgetful subject and rather explore the similarities between their existential analytic of our being as human beings. Death is neither a perishing (the actual physical event of death) nor a demise (the collapse of our worlds that accompanies perishing) for Heidegger but mortality as our essential possibility as human beings.[99] My death is my ownmost possibility: this ownmost possibility is the difficult burden Nund Rishi speaks of which cannot be passed on to someone else (*bōr gōm gob tu' trāvu' kas*). We can now see the limitations of Rahi's criticism that Nund Rishi is crushed by the burden of death and turns his back on the everyday strife of the human situation. Rather, the human situation appears more clearly at stake in Nund Rishi's thinking of death. Yet this takes place in an Islamic eschatological register which shares much in common with Heidegger's philosophy, a philosophy that counterposes the certainty of death to the Cartesian "I think, therefore I am!":

"This certainty, that 'I myself am in that I will die,' is *the basic certainty of Dasein itself*."[100] Nund Rishi turns to this "basic certainty" of human existence in the following *shruk*:

Sarphas tsạlizē astas khandas
Su'has tsạlizē kruhas tām
Dīndāras tsạlizē vaharas khandas
Mōtas tsạlizē nu' achi muhas tām

You can run away from a snake to an arm's length
You can run away from a lion for a few miles
You can run away from a priest for a year
You cannot escape death even by the distance of an eyelash[101]

This *shruk* discloses the same mood of anxiety and anticipation we encounter in such *shruks* earlier as *Ganbar prakat karān chum kāv*. Anxiety brings us face-to-face with our mortality. But this facing up to mortality appears bound up with the owning up to a responsibility for one's actions. As Nund Rishi puts it in a refrain from a longer poem: *Yus kari gọngal suy kariy krāv* (Only the one who sows shall reap). It is to this situation of choosing one's choosing that Nund Rishi's *shruks* push us by holding the self responsible to its mortality. Nund Rishi is critical of any lack of resoluteness in choosing an authentic possibility for the self: *Kyāh karu' kyāh karu' tsoliy nu' zāth* (You could never rid yourself of this "What shall I do? What must I do?"). The legends about Nund Rishi in the different hagiographies speak of his own failure at different human skills before his retreat to the forest: his brothers initiate him into thieving, but he disappoints them and he also loses his apprenticeship with a weaver because of his abstract ruminations about weaving.[102] This failure in the world opens up a more fundamental possibility for action: an authentic relationship to the self and others.

Resolutely facing up to one's mortality involves existing in the face of death. This Heideggerian idea resolves the seeming contradiction between Nund Rishi's dismissal of death as inconsequential and the fear and trembling to which the thinking of death reduces him (which was a matter of unease for Rahman Rahi). The fear of death (anxiety, in Heideggerian terms) brings a sense of urgency to human action. This is why there is no danger of the Sufi (and the Kashmiri) tradition interpreting Nund Rishi's call to "die before you die" as an invitation to suicide. To "die before you die" is the hope of a new life.

A world to which we die is transformed by our dying to it. Nund Rishi calls death the "sweet drink" which "heals": *Margu'c sharbath canu' ros nu' bạliz̤ay* (Death is a sweet drink without which you shall not heal). His thinking of death is not a morbid obsession, as claimed by Shafi Shauq, but a healing that begins with the owning up to one's death.[103] There is yet another question which we need to address: does immortality appear as a solution to the problem of death in Nund Rishi? There are clearly *shruk*s that speak of immortality (as an Islamic afterlife), but it seems clear that what is more immediately at stake is life in the here and now. Even though Nund Rishi does speak of an afterlife, it is the *shruk*s about a dying to the world that give us a better understanding of his idea of death. For Nund Rishi, death is not a transition to an afterlife that takes place at the end of life. Death is existential and not merely actual. The afterlife is a ruse to speak of this life.

Nund Rishi also speaks of the death of others. Arguably, it is often the death of the others that Nund Rishi uses to stage an existential encounter with death in the *shruk*s. Heidegger approaches this phenomenon in Section 47 of *Being and Time*: "In the dying of the Other we can experience that remarkable phenomenon of Being which may be defined as the change-over of an entity from Dasein's kind of Being (or life) to no-longer-Dasein."[104] Nund Rishi brings this transition from being to the nothingness of death into sharp focus through images and metaphors which produce a shock in the reader. But there is no way of experiencing this dying of others except in an objective sense. That is a problem with this idea of death and clearly something which Nund Rishi strives against in his own effort to move from the death of the others to an existential concept of death. For, as Heidegger puts it, "death is in every case mine [death is always essentially my own: the Stambaugh translation]."[105] We must move beyond dying as the death of others to dying as the existential concept of death.[106] There is certainly in Nund Rishi an Islamic concept of death as a state of difficult transition from one mode of being (life) to the other (afterlife). But against this Islamic background, Nund Rishi advances an existential thinking of death.

Death is, for Heidegger, *distinctively* impending (or, an eminent imminence: Stambaugh translation).[107] If Rahi calls death as the fundamental theme of Nund Rishi's mystical poetry, it is death's imminence which I consider to be at stake in Nund Rishi's thinking of death. The reason Rahman Rahi turns often to the Urdu poet Ghalib in speaking of Nund Rishi is the mood of angst, or dread, in relation to death in both the poets. As Ghalib puts it in a couplet from one of his famous *ghazal*s:

> *Maut kā ek din mu'ayan hai*
> *Nīnd kyūñ rāt bhar nahiñ ātī*[108]
>
> A day is fixed for my death
> Why then do I get no sleep at night?

This anxiety about death is not to be confused with fear. As Heidegger puts it:

> Anxiety in the face of death must not be confused with fear in the face of one's demise. This anxiety is not an accidental or random mood of "weakness" in some individual, but as a basic state-of-mind of Dasein, it amounts to the disclosedness of the fact that Dasein exists as thrown Being *towards* its end.[109]

It is from death that life gets its meaning. This is the sense in which Ghalib speaks of death, and this is the death we encounter in Nund Rishi. But in structures of everydayness, death often appears as the idle talk about "one dies."[110] We can call this our ordinary understanding of death. It is this evasion of death in everyday life that is the subject of Nund Rishi's *shruk*s on death. It is the bustle of the bazaar in the day where one finds oneself suddenly abandoned at night. It is the buoyancy of the youth on which rain the arrows of death. But it is not as if everydayness is oblivious of death. Nund Rishi turns to the everydayness of death by speaking of it as water being absorbed by dry clay vessels or as shops at closing time. That is why the risk in traditional theological reading of Nund Rishi is that we might reduce his thinking of death to merely revealing the certainty of death. We encounter this idea of death in the reception of Nund Rishi's thinking of death as "idle talk" about death (for instance, in multiple religious exegeses of his mystical poetry which are published every year by different Islamic presses in Srinagar). But Nund Rishi in his *shruk*s about death uncovers the inappropriate covering up of death in everydayness. We must recall here the legend from Nund Rishi's hagiographies when his wife visits him in the forest and implores him to return home. But when Nund Rishi refuses, she abandons her two children outside his cave – both of whom are later found dead.[111] This is a moment of scandal in Nund Rishi's biography, and he is about to be arrested for this crime. But the police chief who comes to arrest him is converted by Nund Rishi in a single glance.[112]

One way of reading this difficult legend is the way it reveals Nund Rishi's unsettling of the traditional thinking of death as "idle talk" about death.

What is an existential thinking of death? In *Being and Time,* Heidegger poses the possibility of an authentic being-toward-death which he then makes explicit in Section 53, where he proposes the project of an existing being-toward-death:

> ... anticipation reveals to Dasein its lostness in the they-self, and brings it face to face with the possibility of being itself, primarily unsupported by concernful solicitude, but of being itself, rather, in an impassioned *freedom towards death* – a freedom which has been released from the Illusions of the "they," and which is factical, certain of itself, and anxious. (Emphasis in the original)[113]

Nund Rishi's *shruk*s about death do not then disclose a morbid obsession with death ("masochism" in Shafi Shauq's reading) but an impassioned freedom toward death beyond the comforts of all idle talk about it. The *bhaktī* poet Kabir celebrates this moment of reversal in relation to one's attitude to death in these words: "Kabir, death that the world is afraid of, brings me joy/Supreme bliss one attains only upon dying."[114] The existential idea of death in Nund Rishi also helps clarify the seeming contradiction between the impossibility of death and its imminence in Nund Rishi's *shruk*s, where Nund Rishi can at the same time say *Kyāh tagi mōtas* (What can death do?) and *Mōtas tsạlizē nu' achi muhas tām* (You cannot escape death even by the distance of an eyelash). Nund Rishi's *kyāh tagi mōtas* recalls the words of the New Testament: "O death, where is thy victory? O death, where is thy sting?"[115] Nund Rishi keeps calling to *Marnas brōnth mar* (Die before you die) and reminds his readers *Marith martabu' peyi* (Only in losing yourself to death will you find yourself).[116] The ordinary understanding of death is consistently challenged in the *shruk*s and an existential understanding of death presses itself upon us.

What does it mean to "die before you die"? Jacques Derrida, following Socrates, connects the dying before death to nothing less than the task of philosophy:

> The *Phaedo* explicitly names philosophy: it is the attentive anticipation of death, the care brought to bear upon dying, the meditation on the best way to receive, give, or give oneself death, the experience of a vigil over the possibility of death, and over the possibility of death as impossibility.[117]

As Socrates puts it himself: "... those who pursue philosophy aright study nothing but dying and being dead."[118] The scholar of Sufism Annemarie Schimmel reminds us that death is the gateway to life for the Sufis, and the eternal life opened up by death in Islamic poetry is often likened to a spring.[119] For Nund Rishi, a Sufi dying to life is the beginning of a proper relation between the self and God. A call to such a dying is a call to wake up from a complacent slumber to the possibility of a meaningful existence in the world. The relation with death is the condition of possibility for the necessary solitude that makes possible the decisive human action toward self-transformation.

There is a strong resemblance between the Judeo-Christiano-Islamic understanding of death we encounter in Nund Rishi and Heidegger's existential thinking of death. It is not that Heidegger is repeating themes of Christianity at the ontological level or Nund Rishi is doing much the same with Islamic themes but that both Christianity and Islam appear to have at their foundation an existential phenomenon accessible only to a spiritual practitioner (Heidegger, of course, presents such phenomenon in purely existential terms). One could then go as far as to say that not only is Nund Rishi uncovering an existential idea of death but that he is also situating death as the existential phenomenon at the heart of Islam (more so in the moments where he repeats the Qur'ānic thinking of death). As such, Nund Rishi's Sufi understanding of a voluntary death, the call to "die before you die," also draws upon and transforms the more traditional Islamic understanding of death based upon the Qur'ān and the collections of the sayings of Prophet Muhammad called the *ḥadīth*. There are about 165 Qur'ānic verses and thousands of *ḥadīth* that deal with death in Islam.[120] The Sufi call to "die before you die" must then also be read in relation to the traditional Islamic understanding of death. Even more so because Nund Rishi develops his existential thinking of death against the background of medieval Sufi transformations of the traditional Islamic understanding of death.

Death of mortals, in Islam, is a matter of the will of God. Most Muslims recite the Qur'ānic formula "Surely we are for God, and to Him we shall return" (2:156) at a time of difficulty or death, and this gives us the idea that death appears in Islam as a moment of passage in the journey of man, which begins much before his birth and ends much after his death, in relation to a nearness or distance from God.[121] This is a journey predetermined by God. Death is something which is individual in each and every case in the Islamic tradition, but it is also a threshold to a new, albeit different, life. The Apocalypse is, in the Qur'ān, the Event (Al-waqi'ah) to which death points as a provisional stopover after the soul goes into a phenomenological deep-freeze called the *barzakh*. John Bowker writes that Islam "represents the understanding of death, in the western religious history and tradition, at its furthest extreme of formalisation."[122] Clearly that formalization appears time and again in Nund Rishi (for instance, in the *shruks* about the trials and tribulations of the grave, a fundamental theme in the Islamic tradition) but is expressed with much more force in Nund Rishi's engagement with the apocalyptic (a subject I take up in Chapter 4). In one of his *shruks*, Nund Rishi connects the question of death with the practice of reading the Qur'ān. For Nund Rishi, the experience of reading the Qur'ān is, to borrow a phrase from Jacques Derrida, that "which leaves nothing intact":[123]

Qur'ān parān kōnō mūdukh
Qur'ān parān goy nō sūr
Qur'ān parān zindu' kÿthu' rūdukh
Qur'ān parān dod Manṣūr

Did you not die after reading the Qur'ān?
Did you not burn to ashes after reading the Qur'ān?
How did you survive after reading the Qur'ān?
Manṣūr set himself on fire after reading the Qur'ān[124]

There appears in Nund Rishi a relation between the experience of reading the Qur'ān and a dying before death. But such a reading of the Qur'ān is different from any traditional reading and brings the self into a mode of crisis. Reading the Q'urān here is a metaphor for an existential encounter with death. This experience of dying as a living catastrophe is often approached by Nund Rishi as an event in inner space – a cataclysm that leaves nothing intact. Reading must then resemble a dying. There is no other way of reading the Qur'ān but in this coming face-to-face with one's death.

In his classic study *Muhammad's Thoughts on Death: A Thematic Study of the Qur'anic Data*, Thomas O'Shaughnessy points out that the subject of death occupies "a place of growing frequency and importance in the Qur'an as one passes from the Meccan to the Medinan period" of the life of Prophet Muhammad.[125] The earliest uses of death in the Qur'ān are metaphorical and from the Meccan *sūrahs*. O'Shaughnessy quotes two Qur'ānic verses (50:11 and 25:49) that speak of a dead land which is made alive by rain.[126]

The Qur'ān also speaks of a "dead earth."[127] The earliest occurrence of death in the Qur'ān is in relation to these nature metaphors used in what O'Shaughnessy designates as sign passages, and this theme then slides over into the theme of God's omnipotence.[128] The third set of occurrences is traced by O'Shaughnessy to the analogies of the death of disbelief and the death in hell. The Qur'ān in the Medinan period turns gradually from the theme of death to the related one of the transitoriness of life: "the life one leaves behind at death is not a worthy object of attachment, certainly not a thing to be clung to."[129] Nund Rishi directly quotes a Qur'ānic verse which proclaims the universality of death in one of his *shruks*: *Kullu nafsin zaiqat al-maut* (Every soul shall taste death, Qur'ān 3:185).[130] This universality of death is affirmed in the Qur'ān three times in this formula, "Every soul shall taste death," a rabbinic expression that also runs through the New Testament.[131] O'Shaughnessy writes: "'Tasting' is a broad term in the Qur'ān and is often equivalent to 'perceiving' or 'feeling,' for example, God's mercy or grace...."[132] But what does it mean to taste death? Hussam S. Timani quotes the following Prophetic *ḥadīth*:

> God communicated to Adam the following: "O Adam! Go on your pilgrimage before something happens to you." Adam replied: "What is going to happen to me, O God?" Then God answered: "Something that you are not aware of, that is death." "What is death?" Adam replied. God said: "You will taste it."[133]

But what would it mean for the living to taste death? What would be involved in cultivating a taste for one's own death? This is different from a Heideggerian anticipation of death. Sometimes death in the Qur'ān is viewed as a release from a burdensome life.[134] Yet everyone must go through the agony of death. *Sakarat al-maut* (the agony of death) is a phrase which has passed into Kashmiri language from Arabic and is still in use.[135] In Sūrah 50, the Qur'ān speaks of this pain: "The palsy of death will surely come. This is what you wished to avert."[136] The agony of death is not only unpredictable and inescapable but also irrational and oppressive. The Qur'ān also employs *adraka*, "catches up with," in relation to death.[137] Death always catches up with human beings. It is this theme of death's stealthy operations that Nund Rishi invokes through the metaphor of thievery. Death is called *lazal tsūr*, a stealthy thief, by Nund Rishi in one of his *shruks*. Yet there is, as we have already observed, a difference between a voluntary dying and death in Nund Rishi. The call to a voluntary dying in Nund Rishi can be traced to the purported *ḥadīth* widely disseminated by the Sufis: "Die before you die."[138] The question for us is not the authenticity or inauthenticity of this *ḥadīth* but its centrality to the Sufi tradition.[139] Nund Rishi often repeats it in his verses in phrases like *Marnas brōnth mar* (Die before you die). This invitation to one's own death is a fundamental recurring motif in Nund Rishi's poetry. For instance, let us consider the following *shruk*:

Manas khay kās yithu' kāsi ạnas
Tavu' zānas sạt gatshiy zān
Talu' talu' kyāh chhuy shrehuk pānas
Marnas brōnth mar suy chuy gyān[140]

Polish your heart as if a mirror
You will then recognize the Familiar One
Why this deep attachment to the self?
Die before you die: this is true knowledge

A tension emerges here again between the Qur'ānic concept of death as a moment of transition, reckoning, catastrophe that must give way to an Islamic afterlife and the concept of death as a form of knowledge and practice that leads to a transformation of the self. In the Qur'ān, death also carries the meaning of "a symbol of a relatively fixed state of disbelief."[141] "Die before you die," therefore, could also mean to die to the self in order to avoid the death of disbelief and thereby gain a second life in eternity. But it could also hint at a secret knowledge of the self implied in the Neoplatonic idea of polishing the mirror of the heart.

Death is and is not universal. As the Bosnian Islamic Studies scholar Amila Buturovic reminds us:

> Death is subject to appropriation, fascination, and often veneration; it is taken hostage by multiple disciplinary and cultural forms and sensibilities. It is a representational category. It may be universal biologically but it is not universal conceptually.[142]

In the pre-Islamic cultures of Arabia, a socially meaningful life ended with death, but death was also a figure of fate.[143] The Qur'ān (45:24) itself gives us an example of what the pre-Islamic attitudes were like: "Yet they say: 'There is nothing but the life of this world. We die and we live, and only time annihilates us.'"[144] In the same verse, the Qur'ān adds: "Yet they have no knowledge of this: They only speculate."[145] Buturovic comments:

> The *dahr* – translated variably as time, destiny, or fate – is the guiding principle of pre-Islamic cosmology that carries no particular fascination with constructing immortality. Like *maniyya* – fate or destiny – *dahr* is unpredictable and wicked in its workings in the *dunya* (the world), subjecting the living to its whims and leaving them with a feeling of having no control over their existence.[146]

This view of a resigned acceptance of death as fate had determined pre-Islamic Arab life. And it is precisely this resignation to fate that Nund Rishi, following the Qur'ānic revelation, challenges in his meditations on death. But Nund Rishi radicalizes the Islamic understanding of death by going beyond merely affirming faith in a life-beyond-death to death as a head-on existential encounter with the meaning of life in the present. That meaning is hard to tease out between the different registers that the *shruk*s move through rapidly, that is, the Islamic, the Hindu, and the Buddhist. Nund Rishi does not only simply hold out an Islamic hope for an eternal existence in the afterlife (even though many *shruk*s do deal with this subject) but turns to the power of death in transforming individual (and communal) existence. The thinking of death in Nund Rishi's *shruk*s can then be read at the same time as a repetition of traditional Islamic understanding of death as well as an existential understanding of death closely tied to his political thinking.

From al-Ghazālī, Ibn Sīna, to Ibn Miskawayh, a morbid fear of death came to be seen in the history of Islamic philosophy as a moral ill.[147] But the freedom from fear of death did not mean that one did not remember death: remembrance of death and the afterlife remained central to Islamic spiritual practice. Nund Rishi often turns to this remembrance of death, trembling with fear about a final reckoning. In the following *shruk*, he sees the world as a trap and a "dying before death" as the only possibility of action in it:

> *Shiv chuy zạ̄vyul zāl vahạ̄rith*
> *Tiy chuy marun tirath kath*
> *Zindu' nay marakh adu' kavu' zi mạrith*
> *Pānu' manz pān kad vÿtsạ̄rith kath*[148]
>
> Śiva has cast a delicate net
> That is death, not the one that awaits you in a sacred city
> If you don't die before you die, that is no death
> You must search for the self in the self

Nund Rishi invokes Śiva's net and an Islamic eschatological crossing to speak of a mystic self-recognition (*pānu' manz pān kad vỳtsạ̄rith*) which can be traced back to both Kashmiri Śaiva and Sufi traditions. Śiva has woven this world as a thin and delicate net, and the only way to escape it is a voluntary death. Here the dying resembles not a cataclysmic encounter but a kenotic self-emptying. Even though the *shruk* is about death and a dying before death, it also calls for a searching of the self to reach the self. *Vỳtsạ̄r*, or thinking, plays a fundamental role in this searching as a dying. Nund Rishi binds an ascetic searching of the self to *vỳtsạ̄r* (the task of thinking) and a dying before death.

The attitudes to death in Islamic thought kept changing over time. This is at its most obvious in the gradual supplementation of the Qur'ānic notion of the separation of the soul from the body with the idea of the grave as a place for post-mortem punishment. Buturovic writes:

> The tomb, far from being a resting place, had by al-Ghazali's times been conceptualized as a place of change. As Leor Halevi suggests, by the mid-eighth century, the tomb had already come to be understood as the place of punishment and possible redemption of sins although the religious function of that punishment was not entirely clear. Rejecting the Mu'tazalite denial that the tomb houses any real experiences, Muslim traditionists sought to assign to the grave a purgative function for those who had not asked for forgiveness for their sins before they passed away, and a punitive function for those whose sinful and bad acts had taken them to the point beyond redemption. In that sense, the Qur'anic notion of the precipitous ejection of the soul from the body to the outer spheres of existence is gradually replaced, in post-Qur'anic times, by a notion of a more approximate bond between the body and the spirit in the *barzakh* of the grave.[149]

We could read many of the *shruks* on bodily torments after death as Nund Rishi's affirmation of such a traditionalist position. The Qur'ān does not offer us many details on the actual process of death except that the soul of the dying person rises to the throat (56:82) and that death is a kind of a "flooding-in process [*ghamarāt al-maut*] at which time angels stretch forth their hands and ask that the souls be given over to them."[150] The angel of death, 'Izrā'īl, immense and fearsome to behold, appears with death to demand that a human being surrender his or her soul. The wider Islamic tradition adds to this the detailed narratives on the punishments of the grave (*'adhāb al-qabr*) and the questioning by the angels Munkar and Nakīr.[151] These two angels are also fearsome and ask a human being difficult questions about the content of his or her faith.[152] Nund Rishi addresses the theme of the questioning by the angels Munkar and Nakīr in one of the *shruks*:

Nakīr tu' Munkar javābas vasan
Parbat tsasan hābat sāt
Shūblis pānas māran tu' dasan
Bāch tu' pothar mō vasan sāt
Kuniy su' zanis chim āvasun
Lasan pāy natu' maran kāt
Bukri pỳthu' yeli kafan kasan
Saraf tu' gunsu' vasan sāt[153]

The angels Nakīr and Munkar shall descend on you
The mountains shall shrink back in fear
Your beloved body tormented and torn
No companions or children shall be in the grave with you
I must crumble to pieces on my own
I must tread with care
Before the shroud is tightened on my bier
And the snakes and reptiles enter my grave

Nund Rishi turns to the horrific images of traditional Islamic eschatology to shock the listener into a recognition of his self as a being-toward-death. Nund Rishi often turns to the experiences of *adhāb-e qabr* (the punishments of the grave), but he also uses the fear of these punishments of the grave to provoke human beings to reflect on their lives and actions:

Ådijan sapnī anjaru'h panjarō
Tsỳtas pāvay avalim rāth
Pānas chānis gatshi zaru' zarō
Kyāh karu' kyāh karu' tsoluy nu' zāth[154]

Your bones will be shattered and scattered
You shall remember it all on the first night
Your body will be broken into pieces
You never gave up on – What shall I do? What shall I do?

The call to "die before you die" need then be seen not only as an owning up to one's death but also as an owning up to one's life. It is precisely such an owning up which prepares one for death and liberates the self from crippling fear. The fear of death should only be there in those who have not led righteous lives, according to the Qur'ān, and not for those who have led righteous lives.[155] Nund Rishi keeps returning to this idea of righteous living in many of his *shruks* (for instance, in the *shruk* about *sọ zan*, the righteous, and *kọ zan*, the unrighteous, that I discuss in Chapter 4).[156] The question now is not merely about how one lives in the world, or after death, but also of how one must transform oneself to live properly in the world in preparation of death. For instance, Nund Rishi says in one of his *shruks*:

Asi brōnth yim āy timav yotsh patu'
Choni dapu' dapu' manz hāsil kyāt
Maranas chum yūt kyāh trapu' trapu'
Gāsil sọmbrām vāsil kyāt[157]

Those who came before us also wished to die last
You achieve nothing from this empty talk
Why even this mad rush to death?
I gathered mere empty straw, what did I gain from life?

It is then neither in delaying one's death nor in a restless wishing for it that one owns up to one's death. A total absorption in the world might resemble a rush to death. It is in recognizing the transitoriness of life for the sake of life that one owns up to one's death. A life lived without owning up to one's death is like gathering dry stalks of grass. The recognition of life's transitoriness sharpens our engagement with it. Death is then not an event that bookends our life but a certainty that shapes it.

The form of life-beyond-death as a subject has received far more attention in the Islamic intellectual tradition than the theme of a dying before death. Sufism, for instance, transformed the Qur'ānic concept of death by rearticulating the "relationship between God, the dead and the living, as well as ... body, spirit and soul"[158] through the idea of a voluntary dying, a dying before death, and, in certain moments, its rearticulation of the concept of *nafs* (ego or self). The Sufi difference in the articulations of death can be traced back to the seminal text of al-Qushayrī (*Al-Risāla*) that reveals, according to Buturovic, "a qualitative repositioning toward death in Sufi discourse and practice from the one associated with mainstream teachings."[159] One key repositioning is in relation to the *nafs*, which acquires in Sufism the meaning of ego/self, a subtle being, which is the locus of blameworthy traits in an individual as opposed to *sirr* (heart) or *ruh* (spirit), which is the locus of praiseworthy traits.[160] Buturovic writes of the Sufi *nafs*:

> Conditioned by a desire to return to its Creator, the *nafs* experiences the separation as yearning and worship, and the union as the ultimate reward for the spiritual self-discipline and committed self-edification. Evoking the Prophet's dictum "Die before you die!" and the *mi'raj* (the Prophetic ascension story), whereby beatific visions are made possible through an interplay of God's grace on the one hand and a spiritual and ritual wayfaring on the other, the Sufis model the reunion in/with God as a momentary death that brings about a cessation of one's self in the divine self.[161]

Buturovic also quotes the great Sufi poet Rūmī: "The mystery of 'Die before death' is this: After dying come the spoils."[162] This *fanā* (annihilation) is not only difficult to come by but a mystery which depends on grace. It is also the end of all *'ishq* (love). Muḥasibī develops a Sufi psychology around the idea of a spiritual preparation for death: the self arrives at a death, which keeps withdrawing, in transitions from states (*hāl*) to stations (*maqām*) leading up in the end to annihilation (*fanā*) only to rest in eternal perdurance (*baqā*). Dying signifies a change in one's mode of being, and to "die before you die" is only possible across the threshold of a waiting. *Inna'llah ma'a'l ṣābirīn* (Allah is with the Patient), reminds the Qur'ān. Let us turn again to Nund Rishi for a *shruk* which is also attributed to Lal Ded:

Tsālun chuy vuzmalu' tu' traṭē
Tsālun chuy mandnȳn gatu'kār
Tsālun parbatas karni atē
Tsālun chuy manz athas hyon nār
Tsālun chuy pān kadun graṭē
Tsālun chuy khyon veh tu' gār[163]

Patience is to endure thunder and lightning
Patience is darkness at midday
Patience is to move a mountain
Patience is to hold a fire in the middle of your palm
Patience is to be ground in a mill
Patience is to voluntarily drink poison

The theme of patience as a voluntary drinking of poison returns us to Plato's *Phaedo* and to the complex genealogy of dying in the Islamic tradition. Waiting at the *dihlīz* (threshold), with or without patience, for death or God, the powerful Sufi discourse on death is a form of negative theology which, in the words of Derrida, leaves you yet again "without ever going away from you."[164]

Todd LeRoy Perreira argues that the call to "die before you die" was not merely a mystical formula in the Sufi tradition but a spiritual technology of the self.[165] Perreira argues that "dying" as a practice is in use across multiple religious traditions where the transiency of life is turned into an opportunity for spiritual transformation. Death is seen then as not something that happens at the end of our life but a practice which must be renewed again and again. This involves preparing for a death about which it is impossible to know anything. Learning to die was fundamental to the arts of living across religious traditions. To learn dying involved a search for the truth of human existence which, in turn, involved a transformation of the self. Perreira writes:

> What accounts for the particular value of this exercise is the fact that not only must one's entire life be thoroughly transformed but this process is integral to the moral life. Indeed, this is not simply a question of learning how to anticipate death, of being prepared for death, of attaining the proper state of mind at the moment of death, of understanding what happens when you die or after you die, or why you die, or even the hope of achieving a "good death" (*ars moriendi*) in the final moment of life. These are all, of course, immensely important concerns but, in actuality, they are the result of something far more fundamental: the wide-spread recognition that the scandal of death demands of one a transformation of the self as a living subject and moral agent.[166]

It is this transformation of the self as a living subject and moral agent that is fundamentally at stake in the *shruks*. A comparative study of Islam and Buddhism reveals that both Islam and Buddhism stress the transformation of the self prior to death. Ignaz Goldziher had made a case for the strong influence of Buddhism on Sufism in his *Introduction to Islamic Theology and Law*.[167] Goldziher even attributed such Sufi rituals to the influence of Buddhism as "the bestowing of the *khirqa*, that is, the piece of clothing that symbolizes the Sufi's poverty and his flight from the world."[168] The two religions also share the notion of a self that must "die" to itself before the event of physical death. But in "dying," does the self reveal something about its nature? Perreira poses an even more difficult question: "What must one know about oneself in order to be willing to submit to a practice of dying before dying?"[169] Perreira then turns to asceticism studies to juxtapose Gavin Flood's general claim that asceticism as "a voluntary performance of tradition" is aimed at "shaping the narrative of a life in accordance with the narrative of tradition" with the theory of Richard Valantasis that the ascetic "constructs an entirely new agency capable of functioning in a different and resistant way to the dominant culture that defines identity, personality, and social functions."[170] Even though Nund Rishi's asceticism does exemplify the voluntary performance of the mystical tendency in the Islamic tradition in a new context, the rise of Rishi asceticism can be better approached as a movement that was resistant to the dominant political culture of medieval Kashmir.

A minute scrutiny of one's own attitude to death is central to both Sufi and Buddhist asceticism.[171] In the Pali canon, it is Buddha's encounter with a dead man (as well as an old man and a sick man) that turns him to a life of asceticism (the story of the renunciation of the Buddha has strong echoes in Sufi tales of renunciation).[172] In the Theravada Buddhist tradition, not only does the initiation ceremony of a monk mirror a symbolic death but the instruction that a monk receives largely consists of meditations on the body which initiate the process of "dying before dying."[173] The Buddhists, much like the Sufis, encouraged visits to cemeteries to cultivate mindfulness of one's own death. Perreira spells out the key stake in "dying before dying": "If the death that comes at the end of life is the death that separates us from one another, then the death that comes before death is the death that joins us to one another."[174] "Dying before dying" then is not about renunciation but the possibility of "arriving at a profound feeling of being more fully at home in the world" and to live without the fear of death.[175] "Dying before dying" is then a thinking of life that is the gift of an owning up to one's death: it envisions a new political community that is less alienated from the world out of a fear of death.

Death is connected in Islam to the *ākhirāh* (the end) and the promise of an afterlife. This was contrary to pre-Islamic Arab thinking of death, in which the end of all ends was, in the words of Amila Buturovic, "a cul-de-sac that could only be counteracted by a full and fulfilling engagement with life."[176] The pre-Islamic Meccans had almost an Epicurean outlook on death. The Islamic understanding of death openly challenged the pre-Islamic notions of "a chaotic and arbitrary beginning and end of individual life" by evoking the divine justice that "puts order in the seemingly random cycles of life and death...."[177] No longer could it be said that death was not a concern for a human being because he or she is not present at the time of death. Buturovic cites the Qur'ān (6:162) as exhorting to an owning up to one's death. It is in an owning up of one's death that one belongs to God. But it is also in this owning up to death that one gains control over one's life. Death is no longer a dead-end but "a gift from God, and ... related to the nature of God's relationship to human beings."[178] According to Perreira, the Sufi reworking of this Islamic understanding of death as a "dying before dying" introduces two new forms of experience: "The first – that of introspection – appears to be linked to a new knowledge of how one/I/you/we should live our lives, while the other is primarily one of interrogation – the minute level of scrutiny required of one who goes to battle with his own demons."[179] Both these forms of experience are to be found in the *shruks*. But what concerns us here is that the meditation on death in Nund Rishi appears connected to the ethical and political question of how we ought to live in the world. Nund Rishi's call to "die before you die" must be in the end seen as the reshaping of the traditional Sufi idea of death as a spiritual technology into the idea of death as an existential-political transformation of "the self in relation to the dominant culture that otherwise shapes one's personal and social identity."[180] A living with death is solitary, but it prepares the ground for a new form of political existence. The existential idea of death in Nund Rishi seeks to create not only a new ethical subject but also a new political community. Nund Rishi often revisits the past (Islamic and pre-Islamic) in order to open the Kashmiri present to such a utopian political possibility. Such a move is even more obvious in his turn to the idea of the Nothing and the apocalyptic (Chapters 3 and 4).

Notes

1. Plato, *Phaedo*, in Plato, *Euthyphro Apology Crito Phaedo Phaedrus*, tr. Harold North Fowler (Cambridge: Harvard University Press, 2005), 241.
2. Rahi, "Shaikh al 'Ālam sạnz shạ̄'irānā ḥasịyath," 143.
3. Ibid.
4. Ibid., 143–44.
5. Ibid., 136.
6. Ibid., 136–37.
7. Ibid., 136.
8. Ibid.
9. Ibid., 137.

10. Maurice Blanchot, "Literature and the Right to Death," in Maurice Blanchot, *The Work of Fire*, tr. Charlotte Mandell (Stanford: Stanford University Press, 1995), 323–24.
11. Rahi, "Shaikh al 'Ālam sạnz shạ̄'irānā ḥạsiyath," 137.
12. Ibid., 138.
13. Rahi, however, adds that Azad is much more cautious in his judgment than Kaul in not expressing a resounding (*vạ̄yith*) and explicit (*tshạtith*) opinion (*rāi*) but instead stresses on the distinction between the poetry of religious confession and the poetry of spontaneous emotion, which yields a dual exalting (*tamjīdi*) and critical (*tanqīsī*) narrative. Ibid.
14. Ibid.
15. Ibid.
16. Rahman Rahi, *Siyāh rūdu' jarÿn manz* (Srinagar: self-published, 1997). Both the first and the last *nazm* in this collection of poems deal with the question of faith.
17. Rahman Rahi, "Shaikh al 'Ālam sạnz shạ̄'irānā ḥạsiyath," 138.
18. Ibid., 138–39.
19. Ibid., 139.
20. Ibid., 140.
21. Unlike Rahi, I consider Kamil's schema useful in identifying the three basic trends in Nund Rishi's poetry: Islamic, Sufi, and philosophical. If Chapter 1 addressed the Sufism (and Islam) of Nund Rishi's poetry, Chapters 2, 3, and 4 of this book turn more toward a philosophical Nund Rishi.
22. Rahi, "Shaikh al 'Ālam sạnz shạ̄'irānā ḥạsiyath," 140.
23. Ibid.
24. Even as Rahi concedes that the latter verse appears oppositional (*vulte*), he draws the following conclusion: "*Magar toti hÿkov nu' mahaz̤ avu' mọkhu' yiman shāran hạndis qu'vatas yā kotạ̄hī mutalliq kānh fạ̄slu' sạ̄dir kạrith* [But nonetheless we cannot easily decide between the potentiality or error of these two verses]." Rahi, "Shaikh al 'Ālam sạnz shạ̄'irānā ḥạsiyath," 140.
25. Ibid.
26. Ibid.
27. Ibid., 140–41.
28. Ibid., 141.
29. Ibid.
30. Ibid.
31. Qari Saifuddin, *Guldasta: Kalām-e Shaikh al-'Ālam* (Srinagar: Maktaba 'Ilm o adab, 1994), 80. Cited in a different translation in A. H. Tak, *The Eternal Verities: Shaikh Nooruddin Noorani and His Poetry* (Srinagar: Ashraf Book Centre, 1996), 33.

32. See Rahman Rahi, "Lal Dyd tu' Shaikh al-'Ālam: Akh sarsarī taqobulī muṭālu'," in *Kahvạt: Tanqīdī maẓmūnan hạnz sombran* (Srinagar: self-published, 1979), 120.
33. Rahi, "Shaikh al 'Ālam sạnz shạ'irānā ḥạsiyath," 143.
34. Ibid.
35. I discuss the *shruk* from which the line is taken in more detail in Chapter 3.
36. See, for instance, the introduction to Ranjit Hoskote's translations of Lal Ded. Hoskote, *I, Lalla*, ix–lxvii.
37. Rahi, "Shaikh al 'Ālam sạnz shạ'irānā ḥạsiyath," 144.
38. Ibid., 149–50.
39. Ibid., 144.
40. Ibid.
41. Saqi, *Kulliyāt-e Shaikh al-'Ālam*, 40.
42. Rahi, "Shaikh al 'Ālam sạnz shạ'irānā ḥạsiyath," 147. There is another version of this *shruk* which uses *nabī* (prophet) instead of *valī* (saint) underlying the same truth about death. See Saqi, *Kulliyāt-e Shaikh al-'Ālam*, 63.
43. Saqi, *Kulliyāt-e Shaikh al-'Ālam*, 36.
44. Rahi, "Shaikh al 'Ālam sạnz shạ'irānā ḥạsiyath," 144.
45. Ibid.
46. Ibid.
47. Ibid., 144–45. The numbering is my own, but Rahi interprets these *shruks* together and in sequence.
48. Saqi, *Kulliyāt-e Shaikh al-'Ālam*, 93. Rahi gives the following two lines of the *shruk* in his essay, which varies slightly from the version quoted above: *Maut chuy su'h tu' kotū tsalize/Kheli manzu' kadiy tsārith kunh* [*sic*]. See also Rahi, "Shaikh al 'Ālam sạnz shạ'irānā ḥạsiyath," 147.
49. R. Raj Singh, *Death, Contemplation and Schopenhauer* (Burlington, VT: Ashgate, 2006), 1.
50. Ibid., x.
51. Rahi translates *pazar bāsh*, which I have translated as truth-recognition, as sense of reality. Rahman Rahi, "Shaikh al 'Ālam sạnz shạ'irānā ḥạsiyath," 145.
52. Ibid., 146.
53. This *shruk* is either a fragment of a longer poem or a variant of the *shruk* about shops at closing time I have already discussed.
54. Rahi, "Shaikh al 'Ālam sạnz shạ'irānā ḥạsiyath," 146. I have corrected minor spelling inconsistencies in the last line from Rahi's text.
55. The refrain *vạn gatshi vānas phālav dith* (literally, the grocer will lock his shop at night) is a variation on *vạni dith vānan phālav gạyi* quoted earlier and suggests that these *shruks* are culled from a longer poem.
56. Rahi, "Shaikh al 'Ālam sạnz shạ'irānā ḥạsiyath," 146.

57. Ibid., 148.
58. See, for instance, Khaki Muhammad Farooq, *Mubaligh-e Islām: Ḥaẓrat Shaikh Nūruddīn Walī* (Srinagar: Siddiq Publications, 2012).
59. Rahi, "Shaikh al 'Ālam sạnz shạ'irānā ḥạsiyath," 150.
60. Rahi quotes the following couplet from Ghalib which resonates powerfully with the last line of the *shruk* under discussion: *Bojh vo sar se girā hai ki uṭha'e na uṭhe/Kām wo ān paḍā hai ki bana'e na bane* (Such a burden has fallen off my head that I no longer can lift it again/Such a task I face now that I no longer can get it done). Ibid. See also *Divān-e-Ġhālib*, ed. Ali Sardar Jafri (Delhi: Urdu Academy, 2001), 371.
61. Rahi, "Shaikh al 'Ālam sạnz shạ'irānā ḥạsiyath," 150.
62. Ibid., 151–52.
63. Ibid., 152.
64. Personal interview with Rahman Rahi in May 2013.
65. Rahi, "Shaikh al 'Ālam sạnz shạ'irānā ḥạsiyath," 152. Rahi also observed in the personal interview that it was often Kashmir's waterways that gave access to large orchards in the past.
66. Ibid., 154.
67. Ibid.
68. Ibid.
69. Ibid., 159.
70. Ibid., 159.
71. Ibid., 159–60. *Hār* and *poh* are months in the Kashmiri calendar.
72. Ibid.
73. Rahman Rahi, "Lal Dẏd tu' Shaikh al-'Ālam: Akh sarsarī taqobulī muṭālu'," in *Kahvat: Tanqīdī maẓmūnan hạnz sombran* (Srinagar: self-published, 1979), 128.
74. Ibid., 120.
75. Ibid., 121.
76. Ibid.
77. Ibid.
78. Ibid., 122. The transliteration is from the Rahi text. It should be *Gōru' sund* instead of *Gọru' sund*.
79. The translation of this *vākh* is by Ranjit Hoskote. See Hoskote, *I, Lalla*, 12. *Rāvan tyol* is a difficult to translate metaphor which means the burning or scorching of loss.
80. Rahi, "Lal Dẏd tu' Shaikh al-'Ālam: Akh sarsarī taqobulī muṭālu'," 122. There is a slight variation in the last line of the *shruk* in the version cited in Rahi's essay and the one we discussed above. See Ibid., 150.
81. Ibid., 122–23.

82. Ibid., 124.
83. Ibid.
84. This translation is by Sonam Kachru. Sonam Kachru, "'The Words of Lalla: Voices of the Everyday Wild': Translation and Commentary," *Spolia Magazine, The Medieval Issue*, no. 5 (October 2013).
85. Rahi, "Lal Dẏd tu' Shaikh al-'Ālam: Akh sarsarī taqobulī muṭālu'," 124. The *kalkī kāl* (age, or time, of Kalkī) here refers to the time of the prophesied tenth incarnation of Lord Vishnu which ends the fourth and darkest period of a cycle of cosmic existence (Kali Yuga, or the Dark Age).
86. Ibid., 124–25.
87. Ibid., 126–27.
88. Ibid., 127.
89. Ibid., 127–28.
90. Ibid., 129.
91. Ibid., 130.
92. Ibid., 131.
93. Ibid.
94. Ibid., 132.
95. Ibid.
96. See Agha Shahid Ali, *The Veiled Suite: The Collected Poems* (New Delhi: Penguin, 2009), 29.
97. We are not here going to consider the Levinasian position that the beginnings of our thinking of death are in the death of the others. See Emmanuel Levinas, *God, Death and Time* (Stanford: Stanford University Press, 1993), 12.
98. Martin Heidegger, *History of the Concept of Time: Prolegomena*, tr. T. Kisiel (Bloomington, Indiana: Indiana University Press, 1985), 314. See also Martin Heidegger, *Being and Time*, tr. John Macquarrie and Edward Robinson (New York: Harper & Row, 1962), 292.
99. Richard Polt, *Heidegger: An Introduction* (New York: Routledge, 1999), 86–87.
100. Heidegger, *History of the Concept of Time*, 316–17. See also Heidegger, *Being and Time*, tr. Macquarrie and Robinson, 300–02.
101. Parimoo, *Unity in Diversity*, 295.
102. Gauhar, *Kashmir Mystic Thought*, 48–50.
103. Rahi, "Lal Dẏed tu' Shaikh al-'Ālam: Akh sarsarī taqobulī muṭālu'," 130–31.
104. Heidegger, *Being and Time*, tr. Macquarrie and Robinson, 281.
105. Ibid., 284. For the Stambaugh translation, see Martin Heidegger, *Being and Time*, tr. Joan Stambaugh (Albany: State University of New York Press, 1992), 240.
106. In Section 49, Heidegger lets the term *dying* "stand for that *way of Being* in which Dasein *is towards* its death." Heidegger, *Being and Time*, tr. Macquarrie and Robinson, 291.

107. Heidegger, *Being and Time*, tr. Macquarrie and Robinson, 294. See also Heidegger, *Being and Time*, tr. Stambaugh, 241.
108. *Divān-e-Ġhālib*, edited by Ali Sardar Jafri (Delhi:Urdu Academy, 2001), 315.
109. Heidegger, *Being and Time*, tr. Macquarrie and Robinson, 295. Heidegger calls this experience of being thrown into the world which matters to us "thrownness."
110. According to Magda King, a commentator on Heidegger's *Being and Time*, "idle talk" in Heidegger is a form of discourse which gives us "an average explanation of existence and world in everyday being-together." King adds: "It offers the possibility of understanding everything without going into anything. It develops an average understandability to which nothing remains hidden, so that it in advance hinders and closes a deeper and more genuine approach to things." Magda King, *A Guide to Heidegger's* Being and Time (Albany, NY: State University of New York Press, 2001), 85.
111. Gauhar, *Sheikh Noor-ud-Din Wali (Nund Rishi)*, 26.
112. Ibid.
113. Heidegger, *Being and Time*, tr. Macquarrie and Robinson, 311.
114. Cited in Singh, *Death, Contemplation and Schopenhauer*, 1. Charlotte Vaudeville in her 1974 study of Kabir concludes: "Death, its inescapabale, frightful, tragic character, appears to be at the core of Kabir's thought." Charlotte Vaudeville, *Kabir* (Oxford: Clarendon Press, 1974), 147–48.
115. Françoise Dastur, *Death: An Essay on Finitude* (London: Athlone, 1996), 14. This also has some resonance with the thinking of death we find in Epicurus.
116. Parimoo, *Unity in Diversity*, 302–03.
117. Jacques Derrida, *The Gift of Death*, tr. David Wills (Chicago: University of Chicago Press, 1995), 13.
118. Plato, *Phaedo*, 223.
119. Annemarie Schimmel, "Death as the Gateway to Life in the Eyes of the Sufis," in *Reza Ali Khazeni Memorial Lectures in Iranian Studies, Volume 2: Crafting the Intangible: Persian Literature and Mysticism*, ed. Peter J. Chelkowski (Salt Lake City: The University of Utah Press, 2013), 48.
120. Hussam S. Timani, "Death and Dying in Islam," in *Ultimate Journey: Death and Dying in the World's Major Religions*, ed. Steven J. Rosen (Westport: Praeger, 2008), 60.
121. *Al-Qur'ān*, tr. Ali, 30.
122. John Bowker, *The Meanings of Death* (Cambridge: Cambridge University Press, 1991), 127.
123. This phrase is used by Jacques Derrida in different contexts. See, for instance, David Wood and Robert Bernasconi, *Derrida and Différance* (Evanston: Northwestern University Press, 1988), 74.

124. Saqi, *Kulliyāt-e Shaikh al-ʿĀlam*, 37. This *shruk* is given as a set of two *shruks* in the Moti Lal Saqi collection, but I quote here only the first *shruk* as the latter appears to be an interpolation. The first *shruk* quoted here is the one that often circulates in collective oral memory. The reference is to Manṣūr al-Ḥallāj, an Islamic mystic, executed on the orders of the Abbasid caliph for his heterodox beliefs (we have discussed Nund Rishi's relation to Manṣur al-Ḥallāj in Chapter 1).
125. Thomas O'Shaughnessy, *Muhammad's Thoughts on Death: A Thematic Study of the Qur'anic Data* (Leiden: Brill, 1969), vii.
126. Ibid., 6.
127. Ibid., 7–8.
128. Ibid., 77.
129. Ibid., 80.
130. Kamil, *Nūrnāmu'*, 176.
131. O'Shaughnessy, *Muhammad's Thoughts on Death*, 56.
132. Ibid.
133. Timani, "Death and Dying in Islam," 61.
134. O'Shaughnessy, *Muhammad's Thoughts on Death*, 59.
135. Thomas O'Shaughnessy writes: "The word for 'agony' *sakrah*, literally means 'intoxication.' Lane sums up the commentators by defining the word used here as the irrationality and oppression attendant on death, and Bell translates it as 'the drunken sleep of death.'" Ibid., 69.
136. *Al-Qur'ān*, tr. Ali, 447.
137. O'Shaughnessy, *Muhammad's Thoughts on Death*, 75.
138. Chittick, *Sufism*, 179
139. Omid Safi, *Memories of Muhammad: Why the Prophet Matters* (New York: HarperOne, 2011), 168.
140. Kamil, *Nūrnāmu'*, 233.
141. O'Shaughnessy, *Muhammad's Thoughts on Death*, 9.
142. Amila Buturovic, "Death," in *Key Themes for the Study of Islam*, ed. Jamal J. Elias (Oxford: Oneworld Publications, 2010), 123.
143. Ibid., 125.
144. *Al-Qur'ān*, tr. Ali, 429.
145. Ibid.
146. Buturovic, "Death," 124.
147. Ibid., 130–32.
148. Saqi, *Kulliyāt-e Shaikh al-ʿĀlam*, 41.
149. Buturovic, "Death," 130–31.
150. Jane Idleman Smith and Yvonne Yazbeck Haddad, *The Islamic Understanding of Death and Resurrection* (Albany: State University of New York Press, 1981), 31.

151. Ibid., 33.
152. Ibid., 41–42.
153. Gauhar, *Kashmir Mystic Thought*, 401. For a slightly different version of this *shruk*, see Afaqi, *Āʾīnā-e ḥaq*, 117–18.
154. Kamil, *Nūrnāmu'*, 126.
155. Buturovic, "Death," 127.
156. Nund Rishi often returns to this idea of a *sọ zan*, a righteous human being (*sajjan* in Hindi and Sanskrit).
157. Rahi, *Kahvạt*, 160.
158. Buturovic, "Death," 133. The Islamic thinker Fazlur Rahman has contested this interpretation of the term *nafs*. Rahman sees *nafs* as nothing more than a reflexive pronoun in the Qur'ān. For Rahman, the Qur'ān does not recognize a dualism between the soul and the body. The *nafs* refers, for Rahman, to the person of man including a certain life-and-intelligence center as his or her inner identity. The word *nafs* in Nund Rishi, however, is used more in the Sufi sense as a blameworthy ego that must be brought under control. The voluntary death imitates the power of death in relation to the rule of the *nafs*. See Ibid., 132.
159. Ibid., 133.
160. Ibid.
161. Ibid.
162. Ibid.
163. Saqi, *Kulliyāt-e Shaikh al-ʿĀlam*, 35.
164. Derrida, *On the Name*, 85. The idea of the threshold, or *dihlīz*, and waiting at the *dihlīz*, appears powerfully in the work of the great medieval Islamic mystic and philosopher Abu Hamid al-Ghazālī. See, for instance, Moosa, *Ghazālī and the Poetics of Imagination*, 29–30.
165. Todd LeRoy Perreira, "'Die Before You Die': Death Meditation as Spiritual Technology of the Self in Islam and Buddhism," *Muslim World* 100 (April/July 2010): 249.
166. Ibid., 248.
167. Ignaz Goldziher, *Introduction to Islamic Theology and Law* (Princeton: Princeton University Press, 1981), 141–43.
168. Ibid., 145.
169. Perreira, "'Die Before You Die,'" 248.
170. Ibid., 250.
171. Even a Sufi figure as mindful of Islamic orthodoxy as Ghazālī had devised many death meditations as "a training for making death an actuality in one's daily life." Ibid., 252. Al-Ghazālī, for instance, advocates lying in the position of a corpse in the bed, imagining the body as a corpse undergoing decay and remembering the friends who have died. The idea was to instill a *dhawq* (literally, "tasting")

of one's death. As we have seen, this insistence on a tasting of one's death is Qur'ānic in origin. Ibid., 252.

172. Ibid., 255.
173. Ibid., 257.
174. Ibid., 260–61.
175. Ibid., 261.
176. Buturovic, "Death," 124.
177. Ibid., 125.
178. Ibid., 127.
179. Perreira, "'Die Before You Die,'" 248.
180. Ibid., 264.

3

Becoming Nothing

> The death of God is the *final* thought of philosophy, which proposes it as the *end* of religion: it is the thought towards which the Occident (which in this respect excludes neither Islam nor Buddhism) will not have ceased to tend.
>
> —Jean-Luc Nancy[1]

The *shruk*s of Nund Rishi bring us face-to-face with an existential encounter with death's imminence. But what work does the recognition of death's imminence do? We have already seen that Nund Rishi's insistence on death's imminence is a call to a dying before death. The call to a dying before death is often also in Nund Rishi a call to becoming Nothing. Let us turn to the first two lines of a *shruk* taken up by Rahman Rahi in his critical essay on the mystical poetry of Nund Rishi that we also discussed in the previous chapter:

Zū neri brōnṭh tu'lōbh nēri patu'
Gatshan dọn zu' vaṭu', shunya ākār[2]

The first to depart is life and only then greed
The two go on separate paths: the form of the Nothing

Rahman Rahi turns to the modern theatre stage in an attempt to interpret this *shruk*. He sets up a play between *zū*, or *zuv* (life), and *lōbh* (greed), which meet their end in the nothingness of death. *Zū nēri brōnṭh* (the first to leave, or depart, is life) gives us a palpable sense of someone's departure (in this case, *zū*, or life) before that of someone else (*lōbh*, or greed). It is, in other words, impossible for human greed to end before the end of life. *Lōbh*, greed or avaricious desire, has such a tenacious hold over us that it only leaves the stage of existence after life has already departed. What life and desire leave behind is a space of emptiness (*shunya*), and this play has the form of nothingness (*shunya ākār*). The idea that everything is empty (*śūnyatā*, or emptiness) is central to

Mahayana Buddhism, which held sway in Kashmir between the third century BCE to about the fifth century CE (the Sanskrit term *śūnya* also means zero).[3] Such a stance was not seen in the Buddhist tradition as nihilist. Graham Priest identifies the core meaning of the idea of *śūnyatā*: "Nothing exists in and of itself. Everything that exists does so inasmuch as, and only inasmuch as, it relates to other things. It has, so to say, only relational existence."[4] It is this relational idea that is expressed in the *shruk* and Rahi's explication of it that I discuss later.

The Buddhist resonance of this *shruk* appears here in relation to such Meccan Qur'ānic verses as the following from the *Surah At-Takāthur*: "You are consumed with unending desire for more even until you die."[5] It is beyond the threshold of death that the paths of life and greed fork, revealing the form of the Nothing (*shunya ākār*). Or the way *zū* and *lōbh* part *is* the form of the Nothing. Can such a project be undertaken in life before one's death? Is it possible to severe *zū* from *lobh* and become Nothing? Rahi conceives of *zū* and *lōbh* as two characters in a play that depart the stage at its opposite ends. *Zū* exits the stage in one direction and *lōbh* in the other. But the emptiness that is suspended in the space in the middle is in Rahi's reading the form of the Nothing, the *shunya ākār*. Let us turn to Rahi's own words:

> If you look at it carefully *zū* and *lobh* are two ordinary words from everyday Kashmiri speech which are almost synonymous with life and health (*dil bastagī*). But if you look again at these words with the eyes of poetic creation, you would have before you two tragic characters deeply in love separated forever by death and in such a way that both exit the stage in opposite directions. And what remains between them is Nothing. And this Nothing is *shunya ākār* or the space/form of the Nothing.[6]

Much like Rahman Rahi, the Japanese philosopher Keiji Nishitani too turns to the metaphor of the stage to speak of this process of becoming Nothing, which resembles a dying before death:

> Absolute selfhood opens up as nonobjectifiable nothingness in the conversion that takes place within personality. Through that conversion every bodily, mental, and spiritual activity that belongs to person displays itself as a play of shadows moving across the stage of nothingness. This stage represents the near side of the personal self. It is the field commonly seen as "outermost" by the personal self and referred to as the external world actually present in the here

> and now, ever changing. At the same time, it is the field of nothingness bursting forth from within the innermost depths of personal self. It is the ultimate realization and expression of nonobjectifiable – and, in that sense, elementally subjective-nothingness.[7]

The world and its play revealed on the stage of Nothingness bear a relation to the self. The moment the outer world of *zū* and *lōbh* are revealed as the form of the Nothing, the self becomes Nothing; it is one with the Nothing. Nund Rishi speaks of *shunya ākār* also in relation to *samsāra* (the world) in another of his *shruk*s:

Athu' khọr jachām (tạchāyam) athi kūntsh lōgum
Chu' nu' kathu' karān gōs sharamsār
Nạ kạ̄nsi ditsām na kạ̄nsi zōgum
Samsār zōnum me shunya ākār[8]

I worked hard with my two hands and feet
But I could not get hold of him
He refuses to speak to me and I am ashamed
Neither did I give anything to anyone nor did I covet anything from anyone
The world, I gathered, is the form of the Nothing

Nund Rishi reveals the world to have the form of Nothingness (*shunya ākār*) because neither is the self able to give nor is it able to receive at will. The language addressed to the other also echoes and rebounds in silence. There is no answer which leads the self to an understanding of the *samsāra*, world, as *shunya ākār*, the form of Nothingness. The world is not the Nothing but has the form of Nothingness. Here in this *shruk*, we come across a conventional rejection of the world associated with asceticism in all the three major religious traditions of Kashmir: Hindu, Buddhist, and Islamic. This understanding of the world as the Nothing makes exchanges in the world bereft of any meaning. Yet there is a searching for someone in the first line of the *shruk* and the shame of the self which receives no answer.

In the *shruk*s that deal with death and the Nothing, it is not merely enough for Nund Rishi to recognize life as having the form of nothing, but this recognition must turn into a practice I am calling here "becoming nothing" and Nund Rishi calls *Marnu' bronth mar* (Die before you die). How does one become Nothing? *Śūnya*, or the Nothing, in the Buddhist tradition has often been translated as emptiness. To become Nothing resembles a certain kenosis, an emptying out of the self. Nund Rishi alludes to this shade of its meaning in the following *shruk*:

Zū ti otshuy, pavan ti otshuy
Tsӯth ti otshuy, otshuy sār
Yiman padan me vӯtsār gotshuy
Bār khudāyā, pāp nivār[9]

Life is empty, empty is the wind
The search is empty, empty the meaning
These verses of mine call to thinking
This burden of existence!
God, forgive my sins!

The Kashmiri word *otshuy* means empty or hollow. Nund Rishi not only calls *zū* (or life) and *pavan* (or wind) as empty but considers the *tsӯth* (search) of the human and all *sār* (meaning) as empty. He then invites the reader to a *vӯtsār*, or thinking, of his *padas* (or verses). The *shruk* is part of a longer poem which ends with the refrain *Bār khudāyā pāp nivār* (This burden of existence! God, forgive my sins). The refrain is paradoxical because it speaks of a heavy burden (the difficult burden of human existence in the Islamic tradition) which leads the poet to a simple prayer of submission to ask for God's forgiveness. This burden of existence concerns the accountability for human actions which makes a believer tremble in fear. But the *shruk* above approaches existents, and existence, as empty. In the Islamic tradition, the world is treated as transitory, but it does not lack meaning. But here Nund Rishi affirms a meaning held out by the Nothing. The refrain *Bār khudāyā pāp nivār* arrests the movement of the first two lines, which could be read as an affirmation of the emptiness of life, wind, human searching, and meaning by putting this meaninglessness to work for a traditional pietistic surrender. The emptying out is often cast in Nund Rishi in conventional Sufi terms as a surrender of desire. But Nund Rishi often sets up a different encounter with the Nothing just as he does with death. The question of death then is bound up with the question of the Nothing. The Kashmiri word for the Nothing, *kenh nu'*, literally translates as No-Thing. But Nund Rishi also uses *shunya* (Nothing), *nāh* (naught), *nafī* (negation) and *nirguna* (without attributes, often "God without attributes"). As Lal Ded puts it before Nund Rishi: *Kenh na tu' manz kyāhtām drāv* (From the Nothing/Something came to be). In more than one *shruk*, Nund Rishi asks,

Bu' nu' kenh tu' me kyāh nāv? (I am nothing. What is my name?). The Kashmiri tradition also remembers Nund Rishi's rhetorical question in another way: *Bu' kus Rishī me kyāh nāv?* (What Rishi am I? What is my name?).[10] It is through a defamiliarization of the name itself that Nund Rishi approaches the question of becoming nothing. The name is groundless, and so is our being. Nund Rishi turns to the question of the Nothing more explicitly in a famous *shruk, Kunearē bōzakh kuni nō rōzakh* (If you find unity/the One, you will become Nothing). What does it mean to become Nothing? Let us quote the *shruk* in full and turn to it in more detail:

Kunearē bōzakh kuni nō rōzakh
Ȧmị kunearan kōtah dyut jalāv
'Aql tu' fiqr tōr kot sōzakh
Kạm māli chӯth hyok su dạrịyāv[11]

The moment you realize the unity of Being
You become Nothing
This One-ness endlessly emanates
You cannot send your reason or thinking after it
Who, my dear, could drink up the ocean?

Why bring up this *shruk* when it is clearly a *shruk* about the Being of One as much as it is about the Nothing? Nowhere is the question of Nothing as insistent as it is with the question of being.[12] When Nund Rishi says, *Kunearē bōzakh kuni nō rōzakh*, because the Kashmiri word *kunear* has three meanings (the unity of Being, the oneness of human beings, but also solitude), these words could also translate as: "The moment you realize the Unity of Being, Oneness, Nothingness/You become Nothing." There emerges a deep connection between the *kunear* of solitude and the *kunear* of nothingness in becoming Nothing. Does the "unity" here not threaten the absolute transcendence of the monotheistic God so central to the Islamic tradition? Yet again we come upon the paradox involved in searching for God within the Abrahamic faiths. Maurice Blanchot delimits a solution to this problem in the mysticisms of monotheistic faith in relation to Meister Eckhart in these terms:

> God, as he is grasped as identical to the soul where he is revealed, is beyond substance and in no way offers himself as a subject that must be received as such. One must add that this experience that seems to suppress divine transcendence since it asserts the complete unity of the soul in its depths and of God in his

> depths is, in reality, the experience of transcendence. It is in soul itself that the leap is accomplished; it is in the soul that is hollowed out the abyss that no thought, no action, can cross. The beyond is inside us in a way that separates us forever from ourselves, and our nobility rests in this secret that causes us to reject ourselves absolutely in order to find ourselves absolutely.[13]

The *kunear* of solitude opens out the self to an abyss where we reject ourselves in order to find ourselves. This at least is the ascetic imperative. Let us reconsider the *shruk Kuneare̅ bōzakh kuni nō rōzakh*. The Kashmiri verb *bōzun* means "to hear" or "to listen," but it also carries the second meaning of "to consider," "to reflect," "to reckon," often in relation to an impending decision (for instance, in giving someone advice in relation to a decision, we may begin with *Bōzakh hae* ... [If you hear me ...]). A *bōzan wōl* is someone who understands, "one who is by nature accustomed to consider, to act with understanding and intelligence."[14] *Kuneare̅ bōzakh kuni nō rōzakh*: If you were to understand the meaning of the One, you will be dis-placed (*kuni nō rōzakh*). You will lose your station in life. You will become Nothing. For a moment, one is tempted to read *kuni nō rōzakh* as "you will come to nothing," which could also mean that "you will lose everything (culture, faith, meaning)," and the One here seems to be beyond the threshold of a nihilism.[15] *Kuni nō rōzakh* also connotes a limit to experience. It can also mean that your search is going to reveal nothing. And then the line: *Ȧmi̱ kunearan dyut kōtah jalāv* (The One-ness endlessly emanates). It is now revealed that the destitution of the self, its solitude, has a relation with another *kunear*, the *kunear* of Oneness. It is not clear that if this is an external *kunear* (of Oneness or transcendence) or if it is the ecstasy of the *kunear* (solitude) of the self. The One here is beyond measure, and it is given to a giving (*dyut*) which is an emanation (*jalāv*). This is the *jalāv* of the *tajallī-e illāhī* (divine emanation). The "light" is a possible, though not necessary, translation of what emanates. It is not clear what emanates from the Oneness of the One (Is it an [over]flow of light or life, love or care, death or torture?) since everything appears to emanate from the place which is no-place. The emanation here bears witness to the exchange between Neoplatonism and Sufism. But the emanation is also an endless calling. The solitude is in a state of overflowing. We hear an echo of this in Lal Ded: *Zū chum bramān garu' gatshu'hā* (My life spills over with the desire for home). This is consistent with emanationist schemas in Neoplatonism, but in a reversal. Both Nund Rishi and Lal Ded use the word *zū*, which is untranslatable as soul, and can only be translated as life, or the vital life-force (like the Greek *menos*).

The beginnings of knowledge are in the thinking of unity, which is inseparable from human action. But this action is seen in relation to a withdrawal to solitude. In Nund Rishi, the unity (or Oneness) of being is made possible by a certain concealment.

Yus ōs tatī suy chu yatī
Suy chuy prath shāyi ratÿth makān
Suy chuy pyādu' tu' suy chuy rathu'ī
Suy chu sōray gupit pān[16]

The one who is over there is also over here
He is the one who occupies every place
He is the soldier and he the chariot
He is the one hiding everywhere

We are here close to the Sufi idea of the immanence of divinity and the multiplicity of its forms that resonates strongly with Vedantic philosophy. The world here is a world on march, and even its strife discloses a divine unity. We are also not far from Neoplatonic metaphysics, which left a deep impact on Indo-Persian Sufism across the different Persianate Sufi orders and the regional South Asian Sufi orders. The Sufi metaphysics of Ibn al-ʿArabī had, in particular, influenced the Kubrāwiyya Sufi Order with which Nund Rishi must have been familiar, since some hagiographies mention that his parents were disciples of the Kubrāwiyyā Sufi Sayyid Husayn Simnānī.[17] We can conclude that the idea of unity of being (*waḥdat al-wujūd*), often associated with Ibn al-ʿArabī, was also circulating in Kashmir, disseminated by the Kubrāwiyyā Sufis.

The third line of the *shruk Kuneare̅ bōzakh kuni no rōzakh* is: *ʿAql tu' fiqr tōr kot sōzakh*. Here we come across a more familiar Sufi trope. How and where will you send reason (*ʿaql*) and thinking (*fikr*) in search of the One? The One is seen here beyond all searching. There is a difference here between *ʿaql* (reason) and *fikr* (thinking) but both are useless in the search for the One. Yet again, the divinity is disclosed in relation to a spatial metaphor: the *tōr* (that place) is beyond all searching but the impossible possibility that makes possible the unity of all being. The gap between an immanent "here" and the transcendental "there" also alludes to the Qur'ānic narrative of Muḥammad's journey (*mi'rāj*, ascension to heaven) to God. This could also be interpreted as an inner journey, but the metaphor is spatial. This line of the *shruk* resonates not only with the Qur'ānic narratives of Muḥammad's ascension to the heavens where he is drawn close to God but also with the narrative of Moses's encounter with God, which reduces a mountain to ash. Even the prophets cannot draw near to the mystery of Oneness, which is the strongest attribute of God in the Islamic tradition. We have already seen that if one were to know the One, one will be in no (one) place: it would be an absolute transcendence. Both *'aql* and *fikr* are near to us but can never search the One that grounds the One and makes possible the One-ness of the many. The rejection of *'aql* is a common trope that recurs in most South Asian vernacular Sufi poetry. The Kashmiri *kunear* then is also a site of privation: a destitution and solitude.

The Kashmiri word *fikr* is the same as the Arabic *fikr*, which means thinking. But it also connotes in Kashmiri (as it does in Hindi and Urdu) the meaning of anxiety. The *fikr* (thinking) which sets out in search of the One (possibly with the aim of becoming One) comes up against the nothing. But the *fikr* is set on this path by the experience of anxiety that comes over it in its relation to beings as Not-One and its experience of that which grounds it as not a wholeness but a groundless transcendence. The last line of the *shruk* returns us to the everyday: a sage addressing his Kashmiri audience with affection: *Kạm māli chŷth hyok su dariyāv* (Who, my dear, could drink up the ocean?). The child of the *shruk* is the desiring human self. The meaning of *dariyāv* is river in Kashmiri, but it may be proper to translate it here as an "ocean" or "sea," which is already the meaning of the original Persian *dariyā*. It is impossible to drink from this ocean without risking annihilation. Nund Rishi often ends his *shruk*s in a mode of affection, as his piercing advice addressed to his disciples gathers force. In this *shruk*, Nund Rishi affirms a radical finitude in relation to the transcendence of the One and warns against any movement toward infinity. Nund Rishi speaks in this *shruk* of the *kunear*, of Oneness and solitude, but situates it beyond the reach of *'aql* (reason) and *fikr* (thinking). Yet there is no explicit trace of the Nothing in this *shruk* except in the negation of the first line and the privation of the third.

Nund Rishi advances his thinking against the background of multiple traditions which gives rise to paradoxes that may be suppressed in individual attempts to read Nund Rishi solely from the standpoint of one religious tradition or the other. My contention is that Nund Rishi works with these contradictions without fear or anxiety, perhaps even indifferent to the contradictions, as his thought leaps across multiple traditions to think a new moral and political subject. It builds on the insights of different traditions to open up a path to a new thinking of "unity," "oneness," and "solitude" that turns on a dying before death and becoming nothing. This thinking of "unity" also assumes significance against the historical background of sectarian tensions between Hindus and Muslims in the fourteenth century (the word *kunear* came to acquire in contemporary Kashmiri the additional meaning of unity among the members of a family or a community but also between different religious communities).

In yet another *shruk*, Nund Rishi contemplates the source of the *ṣạdur*, ocean. But in the same *shruk*, he also asks of the source or the origin of the Nothing?

'Alimuk āgur chu kalimuk ma'nē
Kreyi hund āgur mīni̱ khen
Shuni̱yuhuk āgur pānay zāne
Ṣạdruk āgur labi nō tshen[18]

The origin of knowledge is the meaning of the *kalimā*
The origin of action is renunciation [measured diet, literally]
The ground of Nothing [*shunya*] only He knows
The origin of the ocean: you'll never find a break

The origins of knowledge, or its beginnings, are in the *kalimā*, which carries the meaning of the Word and is also the name of the first article of the Muslim faith. But the first article of Muslim faith, *Lā Ilāhā illallāh* (There is no god but God), or the *kalima*, also affirms the unity and transcendence of God through negation. It is then a consideration of the *kalimā*, and the negation at the heart of it, that gives access to knowledge of the transcendent. Nund Rishi then connects the origin of all human action to a measured diet (*mīni̱ khen*), or, in other words, to moderation. The path to moderation is made possible by the negation that animates the faith in an unknown God. Nund Rishi then turns to the source or the origin of Nothing (*shuni̱yuhuk āgur*) and concedes that the knowledge of this only belongs to God. The Nothing is then likened in the last line to an ocean without any break. As we have already seen in the earlier *shruk*, the human attempt to send *'aql* and *fikr* after the Nothing is compared by Nund Rishi to a childish attempt to gulp down the ocean. It is not just that the *zū* (life) or the *pavan* (wind) which are *otshuy* (empty), but the words of the *shruk* hold up a mirror to not only the emptiness of signifiers but also that of the signified. The word used here for ocean, *ṣạdur,* is also used by Lal Ded in the following famous *vākh*:

Āmi panu' ṣodrus nāvi chas lamān
Kati bōziy day myōn me ti diyi tār
Āmŷn tākŷn pōni̱ zan shamān
Zū chum bramān garu' gachu'hā[19]

I am towing my boat across the ocean with a thread.
Will He hear me and help me across?
Or am I seeping away like water from a half-baked cup?
Wander, my poor soul, you're not going home anytime soon[20]

In yet another *shruk*, Nund Rishi turns to the play between *fikr* (thinking) and being which reveals the self as nothing:

Tshānjām bonan beyi shŷn dishan
Neb tu' nishanu' lobmas nu' kunē
Pritshām malu' bāban tape rŷshan
Tim lạg būz būz rāvu'nē
Dab yali dyutmas fikreh andeshan
Adu' su dyūnthum bu' nu' kunē[21]

I looked for him within and in six directions
I could not find even a trace
I turned to the *mullah*s, elders and sages
The more they heard me, the more they were lost
But when I searched for him in my anxiety and fears
I could then see him but I was nowhere to be found

Nund Rishi reveals that having searched his inner experience and the six directions, he could not find any trace of God. He then speaks of his questioning of the *mullah*s, dervishes, and *rishī*s but reveals that all of them were at a loss with his questions. But it is only when he wrestles with his thinking and anxiety, he gets the *darshana* (or vision) of the divinity (here invoked by the impersonal pronoun, *su*), but his own self is nowhere to be found (*bu' nu' kunē*: I am nowhere). Nund Rishi invokes the disappearance of his self in this *shruk*, and a few other *shruk*s, as a way of either erasing his own identity as a teacher of spirituality in the Kashmiri tradition (as in the *shruk* where he says *Bu' kus rishī me kyāh nāv*/What Rishi am I? What is my name?) or a forgetting of his name or place. The relation to the Nothing is then connected to this forgetting of both the name and place. In Nund Rishi's mystical poetry, this namelessness or placelessness emerges in relation to becoming Nothing. But this becoming Nothing is not merely an ascetic operation but is connected to our ruinant existence on the planet. Nund Rishi speaks of his experience of becoming Nothing (*nāh*: naught) in unflattering terms in another *shruk*:

Prenis badnas malyun dāgh̲ gōm
Zāgh̲ gōm nīrith bāgh andray
Hārni garmiyi poh tu' māg gōm
Zazaran chọku' hani hani dāh gōm
Gọnāh gạm tsạri̲ tu' kahi̲ ubray
Myūth tu' modur khÿth und siyāh gom
Nāh gom pānas rah kas karay[22]

My pure being stained with impurities
The bird (of the self) has escaped the garden (of the body)
The hot summer of my youth faces the bitter chill of winter
The wounds of decay waste every part of my body
The sins multiply – how can I bounce back?
Addicted to tastes sweet, my inner being is a darkness
And I have become Nothing – who can I blame?

The unstained body of youth is now covered over with stains. The bird (of life) has escaped the garden (of the body). In some versions, the second line appears as *Phāh gōm nīrith har bandray* (the heat escaped from every part of my body). Both lines allude to the slow ruination of the human body over time. This meaning is brought out clearly by the third line which mourns the passing of the *hārni garmiyi* (the heat of summer) which must now face the winter months of *poh* and *māg* (the coldest months of the winter in the Kashmiri calendar from the middle of December to the middle of February). The poet speaks of his state of physical and spiritual decline as the winter months of *poh* and *māg*. But becoming winter also carries a sense of being reduced or diminished. This sense comes across in the last line: *Nāh gōm pānas rah kas karay* (And I have become Nothing – who can I blame?). This idea of a slow ruination appears in Rahman Dar's mystical poem "Shash Rang" (a poem which the writer Akhtar Mohi-ud-Din considered one of the three best works in Kashmiri literature) as late as the twentieth century. Rahman Dar connects this ruination to the experience of love:

Khotsān chu nu' pāpan tay
gạ̄jnas ashqu' tāpan
Pạhi̱ pan bu' vạ̄jnas lạ̄jnas tshẏpan tay
kạri̱has ta 'vīz pan[23]

He has no fear of sins
and has burnt me in the fire of love
I fall weightless like an autumn leaf
helpless, as if in a spell

In the mystical poem by Rahman Dar, the same idea of ruination is invoked where the self is compared to a dry, weightless, autumn leaf which falls in involuntary surrender burnt by the fire of love. The same way the self cannot pass on its existential burden to someone else in the Nund Rishi *shruk* we examined in the previous chapter (*Bōr gōm gob tu' trāvu' kas*: The burden has become heavy/I cannot even leave it for someone else), the self cannot blame anyone for having been reduced to Nothing. It had been destined to become Nothing. This process is unmitigatingly physical: *Zazaran chọku' hani hani dāh gōm* (The wounds of decay waste every part of my body). The death-work of the Nothing is the truth of temporal existence. But Nund Rishi then speaks of the accumulation of sins that make it impossible for him to escape this ruination and the sweetness of appetites that fuel inner darkness. These two lines do not seem to go well with the rest of the *shruk* which could be a later interpolation. The Nothing appears in this *shruk* to be more intimately connected with life. This is a bleak vision of the human condition, and indeed in many of these *shruk*s, Nund Rishi offers us no hope. But the meditation on the work of the Nothing produces a relation to it; a relation expressed through emotions of loss and melancholy.

The slow ruination of human life, and the invocation of this experience of loss in poetry, foreshadows death. But the recognition of the work of death in life can also offer an escape from its terrible, paralyzing grip which can lead to inaction. For Nund Rishi, it is the fear of death that is responsible for forgetting in the world:

Zuvō tsu' bōz tō kanu'vān
Yi hō mạri̱nu'n k̲h̲abar shinvān chay
Kạ̄li̱ hạṇḍis zan ninay puj vān
Yi gāsu' kạ̄n duni̱yahic bramvān chay[24]

My life, please hear this news
This news of death which reduces you to Nothing
A time will come when they'll take you away as a lamb to the slaughterhouse
A dry blade of grass are these works of the world's illusions

In this *shruk*, the slow-approaching Death keeps reducing the being to Nothing (*shinvān* which I translate here as "reduces you to Nothing" literally means "to freeze"). The knowledge of death reduces the self to Nothing: it freezes human action (this recalls the *poh* and *māg*, the winter months, of the earlier *shruk* we discussed). It is striking how Nund Rishi uses a metaphor which was likely to make a powerful impact on the Kashmiri peasantry which faced harsh winters. Nund Rishi exacerbates the effect of terror by reminding his reader that he is going to be carried away by death as a lamb is taken to the slaughterhouse. Such a fate compels the poet to compare the world's play of illusions to a *gāsu' kạn* (a dry blade of grass) which has no weight or value.

The idea of becoming Nothing also appears in Nund Rishi in the form of a relation to the unknown, absent God. In yet another *shruk*, Nund Rishi addresses the *nirguna* (God without form/attributes):

Nirgunu' tsu' royatu' ditam
Chus bu' cyōnay nāv saran
Bhugi Kailāsh khạrith nitam
Chuham tsÿtas tsu' meharbān[25]

Nirguna, give me your face to see
All I do is contemplate your Name
God, carry me to the Mount Kailash
I always remember you the gracious one

Is the *nirguna* here an absent God without attributes or the Nothing? *Nirguna* in monistic Hindu thought is the Brahman (the Supreme Being) without attributes in which all distinctions are obliterated. But there is also here an explicit invocation of the Hindu God Śiva as Nund Rishi prays to the Lord to carry him to the sacred Mount Kailash. To be carried to Mount Kailash here is an allusion to the spiritual liberation that Nund Rishi seeks (Mount Kailash in Tibet is sacred to Hinduism, Jainism, and Buddhism). To attain such salvation is to come face-to-face with the *nirguna*, the Brahman without qualities, which Nund Rishi situates in his *shruk*s in a relation with the unknown God of the Qur'ān. This turn to the *nirguna* Nund Rishi shares with many north Indian saints at the crossroads of Sufism and *bhaktī* such as Kabir, Guru Nanak, and Dadu Dayal.

The *shruks* of Nund Rishi that deal with the Nothing, and becoming Nothing (*nāh gōm pānas*), return us to the lines Jacques Derrida quotes from the Christian mystic Angelus Silesius on becoming Nothing in his collection of essays, *Sauf le Nom*:

> *To become Nothing is to become God*
> Nothing becomes what is before: if you do not become nothing,
> Never will you be born of eternal light.[26]

Let us now turn to Derrida's exegesis of this verse:

> How is this becoming to be thought? *Werden*: at once birth and change, formation and transformation. This coming to being starting from nothing and as nothing, as God and as Nothing, as the Nothing itself, this birth that *carries itself* without premise, this becoming-self as becoming-God – or Nothing – that is what appears impossible, more than impossible, the most impossible possible, more impossible than the impossible if the impossible is the simple negative modality of the possible.[27].

Becoming nothing is the becoming self which remains an impossible possibility. Even an inquiry into the Nothing then is an inquiry into ourselves. When we turn to Nund Rishi's powerful images of Death – water disappearing into new clay vessels, shops after closing time (the image of *fālav*, the long iron crossbars which are used to lock the traditional Kashmiri shops), the scattering-shattering of the arrows of Death – we realize that everything has a fragile meaning in relation to our own meaning as the being which is in a relation to death and the Nothing. Heidegger has an early term for this work of the Nothing which fits our needs well here: ruination (*ruinanz*). This *ruinanz* is later replaced by falling.[28] But ruination captures better the fate of the human subject in the world and it is the task of poetry and philosophy that they combat such ruination. I venture that the *shruk* does not merely intend to terrorize with its themes of death and the Nothing but hopes to combat the hold of death and the Nothing through an invitation to poetic thinking. Heidegger speaks of ruination as larvance and destruction in an early lecture course on Aristotle.[29] The factual life becomes Nothing in ruinant existence. Ruinance is nothing but the temporal movement of life: if ruinance is a movement through emptiness, negative theology's meditation on ruinance can be interpreted as a philosophical counter-ruinance. Nund Rishi repeatedly bemoans the time that is lost in searching for an escape from temporal finitude so that fundamental decisions can be avoided. The subjective experience of ruination is evoked by Nund Rishi in the *shruk* quoted earlier where a pure (*pren*) body is despoiled by stains of impurity and the bird of the self escapes the garden, the pleasant sunshine of a Kashmiri summer suddenly turns to bitter chill of the winter, and all essences abandon the self suddenly struck by a primordial poverty. We get a sense of the spiritual crisis of Nund Rishi in relation to the factical world and its ruination in another oft-cited *shruk* we have discussed in the previous chapter:

Ganbar prakat karān chum kāv
Tīr chanẏm anbar bāvu' kas
Sạri̱ gōm gur tu' wọkhu'li̱ gayạm nāv
Bōr gōm gob tu' trāvu' kas[30]

The crow reveals a serious word that makes it shed
All its feathers that are a heap of dust at its feet
My horse is drowning and my boat has run aground
This burden has become heavy and I cannot even pass it on

The spiritual crisis is brought to life in both Nund Rishi and Lal Ded often in time-images that are images of life stilled and stalled by ruination (a horse drowning in the waters and a boat that has run aground). It is only through an encounter with the Nothing that one can reach authenticity, home, and a life of meaning. We have already noted in the previous chapter that it is an inability to handle beings which is written into the legends of Nund Rishi's traditional biographies: a young Nund Rishi fails at different crafts and trades as he ponders over the contingency of meaning in those domains (as weaver, thief, and peasant). It is the failure to handle beings that stages the human encounter with the Nothing.

The encounter with the Nothing returns us to the question of authentic being. Nund Rishi writes:

Yati ti me tsū'i tati ti me tsū'i
Me tsū'i kartam gulzār
Sạ̄rī trạ̄vith rotukh mye tsū'i
Mye tsū'i hāvtam dīdar[31]

Here you are enough for me; and you are enough for me over there
You alone can make this clay blossom into flowers
I left everything and hold on to you alone
You alone now show me your face

The *me* (mine) is bound up with the Thou (*tsū'i*: only You). But the *shruk* that announces the economy of this relay between I and Thou, where each is sufficient for the other and where the *me* (My) relies on the *tsu'* (You) for a flowering in the desert that is the self, is rent by the homonym *metsū'i* (only clay). This double register is less obvious in the rest of the two lines where a prayer is addressed to the other for a more fundamental disclosure in which God must at least give a *dīdār*, sighting, as God did to Moses). The first two lines can be reread as "Only clay here and only clay there/turn this desert into a flower garden." The meaning also shifts in the last line if we were to take up the other meaning of the homonym where the line could now be read as a call for a revelation, an advent of the other, in the desert of the immanent (*myets*, or clay). The last line can also be translated as "Show me your face in this clay." This *shruk* reveals the striking resemblance negative theology bears at times to radical atheism: the reliance of *mye-tsū'i* (to me, you alone), which carries an echo of the Qur'ānic *Hasbunallahu wa ni'mal wakīl* (You alone God are sufficient for me!), is threatened by the facticity and finitude of *metsū'i* (only clay).

We must now consider the Nothing in the immediate environment in which Nund Rishi's thinking takes place, that is, the Hindu ideas of the Nothing but also the *śūnyatā* (emptiness) of Buddhist thought. Nund Rishi composes his *shruks* long after the decline of Mulasarvastivadin Buddhist thought in Kashmir. Even the different flourishing schools of Śaiva and Vaiśnava thought had shrunk to forms of Trika and Kaula Śaivism (grouped together as Kashmir Śaivism in contemporary scholarship) by the fifteenth century. It is difficult to speculate how many of these ideas informed Nund Rishi's thinking. But the Buddhist concept of *śūnya* is very much there in Nund Rishi's mystical poetry. It is important to remember though that the term *śūnyatā* has a phenomenological thrust in Buddhism: it is used to precipitate a thinking of "the way things really are."[32] Much like early Greek philosophy, the Buddhist thinking on the Nothing did not develop in isolation from a spiritual practice of self-transformation. The Buddhist *śūnya* never implied privation or lack but was a dynamic concept in the tradition. Even though the Buddhist Nothing has been a source of much controversy, it is neither being nor non-being. For negative theology, it is not merely the question of knowing Nothing which is at stake but also becoming Nothing. This becoming Nothing is just beyond the threshold of negative theology. Negative theology decides to go further than knowing and to become Nothing. It knows nothing about the Nothing. Nund Rishi struggles to push language to the limits in search of the Nothing. How does one search for the Nothing? Even an attempt to answer this question can leave speech paralyzed. As Samuel Beckett writes: "What am I to do, what shall I do, in my situation, how proceed? By *aporia* pure and simple."[33] Nund Rishi admonishes the paralyzed self: *Kyāh karu' kyāh karu' tsolay nu' zāth* (What shall I do? What must I do? You never gave up on this). This is a refrain through many of the *shruk*s clustered together by Amin Kamil in his edition of the *Nūrnāmu'*.

Let us now turn to the question of negative theology in Nund Rishi, and the relation it bears to the Nothing, through one of the first few *shruk*s of the Moti Lal Saqi collected edition of the *shruk*s:

Lā Ilāhā illallāh ṣahih korum
Vaḥī korum panun pān
Vojūd trạvith mūjūd myūlum
Adu' bu' vōtus lā makān[34]

I decided on "There is no god but God"
And made of myself a site of revelation
Abandoning existence, I found presence
Thus have I reached the place-less place

There are other variants of this *shruk* given by Saqi that already help us establish an equivalence between certain key terms as interpreted by the tradition. In the second version, *Lā Ilāhā illallāh ṣahih korum* is substituted by *Nafī Isbāt ṣahih korum* (I decided on the negation–affirmation). This makes possible a Sufi interpretation of the *kalimā*, the first article of the Muslim faith (with which Nund Rishi begins the first version), as beginning with a negation followed by an affirmation. The first article of the Muslim faith (*kalimā* or *shahāda*), *Lā Ilāhā illallāh* (There is no god but God), is also considered to be the foundation of Islam expressed in the Islamic concept of *tawhīd*, or unity of God. Elsewhere Nund Rishi speaks of the way his thinking has been shaped by the meditation on the *kalimā*, or the first article of the Muslim faith, and its insistence on *tawhīd* – a fundamental Sufi practice:

Kalimay porum kalimay sōrum
Kalimay korum panunay pān
Kalimay hani hani mōyan tōrum
Kalimÿe sạt votus lā makān[35]

I read the *kalimā,* I contemplated the *kalimā*
I made of myself the *kalimā*
I absorbed the *kalimā* into every hair on my body
And by the *kalimā,* I reached the place-less place

This gives us a sense of the difficulty involved in reading the *kalimā*. To read the *kalimā* which declares the unity of God is no easy task. One must become the *kalimā*. What would it mean to embody the *kalimā* so that it enters you through every pore of your body? To realize the idea of unity (*tawhīd*) at stake, one must first grapple with the negation of *La Illāhā* (There is no god). But let us return to the first line of the key *shruk* which begins the Moti Lal Saqi edition of the *shruks*: *Lā Ilāhā illallāh ṣahih korum*. *Ṣahih korum* could simply mean recitation, avowal, or owning but it also carries the meanings of decision and correction or returning something to its right and proper origin. But what of the alternative *Nafī Is̱bāt ṣahih korum* (I decided on the negation–affirmation). Nund Rishi explicitly takes up the *nafī–is̱bāt* question in another long *shruk* which help us understand better the relation that appears in the Nund Rishi corpus between the *Lā Ilāhā illallāh* (There is no god but God) and *nafī–is̱bāt* (negation–affirmation):

Pānay chu gindān nafī-is̱bātas
Ạkis sātās labÿs nu' tshÿn
Ārạyish ditsu'n prÿth ṣifātas
Zātas lobun nu' marun tu' zyan
Sharaf bak̲h̲shun ḥaẓrat-e insaanas
Trukuy chukh tu' pānai tsÿn
Soruy pānay vuchakh kyā pānas
Rātas labi nu' nyendu'r tu' khÿn
Yimav nu' dyān kor ath gyānas
Ạnis chu hihuy rāth tu' dÿn[36]

He plays himself with affirmation-negation
Not even for a moment you'll find his absence
He adorned every attribute
There is no birth or death for His essence

He gave many gifts to the human
If you are wise, know yourself
He is everywhere, where would you search for him?
You'll find neither sleep nor food at night
The ones who pay no attention to this teaching are blind
There is no difference for the blind between the night and the day

Is the negation–affirmation dialectic of the *kalimā* the same as the *nafī–is̱bāt* of South Asian Sufi traditions? The *nafī–is̱bāt* is not only the problem of predicating God's existence through negations. The way of *nafī–is̱bāt* is also a serious political and theological question in medieval South Asia, as is obvious from the case of Sarmad, whose execution, by the Mughal emperor Aurangzeb (1658–1707), Nauman Naqvi has connected to the controversies around the problem of *nafī–is̱bāt*:

> The most legendary charge [against Sarmad], however, was that which is now synoptically remembered as the matter of negation and assertion (*nafi-o-asbat*). For in reciting the first article of the Muslim faith, the *kalima-e-shahadat* – literally, "the word of witness" – Sarmad Shaheed would merely say, *la ilaha*: no assertion of the singular Divinity (Allah) and the prophethood of Muhammad, just *la ilaha* – "there is absolutely no God." When interrogated by the judge (*qazi*), he explained that he was yet unable to rise to assertion since he had not witnessed – *mushahida* or *shahadat* – the Most High. Needless to say, this was unacceptable under the new dispensation, and so he was executed.[37]

Yet again we witness that the charge that negative theology unproblematically affirms a faith in a Being beyond beings is in question and that negative theology in the Islamic tradition often found itself accused of outright heresy. It is this other tradition of negative theology on the borders of heresy in which we must situate the mystical poetry of Nund Rishi.

Let us now turn to the second line of the *shruk* about the *kalimā* that we have been discussing: *Vạḥī korum panun pān*. This is the second step. To turn one's self into a revelation. *Panun pān* can translate as one's own self. What does it mean to turn one's self into the site of a revelation? This could have two possible meanings: (*a*) to move toward the experience of the self as a site of revelation through an endless kenosis or (*b*) to turn away from all metalanguages toward the finitude of the self itself as the self's only possible transcendence. The third line is even more intriguing. *Vojūd trạvith mūjūd myūlum*: abandoning existence, I found presence. The presence here has less to do with metaphysics and more with the presencing (*anwesen*) of later Heidegger (where presencing is a rising up of things, a temporal unfolding of entities in human experience but also moving in and moving out of presence).[38] To find presence is not to find metaphysical being but a site of unconcealment. One must abandon an existence (*vojūd*) which is an essence for such a presencing: one must become Nothing. There is a sense in which there is here a turn away from the world. This abandoning of existence holds the promise of an arriving at the *lā makān*, the placeless place, which carries an echo of the *khôra* from Plato's *Timaeus*, about which Derrida says that it is not Nothing but "a desert in the desert of which it is neither a threshold nor a mourning."[39]

For Nund Rishi, the *lā makān*, the no-place, is the absence on which all presencing depends. Even the metaphor of being this side of the river, waiting to cross over, meandering on the riverbank, mourning the absences, lacks, and losses that characterize life (metaphors that endlessly proliferate in Kashmiri mystical poetry), reveal to us a subject grappling with nihilations. This sense is deeper and more profound in Lal Ded than it is in Nund Rishi. But in Nund Rishi, it achieves a massive reconfiguration under the sign of an Islamic eschatological thinking. Henry Corbin, the French scholar of Islamic philosophy and mysticism who also happens to be the first French translator of Heidegger, has denounced the tendency toward the "unreality of the ego" in certain forms of Sufism that confuse the unity of *vojūd* (existence) with the unity of *mūjūd* (existents). Corbin writes that "our Iranian metaphysicians of the Avicennian tradition" do not confuse "the transcendental unity of Being or Existence (wahdat al wojud) with an impossible, contradictory and illusory unity of existents or existent being(s) (mawjud, latin ens)."[40] But Nund Rishi affirms the *mūjūd* (present, presence) having abandoned the *vojūd* (existence). As we discussed above, *mūjūd* can be translated as "presence" but does not signify a metaphysical presence. Nund Rishi's affirmation of the *mūjūd* could also be read in relation to Heidegger's idea of presencing. Is this a simple reversal of *vojūd* and *mūjūd* where Corbin and Nund Rishi are in a fundamental agreement about the unity of being? Or is Nund Rishi's understanding of the unity of being different from Corbin's? One way of reading *kunear* (unity) in Nund Rishi is not as a transcendental unity but as a unity which, even if it eludes understanding, grounds temporal finitude. It points to our existence (*vojūd*) as bound up with everything else in the world (*mūjūd*). What is at stake in these difficult, paradoxical utterances? Or these affirmations and negations (the *nafī* and the *is̠bāt*)? Maurice Blanchot writes about Meister Eckhart that he takes "recourse to a violent form because his thinking demands this violence, this 'yes' and 'no' intimately united, but he consciously chooses the most shocking form so that thought can receive it only in a tension that strips away its repose and destroys it and prepares it for silence."[41] Does the preparation for silence that appears to be the purpose behind these affirmations and negations bring us yet again to the threshold of Nothing? Keiji Nishitani explicates these connections in reflecting on the meaning of a Christian creation *ex nihilo*:

> That a thing is created *ex nihilo* means that this *nihil* is more immanent in that thing than the very being of that thing is "immanent" in the thing itself. This is why we speak of "absolute immanence." It is an immanence of absolute negation, for the being of the created is grounded upon a *nothingness* and seen fundamentally to be a nothingness. At the same time, it is an immanence of absolute affirmation, for the nothingness of the created is the ground of its *being*. This is the omnipresence of God in all things that have their being as a *creatio ex nihilo*. It follows that this omnipresence can be said to represent for man the dynamic *motif* of the transposition of absolute negation and absolute affirmation. To entrust the self to this *motif*, to let oneself be driven by it so as to die to the self and live in God, is what constitutes faith.[42]

Faith is this transposition, this translation of the Nothing into being. The nothingness that grounds the being of the created, the nothingness which is immanent in being, is also at the same time the ground of being. There is no difference between an absolute affirmation and an absolute negation. To die to the self, to affirm that the ground of all being is a nothingness that brings us near to God, is what constitutes faith. There is a closing of a gap here between God and Nothingness. But what is becoming Nothing? Nund Rishi speaks of *nāh karun* (to make Nothing) in a way similar to Angelus Silesius' call to *Become Nothing*: to be driven by the motif of nihilation (and its presencing in and as ruination) is to surrender to the other beyond stratagem or renunciation.[43] This is how a Japanese philosopher, Ueda Shizuteru, considers the relations between Meister Eckhart's Nothingness and a "fundamental death" which is a movement away from God toward a Nothingness:

> Hence the soul, in order to return to its original ground, must break through God and out into the nothingness of the godhead. In so doing the soul must "take leave of God" and "become void of God." This is accomplished only if

> the soul lets go of itself as what has been united with God. This is what Eckhart understands by extreme "solitariness," the "fundamental death."[44]

The extreme solitariness, *kunear*, is a "fundamental death," or in the language of Sufism, a dying before death. But one must risk losing God in this fundamental death as much as losing one's self. What is most striking about this dying is that such a movement is not without a purpose or consequence for the world: "In unison with the movement 'away from God to the nothingness of the godhead' goes a movement 'away from God to the reality of the world.'"[45] Becoming Nothing has an irreducibly political dimension. It returns the self to the reality of the world, and for Shizuteru, to "a non-religious religiosity."[46] This "non-religious religiosity" could also be seen as one of the most significant stakes of the Sufi–*bhaktī* upsurge in medieval north India and Nund Rishi remains in relation to a generalized movement toward a "non-religious religiosity" in north Indian religious revolts which nonetheless do not cohere into a universal religion. Shizuteru interprets the affirmation that comes after the negation of negative theology, a return to the world, as what he calls "a coincidence of negation and affirmation, of nothingness and here-and-now actuality."[47] Dying before death is to then come alive to the here-and-now actuality of the world. We must again turn to Keiji Nishitani for a more explicit consideration of the relations between being, the Nothing, and death:

> Our life runs up against death at its every step; we keep one foot planted in the vale of death at all times. Our life stands poised at the brink of the abyss of nihility to which it may return at any moment. Our existence is an existence at one with nonexistence, swinging back and forth over nihility, ceaselessly passing away and ceaselessly regaining its existence. This is what is called the "incessant becoming" of existence.[48]

Negative theology, including that of Nund Rishi, is this proximate awareness of death and the way it is incessantly shaping our existence in the world. But to what end? Should one even posit an end to the Being and Nothing that disclose themselves as "incessant becoming"? The Greek philosopher Epicurus (*Letter to Menoeceus*) declared that "death is nothing to us seeing that when we exist death is not present, and when death is present we do not exist."[49] But Keiji Nishitani makes explicit what is implicit in the "becoming Nothing" of Angelus Silesius or the *nāh karun* ("to make Nothing") of Nund Rishi:

> ... we come to the realization of death and nihility when we see them within ourselves as constituting the basis of our life and existence. We awaken to their reality when we see them as extending beyond the subjective realm, lying concealed at the ground of all that exists, at the ground of the world itself. This awareness implies more than merely looking contemplatively at death and nihility. It means that the self realizes their presence at the foundations of its existence, that it sees them from the final frontier of its self-existence.[50]

Nund Rishi is not merely expressing an awareness or contemplation of death in the *shruk*s but rather reveals that death is to be found at the foundations of human existence. In the Zen Buddhist tradition, Nishitani writes, the stance of a radical doubt toward existence is called "the Great Death" which is absolutely essential for a Zen practitioner.[51] The thinking of negative theology is a phenomenology of that which shows up in relation to our awakening to the reality of death.

Be it the severe and relentless questioning of the *nafs*, the desiring ego, or the questioning of Being itself, negative theology (Muslim, Christian, Jewish, or Greek) is an existential understanding (in the Heideggerian sense) of human existence. Take, for instance, the *nafs*. *Nafs* is neither ego nor self and has a complex genealogy in the Islamic tradition and interpretations vary from the grammatical to the phenomenological. *Nafs* marks reflexive grammatical constructions in Arabic like "He saw himself" but, in Sufism, it suggests the locus of self-centered life.[52] The term *nafs* appears often in the Qur'ān. There is a Qur'ānic verse: "Each *nafs* will be reckoned only according to itself, and no bearer of burdens will bear the burden of another."[53] The death of a *nafs* is in the direct control of God: "... And it does not belong to a *nafs* to die except with the permission of God at a term written down."[54] According to the Qur'ān, each and every *nafs* must taste death. The Islamic thinker Fazlur Rahman contends that the term *nafs* which, in Islamic philosophy and Sufism, came to mean soul as a substance separate from the body, in the Qur'ān only means mostly "himself" or "herself."[55] For Rahman, the Qur'ān does not recognize a dualism between the soul and the body.[56] The word *nafs* in Nund Rishi, however, is used more in the Sufi sense as a blameworthy ego that must be brought under control. For instance, take this *shruk*:

Nafsu'ī myōn chuy madu'h hostuy
Ām hạsi̱ monganam kōtāh bal
Sāsan manzu'h chuy akhā lọstuy
Natu' ạmi̱ hy̆ti̱nam sạ̄rī tal[57]

My *nafs* is a mad elephant
This elephant has drained me of all strength
Only one in a thousand escape its power
Everyone else is trampled under its feet

Nund Rishi subjects the experience of the *nafs* to a radical doubt and calls for a dying of this "ego-self" for a more enduring life. Only one in a thousand escape the power of the *nafs*. The *nafs* here recalls the mad elephant that charged at the Buddha with murderous intent but then suddenly became calm and kneeled before him.[58] The task of the ascetic is to tame the mad, elephantine *nafs*. Nishitani's own synoptic account of Christianity is helpful in approaching the stakes in Nund Rishi's appropriation of the later Sufi theme of the annihilation of *nafs*, or the "lower" self:

> Christianity has long considered the egoistic mode of being that is basic to the reality of man as a form of disobedience against God, as an original sin. The alternative it offers is the way to a new man who, rather than following his own will, forsakes it to follow the will of God, who dies to self in order to live in God.[59]

Nishitani also speaks of a "dying before death" as a rebirth "when we break through nihility."[60] The death involves the dying of a form of willing (such an autonomous willing, in turn, is taken as a sign of ignorance). Such a call to surrender can translate poorly into politics and Sufism can often appear as a call to political quietude.[61] But everything is at stake in the question whether God involved in the surrender is the unknowable God of negative theology or the unknowable God of Islamic theology. Christianity connects the Nothing with the absolute transcendence of God by turning to the idea of a creation *ex nihilo*. As Nishitani writes:

> Christianity speaks of a *creatio ex nihilo*: God created everything from a point at which there was nothing at all. And since all things have this *nihilum* at the ground of their being, they are absolutely distinct from their Creator. This idea is a plain expression of the absolute transcendence of God.[62]

The idea of a *creatio ex nihilo* takes care of the problem of immanence–transcendence of God: God is immanent in creation through the Nothing that is the ground of the being of all entities. To experience the nothingness of things is to draw near to God and at the same time come up against the wall of separation between man and God. Our experience of creation is an experience of the Nothing that calls us to and yet separates us from God:

> If things are telling us that they were created by God, then they also are telling us that they are not themselves God. To that extent, we do not encounter God anywhere in the world. Instead, we find everywhere, at the ground of everything that is, the nihility of the *creatio ex nihilo*. This nihility stands like a great iron wall that absolutely separates all things from God. Accordingly, to encounter this nihility means necessarily to encounter God as an iron wall, to meet with the absolute negativity of God....[63]

The Nothing is not merely that which our thinking comes up against as an iron wall, it is what separates all things, including human beings, from God. There is in becoming Nothing an encounter with the limit that separates us from God but such an encounter has profound consequences. It is undecidable if this is the *kunear*, or unity, that Nund Rishi has in mind. But even in the Christian tradition, according to Nishitani, this encounter with God in all things everywhere can only begin with a self-transformation. Nishitani writes: "Hence for anyone, whoever he happens to be, encountering the omnipresence of God existentially must begin with a sense of having been cast out into the middle of a desert of death."[64] This desert of death calls to our mind the abandoned bazaar at closing time from the previous chapter. One must come up against death in everything with the purpose of being born again in the everyday. For Nishitani, the political-eschatological dimension of death has a clear existential significance which forces a decision on the self:

> The fact that the gospel of the Kingdom of God has an eschatological dimension signifies, from the existential standpoint, that the *motif* of conversion for man implied in divine omnipresence confronts man with an urgency that presses him to a decision on the spot: either eternal life or eternal death. This is the meaning of what was said earlier about the love of Christ being at one and the same time a sword that kills man and a sword that gives man life. It means that there is an undercurrent running through the gospel to the effect that no matter where a man is or what he is doing, he comes into touch with the cutting sword of *de-cision*. Only in this way might eschatology be said to be a problem of human Existenz.[65]

The problem of eschatology is connected to the decision which forever presses on the self. This decision is forced upon the self in its encounter with death.

That is the reason Nund Rishi is mournful of the surrender of this sword of decision: *Kartu'l phạtrạm tu' gạrmạs drạt* (I broke the sword and fashioned sickles out of it).[66] The Nothing not only brings the reader of the *shruk*s to the site of an encounter with the decision but opens up the *de-cision* as the ground of human freedom. For Nishitani, we must speak of God the way Meister Eckhart speaks of God as absolute nothingness.[67]

What are the political stakes of this thinking of the Nothing? Keiji Nishitani, for instance, once claimed that what is at stake for him in negative theology is the possibility that the world "has no specific center...."[68] Michel de Certeau also turns to this relation between the question of Nothing and politics in medieval mysticism:

> The fact that the mystics enclosed themselves in the circle of a "nothingness" capable of being an "origin" is to be explained, first of all, by their having been caught up in a *radical* situation they took seriously. They have translated that situation into their texts, not only in the relation an innovative truth bears throughout with the pain of a loss, but, more explicitly, in the social figures that dominate their discourse, those of the madman, the child, the illiterate.[69]

In this turn to the Nothing in Nund Rishi, there is a serious thinking of political equality at a time when the new Muslim sultanate appears as mired in caste, clan, and race as the order it had displaced. Nund Rishi's critique of theological knowledge and absolutist power gathers momentum in those *shruk*s that deal with the apocalyptic (as we shall see in the next chapter). The *shruk*s that deal with the Nothing point not only to the relationship between the Being of the One and the Nothing (a central problem in Nund Rishi's negative theology) but also turn the thinking of the Nothing into a meditation on the being of the human. Much like death, the Nothing is not only an existential motif. The thinking of the Nothing in Nund Rishi also gives rise to an existential politics. By the rise of an existential politics, I mean the challenge that the thinking of death and the Nothing in Nund Rishi (and Lal Ded from whom he remains inseparable) pose to the positive theological politics that tied monarchical power to Islamic theology. Yet the vision of negative politics in Nund Rishi is neither strategic nor programmatic but utopian – a utopian thinking that imagines a new form of radical equality made possible by facing up to one's death and becoming Nothing. Becoming Nothing here is not an apolitical withdrawal into a transcendental realm; it is a striving for an immanent personal and political possibility. The political impulse in

Nund Rishi is not anarchic but utopian. The relation of this existential politics, and the utopian possibility it iterates, to the *bhaktī* upsurge in north India remains unclear. Unlike many *bhaktī* saints of medieval India, he does not name his utopia but sometimes turns to ideal images of early Islam. Becoming Nothing in Nund Rishi's *shruk*s does not signal an ascetic withdrawal from the political but a new existential politics. The historical memory of this existential politics persists in the political unconscious of Kashmiris. It is this repressed political unconscious, expressed in the *shruk*s and later Kashmiri Sufi poetry, and the question of human freedom at stake in it, that most concerns the contemporary Kashmiri reader of Nund Rishi.

Notes

1. Jean-Luc Nancy, "Des lieux divins," in *Qu'est-ce que Dieu? Philosophie, Theologie: Hommage à l'abbé Daniel Coppieters de Gibson (1929–1983)* (Bruxelles: Facultés Universitaires Saint-Louis, 1985), 561, quoted in and translated by William Franke, "Apophasis and the Turn of Philosophy to Religion: From Neoplatonic Theology to Postmodern Negation of Theology," in "Self and Other: Essays in Continental Philosophy of Religion," *International Journal for Philosophy of Religion* 60, no. 1/3 (December, 2006): 71.
2. Rahi, *Kahvạt*, 144. The full *shruk* is given by Amin Kamil in his *Nūrnāmu'*. See Kamil, *Nūrnāmu'*, 59.
3. There is a slight variation in transliteration here for the same terms in Kashmiri and Sanskrit.
4. Graham Priest, "The Structure of Emptiness," *Philosophy East and West* 59, no. 4 (October, 2009), 468.
5. These are the first two verses of *At-Takāthur*, a Meccan chapter of the Qur'ān, which have been translated by Ahmed Ali in these words: "The avarice of plenitude keeps you occupied. Till you reach the grave." *Al-Qur'ān*, tr. Ali, 549. The poignant translation reproduced above appears in a moving tribute by Talal Asad to his father, Muhammad Asad. See Talal Asad, "Muhammad Asad between Religion and Politics," *Interactive*, last modified April 16, 2020, http://interactive.net.in/muhammad-asad-between-religion-and-politics/ (accessed April 16, 2020).
6. Rahi, *Kahvat*, 144. Fernando Tola and Carmen Dragonetti call *śūnyatā* a metaphor used in the Madhyamika school "to indicate the 'residue' that remains after the abolition of the empirical reality – a 'residue' that neither is nor is not and referring to which nothing can be thought...." Fernando Tola and Carmen Dragonetti, "Nagarjuna's Conception of Voidness (*Śūnyatā*)," *Journal of Indian Philosophy* 9, no. 3 (September 1981): 277.

7. Keiji Nishitani, *Religion and Nothingness*, translated with an introduction by Jan Van Bragt (Berkeley: University of California Press, 1983), 73.
8. Kamil, *Nūrnāmu'*, 160. The transliteration has been slightly modified.
9. Kamil, *Nūrnāmu'*, 58.
10. This *shruk* has been discussed in detail in Chapter 1.
11. Kamil, *Nūrnāmu'*, 37.
12. As Martin Heidegger puts it: "The question about what is not and about Nothing has gone side by side with the question of what is, since its inception." Richard Polt, "The Question of Nothing," in *A Companion to* Heidegger's Introduction to Metaphysics, ed. Richard Polt and Gregory Fried (New Haven: Yale University Press, 2001), 60.
13. Maurice Blanchot, "Master Eckhart," in *Faux Pas*, tr. Charlotte Mandell (Stanford: Stanford University Press, 2002), 26.
14. *Bozanu' yun* is to be visible, or intelligible. George Abraham Grierson, *A Dictionary of the Kashmiri Language* (Calcutta: Asiatic Society of Bengal, 1932), 154.
15. In vernacular usage, *kuni nō rozakh* means "you will be lost," or "you will be without mooring." I am grateful for this insight to Suvir Kaul.
16. Kamil, *Nūrnāmu'*, 249. *Shāyi* (places) will be read in modern Kashmiri as *jāyi*.
17. This biographical detail is unnecessary since the late-fourteenth-century Kashmir was a site of active missionary work by the Kubrāwiyyā Sufis. But many hagiographies are in agreement that either one or both of Nund Rishi's parents were disciples of Sayyid Husayn Simnānī.
18. Kamil, *Nūrnāmu'*, 106. *Kalimā* is the first article of the Muslim faith affirming the unity of God. *Kalimā* can also be translated as the 'word' or 'speech.'
19. Kaul (ed.), *Lal Ded*, 62.
20. This translation is by Ranjit Hoskote. See Hoskote, *I, Lalla*, 6.
21. Kamil, *Nūrnāmu'*, 245. Some versions have *rivu'nē* ("got irritated") instead of *rāvu'nē* ("got lost").
22. Moti Lal Saqi, *Kulliyāt-e Shaikh al-'Ālam*, 43.
23. Basher Bashir, *Raḥmān Ḍār* (New Delhi: Sahitya Akademi, 2003), 65.
24. Saqi, *Kulliyāt-e Shaikh al-'Ālam*, 54.
25. Kamil, *Nūrnāmu'*, 62.
26. Derrida, *On the Name*, 43.
27. Ibid.
28. Polt, "The Question of Nothing," 68.
29. See Martin Heidegger, *Phenomenological Interpretations of Aristotle* (Bloomington: Indiana University Press, 2001).

30. Rahi, "Shaikh al 'Ālam sạnz shạ̄'irānā ḥạsịyath," 150.
31. Kamil, *Nūrnāmu'*, 78. The transliteration has been slightly modified.
32. In Mircea Eliade (ed.), *The Encyclopaedia of Religion*, s.v. "Śūnyam and Śūnyatā."
33. Quoted in Connor Cunningham, "Preface," in *Genealogies of Nihilism* (New York: Routledge, 2002), xii.
34. Saqi, *Kulliyāt-e Shaikh al-'Ālam*, 29. There are many variants of the *shruk*. I have just substituted the last line of the *shruk* from the *Nūrnāmu'* variant quoted by Saqi. The *shruk* appears in this form in B. N. Parimoo's selections (except for the word *myūlum* which is replaced by the word *sōrum*). See Parimoo, *Unity in Diversity*, 124–25.
35. Kamil, *Nūrnāmu'*, 105.
36. Saqi, *Kulliyāt-e Shaikh al-'Ālam*, 48. Saqi gives an alternative to line 3 which I have used here. Ibid., fn. 2. *Ārạyish* means adornment.
37. Nauman Naqvi, "Acts of Askēsis, Scenes of Poiēsis: The Dramatic Phenomenology of Another Violence in a Muslim Painter-Poet," *Diacritics* 40, no. 2 (Summer 2012): 58–59.
38. See the entry on "Presencing (*Anwesen*)" by Richard Capobianco in Mark Wrathall (ed.), *The Cambridge Heidegger Lexicon* (Cambridge: Cambridge University Press, 2021), 603–05.
39. Jacques Derrida, "Faith and Knowledge: The Two Sources of 'Religion' at the Limits of Reason Alone," in *Acts of Religion*, ed. Gil Anidjar (New York: Columbia University Press, 2002), 59. *Makān*, in Arabic, is translated as place and *la-makān* can be translated as 'no-place.'
40. Henry Corbin, "Apophatic Theology as an Antidote to Nihilism," *Umbr(a)* (2007).
41. Blanchot, "Master Eckhart," 25.
42. Nishitani, *Religion and Nothingness*, 39–40.
43. Derrida, *On the Name*, 35–88.
44. Ueda Shizuteru, "Nothingness in Meister Eckhart and Zen Buddhism," in *The Buddha Eye: An Anthology of the Kyoto School and Its Contemporaries*, ed. Frederick Franck (Bloomington: World Wisdom, 2004), 158.
45. Ibid., 159.
46. Ibid.
47. Ibid.
48. Nishitani, *Religion and Nothingness*, 4.
49. Phillip Mitsis, "Where Death Is, There We Are Not," in *The Oxford Handbook of Philosophy of Death*, ed. Ben Bradley et al. (New York: Oxford University Press, 2013), 207.
50. Nishitani, *Religion and Nothingness*, 16.
51. Ibid., 21.

52. Sells, *Early Islamic Mysticism: Sufi, Quran, Miraj, Poetic and Theological Writings*, 147.
53. Bowker, *The Meanings of Death*, 112.
54. Ibid., 123.
55. Buturovic, "Death," 132.
56. Ibid.
57. Kamil, *Nūrnāmu'*, 173.
58. Donald S. Lopez Jr., *From Stone to Flesh: A Short History of the Buddha* (Chicago: University of Chicago Press, 2013), 82.
59. Nishitani, *Religion and Nothingness*, 36.
60. Ibid., 32–33.
61. The idea of surrender is often expressed in Sufism through the concept of *tawakkul*, absolute trust in God.
62. Nishitani, *Religion and Nothingness*, 37.
63. Ibid., 38.
64. Ibid.
65. Ibid., 40.
66. It is ironical then that the line with which the Indian state chose to adorn the first bus it flagged off in 2005 between the disputed regions of a divided Kashmir for a peace initiative with Pakistan was this one from Nund Rishi. It did not occur to anyone that Nund Rishi in the cited *shruk* actually mourns the loss of his sword. For an excellent discussion of this *shruk*, see Nazir Azad, "Kartu'l phạtrạm tu' gạrmạs drạ̄t," *Alamdār* (Kashmiri), 5, no. 5 (2012): 99–113.
67. It is interesting that Meister Eckhart has come to exemplify the position of Christian negative theology, and is used here as elsewhere, as the paradigmatic example of Christian negative theology just as Ibn al-'Arabī and Rūmī mark similar pathways in studies of medieval Sufisms.
68. James W. Heisig, *Philosophers of Nothingness: An Essay on the Kyoto School* (Honolulu: University of Hawaii Press, 2001), 198.
69. de Certeau, *The Mystic Fable*, 24–25.

4

Vernacular Apocalypse*

> As apocalyptist I can imagine that the world will be destroyed. *I have no spiritual investment in the world as it is.*
>
> —Jacob Taubes[1]

The apocalyptic is at the core of the vernacular vision of Islam disclosed in the mystical poetry of Nund Rishi. There is nothing unusual about this as the apocalyptic genre is fundamental to all Abrahamic religions.[2] Even more significantly, it is Nund Rishi's *shruk*s on the apocalyptic that endure the most in Kashmiri cultural memory and have passed on into the Kashmiri language as proverb and prophecy. The apocalyptic mode in Nund Rishi's mystical poetry, it is useful to recall, emerges at a distinct historical moment in medieval Kashmir: a time of transitions from the rule of independent Hindu kings to the establishment of a Muslim sultanate and the beginning of religious conversions to Islam in the region. A close reading of the *shruk*s that deal with the apocalyptic material reveals a translated, and vernacular, apocalyptic in Nund Rishi's mystical poetry that mediates relations between pre-Islamic and Islamic eschatology.

A traditional Muslim apocalyptic is deployed by Nund Rishi and hurled against the political structure of his time (the new Muslim sultanate ruled by the Shahmīrī dynasty). But the elements of a traditional Muslim apocalyptic are also displaced on to metaphors of a sudden inner transformation. The catastrophe of end times intimates hope of a new life. There is a tension in the *shruk*s that deal with the apocalyptic between a traditional Muslim apocalypse and a Sufi apocalypse. This is true of much Islamic mystical poetry,

---

* A version of this chapter was first published in *South Asia: Journal of South Asian Studies*. I thank the journal, and its editor Kama Maclean, for permission to reproduce a revised version of the article.

but what is unique in Nund Rishi's apocalypticism is that the coming hour of reckoning (the Islamic *qiyāmah*, or *qayāmat* in Urdu and Kashmiri) is seen not as the end of history (individual or eschatological) but as the end to an unjust political order *in* history. Even though the currency of Nund Rishi's apocalyptic *shruk*s in popular memory owes much to enduring cycles of violence in Kashmir's recent history, Nund Rishi's apocalypticism is best approached as the translation of classic Islamic eschatology (traditional Muslim apocalyptic) into the Kashmiri vernacular. The preponderance of the theme of the apocalyptic in Nund Rishi's mystical poetry is also conspicuous because other key Islamic eschatological themes such as the Prophet's mystical ascension to heaven, *mi'rāj*, do not appear so significantly in the Nund Rishi corpus. Rather, Nund Rishi translates the Islamic eschaton into the Kashmiri vernacular by bringing it near to the political structure of his time. Or, in other words, Nund Rishi translates the traditional Muslim apocalyptic as a political and ontological reversal that narrows the gap between the self and the world (the end of the world turns out to be a way of speaking of the ends of the individual and a transformation of the world). But what is even more powerfully at stake in this complex moment of translation is the challenge of Nund Rishi's apocalypticism to the reigning Indo-Iranian notions of religious and political authority.

The political stakes of Nund Rishi's *shruk*s are nowhere as explicit as in the ones that deal with the theme of the apocalyptic. By turning to those *shruk*s of Nund Rishi that deal with the apocalyptic, we also turn more explicitly to the relations between the religious and political thinking of Nund Rishi. Let us first turn to the following *shruk* that explicitly deals with the theme of the apocalyptic:

Hā hā aki sangar tār zan wazan
Gunbad wazan dun dun kith
Sọ zan isharu' sạtyen bōzan
Kọ zan bōzan nu' ḍum ḍumu' gath[3]

A single breath and the mountains will blow off like the carder's wool off a string,
The domes resound with the blows
The good shall recognize it from its signs
The evil shall not even hear the revolutions of the drum

This is the *shruk* with which Rahman Rahi begins his seminal essay on Nund Rishi, "Shaikh al 'Ālam sạnz shạ'irānā ḥaṣiyath" (The Poetic Personality of Shaikh al 'Ālam), which we have also discussed in the previous chapters.[4] Even though this is not Rahi's explicit intention, the *shruk* makes possible an understanding of what remains unthought in his own reading of Nund Rishi: *the apocalyptic tone in Nund Rishi's thinking of death*. Nund Rishi's thinking is a form of vernacular apocalypse not only because it signals the appearance of the Muslim apocalyptic in the Kashmiri language but also because it emerges from the peripheries of the Islamic world (*dār al-Islām*). The relation between the apocalyptic mode and the margins is an old one.[5] We will trace here the structure of the apocalyptic in Nund Rishi back to the Judaeo-Christiano-Islamic apocalyptics (Abrahamic apocalyptics) but marked by a difference, which is the promise of their translatability.

The thinking of death in Nund Rishi is often cast in an apocalyptic mode that gathers force in his distinctive use of Kashmiri stress patterns and sound figures. Nowhere is this as obvious as in the *shruk* quoted earlier, which unveils Nund Rishi's vernacular apocalypse (or, what is for the philosopher Jacob Taubes, "an apocalypse from below").[6] Nund Rishi speaks of the day when the mountains will blow off like wool from a carder's string (*sangar tār zan wazan*) and the *gunbad* (domes of buildings, dwellings, tombs) will tremble as everything melts in the heat of the first divine breath (*Hā hā aki*). This is a powerful *shruk* that calls to mind not only the sheer strength of the imagery of the early Meccan revelations in the Qur'ān, which deal with the apocalypse, but also the images of the end in the *bhaktī* and the Sikh traditions. The image of mountains blowing off like wool from a carder's string or the collapse of beautiful buildings are not only the traditional images of Islamic eschatology but also the core elements of Muslim apocalyptic literature. For example, the use of the dome as a symbol emerges in the Muslim historical apocalypses in relation to the Dome of the Rock and the Temple at Jerusalem.[7] One of the characteristics of the Muslim moral apocalypses is "the attack on the building of beautiful buildings."[8] David Cook considers why the apocalyptist targets buildings and their beautiful domes:

> That the builders of these buildings can only be hostile to the apocalyptist is implicit in their willingness to build "permanent" structures: the End is distant, so there is a future for the structures. If this was not so, then they would hardly be willing to put such a huge amount of effort and money into them.

> All of this is totally opposed to the world view of the apocalyptist. He believes that the End is immediate, imminent, and cares nothing for the outer beauty of the structures. They will be destroyed in the apocalyptic wars just around the corner, or at the very latest, when the world ends.[9]

Let us return to the last two lines of the *shruk*:

Sọ zan isharu' sạtyen bōzan
Kọ zan bōzan nu' ḍum ḍumu' gath

The good shall recognize it from its signs
The evil shall not even hear the revolutions of the drum

The poet makes a moral distinction between the good and the evil which turns on their relative competence in reading the signs of the apocalypse. The good need merely a sign, an *isharu'*, to decipher the eschatological message, but the evil do not even hear the imminent call of the end: the revolutions of the drum (*ḍum ḍumu' gath*). The *ḍum ḍumu' gath* is also an allusion to *ḍamaru*, an hourglass-shaped small percussion drum of the Hindu god Śiva associated with the dance of creation and destruction.[10] The dualism between the good and the evil expressed in the last two lines of the *shruk* is the hallmark of apocalypses across different religious traditions. The *shruk* begins with invoking Chapter 101 of the Qur'ān, *Surah Al-Qār'ia*, where the apocalyptic emerges as the disappearance of the ground and the moment when the mountains blow off like wool from a carder's string. Like the *surah*, the *shruk* begins in a hymnic mode with the repetition of similar sound units and, after evoking similes for ontological reversals at end times, turns to the scales of justice upon which human deeds are to be weighed. Michael Sells, in his compelling introduction to the Qur'ān, *Approaching the Qur'ān: The Early Revelations*, points out that the images from *Surah Al-Qār'ia* are "evocative of the inversion of strong and weak that is characteristic of the early revelations."[11] In the *Surah Al-Qār'ia*, the apocalypse is a day when "human beings are like moths scattered/And mountains are like fluffs of wool."[12] Chapter 70 of the Qur'ān, *Surah Al-Ma'arij* (70:6–9), too uses the same metaphor for the cataclysm on the Day of Judgment:

They see it from afar
We see it near

A day the sky will be like molten copper
And the mountains like fluffs of wool[13]

It is clear that an objective description of the last day is not the purpose of the Qur'ān but instead the Qur'ān seeks to instil the fear of a final and cataclysmic event that would involve a final reckoning for each individual. The Qur'ān speaks of "the calamity" (*al-Qār'ia*) in relation to that which overtakes transgressing nations (a detail which makes the appearance of its elements in the Nund Rishi *shruks* as doubly significant because the latter, as I have argued, deploy the apocalyptic against the new political order of sultanate Kashmir).

There appears to be a connection between the violence of natural or political cataclysms and the end: it is as if the political violence of the world prefigures the apocalypse. The natural destruction (*sangar tār zan wazan*: the mountains will blow off like carder's wool) is often used as a metaphor for the destruction to come, but chronologically it is a prelude to the apocalypse. The ending of the *surah* introduces a strange term, *hāwiya*, as the fate of those whose scales weigh light on the Day of Judgment, which Sells translates as "raging fire," but which can also mean "abyss" or "a woman bereft of her child."[14] Nund Rishi turns often to similar figures of sudden human loss in the *shruks*. For instance:

Talu' chuy zyus tay pŷthu' chuk natsān
Wantu' māli vọndu' kithu' patsān chuy
Azāb-e qabras konu' chuk khōtsān
Daptu' māli an kithu' rotsān chuy[15]

There is an abyss at your feet and you dance over it
Tell me, good sir, how do you make this work?
You don't fear the punishments of the grave.
Tell me, good sir, how do you even digest your food?

Nund Rishi considers our very existence as a dance over an abyss. *Zyus* means a pit or a hole but also carries the meaning of an underground (or a ground that slips under the feet). A precarious life is made possible by a forgetting. But Nund Rishi reminds his disciple (whom he addresses in a polite form of address as "father" but translated here as "dear sir") that this situation is so horrific that it should be impossible to even digest one's food. The intimacy between language and the abyss is brought home in Nund Rishi's following line: *Talu' chuy zyus tu' pŷthu' chuk natsān* (There is an abyss at your feet and you dance over it). Like the apocalypse it unravels, the *shruk* too hovers over the abyssal absence of meaning.

There is a moment in Rahman Rahi's long, critical essay on Nund Rishi where he turns his attention again to the apocalyptic tone in Nund Rishi and serially quotes five *shruks* in order to bring forth the cataclysmic movement of the apocalyptic in Nund Rishi's mystical verse. Rahi's effort to establish Nund Rishi's poetic singularity in these five *shruks* allows us to relate the movement of the apocalyptic in Nund Rishi's *shruks* to his thinking of death. Each *shruk* is illustrated by Rahi with a brief comment, almost like a stage direction. Rahi first invites us to look at what he calls the *tāndava* (the Hindu god Śiva's divine dance of destruction) of the first *shruk*:[16]

Sāhÿb dọhu' aki dorāh karē
Yath samsāras kari lur pār
Zamīn tu' āsmān pÿn chari charē
Na gatshÿs insāf na yiyas ār[17]

One day the Master will decide
And shatter the world into pieces
The earth and the sky will scatter in different directions
Neither will he feel any justice nor any mercy

The apocalyptic images of the sky and the earth shattering into pieces as God neither has any compassion (*ār*) nor offers any mercy (*insāf yun*) for his creation are again Qur'ānic in origin. But Rahi relates it to Śiva's divine dance of destruction (*tāṇḍava* in Sanskrit). In Kashmiri, the Arabic-origin word *insāf*, which means "justice," carries the additional meaning of being moved to mercy in the compound verb *insāf yun* (to have mercy). Much like Śiva, the Islamic God is indifferent to the fate of his creation in the moment of its destruction. Rahi then turns to the *pạ̄r pāv ṣūratihāl* (frightening situation) of the following *shruk*:

Tati kyōhō karakh rōz-e maḥsharas
Khāṣan tu' 'āman āsi talvās
Gabran palzan nu' mạ̄li̠ tath qahras
Mọrsal tu' nabī tati khÿn trās[18]

What would you do on the Day of Gathering?
The day the rich are just as helpless as the poor

The fathers cannot save their sons from that calamity
Even the messengers and Prophets will be unavailing

Here Nund Rishi speaks of the helplessness of a human being on *rōz-e maḥshar* (Day of Gathering) when everyone must account for their lives. The Islamic warning that neither wealth nor genealogy (two things which mattered most in pre-Islamic Arabia) is able to rescue an individual on the Day of Judgment is repeated and sealed with the stark reminder that on the appointed day even God's messengers and prophets are going to find themselves helpless. Rahi then invites us to the *'ishq*, or love, of the third *shruk* which he calls a *trati trạv vạrdāth*, a catastrophic event (literally, a lightning strike):[19]

'Ishq chuy māji kun pothur marun
'Ishq chuy gani tulariyo byob barun
'Ishq chuy tez kartaji tsanji darun[20]

Love is the death of a mother's only child
Love is taking the beehive into your cloak
Love is standing up to the blow of a sharp sword

Love is read here as nothing less than a figure of the apocalypse: an overturning that shatters everything. Love is the loss of a mother's only child, to take a beehive into your cloak, to withstand the blow of a sharp sword. Here love is a form of absolute trauma to which the human subject must surrender in radical passivity without any recourse to understanding (*'ishq* is often opposed to *'aql* in Sufi poetry). It is to be hurled into an abyss (*zyus*) which recalls the Qur'ānic *hāwiya* (raging fire or the woman bereft of her child). *Love is the death of a mother's only child*: this line turns on the Qur'ānic meaning of *hāwiya* as an apocalyptic abyss (the worst circle of hell) and a mother bereft of her child. The experience of love is a living hell which one must not try and escape. Everyone must go through his or her own apocalypse of love. This trope is consistent with such medieval Sufi concepts as *fanā* (nihilation) and *fanā al-fanā* (annihilation) of the self (both *fanā* and *fanā al-fanā* are stages of divine love). The fourth example Rahi gives is the one he calls a *matsar boruth iẓtirāb*, a "mad complaint":[21]

Nafsī mōrus tu' vāy
Khạtith rūdum gatay

Athi yiyhy̌m kyāy
Kartạl tshu'nhas hatay[22]

My ego destroyed me
It hides even now in the shadows
If I could only get hold of it awhile
I would put a sword through its neck

The apocalyptic war is revealed here in this *shruk* as the possibility of a decisive battle with the *nafs* (ego) which oppresses the self. Quite consistent with apocalyptic imagery, the sword appears in this *shruk* as a figure of self-transformation and decision. The violence turns out to be inner and primordial: the *shruk* allegorizes the meanings of the Qur'ānic apocalypse, that is, the apocalyptic war is a battle within the self. But in the last example of this cluster of *shruk*s, Rahi introduces a faith (*yatsh patsh*) attuned to bewilderment (*hạrat*) and ecstasy (*shādmạni*):[23]

Kalay karakh kalu'y vuzī
Phulay lagī Allah hū
Tsu' yoru' gatshakh su tor ruzī
Dilay vuzī Allah hū[24]

If you turn to Him in attention
Your mind will echo His Name
You will become a flowering of *Allah hū* (God is)
Wherever you will go, He will be with You
Your heart will resonate with *Allah hū* (God is)

In this *shruk*, we witness remembrance inclining the heart toward the divine, which in turn inclines toward the self. There is a play on *kal* here, which in Kashmiri means an inclination of the heart, and *kalu'*, which means the mind (literally, the head). If you incline toward God, God inclines toward you. We can trace in this set of *shruk*s a movement, through metaphor and similes, parables and symbols, from an apocalyptic eschatology to a Sufi askesis. Indeed we can argue that, for Nund Rishi, just as a thinking of death turns out to be about owning up to death in life, apocalypse too turns out to be a form of metanoia in inner space. Even though this idea of inner conversion is not new in Sufi metaphysics, Nund Rishi's idea of a fundamental inner transformation also retains a connection with a political reversal (a persistent theme in

Muslim apocalyptics). Rahi writes that to reach this dance of expression, Nund Rishi turns to metaphor (*ist'āru'*), simile (*tashbīhu'*), parable (*tamthīl*), symbolism (*'alāmath*), and deliberate images (*hŷs angez shabīhu'*).[25] Further, he also writes that the critic P. N. Pushp is right in pointing out that the greatness of the *shruks* of Nund Rishi is in their concentration.[26] The concentrated force of the *shruks* in turn owes much to the apocalyptic tone in Nund Rishi that remains undecidable between an eschatological event of traditional Islam, which is deferred to the future – the revolutionary Muslim apocalyptics of a political reversal – and the ethico-ontological reversal of the apocalyptic as prayer, spiritual war, and love. The set of *shruks* Rahi quotes also appear to mirror a movement from *fanā* (annihilation) to *baqā* (spiritual perdurance), *maqāms* (stages) in the spiritual journey of a Sufi, which in turn mediate the tension between an "ecstatic" and a "sober" Sufism.[27] The apocalyptic *shruks* of Nund Rishi move between the twin poles of apocalyptic eschatology and Sufi poetics to clear a space beyond both for a new thinking of vernacular Islam that is at the same time political and existential.

By turning to Islam's unknown, unseen God, Nund Rishi opposes the totality of the medieval Kashmiri world with a new totality – justice at end times. The paradox of this situation takes us back to the crisis at the heart of early Islam between messianic hope and worldly ambition. Jacob Taubes, in one of the few references to Islam in his classic study of the apocalyptic, *Occidental Eschatology*, precisely draws attention to this paradox:

> According to an early Islamic viewpoint, God alone is worthy of having dominion over mankind. A human *mulk*, a monarchy, would be anti-God. Even at the time of the Abbasid, the caliphate's lawyers had to seek refuge in legal fiction to reconcile the concept of a hereditary monarchy with feelings deeply embedded in the nation's consciousness.[28]

It is perhaps easier to see now what disturbs Nund Rishi about *vāndar rāj* (the rule of the beasts) which he invokes in one of his *shruks* that remains popular in Kashmiri cultural memory and is still hurled against existing political structures:

Teli māli āsan tithī keran
Tang tsūnth papan tseran sū't
Māji korī kạrith athu'vās neran
Dọh dŷn baran gāran sū't

Khosh yi ḥaqas dunyā lūrun
Su hā māli āsi vāndar rāj[29]

The signs of the times shall be so
The pear and apple shall ripen at the same time as cherries
The mother and the daughter shall go out hand in hand
To spend their days with strangers
It is then that the Real One shall destroy the world
It will be the time of the rule of the beasts

The conservative, even misogynist, tone of the *shruk* about *vāndar rāj* suggests that some of the lines could be a later interpolation as its moral concerns are inconsistent with the ethical philosophy expressed in the rest of the *shruk*s. Nonetheless, the moral "chaos" has always been a sign of the apocalypse in Muslim historical apocalypses. Here the pre-apocalypse society is represented as deviant, and its this-worldly character denounced as "the rule of the beasts." As we have already seen in the *shruk* above, the apocalyptic is a time of reversals not just in the field of the political but also in the order of nature:

Kāvi khÿi gūj tu' kān satu'tis
Nÿpūtis marun pyō kandē
Brạ̄r su'nz lūr peyi̱ kọkar pūtis
Utni balāyi tutis vÿndē[30]

The crow will eat the kernel of the fruit
Just as the arrow will hit the hoopoe
Why will the speechless bird have to pay with her life?
The stick raised against the cat shall fall on the nestling
Someone else will pay for someone else's sins

This is a world in which it is the crow rather than the human who has the rightful share of a fruit or crop. The arrows of death prey on the hoopoe (a symbol of the self in search of the truth).[31] The stick which is wielded against the cat falls on a helpless nestling. It is an inverted world, a world without order.[32] The phrase *Utni balāyi tut* has passed into the Kashmiri language and can be used in any circumstance when someone innocent pays for someone else's mistake. Here the relation with the political is unmistakable: the weak and the vulnerable pay for the sins of the strong. The time is ripe for an apocalyptic reversal.

What were the original linguistic elements which were used to fashion apocalypticism? Or, as Taubes puts it, what are the "base words" of apocalypticism? The first such word taken up by Taubes, in his study of "Occidental eschatology," is alienation. As Taubes puts it: "The theme of self-alienation is to be heard for the first time in the context of apocalypticism."[33] This theme of human self-alienation runs through the history of Kashmiri Sufi poetry: no Kashmiri mystic is in harmony with the world. But there is still hope for salvation: history – or more precisely, the end of history. Taubes adds: "History is the *path* of light into the world, through the world and out of the world."[34] One must respond to the call of a God from whom one is alienated or one must call upon a God who is alienated from the world. Nund Rishi is constantly calling and urging his readers to hear. In the last two lines of the *shruk* with which we began our reading in this chapter, we come across the verb *bōzun*, to hear (or, to consider). For instance, *Kọ zan bōzan nu'*: "The evil shall not even hear the revolutions of the drum." In a rhetorical turn reminiscent of Qur'ānic eschatology, Nund Rishi repeatedly asks why the message of salvation meets with refusal and is often not even heard. There are also some other base words which make the apocalyptic themes more accessible to us. Not only in Nund Rishi but through much of the Kashmiri Sufi tradition, one comes across the words *yati* (here) and *tati* (there). For instance, consider the following line from a *shruk* we discussed in Chapter 3: *Yati ti me tsū'i tati ti me tsū'i* (Here and there: you alone are sufficient for me).[35] Or in the longer poem with the refrain *Haru' tati matu' me zam di* (Do not bring me to shame there, my God!).[36] Jacob Taubes writes:

> The base words *this* and *that* in relation to world are a further symbol of apocalypticism and are closely linked with the theme of self-alienation. The differentiation between "this" and "that" world already implies a valuation.[37]

This and that. *Dunyā* (the world) and *al-ākhirā* (the End). Here and There. A sharp distinction is drawn between the present and the future world to come. Yet it is the question of the when of the apocalypse, and its relations to the present, which is the more urgent one. This is also a sign of the weakness of the apocalyptic: the insistence on the now and the sense of imminence loses its power and appeal over time as the force of the apocalyptic fades away. But the facticity of the imminence of one's own death (apocalypse now) opens a different approach to the apocalyptic. The great Sufi philosopher Al-Ghazālī quotes a Prophetic tradition in which someone who has died is supposed to have gone through his apocalypse.[38] In this sense, the apocalyptic renders my death equivalent to the death of the last person on earth. Despite these moral reversals and ontological revisions, the apocalyptic does not lose its political thrust. What is responsible for this unique political charge of the apocalyptic? Apocalypse is an act of God that first and foremost reduces every human distinction, ruse, strategy to nothing and judges humans from a standard which they cannot judge. It is, in other words, the possibility of justice.

There is a long history of connections between political rebellions and the apocalyptic as a genre. The first Biblical Apocalypse of Daniel appears in relation to the rebellion against the Greek King Antiochus Epiphanes' machinations against the Jews in Jerusalem.[39] Even though Daniel speaks of the end of tyrannical rule of such Babylonian figures as Nebuchadnezzar, Taubes reminds us that "the narratives about earlier rulers, their arrogance and fall, was supposed to hint at what was in store for Antiochus and so strengthen the beliefs of the persecuted."[40] Nund Rishi also speaks of the imperial hubris of Alexander in relation to the transitoriness of human life:

Rāj kor sikandu'ri̱ tājdāran
Tạm kunh māl niyū rạtim sū't
Dil dith tshond di nīlū' mazāran
Asi brōnth asi hī gạmit kū't[41]

The rule of Alexander was majestic
But he left the world with empty hands
Go and mindfully search the lush graveyards
How many like us have passed here before?

Despite the insistence on the imminence of the end, the apocalyptist does not necessarily hasten the end. Sometimes the apocalyptist may even choose a passive political attitude. Perhaps it is for this reason that the apocalyptic emerges in times of historical crisis and in places where there still remains some hope. The apocalyptics, in other words, emerge in a relation with the political but are not always necessarily political. Taubes, for instance, writes of the political passivity of the apocalyptic in certain instances:

> The science of apocalypticism presupposes a passive attitude toward the happenings of history. There is an absence of action. The fate of world history

> is predetermined and there is no sense in trying to resist it. The passive voice predominates in apocalyptic style. In the apocalypses, no one "acts" but rather everything "happens."[42]

There is a tension in the apocalyptics between political passivity and political rebellion that remains undecidable, but nonetheless a political attitude is unmistakable.[43] The passivity is signalled by Nund Rishi in relation to a fundamental helplessness before death, but it also critiques the political conditions in the present, as in the following *shruk*:

Sọnas tu' sartali akuy zalun
Yi dīshith zÿv myāni kalun hyot
Nundÿn lyuth tu' dīthÿn phọlun
Tavay and me tsalun hyot[44]

Gold and bronze have the same shine
I am left speechless beholding this scene
The good are lost to dust and the evil bloom
That is why I chose to depart from this place

The apocalyptists who turn their backs on the world hope to agitate it. Their withdrawal marks an opposition to political hierarchy in the name of a moral hierarchy. This is the essential paradox of the mystic apocalyptist: it is difficult to delimit the mystic's detachment toward an existing political order from revolutionary hope. This is also obvious in the *shruk*s which turn to an inner apocalypse or Sufi apocalypse. The apocalyptic tone in Nund Rishi, therefore, is unmistakably bound up with his concerns about the oppressed in sultanate Kashmir. Let us take, for instance, the following popular *shruk* which we have already discussed in Chapter 2:

Khānan handÿn yiman rōb khānan
Jānan dapān̲ apạri̲ gatsh
Sọndru' vuchmakh harvakh nāvan
Tsamrō sạtÿn duvān latsh
Tạth māli dīthu'm kapas bovan
Nạṣru' me vuch tu' tsu' vuchni gatsh[45]

These intimidating residences of the rich
The moment they see you, they chase you away

I see beautiful women sing in those palaces
And dust being swept with chowries
I see people grow cotton over there
I have seen all this, Nasr, you go and see

The cataclysm announced in the first *shruk* we discussed in this chapter bears a relation to the political situation that appears in the *shruk* cited above. The land with imposing residences of the rich is reclaimed for cultivation. In this *shruk*, it is not the apocalypse but the ruination of time that destroys the iniquities of political order. There is a slow, gradual erosion of worldly power. Is this the real apocalypse? Yet another of Nund Rishi's *shruks* expresses this concern with the poor in a sharp indictment of the rich:

Sạni̱ shuri̱ chi nanỳn wurān
Yạdanu' chi ratān tsākh pan
Tuhind shuri̱ chi sutan muhān
Gạtshith ti divān nārasan[46]

Our children go without clothes
And tie grass ropes against their stomachs to fight hunger
Your children enjoy cotton clothes
Even after they leave this world, they receive lustrations

The *yati* (Here) and *tati* (There) appears to be in a relation to *sạni̱* (ours) and *tuhind* (theirs). *Tsākh pan* is a rope made of grass that poor Kashmiris used to tie against their stomachs to fight hunger. There is a strong moral opposition that Nund Rishi draws here between the children of the poor who have nothing to eat and the children of the rich who grab excessively at everything the world has to offer.[47] This situation is also addressed by Nund Rishi in another *shruk*:

Kentsan hatu' bạd dānik kuchan
An kuchan zag kyāv chotọ
Kentsan vay natu' moṣūm bachan
Pānu' āshan kas kyā ditō[48]

Some have hundreds of granaries of rice
Of various kinds: red and white
Some lack even a daily meal for their children
Only He knows what He gives to whom

The rich have surplus rice of different kinds: red and white. But the poor farmers cannot even afford a daily meal for their children. Even though there is a tone of resignation in the last line of the *shruk*, the oppositions that Nund Rishi sets up in his *shruk*s carry a strong political meaning. The fourteenth century, as we have seen in the Introduction, was an extremely turbulent period in Kashmiri history which began with the Mongol incursions into Kashmir, and the apocalyptic *shruk*s of Nund Rishi record the widespread public disenchantment in late-fourteenth- and early-fifteenth-century Kashmir.[49] These were chaotic times in Kashmir, and we have historical evidence of the rise in tensions among different social groups.[50] Political conditions for the Kashmiri peasantry were bleak, and Nund Rishi's apocalypticism must then be understood in the political register as a message of political salvation, even a proto-communism. As Taubes put it in relation to the early community around Jesus: "There is a clear connection between the enthusiasm for the Kingdom [of God] and communism."[51] Even more significantly, for Taubes, it is the question of freedom that is the fundamental theme of apocalypticism:

> The question of freedom is the fundamental theme in apocalypticism, and all of its motifs point to the turning point, when the structure of this world prison will burst apart. This turn does not refer in the first instance, or exclusively, to the existing social order. Apocalypticism is not at first concerned with changing the structure of society, but directs its gaze away from this world. If revolution were to mean only replacing an existing society with a better one, then the connection between apocalypticism and revolution is not evident. But if revolution means opposing the totality of this world with a new totality that comprehensively founds anew in the way that it negates ... then apocalypticism is by nature revolutionary.[52]

The question of freedom appears in Nund Rishi in opposition to the totality of the medieval Kashmiri world, and he seizes upon the potentiality of traditional Muslim apocalypticism. The demonic, earth-shaking experience of the traditional Muslim apocalypse – an imminent and violent end to the world – made immense sense in an area pulverized by Mongol invasions in what the historian Richard Eaton has called "Kashmir's volatile fourteenth century."[53] The topsy-turviness of the world is a constant theme in the Nund Rishi corpus, and it is the *shruk*s that deal with such topsy-turviness that remain the most popular among Kashmiris. No doubt the popularity of such *shruk*s has meant that the apocalyptic sub-genre in Nund Rishi's oeuvre has expanded because of later interpolations. Their popularity is also no guarantee that this is not because of the dubious moral and political uses to which a prophecy could be put, as is the case with many of the historical Muslim apocalypses.[54] But what is more interesting for us is the work that such *shruk*s accomplish: the work of a reversal. The topsy-turviness of the world in some of Nund Rishi's *shruk*s is a hope for a reversal anticipated in Jesus's: "The last will be first, and the first last."[55] The apocalyptic is about this hope. Perhaps it is about this hope more than anything else. The spiritual breakthrough in the *shruk*s is inseparable from this worldly hope:

Dỳn gāsh dyunthum vanu' kithu' gatu'
Babray langas vanu' sọyi kāṭh
Diluk darvāzu' kithu' māli vatu'
Sọnas kithu' dimu' katsuk vāṭh
Khọdāy dyūnṭhum kas māli khatu'
Jānas sạt chum jānas sangāṭh[56]

I have seen the clear daybreak, how shall I call it darkness?
How shall I call the sweet basil a bramble of stinging nettle?
How shall I close the open doors of the heart?
Can I join gold with glass?
I have seen God, how can I hide this from the others?
Life is joined after all to life

The revolutionary hope then is not separable from the spiritual breakthrough which appears as a new dawn (*dỳn gāsh*: clear light of day). The judgment to discern good from evil (the sweet basil and the stinging nettle or the gold and the glass) is a gift from God. One can no longer close the doors of the heart that have been thrown open by this knowledge. This knowledge can only impel one to act for the sake of life, which is joined to all life.

One might conclude then that the vernacular apocalypse of Nund Rishi is concerned not merely with the destruction at end times but also with the possibility of a new life. Yet there is still a question that one must address: why such a terrible and fearsome imagery? Why the apocalyptic tone? Let us take, for example, the following *shruk* by Nund Rishi:

Ādijan sapanī anjaru'h panjarō
Tsỳtas pāvay avalim rāth

Pānas chạ̄nis gatshi zaru'h zarō
Kyāh karu' kyāh karu' tsoluy nu' zāth[57]

Your bones will be shattered and scattered
You shall remember that first night in the grave
Your body will be broken into pieces
You never gave up on – What shall I do? What must I do?

Or take, for instance, the following *shruk*:

Tsu' chukh bihith pẏth rōbu' khānas
Mehmānas jāy kati dikh
Chān yeli vasī tsandan tānas
Tọr kis chānas van kyā dikh[58]

You are sitting on top of a towering house
You have no room for any guest
When the carpenter goes to work on your sandalwood body
What will you offer to the carpenter of the other world?

For Nund Rishi, the physical ruination of a human body is an eschatological metaphor for an apocalyptic end, but this is still an end that opens out toward a future. It puts into question the architectural efforts of human life. The experience of this calamity is corporeal but also reorders our relationship to the transcendent. The body, imperial and autochthonous, is destroyed in the grave. A political paralysis ("What shall I do? What must I do?") is of no avail to the self. Nund Rishi clearly wants to shift our attention to the *chān* (carpenter) of the invisible world so that we may pay attention to the *chān* (carpenter) of this world.[59] The *chān* is also here a figure of sovereign power. The apocalyptic does not reduce the future to a formula, but rather the future has an open character in the apocalyptic, which is forever, and irreducibly, other.[60] This open character of the apocalyptic is also the promise of the political. It is unclear if it is a slow ruination or cataclysmic destruction that is the true sign of the apocalyptic. But the apocalyptic gives a structure and meaning to human history as the history of ruination. This ruination is not merely historical but also appears in the *shruk*s as the fate of the self as body in the world. However, ruination's relations to the apocalyptic are not always clear.

Some of the most popular *shruk*s in the apocalyptic genre are those that deal with the signs and portents of end times.[61] Most such signs in the traditional

Muslim apocalyptic deal with the supposedly unnatural occurrences or reversals of natural order before a complete destruction of the natural world.[62] The theme of moral decay and strong condemnation of sin is a common theme in the *shruk*s that deal with these signs and portents of the coming hour of reckoning. One of the most popular refrains from the Nund Rishi oeuvre that has passed into ordinary Kashmiri as a popular idiom, which we briefly discussed earlier, is *Su hā māli āsi vāndar rāj* (It will be, dear sir, the time of the rule of the beasts).[63] In another *shruk* with the same refrain, addressed to his disciple Bābā Nāṣir al-Dīn, Nund Rishi makes an apocalyptic prophecy about a topsy-turvy world:

Nasr Bābu' tsu' bōz goru' sạnd vatsan
Sōru' sạnz vọdi āsi moru' sund tāj
Vÿthu' họkhan tu' hanÿr grÿzan
Su hā māli āsi vāndar rāj[64]

Nasr, listen to your teacher's words
The peacock's crown shall be on the head of a pig
The rivers shall dry up but gutters will overflow
It will be, dear sir, the time of the rule of the beasts

The political tone of the *shruk* is unmistakable. The illegitimacy of rule is a true sign of the apocalyptic. Chaos in nature is preceded by a moral and political chaos of which many Islamic theologians speak of in a conservative tone. Moral decay leads to natural disaster, which in turn acts as a prelude to punishment or reward in the hereafter. The bare economy of the Qur'ānic apocalypse gave rise to a wildly proliferating genre, in which accretions and emendations could be made to develop a corpus more moralistic and conservative than Qur'ānic eschatology. It is, therefore, not surprising that this strain of the apocalypse (moral and political chaos) is the dominant one in Nund Rishi's apocalypticism. I do not intend to suggest that the conservative tone of the *shruk*s in this refrain in Nund Rishi (and other *shruk*s in this vein) emerges only because of later interpolations, or expresses Nund Rishi's true beliefs, but rather to assert that such conservatism is the signature of the moral apocalyptic.

We find a slightly different thematic in the *shruk*s that deal with a Sufi apocalypse.[65] In the traditional Muslim apocalyptics, moral disintegration is often conjoined with the political situation of the Muslim community: the political always lurks in the background of the apocalyptic.[66] But these meanings of the apocalyptic are interrupted and transformed by the Sufi enunciations of the apocalypse as an inner event. The way Nund Rishi draws on the political charge of the apocalyptic but at the same time affirms the Sufi reversal of the traditional apocalyptic opens out another path to understanding his political thinking. Nund Rishi does not give an outright call to political rebellion but pushes the limits of the Sufi hermeneutic to accommodate local Kashmiri spiritual practices of self-transformation as a source for an ethic of non-violent political struggle. The Islamic apocalyptic materials are harnessed to effect a strident political critique, and the Sufi apocalypse is repurposed for a radical but passive political struggle. The apocalyptic mode in the *shruk*s does not yield a religious politics but a political spirituality. I am not trying to suggest that such an approach to Islam as an apocalyptic religion exhausts Nund Rishi's political thinking, but that this is one way we can read the apocalyptic tone of Nund Rishi's *shruk*s.

The natural audience of the apocalyptist, as Cook reminds us, is not the *'ulamā*, or the religious elite, but the general populace.[67] Cook writes that the apocalyptist "spoke for those whose feelings did not enter into the court history books, nor into the orthodox theological tomes."[68] The apocalyptist, who functions as a critic of the government, often turns against "formal Islam" (by critiquing the *mullah*s, for instance!) and declaring the latter to be corrupt.[69] This was often done by invoking the Islam of the Prophet's time against the prevailing norms and practices. The Sufi shared with the Muslim apocalyptist the desire to return to the Islam of the Prophet's time: "Things must be returned to the simple form that existed during the mythical time of the Prophet and the orthodox caliphs."[70] But the Muslim apocalyptists disagreed about the nature and meaning of this return. What Nund Rishi manages to do in the *shruk*s dealing with the apocalyptic is to translate the persistent anti-*'ulamā* themes of Sufi poetry, and the force of traditional Muslim apocalypticism, into his own situation: a time of historical and cultural transitions in which the most vulnerable and the weakest in Kashmir were also the most at risk.[71] Nonetheless, the *shruk*s continue to evince a tension between the Sufi apocalypse and the traditional Muslim apocalyptic. A tension also persists between asceticism and apocalypticism. The two are sometimes put in relation to each other, even reduced to one another, but the problem is never resolved. Even though asceticism appears at times as a waiting for the apocalypse, asceticism and apocalypse herald the promise of a new life. The apocalyptic in Nund Rishi is not about an irreversible collapse or a cataclysmic end but a future of hope.

That is why generations of Kashmiri readers of Nund Rishi have turned to his *shruks* not in despair but hope. Both Nund Rishi's existential thanatology and his apocalypticism proclaim a new political life.

I am not trying to interpret the Rishi movement solely as an apocalyptic group with political ambitions but arguing for situating its apocalypticism in the social upheaval which gave rise to it. War, economic upheaval, sectarian strife, rise in cross-cultural contact (a time of crisis "when all is forfeit to chaos") form the background to the rise of the Rishi movement.[72] The apocalyptic language lends itself to such situations of conflict. The rise of negative theology at multiple times in Kashmir's history (and the irruptions of apocalyptics within that negative theology) can be read against the history of such crises from the fourteenth–fifteenth to the nineteenth–twentieth centuries. We witness a proliferation of negative theology in Kashmiri Sufi poetry again in the nineteenth century as Kashmir first came under Afghan and then Sikh rule culminating in the British sale of Kashmir to its Dogra allies in 1846.[73] As the political crisis engulfed Kashmir again toward the middle of the twentieth century, negative theology emerged yet again in Kashmiri poetry (sometimes disguised in an existentialist idiom).[74]

There is nonetheless a problem with the apocalypse. The apocalypse fails on account of its worldliness (the apocalyptic concerns itself with not just a worldly after*life* but also an after*world*). The traditional Muslim apocalyptic does not merely anticipate an after*life* but an after*world*. The after*world* of the Islamic *eschaton* turns out to resemble this world. Nerina Rustomji writes that "Islamic eschatology provides an after*world*, while Christian eschatology focuses on an after*life*."[75] Rustomji contends that unlike an abstract afterlife, "the afterworld provides a setting," a world.[76] The life of a Muslim is in relation to an afterlife in the after*world*. This move away from the nebulous state of the afterlife to the architectonics of an after*world* is what makes Islamic eschatological thought distinctive in the three Abrahamic faiths. The difference between the after*life* and the after*world* nonetheless helps us develop our understanding of the political origins of the Muslim Apocalyptic: "... the afterlife is a part of the future, but the afterworld is a place that can be brought near during apocalyptic time...."[77] The attempt to bring the after*world* near opens up the world to the possibility of an apocalyptic reversal.[78] The after*world* begins to haunt the iniquities and injustices of the world. It is the material character of the Islamic after*world* which "allowed human longings for and fears of a future life to actualize into visions of a future world."[79] Nund Rishi also turns to the materiality of the after*world* in some of his *shruk*s:

Kọng chuy gāsu' zamīn sōbā
Sọrgay gatshī tu' kray kar
Sọrgas bar pỳṭh darkh-e Tūbā
Su habā sọrguk gvāshur[80]

The saffron is the grass of Paradise
If you dream of Paradise, you must work for it
The Tree of Tuba is at the gates of Paradise
The Tree which lights up Paradise

One of the material objects of Paradise here, that is, saffron, belongs to the Kashmiri landscape. In another *shruk*, Nund Rishi speaks of the roots of this tree of Paradise as being nourished by a milky spring of *amrita* (a drink of the gods in the Hindu tradition which confers immortality). The word he uses for paradise here is not the Persian *firdaws* or the Arabic *jannah* but the Sanskrit *svarga* (a heavenly *loka*, or realm of existence). The material after*world* in the *shruk*s is Kashmiri, and Paradise itself is refigured as an inner space:

Mūlan tal chus boḍ nāgu'rādā
Dọdu'h rang tu' amrỳtu' tar
Karshanu' bọyakh asan vādā
Darshanu' kasỳkh vọndu'c thar[81]

Under its roots is a huge spring
milky in colour and ambrosiac
Your actions become your joy
The vision of the divine burns away
the bitter chill of winter

The *shruk* expresses hope not merely for a paradisiacal immortality but the possibility of self-transformation in this world. The "bitter chill of winter" (*vọndu'c thar*) is a metaphor from the Kashmiri material world which could as easily allude to the political conditions of Kashmiris (as it was later used in the early twentieth century by the Urdu poet Muhammad Iqbal).[82]

The apocalyptics are almost always calling for an insurrection against the world, and it is because of this reason that traditional theologians – Jewish,

Christian, or Muslim – are opposed to them. But such an insurrection does not only have worldly concerns for its end. This tension marks all apocalypses, and Nund Rishi's apocalypticism is no exception. The apocalypse must be other-worldly if it is to call for a complete change in the world, but such a demand remains an irreducibly worldly demand. This paradox is the condition of possibility of the apocalypse. There are also real consequences, if in a concrete historical situation, an apocalyptic movement fails to bring about a public redemption. It then has no choice but to either retreat or turn inward. All apocalypses turn into inner apocalypses. Perhaps what Nund Rishi's apocalypticism also discloses is a possible way out of the violence of history. We could then claim the Kashmiri vernacular apocalypse for what the feminist theologian Catherine Keller calls a "counterapocalypse."[83] Such a counterapocalypse turns an "emergency into an emergence": it bequeaths to us the potentiality of the Kashmiri language.[84]

The apocalypticism of Nund Rishi is as much about the present as it is about the future. It poses the question of the eschaton as the question of the political. Nund Rishi's apocalypticism is not born out of despair but is a call for a passive political struggle ("Sufi intervention" in a history seen as a mere succession of empires) to correct political injustice or minimally to offer consolation to those on the margins.[85] Catherine Keller, following James Scott, calls apocalypticism a hidden transcript of rebellion.[86] Nund Rishi interpreted the bleak political conditions of fourteenth-century Kashmir on the basis of the apocalyptic scenario. The Rishi movement inaugurated by Nund Rishi must then be read not just as a spiritual movement but also as a political movement of the Kashmiri dispossessed and poor. Clearly it is in this context that we can read both Nund Rishi's imprisonment in the early sultanate period and the accounts of exile of his disciple Zain al-Dīn Rishi to Tibet that we come across in the historical and hagiographical literature.[87] A case in point is the legend of *Yāvan Mạts*. Many hagiographies of Nund Rishi relate that some enemies of Nund Rishi sent Yāvan Mạts, a beautiful Kashmiri dancer, to seduce Nund Rishi, but she, in turn, became one of his disciples soon after her first encounter with the Sufi. By changing just one vowel, Nund Rishi puns on her name in his address to her that has passed on into Kashmiri legend:

Yāvan Mạtsī yāvan motsī

Yāvan Mạtsī, your youth shall shrink (*motsī*)[88]

Yāvan Maṭs can also be translated as Mad Youth. Yāvan Maṭs, the dancer, is addressed in the vocative (*Yāvan Maṭsī*), and Nund Rishi passes a sharp moral judgment: "your youth shall shrink (*yāvan motsī*)." According to legend, this event had taken place when Nund Rishi was passing through Srinagar.[89] The legend also corroborates the historical fact that the Persianate Sufi orders were strong in Srinagar, but it is the Rishis who held sway in the countryside. G. N. Gauhar, an independent researcher who spent a lifetime researching Nund Rishi, has this conclusion to offer: "His [Nund Rishi's] mass popularity was threatening power of the officials, his defending local traditions and culture was an affront to those foreign elements who looked down upon Kashmiris and boasted of their own high descent, superior learning and sophisticated culture."[90] Gauhar also writes that Nund Rishi was struggling against the atmosphere of religious extremism that prevailed under Sultan Sikandar (r.1389–1413).[91] The *Yāvan Maṭs* legend, the historical context of Nund Rishi's arrest, and similar events (such as the dialogue of Nund Rishi and his disciples with Mīr Muḥammad Hamadānī, the son of Mīr Sayyid 'Alī Hamadānī) reveal the contestations over the meanings of Islam that shaped the new Muslim sultanate. Writing about the meeting between Nund Rishi and Mīr Muḥammad Hamadānī, Mohammad Ishaq Khan claims that the companions of Mīr Muḥammad Hamadānī considered Nund Rishi to be ignorant (*nadān*) because he was "practising austerities in the manner of the Hindu saints" and were unhappy about their teacher expressing a desire to meet Nund Rishi.[92] It is significant that the historians have recorded that Nund Rishi attended this meeting with two of his women disciples (the tradition does not recount any woman among the Kubrāwiyyā Sufis that had come to meet Nund Rishi).[93] Even though Khan concludes that the meeting ended with Nund Rishi offering his allegiance to Mīr Muḥammad Hamadānī, it is quite clear that the Rishis pursued an understanding of Islam which was different from that of the Persianate Sufi orders.[94] As we have seen in Chapter 1, the Persianate Sufi orders insisted that the sultans of Kashmir strictly adhere to the Sharī'ah, or Islamic Law, in the matters of state.[95] The political challenge the Rishis posed to the new sultanate revolved around the actual condition of the Kashmiri peasantry, not merely matters addressed by the Sharī'ah (for instance, on the question of the relations between Muslims and non-Muslims). These contestations over the meanings of Islam in medieval Kashmir have been discussed in detail in Chapter 1. Nund Rishi's apocalypticism is an intervention in these contestations that turns the energies of the traditional Muslim apocalyptic against the authoritarian tendencies of the new monarchy with a view to translating Islam in the Kashmiri regional world as a thinking of justice. Across medieval South Asia, we see such attempts to challenge imperial power in the name of a justice grounded in a personal relationship to the transcendent that opens up the political to the demands of the subaltern. The Rishi movement must then be understood first and foremost as a religio-political movement of the Kashmiri subaltern. Nund Rishi is the *'alamdar* (flagbearer) of Kashmiri subaltern meanings, beyond Persian and Sanskrit cosmopolitanisms, thrown up by the Rishi resistance at a time of intense sectarian conflict in Kashmir. It is in this context that we must understand why the name of Nund Rishi has moved close to the name of Lal Ded in Kashmiri cultural memory, and it is in this context that we must understand the beginnings of Kashmiri literature.

Notes

1. Quoted in Marin Terpstra and Theo de Wit, "'No Spiritual Investment in the World as It Is': Jacob Taubes's Negative Political Theology," in *Flight of the Gods: Philosophical Perspectives on Negative Theology*, ed. Ilse. N. Bulhof and Laurens ten Kate (New York: Fordham University Press, 2002), 336.
2. By the apocalyptic, I mean apocalyptic literature that concerns itself with the end times (and the ends of human life and history) with its origins in Judaism, Christianity, and Islam. As John Joseph Collins writes: "Apocalypticism is born of fears and hopes that are endemic to the human condition." See John J. Collins, 'What Is Apocalyptic Literature?', in *The Oxford Handbook of Apocalyptic Literature*, ed. John J. Collins (New York: Oxford University Press, 2014), 13. The Greek word *apokaluptō* carries with it a strong element of destruction which is sometimes obscured in its translation as "unveiling" or "revelation." The theologian Bernard McGinn writes:

   > Apocalyptic texts from various religious backgrounds and different ages display family resemblance in key areas that include: first, a sense of the unity and structure of history conceived as a divinely predetermined totality; second, pessimism about the present and conviction of its imminent crisis; and third, belief in the proximate judgment of evil and triumph of the good, the element of vindication.

   Bernard McGinn, *Visions of the End: Apocalyptic Traditions in the Middle Ages* (New York: Columbia University Press, 1979), 30.
3. Rahi, "Shaikh al 'Ālam sạnz shạ'irānā ḥạsiyath," 136. Also see Kamil, *Nūrnāmu'*, 284. I have slightly modified the transliteration.

4. The *shruk* does not bear any immediate relation to Rahi's reading of Nund Rishi's thinking of death in the essay which is why his choice of beginning the essay with this *shruk* presses itself on the reader.
5. The apocalyptic has often gone hand in hand with the political critique of imperial power.
6. See Joshua Robert Gold, "Jacob Taubes: 'Apocalypse from Below,'" *Telos*, no. 134 (2006): 141–42.
7. David Cook, *Studies in Muslim Apocalyptic* (Princeton: The Darwin Press, 2002), 54–55. Cook adds:

   > It should be noted that the connections between the Dome of the Rock and the Temple are strong and well documented in the various praise compilations (*faḍā'il*) on Jerusalem.... It should be noted, however, that it is by no means clear that the builders of the Dome (the Umayyads 'Abd al-Malik and al-Walīd I) had this messianic concept in mind when they built it.

   Ibid.
8. Ibid., 232.
9. Ibid., 233.
10. The political meanings of the drum (*damāmā*) become more explicit in Nund Rishi's contemporary, Kabir, who speaks of a *gagan damāmā*) (a drum in the sky) that gives the call for a decisive spiritual war. See Purushottam Agarwal, *Akath kahānī prem kī* (New Delhi: Rajkamal Prakashan, 2016), 431. For more on the *ḍamaru*, see Corinna Wessels-Mevissen, "Divine Attributes and Emblems," in *Brill's Encyclopedia of Hinduism, Volume V* (Leiden: Brill, 2013). The *ḍamaru* emanates creative energy and is also associated with the sacred sound of creation, *Om*, but in the *shruk* under discussion it brings to mind the destructive power of Lord Śiva. Please also see Theodore Gabriel, "Dance," in *Encyclopedia of Hinduism* (New York: Routledge, 2018).
11. Michael Sells, *Approaching the Qur'ān: The Early Revelations* (Ashland, Oregon: White Cloud Press, 1999), 24–25.
12. Ibid., 112. The translation of the verses from *Surah Al-Qār'ia* are by Michael Sells.
13. Ibid.,119. The translation of the verses from *Surah Al-Ma'arij* are by Michael Sells.
14. Ibid., 26.
15. Kamil, *Nūrnāmu'*, 133. The Kamil text gives us *chuk* in the first and third lines which should be read as *chukh*. This quatrain is often also attributed to Lal Ded.
16. Rahi, "Shaikh al 'Ālam sạnz shạ'irānā ḥạsiyath," 155.
17. Ibid.

18. Ibid.
19. Ibid.
20. Ibid. Rahi has collapsed this *shruk* into a rhyming tercet. The full *shruk* is available in the Amin Kamil edition of Nund Rishi's mystical verse. See Kamil, *Nūrnāmu'*, 199. I have not quoted the full *shruk* here to closely follow Rahi's reading of the apocalyptic tone in Nund Rishi's mystical poetry. Rahi's transcription of the *shruk* is different from Kamil. We have already discussed this *shruk* in Chapter 1.
21. Rahi, "Shaikh al 'Ālam sạnz shạ̄'irānā ḥạsiyath," 155.
22. Ibid., 155–56.
23. Ibid., 156
24. Ibid. *Allah ḥū* is a Sufi chant. The *ḥū* is the desinence produced by the repeated chanting of *Allah-u* (God is) which often ends in Sufi practice with the invoking of the divine name al-Ḥaq (the Truth).
25. Ibid.
26. Ibid.
27. For more on the polemics between an "ecstatic" and a "sober" Sufism – an ingredient of the debates on and oppositions to Sufism – see Carl Ernst, *Words of Ecstasy in Sufism* (Albany: State University of New York Press, 1985). Also see Jong and Radtke, "Introduction."
28. Jacob Taubes, *Occidental Eschatology*, tr. David Ratmoko (Stanford: Stanford University Press, 2009), 9. It is these "feelings deeply embedded in the nation's consciousness" which appear to drive many nineteenth- and twentieth-century Muslim revivalist movements.
29. Afaqi, *Ā'īnā-e ḥaq*, 362. This *shruk* is given in a slight variation in Amin Kamil's *Nūrnāmu'*. See Kamil, *Nūrnāmu'*, 274. The *shruk* is given in Asadullah Afaqi's collection of Nund Rishi's mystical poetry as part of a longer narrative poem with the refrain *Su hā māli āsi vāndar rāj* (It will be the time of the rule of the beasts).
30. Kamil, *Nūrnāmu'*, 282.
31. The hoopoe (Ar. *hudhud*) appears in Qur'ānic narrative on the Prophet Solomon and Farīd al-Dīn 'Aṭṭār's epic poem, *Manṭiq al-ṭayr* (Conference of the birds). See Farīd al-Dīn 'Aṭṭār, *The Conference of the Birds*, tr. Dick Davis (New York: Penguin, 2011).
32. In her preface to Arvind Krishna Mehrotra's translation of the *bhaktī* poet Kabir's poems, Wendy Doniger draws attention to what she calls Kabir's "twilight language" or "upside-down language." See Wendy Doniger, "Preface," in Arvind Krishna Mehrotra, *Songs of Kabir* (New Delhi: Hachette, 2011), xv.
33. Taubes, *Occidental Eschatology*, 26.
34. Ibid., 27.

35. Kamil, *Nūrnāmu'*, 78.
36. Saqi, *Kulliyāt-e Shaikh al-'Ālam*, 204.
37. Taubes, *Occidental Eschatology*, 28.
38. See William C. Chittick, "Eschatology," in *Islamic Spirituality: Foundations*, ed. Seyyed Hossein Nasr (New York: Routledge, 1987), 398. Chittick writes:

    > Al-Ghazzāli had already brought this type of commentary under the protective wing of mainstream Islam in his *Iḥyā'*: "I mean by 'Lesser Resurrection' the state of death, for the Prophet – God bless him and give him peace – said, 'He who has died has undergone his resurrection.'" He explains that all the terms that refer to the Greater Resurrection have their equal (*naẓīr*) in the Lesser Resurrection. Thus the earth corresponds to the body, mountains to bones, the sky to the head, the sun to the heart, the stars to the senses, grass to hair, trees to limbs, etc.

39. Taubes, *Occidental Eschatology*, 43–44.
40. Ibid., 44.
41. Kamil, *Nūrnāmu'*, 132.
42. Taubes, *Occidental Eschatology*, 32.
43. The tensions between a revolutionary and a passive political attitude in Nund Rishi's apocalypticism resemble tensions at the very heart of early Islamic history.
44. Afaqi, *Ā'īnā-e ḥaq*, 361.
45. Rahi, "Shaikh al 'Ālam sạnz shạ'irānā ḥasiyath," 146.
46. Saqi, *Kulliyāt-e Shaikh al-'Ālam*, 73. Saqi has transcribed *ti* in the last line as *tu'* which appears incorrect.
47. The *shruk* echoes Qur'ānic attitudes from the Meccan period as in the following verses from *Surah At-Takāthur*: "The avarice of plenitude keeps you occupied/ Till you reach the grave." See *Al-Qur'ān*, tr. Ali, 549.
48. Saqi, *Kulliyāt-e Shaikh al-'Ālam*, 182.
49. Hasan, *Kashmir under the Sulṭāns*, 36–45.
50. The primary social tension that emerged is the one between the immigrant Sufis and the new Muslim converts on the one hand and the Hindus of Kashmir on the other. The historian Walter Slaje writes of the reign of Sultan Sikandar (1389–1413):

    > ... a wave of systematic destruction of Hindu and Buddhist sacred buildings and idols was unleashed by Šihāb ad-Dīn's nephew, sultan Sikandar (1389–1413). It earned him the honorific title of "a destroyer of false gods" (*butšhikān*) and lasted for decades. Before Sikandar had come to power, considerable resistance seems to have been offered by the Hindu population against such iconoclastic endeavours.

Slaje, *Brahmā's Curse*, 32. One could speculate if the apocalyptic material in Nund Rishi's mystical verse is from the period of Sultan Sikandar's reign rather than of Sultan Zain al-'Ābidīn, that is, if the apocalyptic material is from the early years of Nund Rishi's life. It is hard, however, to situate the *shruks* within a clearly demarcated chronology.

51. Taubes, *Occidental Eschatology*, 67.
52. Ibid., 9. Taubes further writes: "Theocracy is built upon the anarchic elements in Israel's soul. It expresses the human desire to be free from all human, earthly ties and to be in covenant with God. The first tremors of eschatology can be traced to this dispute over divine or earthly rule." Ibid., 19.
53. Richard Eaton, *India in the Persianate Age 1000–1765* (New Delhi: Allen Lane, 2019), 91. As Eaton reminds us, the fourteenth century "saw the end of the indigenous Lohara dynasty (1003–1320), Mongol invasion, and the fitful beginnings of the Kashmir sultanate." Ibid. In an article about the Mongol invasions of Kashmir, Karl Jahn writes that "the Mongols not only repeatedly invaded Kashmir, but they even succeeded temporarily in subjugating the country and in appointing the kings." See Karl Jahn, "A Note on Kashmir and the Mongols," *Central Asiatic Journal* 2, no. 3 (1956): 176. The historian André Wink writes that the Mongols had already invaded Kashmir three times in the thirteenth century before they did so again in the early fourteenth century. Andre Wink, *The Making of the Indo-Islamic World, C700–1800 CE* (Cambridge: Cambridge University Press, 2020), 102. The Indian historian Mohibbul Hasan also discusses the condition of Kashmir before and after the Mongol invasions in his classic, *Kashmir under the Sulṭāns*. See Hasan, *Kashmir under the Sultans*, 36–38. Hasan writes: "After the withdrawal of the Mongols the inhabitants returned to the Valley from the mountains whither they had fled to escape massacre or enslavement. They witnessed the havoc which the invaders had caused. Many found themselves without houses, without relations, and without friends." Ibid., 36.
54. I use the term "historical Muslim apocalypses" in a heuristic sense, following David Cook, who discusses it in a separate chapter and distinguishes it from other subgenres such as the metahistorical, messianic, Shi'ī, moral and Qur'ānic apocalypses. See Cook, *Studies in Muslim Apocalyptic*. Cook writes that historical apocalypses are those in which "there exist recognizable historical personalities, and a historical sequence of events that leaves reality at a particular point and moves into the realm of fantasy." Ibid., 34.
55. Taubes, *Occidental Eschatology*, 51.
56. Rahi, "Shaikh al 'Ālam sạnz shạ̄'irānā ḥaṣiyath," 142. Amin Kamil gives the second line as *Babray langas dapu' sọyi kāṭh*. There is hardly a difference between *dapun* (to tell) and *vanun* (to say) in Kashmiri. See Kamil, *Nūrnāmu'*, 252.

57. Kamil, *Nūrnāmu'*, 126. *Zāh*, a variant of the adverb *zāth*, is more commonly used in everyday Kashmiri.
58. Saqi, *Kulliyāt-e Shaikh al-'Ālam*, 116. It should be *tōr* instead of *tọr* in line 4 but I have followed Saqi's transcription here.
59. The figure of the *chān* also appears in a Lal *vākh* where it alludes both to a mind struggling for enlightenment and a ruler that reigns over chaos. For a longer discussion of the Lal *vākh*, see Abir Bazaz, "'Dancing Naked': Gender, Trauma and Politics in the mystical poetry of Lal Ded," *South Asian Review*, DOI: 10.1080/02759527.2021.2002238. Lal Ded calls the architect of the capital city (*razdạn*) a foolish carpenter (*abakh chān*). See also Kaul (ed.), *Lal Ded*, 64.
60. William Franke, *Poetry and Apocalypse: Theological Disclosures of Poetic Language* (Stanford: Stanford University Press, 2009), 8.
61. David Cook writes: "For the most part the Muslim apocalyptist is quite cautious as far as saying exactly when the End will occur.... One widely quoted tradition says that the Prophet does not know when the Hour will come: literally, that he does not know any more than the one asking the question." Cook, *Studies in Muslim Apocalyptic*, 18–19. Many Qur'ānic verses state unambiguously that only God knows when the end will come. Ibid. It is perhaps for this reason that there appears to be more of an emphasis on the signs or portents of the end in the Muslim apocalyptic.
62. As Jane Idleman Smith and Yvonne Yazbeck Haddad put it: "Preceding the final judgment will come signs (both cosmic and moral) signalling the arrival of the Hour as well as the specific events of the resurrection and assessment. Within this overall structure is the individual cycle which specifies the events of creation, death, and resurrection." Smith and Haddad, *The Islamic Understanding of Death and Resurrection*, 5. The Qur'ān calls the signs of the end as the signs of the Hour, or *ishārāt al-sā'a*. The cataclysmic events which bring about the end of the world, called the greater signs or *'alāmāt al-sā'a*, are events "that will literally devastate the earth and reverse the natural processes, which throughout the Qur'ān are consistently cited as proof of God's ordinance and authority." Ibid., 65–66.
63. The line can also be translated as: "It would then be a topsy-turvy world." *Māli*, here translated as "dear sir," literally means "dear father," a form of affectionate address.
64. Afaqi, *Ā'īnā-e ḥaq*, 362.
65. There is some tension at times between the apocalyptic tone and an anti-apocalypticism even in the *shruk*s that are in the apocalyptic mode. Sometimes the *shruk*s which are not in the apocalyptic mode undergo an apocalyptic modulation.

66. The term *fitān*, the political trials before the apocalypse, also allude to civil wars that shall anticipate the end times. Smith and Haddad, *The Islamic Understanding of Death and Resurrection*, 67.
67. Cook, *Studies in Muslim Apocalyptic*, 234.
68. Ibid., 267. Cook writes: "The call for just government was, and is today, the hallmark of every revolutionary apocalyptic and messianic Muslim group and needs to be recognized as such." Ibid., 234–35.
69. Ibid., 235. We have discussed in Chapter 1 a few *shruk*s that take up this theme.
70. Ibid., 234.
71. David Cook has also pointed out the connection between apocalyptics and border regions and the ambivalence toward capital cities and regions of Islam. Ibid., 254. We do not, however, encounter in the *shruk*s any serious engagement with such elements of Muslim apocalypticism as the Dajjāl (Anti-Christ), Jesus's Second Coming, the Mahdī (the Muslim Messiah), the anti-Mahdī (Sufyānī), the *dabba* (the Beast that speaks to humans and is a sign of end times) or the Gog and the Magog. What we have is an apocalyptic tone that merges ceaselessly with Nund Rishi's powerful discourse on death and at times even draws on some of the traditional themes from the Muslim apocalyptic such as the events of the grave, the gathering of human souls on the Day of Judgment, the Garden of Paradise, and the Fire of Hell. For instance, Nund Rishi takes up the theme of the difficult crossing of the *aṣ-ṣirāṭ,* or *pul-e ṣirāṭ* (the precarious, hair-narrow bridge that stretches over Hell which one must pass on the day of resurrection): *Bay chum tami sumi and ku'hi̱ vatu'/Yemi tạl pakān nāru'v kọl* (I fear how I will cross the bridge to the other side/under which rages a river of fire). See Saqi, *Kulliyāt-e Shaikh al-ʿĀlam*, 41.
72. McGinn, *Visions of the End*, 30.
73. I have here in mind the rise of such Sufi poets as Shamas Faqīr (1843–1901) and Wahab Khār (1842–1912).
74. I have here in mind not just a Sufi poet like Ahad Zargar (1882–1984) but also modernist poets like Amin Kamil (1924–2014).
75. Nerina Rustomji, *The Garden and the Fire: Heaven and Hell in Islamic Culture* (New York: Columbia University Press, 2009), xvi. Rustomji writes:

> The afterworld is not just the eschatological space where one happens to live after life; instead, it is a place that operates according to a distinct logic ... afterworlds are typically unambiguous about one idea: life after death is not a nebulous state accessed only by the soul or the mind. Instead, an afterworld offers the structure of a world, the rhythm of daily life, and the complexity of interaction experienced in the earthly world.

Ibid, 21.

76. Ibid.
77. Ibid., 21–22.
78. John J. Collins writes: "The anticipated reversal of 'ordinary history' is a source of great comfort for millions of true believers living in conditions of squalor, relative deprivation, or moral decadence." See John J. Collins, "What Is apocalyptic literature?" in *The Oxford Handbook of Apocalyptic Literature*, ed. John J. Collins (New York: Oxford University Press, 2014), 12.
79. Rustomji, *The Garden and the Fire*, 162.
80. Kamil, *Nūrnāmu'*, 150.
81. Ibid., 151.
82. See Pankaj Mishra, *Temptations of the West: How to Be Modern in India, Pakistan and Beyond* (London: Picador, 2006), 240. The Kashmiri *darshan* is borrowed from the Sanskrit *darśana*, and can also mean "a way of seeing." What is at stake in *darshan* is to see and being seen. Yet *darshan* is also about a personal relationship with the deity unmediated by the priests. Please see Cynthia Bradley, "Darśana," *Encyclopedia of Hinduism* (New York: Routledge, 2018).
83. Catherine Keller, *Apocalypse Now and Then: A Feminist Guide to the End of the World* (Minneapolis: Fortress Press, 2005), ix–x.
84. Ibid., xi.
85. The historian Muzaffar Alam speaks of a deliberate "Sufi intervention" in medieval India "not merely in society and the social order, but equally in politics, as an attempt at defining political directions." See Alam, *The Languages of Political Islam in India*, 83. See also McGinn, *Visions of the End*, 30. Bernard McGinn calls apocalypticism a mirror held up to a particular age. Ibid., xiv.
86. Keller, *Apocalypse Now and Then*, 9–10. Keller also reminds us of the connection eschatological narratives bear to "agrarian narratives of cyclical death and renewal." Ibid., 20. John J. Collins also writes that many of the Jewish and Christian apocalypses, for instance, are revolutionary and involve resistance to imperial power. See Collins, "What Is Apocalyptic Literature?" 6.
87. The controversy among contemporary historians in relation to the restrictions that were placed upon Nund Rishi during the reign of Sultan Sikandar signals the entanglement of history with politics in Kashmir. I have here in mind the debate between the Kashmiri historians Abdul Qaiyum Rafiqi and Mohammad Ishaq Khan about the early history of the Rishi movement. The disagreement between the two even about as serious a subject as the restrictions that had been placed on Nund Rishi (clearly cited, however, in an original source for the period!) is suggestive of the political stakes in any interpretation of Rishi history. Rafiqi in an introduction to a new edition of his book, *Sufism in Kashmir: From the Fourteenth to the Sixteenth Century*, discusses the debate and defends

his claim that restrictions had once been put into place against Nund Rishi. See "Introduction" in Rafiqi, *Sufism in Kashmir*. See also ibid., 186–87, 197–98.

88. *Yāvan Mạtsī* is also addressed in a long narrative poem consisting of many *shruks*. See Saqi, *Kulliyāt-e Shaikh al-'Ālam*, 185.

89. G. N. Gauhar goes so far as to give us a date (1417–18) and a location for this incident (Soura on the northern outskirts of Srinagar). See Gauhar, *Kashmir Mystic Thought*, 60–61.

90. Ibid., 156.

91. Ibid., 158.

92. Khan, *Kashmir's Transition to Islam*, 163.

93. Ibid. As Annemarie Schimmel puts it, the attitude of Sufism to women "was ambivalent" but Sufism "was more favorable to the development of feminine activities than were other branches of Islam." See Schimmel, *Mystical Dimensions of Islam*, 426.

94. Khan, *Kashmir's Transition to Islam*, 163.

95. Sayyid 'Alī Hamadānī (1314–84), the Kubrāwiyyā Sufi, who visited Kashmir in the reign of Sultan Qutb al-Dīn (r. 1373–89), had also composed a treatise on ethics (*a<u>kh</u>lāq*) and government, *Za<u>kh</u>irat al-Mulūk*, a text 'for those Muslim rulers and state officials who wished to set right the affairs of religion (*istiṣlāḥ-i umūr-i dīn*)'. Alam, *The Languages of Political Islam*, 43.

Conclusion

We have so far in this book witnessed Nund Rishi's poetic thinking irrupt into a form of negative theology – a negative theology that not only posed a challenge to positive Islamic theology championed by immigrant Persian Sufis but also questioned the political structure of the new Muslim sultanate. From Manṣūr al-Ḥallāj in Caliphate Baghdad to Sarmad in Mughal South Asia, Sufi poets often had to pay the ultimate price of their life for questioning the proximity between positive Islamic theology and political power. It is, therefore, no coincidence that Islamic negative theology (in Kashmir and elsewhere) emerged in moments of political crises. The themes of Islam, death, the Nothing, and the apocalyptic in Nund Rishi's poetry – the negative theology of Nund Rishi – reveal a situation of deep political crisis in medieval Kashmir over the question of the relations of the past to the present, of the Hindus to the Muslims, of upper castes to lower castes, and of peasants to the ruling elites. The emergence of negative theology in vernacular South Asian Sufi poetry more generally signals a contestation over the very idea of Islam precisely at a time when Muslim imperial powers turned to a positive, albeit Sufi, theology for political legitimation.

One of the more significant stakes of the negative theology of Nund Rishi is that its turn to an unknowable God makes possible a conversation across religious traditions in Kashmir. The transformations, and translations, such an interreligious conversation made possible open out to a thinking of new universals such as the idea of *sahaja* that reconcile singularity with difference (one example of this is the phenomenon we sometimes approach with the academic shorthand of the Sufi–*bhaktī* movement). It is to be regretted that these movements have largely been studied only in the framework of the history of religions or literary studies and not as significant milestones in the history of thought in South Asia. We can go so far as to say that the Sufis of South Asia achieve for Islam in the region what St. Paul achieved for Christianity:

the universalization of its message of salvation.[1] If this possibility appears around the figure of Guru Nanak or Kabir in one region, it bears the name of Nund Rishi in another.

For Nund Rishi, Islam is not a stranger in South Asia because it is a stranger everywhere (recall the Prophetic *hadīth* in which Prophet Muhammad calls Islam a stranger).[2] He speaks of Muhammad and 'Uways in the same poem in which he speaks of the Kashmiri *rishīs*. My point is that it is not merely the constitution of a moral subject but also of a political subject (of responsibility, and not just freedom) which is at stake in Nund Rishi's poetry. Even though Nund Rishi turns inward for an ethical transformation of the self, his poetic thinking also calls for a political transformation. This is what makes reading, and rereading, Nund Rishi's mystical poetry an urgent task in a region which still remains sharply divided on questions of the religious and the political.

In the Muslim world, the battle over the meanings of Islam between political theology and poetic thinking is an old one. The tensions between the claims of poetry and those of politics in Islamic South Asia also go back to medieval times. To be a Muslim poet in medieval Kashmir was to enter the realm of these contestations. Even though the form of these contestations have changed in the postcolonial period, the politics of reading mystical poetry, or Islam, must still negotiate these dichotomies. Nowhere are the stakes as evident as in Kashmir where mystical poetry interrupts political theology to reclaim Islam for an alternative thinking of the political. In Nund Rishi's *shruks*, an alternative thinking of the political emerges which foregrounds questions of mortality, negation, temporality, and faith. It reads Islam as a negative political theology.[3]

Be it in the moment of vernacularization in the fourteenth and fifteenth centuries (the time of Lal Ded and Nund Rishi) or the crisis of rule in the nineteenth and twentieth centuries (the time of poets like Samad Mir and Wahab Khar), mystical poetry has played a fundamental role in expressing Kashmiri concerns. But what is unique about Nund Rishi is that his poetic expression not only intervened in the new Muslim society in medieval Kashmir but continues to shape Kashmiri society in the present. Negative theology has an affinity to relationality, and, in the case of Nund Rishi, it transformed Kashmir's encounter with Islam into a breakthrough thinking of a new, and inclusive, Kashmiri community (free from the control of the Brahmans criticized by Lal Ded and the power of the *mullāhs* castigated by Nund Rishi, and above all, free of caste, class, and race). When Nund Rishi says, *Kan thāv shrukӯn tu' panj sūran* (Pay attention to the *shruk*s and the five Sūrahs), he clearly establishes not only a relation between poetry (*shruk*s) and revelation (the five oft-recited Surāhs of the Qur'ān) but urges reading the latter in the light of the former.

The example of Ghalib, cited by Rahman Rahi in his reading of Nund Rishi, is sufficient here to establish that the centrality of poetry in public life has been a significant feature of South Asian Muslim societies and one of the key elements in the rise of an Indo-Muslim modernity (even an Indian modernity). It is not that we do not find a reified Islamic God in Nund Rishi's mystical poetry but that there is also an unsaying of such reification. Nund Rishi is engaged in a struggle to reinterpret the traditional Islamic understanding of his time, but it is also important to remember that the struggle never breaks out into open rebellion. This is perhaps why, even as Nund Rishi declares an unambiguous allegiance to Manṣūr al-Ḥallāj, he keeps his distance from Manṣūr's open disclosure of the "secret" of the relation between the self and an unknowable God, a secret that must not be revealed at all costs. There is, I hope, enough of a hint in my reading of Nund Rishi about how we might approach thinking about such a secret.

There are several themes in Nund Rishi such as the *nafs* (ego), *'ishq* (love), *'ilm* (knowledge), and *faqr* (asceticism) which were barely discussed in this book and deserve a separate treatment. Even some of the themes discussed in this book such as *sahaja* need a more detailed discussion. Lastly, I would also like to stress that a comprehensive study of Nund Rishi, and the Rishi Order of Kashmiri Sufism, needs to be even more interdisciplinary than this project and engage with the fields of South Asian history, anthropology, Indology, Islamic studies, Buddhist studies, comparative mysticism, Dalit studies, continental philosophy, and postcolonial theory. But even more significantly, the "ideal linguistic equipment," to borrow a phrase from Hans Harder, must include Sanskrit, Prakrit, Persian, and, above all, Kashmiri.[4] We will also need to explore the relation the language of the *shruk*s bears to such dialects of Kashmiri as Kishtwari and Pogali. Perhaps this is the reason why few detailed studies of Nund Rishi have been attempted despite his significance to the literary and religious history of Kashmir.

No one book can provide an exhaustive study of the mystical poetry of Nund Rishi. I chose to study in this book a few key themes from the *shruk*s with a view to making a small contribution to our understanding of the linguistic and cultural resources that inform the Kashmiri pasts and,

I hope, offer clues to alternative futures. I may have raised more questions here than I have answered. But it is in the hope that future researchers are able to present a more complex and fuller picture of the intellectual and political legacy of this revered Kashmiri saint, popularly called the *'alamdār*, or the flagbearer, of Kashmir.

"I could think of another Abraham for myself." These are the words of Franz Kafka.[5] Reading Ratan Lal Shant's short story "Byākh Rishīnamu'" (Another *Rishināmā*) from the collection titled *Rạ̄vmu't ma'nē* (Lost Meanings), I am tempted to end with the hope that in the long night of Kashmir's lost meanings, it is still possible to think of another Nund Rishi, a Nund Rishi of Kashmir's future to come.[6]

Notes

1. See Jacob Taubes, *The Political Theology of Paul*, tr. Dana Hollander (Stanford: Stanford University Press, 2004).
2. Prophet Muhammad said: "Islam began as a stranger and it will become a stranger, so blessed are those who are strangers." See Richard Kearney, "Imagining the Sacred Stranger: Hostility or Hospitality?" in *Politics and the Religious Imagination*, ed. John Dyck, Paul Rowe, and Jens Zimmermann (New York: Routledge, 2010), 23.
3. The term is associated with Jacob Taubes' thinking on Paul. See Taubes, *The Political Theology of Paul*, 134. Also see Terpstra and de Wit, "No Spiritual Investment in the World as It Is," 336.
4. Harder, *Sufism and Saint Veneration in Contemporary Bangladesh*, 6.
5. Quoted by Jacques Derrida in an essay on his "Judeities." See Jacques Derrida, "Abraham, the Other," in *Judeities: Questions for Jacques Derrida*, ed. Bettina Bergo, Joseph Cohen, and Raphael Zagury-Orly, tr. Bettina Bergo and Michael B. Smith (New York: Fordham University Press, 2007), 1.
6. Ratan Lal Shant, *Rạ̄vmu't ma'nē* (Jammu: Neehar Prakashan, 2003). This is a story about the Rishi philosophy of itinerancy and everyday life. A driver, presumably a modern-day Rishi, advices his impatient and resentful old passenger toward the end of the story: "To survive somehow. Just survive. To live in the present moment alone. Who knows about tomorrow?" Ibid., 76.

Bibliography

Accardi, Dean. "Embedded Mystics: Writing Lal Ded and Nund Rishi into the Kashmiri Landscape." In *Kashmir: History, Politics, Representation*, edited by Chitralekha Zutshi, 247–64. New Delhi: Cambridge University Press, 2018.

Afaqi, Asadullah. *Ā'īnā-e ḥaq: Kulliyāt-e Shaikh al-'Ālam*. Srinagar: Life Foundation, 2008.

———. *Ta'līmāt-e Shaikh al-'Ālam, Volumes 1 and 2*. Tsrār: self-published, 1998.

Aggarwal, Neil. "Kashmiriyat as Empty Signifier." *Interventions* 10, no. 2 (2008): 222–35.

Agrawal, Purushottam. *Akath kahānī prem kī*. New Delhi: Rajkamal Prakashan, 2016.

Ahmad, Aziz. "Conversions to Islam in the Valley of Kashmir." *Central Asiatic Journal* 23, nos. 1/2 (1979): 3–18.

———. *Studies in Islamic Culture in the Indian Environment*. London: Oxford University Press, 1964.

Ahmad, Irfan. *Islamism and Democracy in India: The Transformation of Jamaat-e-Islami*. Princeton: Princeton University Press, 2009.

Ahmed, Shahab. *What Is Islam? The Importance of Being Islamic*. Princeton: Princeton University Press, 2016.

Alam, Muzaffar. *The Languages of Political Islam in India*. Delhi: Permanent Black, 2004.

al-Hujviri, 'Ali ibn 'Usman. *The Kashf Al-Maḥjūb: The Oldest Persian Treatise on Sufism*. Translated by R. A. Nicholson. Lahore: Islamic Book Foundation, 1976.

'Alī, Sayyid. *History of Kashmir: Tarikh-i-Kashmir of Saiyid 'Ali*. Edited by Abdul Qaiyum Rafiqi. Srinagar: Gulshan Books, 2011.

Ali, Ahmed. *Al-Qur'ān: A Contemporary Translation*. Princeton: Princeton University Press, 1988.

Altizer, Thomas J. J. *History as Apocalypse*. Albany: State University of New York Press, 1985.

Anjum, Tanvir. *Chishtī Sufis in the Sultanate of Delhi, 1190–1400: From Restrained Indifference to Calculated Defiance*. Karachi: Oxford University Press, 2011.

Aquil, Raziuddin. *Sufism and Society in Medieval India*. New Delhi: Oxford University Press, 2010.

Arjomand, Said Amir. "Messianism, Millennialism and Revolution in Early Islamic History." In *Imagining the End*, edited by Abbas Amanat and Magnus Bernhardsson, 106–25. New York: I.B. Tauris, 2002.

Azad, Jagannath. *Iqbāl aur Kashmīr*. Srinagar: Ali Muhammad and Sons, 1977.

Azad, Nazir. "Kartu'l phạtrạm tu' gạrmạs drạ̄t." *Alamdār* (Kashmiri) 5 (2012): 99–113.

Badiou, Alain. *The Age of the Poets: And Other Writings on Twentieth-Century Poetry and Prose*. Edited by Bruno Bosteels. London: Verso, 2014.

Baldick, Julian. *Imaginary Muslims: The Uwaysi Sufis of Central Asia*. New York: New York University Press, 1993.

Bangha, Imre. "Early Hindi Epic Poetry in Gwalior: Beginnings and Continuities in the Rāmāyan of Vishnudas." In *After Timur Left: Culture and Circulation in Fifteenth-Century North India*, edited by Francesca Orsini and Samira Sheikh, 365–402. New Delhi: Oxford University Press, 2014.

Bashir, Shahzad. *Messianic Hopes and Mystical Visions: The Nūrbakhshiyā between Medieval and Modern Islam*. Columbia, SC: University of South Carolina Press, 2003.

Benjamin, Walter. *Illuminations: Essays and Reflections*. Translated by Harry Zohn and edited with an introduction by Hannah Arendt. New York: Schocken Books, 1968.

Bhat, R. L. "Political Content in the Vaakhs of Lal Ded." In *Cultural Heritage of Kashmiri Pandits*, edited by S. S. Toshakhani and K. Warikoo, 190–204. New Delhi: Pentagon Press, 2009.

Blanchot, Maurice. *The Work of Fire*. Stanford: Stanford University Press, 1995.

Boon, Marcus, Eric M. Cazdyn, and Timothy Morton. *Nothing: Three Inquiries in Buddhism*. Chicago: University of Chicago Press, 2015.

Bose, Sumantra. *Kashmir: Roots of Conflict, Paths to Peace*. Cambridge, MA: Harvard University Press, 2003.

Bowker, John. *The Meanings of Death*. Cambridge: Cambridge University Press, 1991.

Boyarin, Jonathan. "At Last, all the *Goyim*: Notes on a Greek Word Applied to Jews." In *Postmodern Apocalypse: Theory and Cultural Practice at the End*, edited by Richard Dellamora, 41–58. Philadelphia: University of Pennsylvania Press, 1995.

Bradley, Arthur. "Thinking the Outside: Foucault, Derrida and Negative Theology." *Textual Practice* 16, no. 1 (2002): 57–74.

Bulhof, Ilse and Laurens ten Kate. "Echoes of an Embarrassment: Philosophical Perspectives on Negative Theology – An Introduction." In *Flight of the Gods: Philosophical Perspectives on Negative Theology*, edited by Ilse Bulhof and Laurens ten Kate, 1–57. New York: Fordham University Press, 2000.

Burchett, Patton. E. *A Genealogy of Devotion: Bhakti, Tantra, Yoga and Sufism in North India*. New York: Columbia University Press, 2019.

Buturovic, Amila. "Death." In *Key Themes for the Study of Islam*, edited by Jamal J. Elias, 123–40. Oxford: Oneworld Publications, 2010.

Callewaert, Winand M. and Peter G. Friedlander, *The Life and Works of Raidās*. New Delhi: Manohar, 2020.

Caputo, John D. *The Prayers and Tears of Jacques Derrida: Religion without Religion*. Bloomington: Indiana University Press, 1997.

Certeau, Michel de. *The Mystic Fable, Volume 1.* Chicago: University of Chicago Press, 1992.

———. "Mysticism." *Diacritics* 22, no. 2 (Summer, 1992): 11–25.

Chakrabarty, Dipesh. *Provincializing Europe: Postcolonial Thought and Historical Difference*. Princeton: Princeton University Press, 2000.

Chittick, William. "Eschatology." In *Islamic Spirituality: Foundations*, edited by Seyyed Hossein Nasr, 378–409. New York: Routledge, 1987.

———. *Sufism: A Beginner's Guide*. Oxford: Oneworld Publications, 2007.

Collins, John J. "What Is Apocalyptic Literature?" In *The Oxford Handbook of Apocalyptic Literature*, edited by John J. Collins, 1–16. New York: Oxford University Press, 2014.

Cook, David. *Studies in Muslim Apocalyptic*. Princeton: The Darwin Press, 2002.

Corbin, Henry. "Apophatic Theology as an Antidote to Nihilism." *Umbr(a)* (2007): 59–84.

Dasgupta, Shashibhushan. *Obscure Religious Cults as Background of Bengali Literature*. Calcutta: University of Calcutta, 1946.

Dastur, Françoise. *Death: An Essay on Finitude*. London: Athlone, 1996.

Davidson, Ronald M. "Reframing *Sahaja*: Genre, Representation, Ritual and Lineage." *Journal of Indian Philosophy* 30, no. 1 (2002): 45–83.

Derrida, Jacques. "Faith and Knowledge: The Two Sources of 'religion' at the Limits of Reason Alone." In *Acts of Religion*, edited by Gil Anidjar, 40–101. New York: Columbia University Press, 2002.

———. *The Gift of Death*. Translated by David Wills. Chicago: University of Chicago Press, 1995.

———. "How to Avoid Speaking: Denials." In *Psyche: Inventions of the Other, Volume II*, edited by Peggy Kamuf and Elizabeth Rottenberg, 143–95. Stanford: Stanford University Press, 2008.

———. *Learning to Live Finally: An Interview with Jean Birnbaum*. Edited by Jean Birnbaum. Hoboken, NJ: Melville House, 2007.

———. "Letter to a Japanese Friend." In *Psyche: Inventions of the Other, Volume II*, edited by Peggy Kamuf and Elizabeth Rottenberg, 1–6. Stanford: Stanford University Press, 2008.

———. "Of an Apocalyptic Tone Recently Adopted in Philosophy." *Semeia* 23 (1982): 63–97.

———. *On the Name*. Stanford: Stanford University Press, 1995.

———. "Post-Scriptum: Aporias, Ways and Voices." In *Derrida and Negative Theology*, edited by Harold Coward and Toby Foshay, 283–323. Albany: State University of New York Press, 1992.

———. *Specters of Marx: The State of the Debt, the Work of Mourning, and the New International*. New York: Routledge, 1994.

DeWeese, Devin. "Sayyid ʿAli Hamadānī and Kubrawī Hagiographical Traditions." In *The Heritage of Sufism, Volume II: The Legacy of Medieval Persian Sufism (1150–1500)*, edited by Leonard Lewisohn, 121–58. Oxford: Oneworld Publications, 1999.

Dhulipala, Venkat. *Creating a New Medina: State Power, Islam, and the Quest for Pakistan in Late Colonial North India*. Delhi: Cambridge University Press, 2014.

Digby, Simon. "Between Ancient and Modern Kashmir: The Rule and Role of Sultans and Sufis (1200/1300–1600)." In *The Arts of Kashmir*, edited by Pratapaditya Pal, 114–25. New York: Asia Society, 2007.

Djurdjevic, Gordan and Shukdev Singh. *Sayings of Gorakhnāth: Annotated Translation of the* Gorakh Bānī. New Delhi: Oxford University Press, 2019.

Dressler, Markus and Arvind-Pal Singh Mandair. *Secularism and Religion-Making*. New York: Oxford University Press, 2011.

Eaton, Richard. "Approaches to the Study of Conversion to Islam in India." In *Approaches to Islam in Religious Studies*, edited by Richard C. Martin, 106–23. Oxford: Oneworld, 2001.

El-Hibri, Tayeb. *The Abbasid Caliphate: A History*. Cambridge, UK: Cambridge University Press, 2021.

Ernst, Carl W. *Eternal Garden: Mysticism, History, and Politics at a South Asian Sufi Center*. Albany: State University of New York Press, 1992.

———. "From Hagiography to Martyrology: Conflicting Testimonies to a Sufi Martyr of the Delhi Sultanate." *History of Religions* 24, no. 4 (May 1985): 308–27.

———. "Rūzbihān Baqlī on Love as Essential Desire." In *God Is Beautiful and He Loves Beauty: Festschrift in Honour of Annemarie Schimmel Presented by Students, Friends and Colleagues on April 7, 1992*, edited by Alma Giese and J. Christoph Bürgel, 181–89. New York: Peter Lang, 1994.

———.*Hallaj: Poems of a Sufi Master*. Translated from the Arabic by Carl W. Ernst. Evanston, IL: Northwestern University Press, 2018.

Ernst, Carl W. and Bruce Lawrence. *Sufi Martyrs of Love: The Chishti Order in South Asia and Beyond*. New York: Palgrave Macmillan, 2002.

Franke, William. "Apophasis and the Turn of Philosophy to Religion: From Neoplatonic Theology to Postmodern Negation of Theology." *International Journal for Philosophy of Religion* 60, nos. 1/3 (December 2006): 61–76.

———. *Poetry and Apocalypse: Theological Disclosures of Poetic Language*. Stanford: Stanford University Press, 2009.

Frembgen, Jürgen Wasim. "Dhamāl and the Performing Body: Trance Dance in the Devotional Sufi Practice of Pakistan." *Journal of Sufi Studies* 1, no. 1 (2012): 77–113.

Gandhi, Supriya. *The Emperor Who Never Was: Dara Shukoh in Mughal India*. Cambridge, MA: Harvard University Press, 2020.

Ganjoo, T. N. "Lallu' vākh lisạni zạvijār." *Shīrāzu', Lal Ded Number* 16, no. 6 (2002): 138–51.

Gauhar, G. N. *Kashmir Mystic Thought*. Srinagar: Gulshan Books, 2009.

———. *Sheikh Noor-ud-Din Wali (Nund Rishi)*. New Delhi: Sahitya Akademi, 1988.

Ghai, Ved Kumari. *Nilamatapurana, Vol. I*. Srinagar: J&K Academy of Art, Culture and Languages, 1968.

Gold, Joshua Robert. "Jacob Taubes: 'Apocalypse from Below.'" *Telos* 2006, no. 134 (2006): 140–56.

Goldziher, Ignaz. *Introduction to Islamic Theology and Law*. Princeton: Princeton University Press, 1981.

Green, Nile. *Making Space: Sufis and Settlers in Early Modern India*. New Delhi: Oxford University Press, 2012.

Hamadānī, Sayyid 'Alī. *Letters of Mir Saiyid 'Alī Hamadani: An Annotated Edition with English Translation and Historical Analysis*. Edited by Abdul Qaiyum Rafiqi. Srinagar: Gulshan Books, 2007.

Hangloo, R. L. *The State in Medieval Kashmir*. New Delhi: Manohar Publishers & Distributors, 2000.

Harder, Hans. *Sufism and Saint Veneration in Contemporary Bangladesh: The Maijbhandaris of Chittagong*. New York: Routledge, 2011.

Hasan, Mohibbul. *Kashmīr under the Sulṭāns*. Calcutta: Iran Society, 1959.

Hasan-Rokem, Galit and David Shulman, eds. *Untying the Knot: On Riddles and Other Enigmatic Modes*. New York: Oxford University Press, 1996.

Hawley, John Stratton. *A Storm of Songs: India and the Idea of the Bhakti movement*. Cambridge, MA: Harvard University Press, 2015.

Heidegger, Martin. *Being and Time*. Translated by John Macquarrie and Edward Robinson. New York: Harper & Row, 1962.

———. *History of the Concept of Time: Prolegomena*. Translated by T. Kisiel. Bloomington, IN: Indiana University Press, 1985.

———. *Phenomenological Interpretations of Aristotle: Initiation into Phenomenological Research*. Bloomington: Indiana University Press, 2001.

Heisig, James W. *Philosophers of Nothingness: An Essay on the Kyoto School*. Honolulu: University of Hawai'i Press, 2001.

Hoskote, Ranjit. *I, Lalla: The Poems of Lal Dĕd*. New Delhi: Penguin Books, 2011.

Hussain, Shahla. *Kashmir in the aftermath of Partition*. New Delhi: Cambridge University Press, 2021.

Hussanini, A. S. "Uways Al-Qaranī and the Uwaysī Ṣūfīs." *Muslim World* 57, no. 2 (1967): 103–13.

Jones, Richard H. *Philosophy of Mysticism: Raids on the Ineffable*. Stony Brook: State University of New York Press, 2016.

Jong, F. and Bernd Radtke. *Islamic Mysticism Contested: Thirteen Centuries of Controversies and Polemics*. Leiden, Netherlands: Brill, 1999.

Kabir, Ananya Jahanara. *Territory of Desire: Representing the Valley of Kashmir*. Minneapolis: University of Minnesota Press, 2009.

Kachru, Sonam. "'The Words of Lalla: Voices of the Everyday Wild' – Translation and Commentary." *Spolia Magazine, The Medieval Issue*, no.5 (October 2013).

Kaul, J. L. *Lal Ded*. New Delhi: Sahitya Akademi, 1973.

———, ed. *Lal Ded*. Srinagar: Jammu & Kashmir Academy of Art, Culture and Languages, 1984.

Kamil, Amin. *Javāban chu 'arẓ* Srinagar: self-published, 2000.

———. *Nūrnāmu'*. Srinagar: Jammu and Kashmir Academy of Art, Culture and Languages, 1966.

Karamustafa, Ahmet T. *God's Unruly Friends: Dervish Groups in the Islamic Middle Period 1200–1550*. Oxford: Oneworld Publications, 2013.

Kars, Aydogan. "What Is 'Negative Theology'? Lessons from the Encounter of Two Sufis." *Journal of the American Academy of Religion* 86, no. 1 (March 2018): 181–211.

———. *Unsaying God: Negative Theology in Medieval Islam*. New York: Oxford University Press, 2019.

Kashmiri, Hamidi. *Shaikh al-ʿĀlam: Ḥayāt aur shāyarī*. Srinagar: Idara-e Adab, 1997.

Kaviraj, Sudipta. "The Sudden Death of Sanskrit Knowledge." *Journal of Indian Philosophy* 33, no. 1 (2005): 119–42.

Keller, Catherine. *Apocalypse Now and Then: A Feminist Guide to the End of the World*. Boston: Beacon Press, 1996.

———. *Cloud of the Impossible: Negative Theology and Planetary Entanglement*. New York: Columbia University Press, 2015.

Khan, Muhammad Ishaq. *Crisis of a Kashmiri Muslim: Spiritual and Intellectual*. Srinagar: Gulshan Books, 2008.

———. *Kashmir's Transition to Islam: The Role of Muslim Rishis, Fifteenth to Eighteenth Century*. New Delhi: Manohar Publishers & Distributors, 2002.

———. "The Impact of Islam in the Sultanate Period (1320–1586)." In *India's Islamic Traditions 711–1750*, edited by Richard Eaton, 342–62. New Delhi: Oxford University Press, 2003.

———. *Sufis of Kashmir*. Srinagar: Gulshan Books, 2011.

Khawaja, G. M. and Gulshan Majeed. *Approaches to Kashmir Studies*. Srinagar: Gulshan Books, 2011.

Knysh, Alexander D. *Islamic Mysticism: A Short History*. Leiden, Netherlands: Brill, 2000.

Kothari, Rita, ed. *A Multilingual Nation: Translation and Language Dynamic in India*. New Delhi: Oxford University Press, 2018.

Koul, Anand. "A Life of Nand Ṛishi." *Indian Antiquary* 58 (October 1929): 194–98.

Kværne, Per. "On the Concept of Sahaja in Indian Buddhist Tantric Literature." *Temenos* 11 (1975): 88–135.

Lapidus, Ira. M. *A History of Islamic Societies*. Cambridge: Cambridge University Press, 2002.

Lawrence, Bruce B. "Islam in India: The Function of Institutional Sufism in the Islamization of Rajasthan, Gujarat and Kashmir." *Contributions to Asian Studies* 17 (January 1, 1982): 27–43.

———. *Notes from a Distant Flute: The Extant Literature of Pre-Mughal Indian Sufism*. Tehran: Imperial Iranian Academy of Philosophy, 1978.

Lawrence, Walter. *The Valley of Kashmir*. London: Henry Frowde, 1895.

Lévinas, Emmanuel. *God, Death, and Time*. Stanford: Stanford University Press, 2000.

Lorenzen, David, ed. *Religious Movements in South Asia 600–1800*. Delhi: Oxford University Press, 2004.

Maharaj, Ayon. *Infinite Paths to Infinite Reality: Sri Ramakrishna and Cross-cultural Philosophy of Religion*. New York: Oxford University Press, 2018.

Mandair, Arvind-Pal Singh. *Religion and the Specter of the West: Sikhism, India, Postcoloniality, and the Politics of Translation*. New York: Columbia University Press, 2009.

Marion, Jean-Luc. "Introduction: What Do We Mean by 'Mystic'?" In *Mystics: Presence and Aporia*, edited by Michael Kessler and Christian Sheppard, 1–7. Chicago: University of Chicago Press, 2003.

Mason, Herbert. *Al-Hallaj*. Richmond, Surrey: Curzon Press, 1995.

Massignon, Louis. *The Passion of Al-Hallāj: Mystic and Martyr of Islam, Vols. 1–4*. Translated by Herbert Mason. Princeton: Princeton University Press, 1982.

McGinn, Bernard. *Visions of the End: Apocalyptic Traditions in the Middle Ages*. New York: Columbia University Press, 1979.

McGregor, Ronald. S. *Hindi Literature from its Beginnings to the Nineteenth Century*. New Delhi: Manohar, 2021.

McLeod, W. H. *The Sikhs: History, Religion, and Society*. New York: Columbia University Press, 1989.

Michot, Yahya. "Life After Death from a Muslim Perspective." In *Abraham's Children: Jews, Christians, and Muslims in Conversation*, edited by Norman Solomon, Richard D. Harries, and Tim J. Winter, 307–18. New York: T & T Clark, 2005.

Mitsis, Phillip. "Where Death Is, There We Are Not." In *The Oxford Handbook of Philosophy of Death*, edited by Ben Bradley, 200–17. New York: Oxford University Press, 2013.

Mohi-ud-Din, Akhtar. *A Fresh Approach to the History of Kashmir (Source Material Drawn Mainly from the Kashmiri Language)*. Srinagar: Book Bank, 1998.

Moosa, Ebrahim. *Ghazālī and the Poetics of Imagination*. Chapel Hill, NC: University of North Carolina Press, 2005.

Naqvi, Nauman. "Acts of Askēsis, Scenes of Poiēsis: The Dramatic Phenomenology of Another Violence in A Muslim Painter-Poet." *Diacritics* 40, no. 2 (Summer 2012): 50–71.

Nishitani, Keiji. *Religion and Nothingness*. Berkeley: University of California Press, 1982.

Nizami, Khaliq Ahmad. *Some Aspects of Religion and Politics in India during the Thirteenth Century*. Bombay: Asia Pub. House, 1961.

———. *Tarīkh-e Mashaikh-e Chisht*. Karachi: Oxford University Press, 2007.

Noorani, A. G. *The Kashmir Dispute, 1947–2012*. New Delhi: Tulika Books, 2013.

O'Connell, Joseph T. "Were Caitanya's Vaiṣṇavas Really Sahajiyas? The Case of Rāmānanda Rāya." In *Shaping Bengali Worlds, Public and Private*, edited by Tony K. Stewart, 11–22. East Lansing, MI: Asian Studies Center, 1989.

Odin, Jaishree Kak. *Mystical Verses of Lalla: A Journey to Self-realization*. Delhi: Motilal Banarsidass, 2007.

———. *Lallā to Nūruddīn: Rishī-Sufī Poetry of Kashmir*. Delhi: Motilal Banarsidass, 2013.

Ogura, Satoshi. "In This Corner of the Entangled Cosmopolises: Political Legitimacies in the Multilingual Society of Sultanate and Early Mughal Kashmir." *Journal of Persianate Studies* 12, no. 2 (2019): 237–60.

Orsini, Francesca and Samira Sheikh, eds. *After Timur Left: Culture and Circulation in Fifteenth-Century North India*. Delhi: Oxford University Press, 2014.

O'Shaughnessy, Thomas. J. *Muhammad's Thoughts on Death: A Thematic Study of the Qur'anic Data*. Leiden: Brill, 1969.

Parimoo, B. N. *Unity in Diversity*. Srinagar: J&K Academy of Art, Culture and Languages, 1984.

Pepper, Thomas Adam. *Singularities: Extremes of Theory in the Twentieth Century*. Cambridge: Cambridge University Press, 1997.

Perreira, Todd LeRoy. "'Die before You Die': Death Meditation as Spiritual Technology of the Self in Islam and Buddhism." *Muslim World* 100 (April/July 2010): 247–67.

Pirbhai, M. R. *Reconsidering Islam in a South Asian Context*. Leiden: Brill, 2009.

Plato. *Phaedo*. In *Euthyphro Apology Crito Phaedo Phaedrus*. Cambridge: Harvard University Press, 2005, 193–403.

Pollock, Sheldon. "Literary History, Region and Nation in South Asia." *Social Scientist* 23, no. 269–71 (October–December 1995): 1–7.

Polt, Richard. *Heidegger: An Introduction*. New York: Routledge, 1999.

Polt, Richard and Gregory Fried. *A Companion to Heidegger's* Introduction to Metaphysics. New Haven: Yale University Press, 2001.

Puri, Balraj. "Kashmīriyat: The Vitality of Kashmiri Identity." *Contemporary South Asia* 4, no. 1 (1995): 55–63.

Qadri, Shafi Ahmad. *Kashmiri Sufism*. Srinagar: Gulshan Publishers, 2002.

Rafiabadi, Hamid Naseem. *Sufism and Rishism in Kashmir: The Lesser Known aspects of some Sufi Orders*. Srinagar: City Book Centre, 2011.

Rafiqi, Abdul Qaiyum. *Sufism in Kashmir: Fourteenth to the Sixteenth Century*. Sydney: Goodword Media, 2003.

———. *Letters of Mir Saiyid Ali Hamadani*. Srinagar: Gulshan Books, 2007.

Rahi, Rahman. "Lal Dýd tu' Shaikh al-'Ālam: Akh sarsarī taqobulī muṭālu'." In *Kahvạt: Tanqīdī maẓmūnan hạnz sombran,* 120–35. Srinagar: self-published, 1979.

———. "Shaikh al 'Ālam sạnz shạ̄'irānā ḥasiyath." In *Kahvạt: Tanqīdī maẓmūnan hạnz sombran.* Srinagar: self-published, 1979.

———. *Siyāh rūdu' jarýn manz.* Srinagar: self-published, 1997.

———. "Vākh tu' shruki: Akh ḥayạ̄tī muṭāllu' tu' sām." *Anhār* (1997).

Rahman, Fazlur. *Islam*. Chicago: University of Chicago Press, 1979.

Rai, Mridu. *Hindu Rulers, Muslim Subjects: Islam, Community, and the History of Kashmir*. London: C. Hurst, 2003.

Ramanujan, A. K. "Is There an Indian Way of Thinking? An Informal Essay." *Contributions to Indian Sociology* 23, no. 1 (1989): 41–58.

Ramsey, Charles. "Rishīwaer: Kashmir, the Garden of Saints." In *South Asian Sufis: Devotion, Deviation, and Destiny*, edited by Clinton Bennett and Charles M. Ramsey, 285–92. New York: Continuum, 2012.

Rao, Aparna. *The Valley of Kashmir: The Making and Unmaking of a Composite Culture?* New Delhi: Manohar Publishers & Distributors, 2008.

Ricci, Ronit. *Islam Translated: Literature, Conversion and the Arabic Cosmopolis of South and Southeast Asia*. Chicago: University of Chicago Press, 2012.

Rotman, B. *Signifying Nothing: The Semiotics of Zero*. New York: St. Martin's Press, 1987.

Rustomji, Nerina. *The Garden and the Fire: Heaven and Hell in Islamic Culture*. New York: Columbia University Press, 2009.

Sands, Kristin Zahra. *Ṣūfī Commentaries on the Qur'ān in Classical Islam*. New York: Routledge, 2006.

Sanyal, Usha. *Ahmad Riza Khan Barelwi: In the Path of the Prophet*. Oxford: Oneworld Publications, 2005.

Saqi, Moti Lal. *Kulliyāt-e Shaikh al-'Ālam*. Srinagar: Jammu and Kashmir Academy of Art, Culture and Languages, 1985.

Schimmel, Annemarie. "Death as the Gateway to Life in the Eyes of the Sufis." In *Crafting the Intangible: Persian Literature and Mysticism*, edited by Peter J. Chelkowski, 43–69. Salt Lake City: The University of Utah Press, 2013.

———. "The Martyr-Mystic Ḥallāj in Sindhi Folk Poetry: Notes on a Mystical Symbol." *Numen* 9 (November 1962): 161–200.

———. *Mystical Dimensions of Islam*. Chapel Hill: University of North Carolina Press, 2011.

———. *Islam in the Indian Subcontinent*. Leiden: Brill, 1980.

Sells, Michael Anthony. *Approaching the Qur'an: The Early Revelations*. Ashland, OR: White Cloud Press, 1999.

———. *Early Islamic Mysticism: Sufi, Qur'an, Mi'raj, Poetic and Theological Writings*. Mahwah, NJ: Paulist Press, 1996.

———. *Mystical Languages of Unsaying*. Chicago: University of Chicago Press, 1994.

Shauq, Shafi. *Lalla Dyad: The Mystic Kashmiri Poetess*. Srinagar: Gulshan Books, 2015.

———. *Nund*. Srinagar: KBD Books, 2022.

Shihadeh, Ayman, ed. *Sufism and Theology*. Edinburgh: Edinburgh University Press, 2007.

Shizuteru, Ueda. "Nothingness in Meister Eckhart and Zen Buddhism." In *The Buddha Eye: An Anthology of the Kyoto School and Its Contemporaries*, edited by Frederick Franck, 157–70. Bloomington: World Wisdom, 2004.

Sikand, Yoginder. "The Emergence and Development of the Jama'at-i Islami of Jammu and Kashmir (1940s–1990s)." *Modern Asian Studies* 36, no. 3 (2002): 705–51.

———. *The Role of Kashmiri Sufis in the Promotion of Social Reform and Communal Harmony, 14th–16th Century*. Mumbai: Centre for Study of Society and Secularism, 1999.

Singh, R. Raj. *Death, Contemplation and Schopenhauer*. Burlington, VT: Ashgate, 2006.

Skaria, Ajay. *Unconditional Equality: Gandhi's Religion of Resistance*. Minneapolis: University of Minnesota Press, 2016.

Skyhawk, Hugh van. *Well Articulated Better Paths: Sufi Saints as Links between Religious Communities*. Edited by Friedrich-Naumann-Stiftung für die Freiheit. Islamabad: Friedrich Naumann Foundation for Freedom, 2014.

Slaje, Walter. *Medieval Kashmir and the Science of History*. Austin: South Asia Institute, The University of Texas at Austin, 2004.

———. *Brahmā's Curse: Facets of Political and Social Violence in Premodern Kashmir*. Halle an der Saale: Universitatsverlag Halle-Wittenberg, 2019.

Smith, Jane Idleman and Yvonne Yazbeck Haddad. *The Islamic Understanding of Death and Resurrection*. Albany: State University of New York Press, 1981.

Steinfels, Amina M. *Knowledge before Action: Islamic Learning and Sufi Practice in the Life of Sayyid Jalāl al-Dīn Bukhārī Makhdūm-i Jahāniyān*. Columbia, SC: University of South Carolina Press, 2012.

Stewart, Tony. K. "In Search of Equivalence: Conceiving Muslim–Hindu Encounter through Translation Theory." *History of Religions* 40, no. 3 (February 2001): 260–87.

Suvorova, Anna. *Muslim Saints of South Asia: The Eleventh to Fifteenth Centuries*. New York: RoutledgeCurzon, 2004.

Taubes, Jacob. *Occidental Eschatology*. Translated by David Ratmoko. Stanford: Stanford University Press, 2009.

———. "The Realm of Paradox." *Review of Metaphysics* 7, no. 3 (March 1954): 482–91.

Temple, Richard Carnac. *The Religion and Teachings of Lalla*. New Delhi: Vintage, 1990.

Terpstra, Martin and Theo deWit. "No Spiritual Investment in the World as It Is": Jacob Taubes's Negative Political Theology." In *Flight of the Gods: Philosophical Perspectives on Negative Theology*, edited by Ilse N. Bulhof and Laurens ten Kate, 320–53. New York: Fordham University Press, 2002.

Thanvi, Ashraf Ali. *Sharīʿat va ṭarīqat*. Mumbai: Maktabah al-ḥaq, n.d.

Tikku, Girdhari L. *Persian Poetry in Kashmir, 1339–1846*. Berkeley: University of California Press, 1971.

Timani, Hussam S. "Death and Dying in Islam." In *Ultimate Journey: Death and Dying in the World's Major Religions*, edited by Steven J. Rosen, 59–82. Westport: Praeger, 2008.

Trimingham, J. S. *The Sufi Orders in Islam*. Oxford: Clarendon Press, 1971.

Turner, Denys. *The Darkness of God: Negativity in Christian Mysticism*. Cambridge: Cambridge University Press, 1995.

Varma, Saiba. "Where There Are Only Doctors: Counselors as Psychiatrists in Indian-Administered Kashmir." *Ethos* 40, no. 4 (December 2012): 517–35.

Vaudeville, Charlotte. *A Weaver Named Kabir: Selected Verses with a Detailed Biographical and Historical Introduction*. New Delhi: Oxford University Press, 1993.

Vries, Hent de, ed. *Religion: Beyond a Concept*. New York: Fordham University Press, 2008.

Wakankar, Milind. *Subalternity and Religion: The Prehistory of Dalit Empowerment in South Asia*. New York: Routledge, 2010.

Wani, Muhammad Ashraf. *Islam in Kashmir: Fourteenth to Sixteenth Century*. Srinagar: Oriental Pub. House, 2004.

Wani, Mushtaq Ahmad. *Muslim Religious Trends in Kashmir in Modern Times.* Patna: Khuda Bakhsh Oriental Public Library, 1997.

Wilson, Robert R. "The Biblical Roots of Apocalyptic." In *Imagining the End*, edited by Abbas Amanat and Magnus Bernhardsson, 56–66. New York: I.B. Tauris, 2002.

Zutshi, Chitralekha. *Kashmir's Contested Pasts: Narratives, Sacred Geographies, and the Historical Imagination*. New Delhi: Oxford University Press, 2014.

———. *Languages of Belonging: Islam, Regional Identity, and the Making of Kashmir*. London: C. Hurst, 2004.

———, ed. *Kashmir: History, Politics, Representation*. New Delhi: Cambridge University Press, 2018.

———. *Kashmir*. New Delhi, Oxford University Press, 2019.

Index